Driven Back to the Text

Driven Back to the Text

The Premodern Sources
of Levinas's Postmodernism

Oona Ajzenstat
(Oona Eisenstadt)

Duquesne University Press
Pittsburgh, Pennsylvania

Library of Congress Cataloging in Publication Data

Ajzenstat, Oona, 1964–
    Driven back to the text: the premodern sources of Levinas's
postmodernism/Oona Ajzenstat.
        p. cm.
    Includes bibliographical references and index.
    ISBN 0-8207-0325-7 (alk. paper)
    1. Levinas, Emmanuel. 2. Judaism and philosophy.
    3. Holocaust (Jewish theology)   I. Title.
    B2430.L484 A49 2001
    194—dc21

                                        2001000810

Printed in the United States of America.
Printed on acid-free paper.

CONTENTS

v

ACKNOWLEDGMENTS

Travis Kroeker of McMaster University and Robert Gibbs of the University of Toronto bear together the responsibility for introducing me to Levinas. Both read drafts of this book and offered immeasurably useful criticism. The Department of Religious Studies at McMaster University was home to me when I started to write; despite the contempt with which it has in recent years been treated by the university administration, it remains a bastion of civilization. The Jewish Studies Programme at the University of Toronto provided the hospitable space in which I finished the book; my thanks are particularly due to the Wolfe family for endowing the Ray D. Wolfe Memorial Fellowship there, an example of true liberality. A number of people helped in more particular ways: the anonymous referees, one of whom lurks behind note 8 to chapter four and note 36 to chapter five; Wendell Dietrich, who brought to my attention the Neusner article I use in chapter four; Jill Robbins, who read a draft and saved me from a couple of gaffes; Susan Wadsworth-Booth from Duquesne University Press who pulled the manuscript into shape with efficiency. The work of Susan Handelman lays the ground for my endeavor, and those of others. The greatest thanks go to those who talk to me philosophically about everything except Levinas: foremost among them are Sam and Janet Ajzenstat and Zdravko Planinc.

KEY TO ABBREVIATIONS FOR WORKS BY EMMANUEL LEVINAS

BPW   *Basic Philosophical Writings*, edited by A. Peperzak, S. Critchley, and R. Bernasconi. Bloomington: Indiana University Press, 1996.

BTV   *Beyond the Verse*. Trans. G. D. Mole. Bloomington: Indiana University Press, 1994.

CPP   *Collected Philosophical Papers*. Trans. A. Lingis. Phaenomenologica 100, Dordrecht: Martinus Nijhoff, 1987.

DEHH   *En decouvrant l'existence avec Husserl et Heidegger.* Paris: J. Vrin, 1949.

DF   *Difficult Freedom: Essays on Judaism.* Trans. S. Hand. London: The Athalone Press, 1990.

EDM   "Entre deux mondes." In *La Conscience juive*. Vol. 1. Les Presses Universitaires de France, 1962. (See note 1 to chapter four.)

EE   *Existence and Existents*. Trans. A Lingis. The Hague: Martinus Nijhoff, 1978.

EI   *Ethics and Infinity: Conversations with Philippe Nemo*. Trans. R. Cohen. Pittsburgh: Duquesne University Press, 1982.

EN   *Entre Nous*. Trans. M. B. Smith and B. Harshav. New York: Columbia University Press, 1998.

EV   *De l'évasion*. Montpellier: Fata Morgana, 1982.

GCM *Of God Who Comes to Mind.* Trans. B. Bergo. Stanford: Stanford University Press, 1998.

ITN *In the Time of Nations.* Trans. M. B. Smith. Bloomington: Indiana University Press, 1994.

LR *The Levinas Reader*, edited by S. Hand. Oxford: Blackwell, 1989.

NTR *Nine Talmudic Readings.* Trans. A. Aronowicz. Bloomington: Indiana University Press, 1990.

OB *Otherwise Than Being or Beyond Essence.* Trans. A. Lingis. The Hague: Martinus Nijhoff, 1981.

PL with others. *The Provocation of Levinas: Rethinking the Other*, edited by R. Bernasconi and D. Wood. New York: Routledge, 1988.

PN *Proper Names.* Trans. M. B. Smith. Stanford: Stanford University Press, 1996.

RK with Richard Kearney. "Dialogue with Emmanuel Levinas." In *Face to Face with Emmanuel Levinas*, edited by R. A. Cohen, 13–34. New York: SUNY Press, 1986.

RM with Raoul Mortley. "Levinas." In *French Philosophers in Conversation: Levinas, Scheieder, Seres, Irigaray, Le Doeff, Derrida*, 10–13. London: Routledge, 1991.

RPH "Reflections on the Philosophy of Hitlerism." *Critical Inquiry* 17 (1990): 63–71.

TI *Totality and Infinity.* Trans. A. Lingis. Pittsburgh: Duquesne University Press, 1969.

TO *Time and the Other.* Trans. R. Cohen. Pittsburgh: Duquesne University Press, 1987.

TrO "The Trace of the Other." In *Deconstruction in Context: Literature and Philosophy*, edited by M. C. Taylor, 345–59. Chicago: University of Chicago Press, 1986.

WO "Wholly Otherwise." In *Re-reading Levinas*, edited by R. Bernasconi and S. Critchley, 3–10. Bloomington: Indiana University Press, 1991.

Introduction

Emmanuel Levinas was born on 12 January 1906[1] in Lithuania, a country where, as he explains, "Jewish culture was intellectually prized and fostered and where the interpretation of biblical texts was cultivated to a high degree" (RK 17). At home and in his secular schools he spoke Russian and read the great Russian novelists, but in addition he began at an early age to study Hebrew and to read the texts of the Jewish tradition; indeed, he describes his childhood as an immersion in the way of life of the Lithuanian Jew, a way that rested "in a tremendous curiosity for books."[2] In 1915, when Levinas was 11, the Jews of Lithuania were expelled by government decree and his family moved to the Ukraine. Here, despite the anti-Semitic pogroms that occurred during the general upheaval caused by the revolution, he was able to attend high school. By 1920, the revolutionary government had revoked the decree of expulsion and Levinas's family returned to Lithuania where he finished his early schooling.

He left in 1923 for France, where he enrolled at the University of Strasbourg and studied under a number of professors, among them Charles Blondel. With Blondel he read Henri Bergson, who was probably his earliest philosophical

1

influence: Levinas was impressed by Bergson's theory of time and his reflections on technology. In the mid-1920s he became interested in Husserl and went to Freiburg to study with him for the academic year of 1928–29. There he also studied with Heidegger, who had published *Being and Time* in 1927 and had thereby become "the leading light in German philosophy" (RK 14). He returned to France in 1930, this time to Paris, and completed his dissertation, *The Theory of Intuition in Husserl's Phenomenology*, under the tutelage of Jean Wahl. It was this book, together with a number of Levinas's early articles and his 1931 translation (with Gabrielle Pfeiffer) of Husserl's *Cartesian Meditations* that, it is generally agreed, introduced phenomenology to France.

Beginning in 1930, Levinas taught at the Alliance Israélite Universelle, an organization that had as its goal the spread of Jewish education in the countries of the Mediterranean. He married Rachel Levy, a friend from his childhood in Lithuania, and eventually had a daughter, Simonne (b. 1936) and a son, Michael (b. 1948). During the 1930s he occasionally attended lectures at the Sorbonne, those of Brunschvicg regularly and those of Kojève irregularly; he also attended Gabriel Marcel's soirées. He began, in the early thirties, to write a book on Heidegger but abandoned it when Heidegger announced his support for the Nazi party, producing instead a short article called "Some Reflections on the Philosophy of Hitlerism" in which he began subtly to trace connections between the Heideggerian and Nazi comprehensions. Then, in 1935, he published the essay *"De l'évasion,"* in which he took up for the first time what would become his lifelong question: whether it is possible, contra Heidegger and certain other philosophers, to think outside of ontology, or to "otherwise than be." Already, he was beginning to come to the idea that to think outside of ontology must be to think ethically first.

He fought for France in the war, serving as an interpreter of Russian and German, but was taken prisoner in 1940.

Because the Nazis treated Jews who were army officers under the laws of the Geneva convention, he spent the rest of the war in a labor camp in Germany for Jewish POWs. There he wrote the bulk of *Existence and Existents*, which further describes his movement away from ontology and begins to make use of the idea of the Good Beyond Being. Levinas's parents and their family, still in Lithuania, were killed early in the war, but Maurice Blanchot — who had been his closest friend since the Strasbourg days and remained so for the rest of his life — arranged to have his wife and daughter hidden and cared for in the monastery of Saint Vincent de Paul near Orleans for the duration of the war. When Levinas was released, he rejoined them and went to work for a branch of the Alliance, the Oriental Israelite Normal School, of which he was appointed Director in 1947. He continued to pursue the philosophical question of how one might move beyond being; in 1946, Jean Wahl invited him to give the series of lectures, later published as *Time and the Other*, in which he rethought human relation as a function of temporal lapse. In addition, he became seriously interested for the first time in Jewish thought. The awakening of this interest that had previously been "latent — I might even say dormant" (RK 18) is attributable to his acquaintance with "the prestigious and merciless" (DF 291) Mordachai Chouchani, who taught him Talmud and other texts between 1947 and 1951. In 1960 Levinas gave his first talmudic lecture to the Colloquium of French Jewish Intellectuals and gave another almost every year for 30 years; all his talmudic interpretations are offered, he explains, "in the shadow of [Chouchani's] shadow" (RK 18).[3] In 1961, he published *Totality and Infinity*. He was awarded the *doctorat d'état* with this text as primary thesis and the bulk of his previously published work as secondary thesis. He was offered a professorship at the University of Potiers, and then in 1967 at the University of Paris — Nanterre, and then in 1973 at the Sorbonne.

This is as far as Levinas sketches his life in the catalog of deeds that opens the autobiographical essay "Signature" (DF 291–95). What happens afterward is more difficult to lay out; his doings are those of the mind, and an account of them would require at the very least an exegesis of *Totality and Infinity* and an explanation of its relation to his second great book, *Otherwise Than Being or Beyond Essence*, published in 1974 — tasks I do not intend to take on. Levinas wrote a great deal during the sixties, seventies, and eighties, largely perhaps because he received a great number of invitations to speak. A complete bibliography of his work would include more than 400 entries. In addition, he traveled in a wide circle: among others he knew Sartre, de Beauvoir, Hyppolite, Ricoeur, Marcel, Maritain, Derrida — in effect, the whole intellectual community of Paris. His influence on many of those he knew and on their students is considerable, although its extent will not properly be determined for several more decades. In short, he introduced to French philosophy the idea of the other as the rupture of the same, the idea that was to become the foundation of late twentieth century (and perhaps twenty-first century) continental thought.[4] He died on 25 December 1995, about a year after the death of his wife. Their daughter, a doctor, and their son, a pianist and composer, are still living.[5]

The intent of this book is to watch Levinas reading certain of the foundational texts of the Jewish tradition in an effort to determine how he reads and why he reads the way he does. We watch him read certain verses of the Bible, certain motifs of the Kabbalah, a discrete collection of passages from the Talmud, and, finally, certain broken tales, images, or after effects of the Nazi period. And we see that he reads them all in a particular way, a way that is almost devoid of historical concern but is deeply philosophical and deeply ethical, a way of reading the goal of which is to tell the truth, or rather the *truths*, of human existence in relation.

The truths rather than the truth. This is to say, first, that Levinas tries to conceive of beings in terms more foundational than those of the fixed structures of the comprehensions he designates as *ontologies* — comprehensions that try to subordinate individuals to larger categories — and, second, analogously, that he tries to conceive of persons in terms more foundational than those of the egalitarian or hierarchical groupings necessary to political thought or public action. In short, he tries to think as much as possible of a given being before thinking of the whole of being and its parts, or of the existent before existence. And for him this means thinking of the other before the self, which is to say, thinking ethically. Thinking of the other before the self is his route out of ontology because, according to the structures of his thought, the respect for the infinite uniqueness of the human being that breaks the certainty or priority of one's categorizations and groupings cannot arise for the autonomous subject, but comes to the subject only from the otherness of the other. Levinas's philosophical writings consist largely, then, of trackings back from a great many different manifestations of ontology, categorization, classification, unity, truth, coherence, sameness — in short, from all the varieties of what he calls *totality* — to a fundamental point in which "totality breaks up," in which we are called by the other to ethical responsibility.[6] He seeks always to move back out of the historical, theoretical, 'interested' self with its conception of truth as a graspable totality to this prior 'disinterest' — or from the indifferent self tied up in itself to this prior 'non-indifference' — and, subsequently, to draw a connection between this prior disinterest or nonindifference and what stands outside of the dominant ontological modes of thought and outside of political forms, that is to say, the human being who can "otherwise than be" and the Good Beyond Being, the God who is never present in time or space but appears only in the response to his command. And to show others that movement is the challenge Levinas sets himself.

In a sense he is not tremendously successful. As part of his trackings back, he offers an account of human relation in which the ethical impulse always precedes the selfish or murderous impulse; an account, moreover, in which this prior impulse bespeaks an extraordinary responsibility by which the subject finds herself[7] called to preserve the otherness of the other even at the cost of her bread and breath; an account, to cap all, in which this always prior ethical impulse represents the trace of the absent God. Many readers find these descriptions inadequately supported by evidence; indeed, Levinas's ethics must almost certainly appear to fans of evidence as naive. But Levinas himself is not a fan of evidence. He shows his movement back by walking through it; his philosophy is fundamentally appeal, an offering up of ideas for the taking. He does not intend to impress us with the facticity of his understanding, but rather with its ethical nature. Indeed, to say, as Levinas often does, that "ethics is first philosophy" is to make an ethical statement rather than a factual or logical statement; more precisely, to say that "ethics is first philosophy" is quite simply to perform an ethical act. Thus, insofar as I defend Levinas in this book, I do not attempt to adduce proof for his ethics drawn from experience or to display in the ethics an analytic coherence. Rather I pronounce myself persuaded. In other words, I suggest that we consider his ideas seriously because they offer ethical address to the philosophical and political falsehoods and perversions of our age.

This is not to say that Levinas is as critical of falsehoods and perversions as is sometimes made out. Admittedly, he regularly expresses his ideas as a critique of all, or almost all, of the Western philosophy (and theology) that precedes him; in fact, he takes this pose so often that one commentator,

Richard Cohen, defines it is as one of the two basic aspects of Levinas's work, the "negative" or "critical" aspect as opposed to the positive description of ethical responsibility. "Negatively," Cohen writes, "[Levinas] opposes the primacy which philosophy quite naturally accords to ontological . . . interests, the hegemony to which it raises the quest for truth," and Cohen continues by telling us that "basically the West is a will to truth, the quest for universal knowledge of the real, [i.e. for] reason," a quest with which Levinas wants little to do.[8] But this way of understanding Levinas, although true enough to the way he sometimes speaks, is not fruitful. For the West is, in actuality, *not* a will to ontological truth. Levinas himself finds the otherwise than being in the Hebrew Scriptures and New Testament, in the rabbinic texts, in Plato, in Augustine, in the Pseudo-Dionysius, in Descartes, in Kant, in Dostoyevsky, in Bergson and perhaps even, to some extent, in Heidegger.[9] Robert Bernasconi is correct to point out that "Levinas is at his weakest when he sets himself up against individual philosophers or philosophy in general [and] at his most penetrating when he finds the otherwise than being within philosophy"[10] — to which we may add, *also within theology*. The strong or "penetrating" Levinas does not criticize everything that came before him. In fact, he does not even criticize all forms of totality or ontology. This must be understood before one can proceed to find out where Levinas's real critique lies and at what it is directed.

Levinas is concerned to combat certain ways of reading and thinking prevalent in our age, ways that, as he puts it, "prevent speech." These ways constitute a basic catalogue of reductivist rubrics — ideologies, sociologies, psychologies, politicizations, historicisms, dialectical structures, orders of being, theologies — all of which share the basic characteristic of subsuming the individual into a scheme or categorization from which she is understood to draw her meaning. They are supported, as he sees it, by a hermeneutic of reification, that is, the wrapping up or fixing of the symbols that express ethical relation in a time-in-a-history and a place-in-a-hierarchy. In Levinas's understanding, what is concrete to experience is without a time in an order-of-time or a place in an order-of-place; what is concrete is a clash and a breaking, a constant questioning, a reversal in the psyche in which what 'I' come into contact with is constantly being revealed as devastatingly new and 'higher.' To say that such an experience is fundamentally the experience of such-and-such an object in such-and-such a place and time is to abstract the experience, and thereby to risk losing altogether its novelty and its capacity to devastate. It is also, potentially, to *sacralize* the experience, to subsume it into a reductivist rubric. For if one holds that the most significant aspect of an experience is its place or time in a larger order of place or time, one is in danger of creating with this order a fully articulated second reality, a screen through which things can be seen and explained and by means of which the foundations of experience can increasingly be ignored. The second reality takes the form of a sacral system, apparently giving its adherents a God's eye view of the world or of history, which is to say that a reductivist ideological second reality is already a certain type of theology: a "sacred grove" (DF 232). Such second realities are the mark of our age. If one wishes to create and impose one, one must abstract experience by reifying its components and placing them in a larger order. If, on the other hand, one wishes to combat second realities, one must deconstruct the abstractions. To this effect, Levinas offers us experiences without referential objects, meanings without reference to an ontology, or, as he puts it, "signification without a context" (TI 23).

Among the sacred groves against which Levinas stands, I am particularly concerned with three: Hegelianism, totalitarianism, and modern progressivist liberalism. A Levinasian framework allows us to see that each of these systems views reality through a single unifying lens. Hegelianism is a monism or ontology that explains everything by means of the overarching rubric of the historical plan thus undermining particularity and individuality; and totalitarianism and progressivist liberalism put this kind of thinking into practice — since both ideologies see world history as marching toward a time when human beings will be fulfilled because they have everything in common. Many critiques are brought against these systems, critiques that seek to replace them with a different 'more responsible' way of thinking or a different 'more responsible' form of politics. But Levinas's critique is the first to suggest that responsibility emerges from the disruption of system qua disruption, from difference, from what is uncommon in human beings, from what is unlike me in the other. This is what has persuaded me of his ethics; or, to be precise, this is what has persuaded me that it is ethical to adopt his ethics. Any critique of sameness that accepts the assumption — common to Hegelians, totalitarians, and liberals as well as to most of their critics — that difference gives rise to antagonism, will not be able to maintain a strong front against Hegelian, totalitarian, or liberal sameness. A critique that assumes that difference gives rise to ethics is stronger, and for this reason alone is worth pursuing.

To speak broadly, Levinas's thought is enormously attractive in an age characterized by three apparently conflicting phenomena: first, by the justification of oppression on the basis of differences between human beings or cultures; second, by the growing homogenization of human beings and cultures justified by the shibboleths of democracy, universal justice, and peace; and third, by a backlash against this homogenization in the name of distinct groups within the whole that insist on their autonomy. Levinas undercuts the primacy of all such ways of thinking, and offers an alternative: an ethics of each-to-each-other commenced in the face-to-face.[11] And this alternative ethics is a real alternative precisely because it is not a reaction to the above mentioned phenomena; it is not designed as a band-aid for contemporary problems. It is always already there in human experience. Moreover, it is best expressed in old books, particularly, as Levinas sees it, the foundational texts of the Jewish tradition.

As Levinas sees it — but is he right? Levinas's relation to the text is as ambiguous as his descriptions of relations between human beings. He struggles to remain open to it but he is also conscious of his responsibility to its 'other others', that is, to previous interpreters and to us. What results from this responsibility — spread wide and thin as it must be — is a way of reading that is neither strictly exegetical nor strictly eisegetical nor precisely a combination of the two, a way that tries, as I said, to tell the *truths*. His responsibility to the text and the text's previous interpreters is, I think, straightforward; his deepest ideas are illuminated primarily through biblical reference or kabbalistic motif and his Bible and Kabbalah are read from the perspective of the Talmud. But his responsibility to us is more complex. It emerges in a hermeneutic that I will at times call 'deontologization', at times 'deontologization and dehistoricization', and at times 'desacralization', a hermeneutic that combats the reification and sacralization characteristic of our age by pulling from stories and symbols their ground in the experience of ethical rupture. A number of the central symbols of the Jewish tradition will serve as brief examples. Levinas's *creation* is createdness: an expression of the experience of not being one's own origin, and thus of being responsive to revelation. His *revelation* is the experience of being called into question by the trace of God in the other. His *election* is the experience that this calling into question comes from without, that it is not a matter of choice but rather of being chosen. And finally his *messianism* is the result of these experiences: ethical responsibility. This is not to say that Levinas denies that God created the world in the beginning, chose the Jews, revealed his Torah at Sinai, and will send a messiah at the end. But these events, qua events, are, as he sees it, matters of evidence or objective fact and therefore not subjects of philosophical discussion; in short, they are less interesting than the ethical experiences that are expressed in the symbols.

For Levinas these asacral understandings or interpretations are embedded in the texts themselves, in the experience of alterity that underlies the texts' symbols and narratives. But they are also very much 'what we need to hear today'. In his understanding, the rigidities of the prevailing modern comprehensions can be broken or at least called into question by an encounter with ancient Judaism, and *that* encounter is the one he provides, at the cost perhaps of other possible kinds of encounters with the old books. Levinas tells ethical truths, now; it is on this basis that he is defensible and on this basis that he should be read. And he tells them through and with the sources of his religion.

Chapter one of this book lays the groundwork for the arguments of subsequent chapters by detailing what I understand to be the philosophical structure most basic to Levinas's thought: the dynamic in which the rupturing relation between two human beings both conditions and also gives way to the nonrupturing social relation. I discuss this structure using various pairs of terms — ethics and politics, saying and said, and infinity and totality — and then take up some of the structure's difficulties — notably the problem of order or whether rupture or nonrupture comes first, and the reasons for the apparently strict distinction between ethics and politics. In the course of these discussions I begin to clarify the place in Levinas's thought of what I have just called the 'second reality' and call in the body of the book the 'avoidable totality'. I explain that totalities may be classified in many ways and choose from these ways a distinction between the

'endemic totality', i.e. the kind of categorization necessary
to political life or a book like this one, and the 'avoidable
totality', i.e. the kind of categorization that claims completeness and forgets its origin in rupture. I imply that because
Levinas's critique of the second reality or avoidable totality
is a critique of a forgetting, the critique must be enacted as
an anamnesis: a reading and recalling of old books that
grounds a reading and recalling of the origins of experience.
And, as I begin to show in the final section of chapter one, for
Levinas, the old books are the sources of Judaism and the
experiences are Jewish experiences. Levinas's Jewishness is
at the core of his philosophy.

Chapter two begins the process of watching Levinas read.
Here I turn to the fifth chapter of *Otherwise Than Being or
Beyond Essence* which contains a series of biblical references
dense enough to form a subtext of midrash. I begin with an
analysis of some of the philosophical themes of the chapter, an
analysis intended to supplement the account of the basic structure of Levinas's thought from chapter one and to clarify —
insofar as is possible — the role of God in that structure.
This involves some discussion of a structure secondary but
critical to the basic structure, namely, the 'witnessing structure' whereby God is withdrawn and his command appears
only as the response of the commanded one. I then move on
to the midrash on which I comment speculatively and un-
restrictedly. My argument with respect to the midrash has
two parts, though they are presented at once, together, in
the play of midrashic analysis. First, I am curious to see how
many of Levinas's basic ideas are illuminated with biblical
reference, including metaphysical desire, the trace of the
absence of God in the face of the other, the ethical turn to the
other as the path to the withdrawn God, the occurrence of
this ethical relation as speech, and, finally, the necessity of
having a nonrupturing politics as well as a rupturing ethics
and the moral dilemmas raised by this necessity. Second, I

look to see how Levinas reads the Bible in order to draw these ideas from the text. Clearly he stands here in the tradition of homiletical midrash, a freewheeling method of sermonizing in which biblical verses are expounded or manipulated in a sequence governed not by their biblical order but by the train of the midrashist's thought. But I argue that Levinas also understands himself to stand in an Isaianic tradition, wrenching images and verses from their original context and rearranging them so as to make the hearts of his readers fat and their ears heavy and their eyes shut (Isaiah 6.10). This analysis constitutes the beginning of my exposition of Levinas's attack on the modern tendency to reify expressions of ethical experience into locatable things and ideas thereby relinquishing any ability to reexperience the ambiguities of the alterity expressed in the text. Levinas draws on Isaiah's negative theology, and yet feels that in order to be responsible to the understandings and misunderstandings of his contemporary readers he must go further than Isaiah, into a theology that is neither negative nor positive, a theology of the God who was never 'here.'

Chapter three takes up certain kabbalistic motifs in Levinas's thought. I begin with an extended defense of this endeavor, a defense that is necessary, in general, because Levinas is highly critical of what he calls 'mysticism', and, particularly, because Levinas's critique of this 'mysticism' is one of the general premises of this book, which precisely watches him dispose of sacred groves and God's-eye views. Levinas uses the term 'mysticism' to refer to the sacred grove, but I argue that this is not actually the nature of Jewish mysticism, and that Levinas knows it. Indeed, Jewish mysticism, even the unitive mysticism found in Abulafia and Luria (as opposed to the *Mitnagdic* school of mysticism on which Levinas overtly draws) has more in common with Levinasian relation than it does with the obfuscatory ontology Levinas calls 'mysticism.' I show this by means of two comparisons, one between Levinas and Abulafia and the other between Levinas and Luria. Both are intended to be broad and tentative; they sketch the outlines of further work to be taken up. But, that said, I believe that there are enough proximities between Levinas and these kabbalists to suggest a deliberate textual relation: a withdrawal of God, a rupturing connected to a height, an extraordinary responsibility, and a connection between ethics and difference or particularity. Moreover, there is, in Abulafia, the basis for a hermeneutic that would take up where Isaiah left off — a hermeneutic not only based in negative theology but suggesting, moreover, that experiences of God can only be understood as broken — and concomitantly, a critique of any understanding of such experiences in the static terms of a hermeneutic that reifies. I argue for a similarity between this hermeneutic and that of Levinas, and, further, that in the same way that Levinas feels it necessary to push the Isaianic envelope because of certain unsalutary modern hermeneutical tendencies, he feels it necessary to push Luria into an Abulafian aontologization and ahistoricism.

In chapter four I treat Levinas's first three lectures to the Colloquium of French Jewish Intellectuals, the first of which, "Between Two Worlds" is an exposition of Franz Rosenzweig's life and thought, and the second and third of which, later published together as "Messianic Texts," constitute Levinas's first talmudic reading. This chapter is the only one in which I watch Levinas engaged explicitly in the act of reading; therefore many of the issues that have lain under my analysis to this point now come to the fore. Levinas presents a desacralized conception of Judaism, but, unlike in the other passages in question in this book, he has an opportunity here to explain to his listeners that this *is* his conception — moreover, he makes a strong argument that it is also the talmudic conception. In order to do this, he turns to the talmudic texts that are perhaps most difficult to claim as asacral, that is, the texts on messianism. Levinas brings from these texts (drawn from close to the end of *Tractate Sanhedrin*) an ahistorical, aontological understanding of messianism, in which the coming of the messiah has nothing to do with ontological transformation in a historical future and everything to do with ethical transformation in the here and now. He is convinced that these texts are expressions of a profound experience that is neither contingent on the circumstances in which the rabbis lived, nor based on vain speculation about the beginning of time or the end of time. They are, moreover, expressions that can only be offered in the open forum of dialogue and debate.

Not only are Levinas's rabbis ahistorical and aontological, they can also, as it were, see ahead to the deformations supported by the modern reifying hermeneutic, the deformations of our second realities or avoidable totalities. As I have said, the contemporary avoidable totality takes several forms in Levinas's thinking — the two most notable philosophical forms being Heidegger's ontology (which I do not treat in this book) and Hegel's historicism. In these lectures on talmudic messianism, Levinas reveals the rabbis to be proto-anti-Hegelians, questioning the idea of an End of History because they are aware that the idea relativizes ethical judgment in the present. Certainly the rabbis explore what seem to modern readers to be Hegelian questions — the nature of the end of history, the growing universalism and commonality that heralds its advent, the matter of how human beings might bring it about or how they might be pawns in its unfolding — but these questions, read with the desacralizing hermeneutic that Levinas claims is the rabbis' own, are revealed as speculative discourse about the ever-present issues of ethical philosophy rather than assertions about historical, ontological transformation. Levinas attacks the modern sacred grove or ontology that is Hegelian historicism, and insists, as he sometimes puts it, that Jews must stand outside the course of world history, or, as he puts it at other times, that Jews must understand there to be no Meaning of History.

Chapter four returns to a part of the basic structure presented in chapter one, a part that was followed through in chapter two with the midrashic commentary on the dilemma of ethical politics but left behind in chapter three since the Kabbalah, at least as Levinas uses it, is largely apolitical. The critical point here is that Levinas accepts Hegel's central insights, including a link between dialectics and historical reality. Experienced reality, especially in the modern progressivist liberal state with its universality and homogeneity, is a totality best explained by Hegel, but the totality, as Hegel explains it, is grotesque, and therefore it is necessary for us to search for meaning outside Hegelian rubrics, and outside totality. In short, chapter four finishes the exposition of the basic structure by showing the extent to which we live in the sameness of the endemic totality (of which Hegel is the single best expositor) while at the same time being aware of the difference in the same, or the brokenness of the totality (which Hegel was not). We avoid the second reality of the avoidable totality by living in the endemic totality and understanding it to be broken, in other words, by living in it and outside of it at the same time. Levinas presents this case in the names of Rosenzweig and the rabbis of the classical period. For him, they present a way of life and thought that is an alternative to ontology, and they do it both by continuous reassertions of the ethical face-to-face and also by erecting and then breaking Hegelian-type totalities.

Chapter five, my final chapter, is a different kind of account of how Levinas reads. Here I ask two questions: why is Levinas so concerned about the breaking of sacred groves? and why does Levinas present and advocate an ethics of difference and infinite responsibility? I answer both by examining Levinas's reflections on the Holocaust, reflections that, as I see it, shape and provide a space for the readings of the old texts at which we have looked. Levinas's attack on ontology and history — his attack on system — is an attack on the Nazis in two senses: first, in the sense that the Nazis almost won and therefore that the rubric of progressive history in which success is the guarantor of virtue must be abandoned, and, second, in the sense that the Holocaust revealed, once and for all, that those groups or regimes that understand themselves to be the beginning of the culmination of a historical plan or attempt to create an ontological utopia are the most inhuman in their actions. In other words, the Holocaust ruptures any idea of an overarching system, first, by wiping away historical hope from the world in the repletion of suffering, and second, because the Nazis, not their victims, were the quintessential systematizers. There must now be no more systems, and above all, no ethical systems. Levinas's ethics is and must be one that 'does not work,' that does not provide room for judgment of the other — this is accomplished in by his focus on difference and his demand for infinite responsibility. And yet, there must a way to judge the Nazis — this is accomplished by the distinction between ethics and politics with an exposition of which this book began.

Chapter five, more specifically, begins with four stories from the Nazi period (three of which are drawn from Levinas's works) all of which describe a shift from second reality or avoidable totality to ethical responsibility, and the abandoning of the God of history or providence in favor of a God who arises in human relation. After this, I take up Levinas's most detailed essay on the Holocaust, "Useless Suffering," and draw out his strong criticisms of the philosopher Emil Fackenheim, a defender of providence. From here, I turn to more general questions about what it means to live without a God of history, to live in the world in a Levinasian way, to otherwise than be.

If Levinas's work is an anamnesis, a thinking back out of totality to its ground and back out of the modern world to old books, then this book also constitutes an anamnesis. I read Levinas backwards: beginning with *Otherwise Than Being* (1974) with its biblical references and its references to Abulafia; then *Totality and Infinity* (1961), from which I draw the comparisons to Luria; then "Between Two Worlds" and "Messianic Texts" (1959–61); and finally Levinas's reflections on the Holocaust. Like Levinas's thought, then, this book is a structure seeking to unravel itself in its origin in the past, a structure which, however, is also directed concretely at present conditions and at the future. Levinas's Judaism has little to do with the questions Jews often ask themselves — who is a Jew? or, what is required of a Jew ethically or *halachically*? — and everything to do with the fundamental question that Jews and everyone should ask, now more than ever: what am I to do for the different one who stands before me? This question, for Levinas, is a Jewish question that nevertheless grounds the philosophy and the way of life of anyone who asks it. All of Levinas's arguments are slanted, overstated, iterated and reiterated — all in order to force, cajole, encourage, and manipulate his readers into asking this question. All his readings are what Harold Bloom would call strong readings; they alter the surface of the text at issue — but the intent is to preserve and convey the text's meaning, which always bears on the necessity of asking the ethical question. Levinas is aware of the conditions under which his readers read and addresses them, partly simply by drawing us back through his hermeneutical anamnesis — by responding, for instance, to questions about Hegel with answers about the Talmud — in order to pave the way for an existential anamnesis, and partly by offering a strong clear critique of modern sacred groves, a critique that is already a turn to the other on his part and can subsequently be adopted as a turn to the other on the part of his readers. Levinas's writing, both hortative and critical, is an ethical and a political act.

ONE

The Structure of Levinas's Thought

When Levinas thinks back phenomenologically, he is thinking from all the various human structures that give reality a cast of 'sameness' to a prior point where sameness breaks up and reveals primary, underlying differences. The structures of sameness from which he thinks back may be said to fall into three types, types that are, however, not terribly distinct and certainly not mutually exclusive. Some involve participation, in which different components of reality are understood to come together in an intimacy or an identity: thus ecstatic conceptions, certain eschatological conceptions, theoretical structures that accord all beings a place or a function in an ontology, the understanding of human relation Plato attributes to Aristophanes, interpretations of the thought of Hegel that emphasize Hegel's telos (that is, absolute knowledge or the universal and homogeneous state), and also certain interpretations of the thought of Heidegger. Some involve what Levinas terms 'egology': thus simple consciousness and self-consciousness, commonplace egotism, megalomania, solipsism, and also a certain interpretation of Husserlian phenomenology. Finally, some involve an opposition in which the terms opposed to one another are defined against one another and in this way together form a whole: thus interpretations of Hegel that emphasize the dialectic, and war in all its variations — including definitions of social relations as tradeoffs of power. Most of what we do, according to Levinas, fits into one, two or all three of these categories, and thus involves the imposition of some sort of sameness on the differences that exist in reality. Politics, for instance, always takes the three forms: it is always in some sense a participation in which individuals insofar as they are political beings take their places as parts of a collective; it always involves at least to some extent the imposition of the egos of a few individuals on the rest; and it is always at least partly founded on the provisional peace of a temporary ceasefire in the war of all against all. But the political realm is not the only realm of the same in Levinas's thinking. All ideologies or theories impose sameness; so too does the attempt of conceptual thought to be comprehensive and consistent, and even the coherence necessary to linguistic communication. One of Levinas's key ideas is the link he draws between the three kinds of sameness: participation, egology and war are all effectively the same for him since they are all same-making. What he seeks is the space where individual human beings stand outside the realm of the same, a space before the realm of the same. He finds it in the relation between two human beings, a relation in which — at least at the beginning or in the approach — the two parties neither come together as a whole, nor stand alone as autonomous egos, nor are defined against one another. In relation one meets up with what is not the same: one meets the 'other'.[1]

The most basic structure in Levinas's thinking, then, involves the interaction of the same and the other. The same occurs in the three forms delineated above (and might also be categorized in other ways, one of which I will describe in a moment), but otherness or difference cannot be categorized; it takes an infinite number of forms, since each other being one meets is infinitely different or unique. The discovery of these infinite differences, the respect for them, the service of the other in his otherness is, according to Levinas, ethics. This is an ethics that has no fixed rules but involves the rupture of all fixities or samenesses, a rupture that emerges from the encounter with unique particularities. 'Same and other', then, can also be called 'same and ethical'; these are the parts of the structure most basic to Levinas's thought, and the structure itself is the interaction of these parts. We will now describe the structure more slowly.

The basic structure: same and other

Ethics, according to Levinas, is discovered in the context of the interaction of two people, that is, the face to face encounter. In my coming into 'proximity' with or facing another human being, I discover, very simply, that he is other. I can come to him with a vast variety of different intentions but in all cases his otherness — or, to use Levinas's technical term, his 'alterity' — strikes me, both because it is an otherness per se, or a not-me-ness, and also because it is the other's particular unique otherness. I am arrested by it, and my intentions, whatever they were, are called into question. Who am I to have intentions toward the other? Who am I to have intentions at all? For Levinas, everything human beings do suggests that these questions at all times both underlie and undercut our intentions, and also that these questions, if they are asked meaningfully, can only have arisen out of the shocking discovery of the otherness of another human being.

Levinas often says that I see in the other's eyes or face — which are, for him, the seat of the other's otherness[2] — the command: thou shalt not kill. This becomes a relatively useful way to verbalize the effect that the other has on me only when it is understood that 'thou shalt not kill' has at least two meanings. It may be that I do actually approach the other murderously, which is to say that I approach him, whether deliberately or in ignorance, with the intention to subsume him into a sameness. If I cherish the notion that I might become one with him or if I conceive of him as a part of a whole — be that whole political or conceptual, harmonious or made up of parts seen as oppositive — then I approach him with the various tools of the makers of the sameness, one of which is my ability actually to bring about his death and all of which can figuratively be described as murderous. And I am tempted all the more in this direction by the fact that his face is vulnerable; it reveals to me some of what he is; it allows me to imagine that I can understand him, subsume his differences, or kill him. But the temptation is cut short, for I see, suddenly, that I cannot touch his differences, that his otherness belongs to him and cannot be made part of a same, that even were I to kill him physically I would not rid myself of it. "This temptation to murder and this impossibility of murder constitute the very vision of the face. To see a face is already to hear 'thou shalt not kill'" (DF 8). "The solipsistic restlessness of consciousness, in all of its adventures finding itself captivated by the self, here terminates: true exteriority is the look which prohibits me from embarking on any sort of conquest. . . . I simply *cannot any more*" (DEHH 173). The first meaning of 'thou shalt not kill' refers, then, to what I will call the *asymmetry of identity*: the fact that the other is different from me and from all samenesses, and that I 'simply cannot' make him same.

But once my murderous intentions have been arrested by the command, or in a case where I approach the other with intentions that are as close to nonmurderous as possible, the command takes on another layer of meaning. This second 'thou shalt not kill' begins in my awareness that the otherness of the other — the striking fact that I know nothing of importance about him — calls all my theories and convictions into question, including my theories and convictions about justice. I may believe that ultimately God will take care of justice, but God is not here, and I am. I may believe that the other is a victim of the patriarchy, or of capitalism, or of the medical profession, or of the grinding numbness of the American TV to which he has been exposed — I may have a number of ideas that go some distance toward explaining his needs. But all such are ideas are just more postulations of sameness, and are suddenly momentarily rendered absurd or, at least, inadequate to his unique him-ness. How do I know anything of his needs? What makes me think my abstract notions of what constitutes justice will do him any concrete good? In any case, the perpetrators of these injustices are not here, and I am. In this moment, I find myself infinitely responsible for the other, for no other reason but that I am on the scene.

And the second meaning of 'thou shalt not kill' does not stop here. It goes on to remind me that I *have* killed. "Was not my 'in the world' or my 'place in the sun' and my home a usurpation of places that belong to the other man, already oppressed by me or hungry?" (GCM 175).[3] The simple fact that I have not always done everything for the other means that I must consider whether I have not, at some time or in some way, taken from him what might have been his sustenance and his life, that is, whether I have not participated in various structures that force others into a mold of sameness, that oppress others in economic or other terms. This is not to say that Levinas is engaged here in casting blame; his meaning is larger in scope. When I find myself forced by the other to ask whether I have not participated in structures of the same, I am not so much asking whether I have done something wrong as simply whether I have done *something*, anything. Levinas writes of "a guiltless responsibility, where I

am nonetheless open to an accusation of which no alibi, spatial or temporal, could clear me" (LR 83), and elsewhere that
"it is *as though* I were responsible for [the other's] mortality
and guilty for surviving" (OB 91, my emphasis). The other
judges my very existence and his judgment is always harsh.
To be before the other is to be unjustified.

So, to the *asymmetry of identity* — to the fact that I can no
longer assume that the other is like me — is added, in the
second meaning of 'thou shalt not kill', an *asymmetry of responsibility*. The latter follows directly from the former: it is
because the other's difference has struck me that I become
aware of the inadequacy of all abstract or same-making theories in which responsibility is, if not simply passed off, at
least spread wide and thin, and also of my participation, by
virtue of my existence, in the same-making structures called
into existence by such theories. His difference commands me
to service, and my "power and emprise [are now] positively
produced as the possession of a world I can bestow as a gift
on the other. . . . For the presence before a face, my orientation toward the other, can lose the avidity proper to the gaze
only by turning into generosity, incapable of approaching
the other with empty hands" (TI 50). This movement can
also be described as the realization that the other is spiritually unbridgeably higher than me, that he is my judge; while
at the same time being economically unbridgeably lower than
me, the one to whom I must give all I have, the destitute one,
the widow or orphan or stranger. In other words, I find myself responsible before him in several ways. I am responsible
to him because he knows things I do not and can judge me in
ways I cannot judge myself. I am responsible *for* him because
any material needs he has are mine to fulfill, to the point
where I must 'feed him with bread from my own mouth' (OB
55, 77, 142). And, above all, I am responsible *for* him in the
sense that in order to make a space for his difference or to
make him free I must bear his responsibility; I must answer

for him and take his punishment.[4] I find myself, then, his breadwinner, his keeper, his hostage, his martyr, and his 'substitute'. And through it all the command 'thou shalt not kill' continues to loom over me, both in its negative form in which it stands for my awareness that I cannot murder him or make him same, and in its positive form in which it stands for my awareness that not to murder him means to serve him. Ultimately, as Levinas sometimes says, it means that the other cannot be left to die alone (RK 24, GCM 175), which is to say that I must stay with him and always do more until there is no more to do. Responsibility "increases infinitely, living infinitely, an obligation more and more strict in the measure that obedience progresses and the distance to be crossed untraversable in the measure that one approaches" (OB 142). The continuous pressure of the command from the other's face is never allowed to give way to pride in its fulfillment; the command disqualifies apology.

So much for a preliminary account of the face to face encounter and the birth of responsibility. I will summarize the account (without attempting to defend it) as follows. When I meet the other, all my certainties, theories, conceptions, motivations, expectations, predictions, judgments, needs, or wishes — all my samenesses — are called into question, and all my resources are put to his service. The other and I do not blend with one another, though a blending of some sort was likely one of my intentions before the encounter; we do not find one another equal, though this, too, might have been in my mind. Rather, the encounter is an epiphanic, traumatic, and terrible celebration of difference, in which I discover an absolutely unbridgeable gap between us, a gap that can be described spatially (he is higher and lower, my judge and the destitute one) or, as we will see, as an aspect of language, or as an aspect of time. This gap or difference strikes me as forcefully as it is possible to be struck, appearing as an ethical command, or as the command to an ethics of difference, an ethics that has as its purpose to preserve his difference by giving to him, answering to him, and answering for him. This is not a series of movements that occur in a particular order. The other's alterity *is* the rupture of my same, *is* my service. We move on now to politics.

The encounter with the other engenders the extraordinary response of infinite service, but the encounter takes place in the everyday world in which such responses are quite simply impractical. We will set aside for the moment the obvious and apparently problematic fact that I may refuse the command 'thou shalt not kill' and slit the other's throat. According to Levinas, even before I make any decisions about accepting or refusing the command, a prior problem, a ubiquitous problem, intrudes on my desire to serve the other, namely, the conflict of competing responsibilities. For the other and I do not inhabit the world to ourselves. The existence of other things, and especially of other people — which Levinas describes by speaking of the 'third' — necessitates certain impositions of sameness. The third "is of itself the limit of responsibility and the birth of the question: What do I have to do with justice? A question of consciousness. Justice is necessary, that is, comparison, coexistence, assembling, order, thematization, the visibility of faces, and thus intentionality and the intellect, and in intentionality and the intellect, the intelligibility of a system, and thence also a copresence on an equal footing before a court of justice" (OB 157). To put the matter bluntly, if I give everything I have to the first other I come across, I will have nothing left for the next one. When there is more than one other person to consider, asymmetry must give way to symmetry, difference to equality, and infinite service to the other to calculation of how best, in necessarily finite ways, to serve the needs of the many. Moreover, the third is always there, and not just because the other and I happen to live in society. The third is there in the very face of the other; as Levinas sometimes puts it, "I see the other's other in the eyes of the other." In fact, in the eyes of the other I see all the other's others, and their others, and so on and so forth until I see in the eyes of the other that if I wish to be responsible for him I must also be responsible for the whole world: "in the proximity of the other, all the others than the other obsess me, and that obsession already cries out for justice" (OB 158). So the face to face, for all that it *ruptures* impositions of sameness, also *calls for* imposition of sameness in the form of universal, egalitarian justice, or calculative reason, or the postulation of models of behaviour, or expectation, prediction, and judgment; indeed, the face to face calls for the imposition of the very economic structures that usurp the livelihood of the other, since these structures — for all that they are unjust — were almost certainly instituted at first for the sake of the third with the intention of distributing necessities over the widest possible field. The ethical encounter itself demands the imposition of the samenesses that compromise or even betray ethics by overlooking the uniqueness of *each other* in a vision of *all the others*; the ethical encounter demands politics.[5]

Is politics, then, the end of the story? It is certainly an end in a sense. Politics is one of the structures of the same that Levinas thinks back from; he is deeply interested in the question of how politics is grounded in the ethical experience. But if, as I have so far laid matters out, politics is founded on the experience of the rupture of the structures of the same in the ethical encounter, then it will be a ruptured politics, a politics full of doubt and self-examination. Since each member of the political order is an ethical being in the deepest sense, a being who has had and continues to have ethical encounters, the political structure, though a structure of the same, is constantly being reminded of its origin in brokenness or broken anew. Levinas's basic structure, the interaction of same and other, is an extraordinarily complex dynamic, involving degrees of rupture, repeated rupture, and above all the memory of rupture. But before we examine it more closely, I want to mention some other sets of terms by which the structure can be described, beginning with 'saying' and 'said'.

According to Levinas, my encounter with the other is played out in discourse, since discourse — whether verbal or constituted by gesture — is the way the other and I can come into relation without merging into a unity. The motivation for discourse is my impulse toward something I do not already know, something other than me; what moves me to converse is the desire to hear the other express his differences, to hear him surprise me. Thus for Levinas all discourse begins, and to a large extent continues, in listening; it begins and continues when I make space for the other, when I give him my ear, when I expose myself to him. The role of subjectivity in discourse — *my* role — can be described as taking instruction, but taking instruction is actually not a taking but a giving; instruction is taken when I offer myself to the other to be stamped by his words. The other, then, is among other things my teacher, a teacher who teaches me about himself. Teaching is a facet of his judgment over me or his height; his presence "dominates him who welcomes it, comes from the heights, unforeseen, and consequently teaches its very novelty" (TI 66). But the other and I cannot spend an entire conversation expressing our differences to one another. We find immediately, or always already, that since we two are not alone in the world, we are discussing other things. And because discourse involves talking about something, it involves having a topic and thus 'thematizing', that is, explaining as a theme, placing under a category, making same. Levinas uses the term 'said' to describe the aspect of speech that is thematization. He uses the term 'saying' to describe the self-exposure that motivates and underlies the speech, the aspect of speech that is the willing expression of openness to teaching.

The saying is nothing miraculous or fantastic or particular to certain modes of discourse. It is merely the generosity of everyday speech, the impulse to cover for the other, to put the other at his ease — not in a vulgar sense or for a vulgar purpose, but with the intention simply to let him know that his words are of value. It begins with the uneasiness of silence into which one interjects a remark, and then continues with saying and saying again, saying 'saids' to be sure, but saying 'saids' in order to say. The openness of the saying is not a springboard; the idea is not to move into saying something important, nor is it even to move into greater intimacy with the other. The saying *is* the intimacy; the whole of oneself is already offered in the word of approach. As the conversation continues after the approach, the said functions to make something — an appearance or theme or object or struc-ture — manifest, to disclose it or bring it to light. But under-neath this there remain the two interlocutors, naked of themes and structures, revealing to one another what cannot be brought to light, their otherness that in its infinity and absolute alterity evades disclosure; they reveal to one another glimpses of what nevertheless remains in its essence always concealed; they offer themselves. On the level of the said, where discourse is the work of disclosure, questions arise over whether the interlocutor tells the truth or lies, questions of objectivity. But on the level of saying, where discourse is the work of revelation, there is no dissembling; there the face or the eyes speak of themselves, always uniquely, in frankness.

The underlying level could not exist without the superficial trappings of discourse; the saying requires the said as its vehicle and so it calls for the said. But, too, the saying and the said vie with one another. The said always dissimulates the saying, covering it over until the saying is indiscernible; at times it even betrays the saying by trying to make alterity itself into a theme. And the saying, in return, undermines the said; it "always seeks to unsay that dissimulation — that is its very veracity" (OB 152). The structure represented here is another version of the structure that relates ethics and politics. There is a moment of approach or inception in which I find that I offer myself to the other, exposing myself to him in his uniqueness: this is the saying as well as the ethical 'thou shalt not kill'. This moment calls for a structure of sameness to be imposed: this is the said as well as politics. The sameness compromises its ethical origin: the said compromises or betrays the saying just as politics compromises or betrays ethics. And the initial or primary moment continues to reside in the structure of sameness, breaking it again or reminding it that it was born in brokenness: the saying 'unsays' the said just as ethics ruptures politics. We now have two accounts of how the ethical that is the service of otherness calls for us to impose a same-making nonethical and yet vies with it, both in the sense that the ethical is threatened by the nonethical it has called forth, and also in the sense that the ethical ruptures the nonethical it has called forth. This is the complete form of what I am calling the basic Levinasian structure. Levinas at one point calls it (or a part of it) "the great paradox of human existence," and describes it by saying that "we must use the ontological for the sake of the other; to ensure the survival of the other we must resort to technico-political systems of means and ends" (RK 28). He omits here the remainder of the structure: that those ontological or technico-political systems undermine otherness, but otherness also undermines them.

Levinas coopts a great many words to serve as technical terms for the parts of the paradoxical structure. In the camp of the same or the political, we have already come across: symmetry, participation, collectivity, identity, egology, objectivity, war, thematization, the said, system, ideology, ontology, theory, conceptual thought, comparison, assembling, copresence, disclosure, vision or visibility, intentionality, and the third. And in the camp of the other or ethics we have:

difference, alterity, relation, novelty, teaching, asymmetry, height, destitution, revelation, listening, saying and un-saying. I want briefly to note three things about these lists. First, some of these terms are more or less synonymous in Levinas's understanding — for instance ontology and sys-tem — while others bring their own nuances to the struc-ture. Second, all the terms carry some form of their common meanings; it is their juxtaposition that allows us to see them in Levinas's way. For instance, the link between sameness and disclosure encourages us to see disclosure as the con-veying of a piece of knowledge already in some sense present, while the juxtaposition of disclosure to revelation allows us to see that what is critical about the revelation conveyed by alterity is its novelty. Finally, all the terms offered here share a particular virtue: they never switch sides and take up places in the opposing camp. This is not true of all of Levinas's words. Justice, for instance, switches from its place as an ethical term or a term of otherness to a political term or a term of sameness at a certain point in Levinas's thinking life. Phi-losophy, morality, religion, responsibility, and the good all occasionally play both sides.[6]

One more critical set of terms must be added to the list: totality, as a synonym for the same, and infinity, as a descrip-tion of otherness or othernesses. In common parlance, total-ity and infinity can at times be used interchangeably, since both are synonyms for 'everything'. They refer, however, to different aspects of 'everything': totality's everything is closed or finished while infinity's everything is ever-increasing and always incomplete. The two terms thus express the nature of same-making as the attempt to bring a kind of closure or fixity to the beings in reality, and the nature of otherness as a rupture of that closure. We will move, with these terms, into a discussion of some of the basic structure's difficulties.

The problems of narrative order

I will begin by categorizing the modes of the same in a new way, taking as my guide Adriaan Peperzak's attempt to offer an introductory definition of the term *totality*. Peperzak begins as follows:

> Levinas presents a critique of the whole of Western civiliza-
> tion, which he sees as dominated by the spirit of Greek phi-
> losophy. Western thought and practice in his view are marked
> by a striving for totalization, in which the universe is reduced
> to an originary and ultimate unity by way of panoramic
> overviews and dialectical syntheses. This kind of monism,
> according to Levinas, must be criticized from the point of view
> of a thinking which starts from phenomena as they present
> themselves. Such a critique is consonant with ancient tradi-
> tions of thought that reach back to Biblical and Talmudic
> sources, but it also occurs in Plato and Descartes.

This description (comparable in some measure to Richard Cohen's "negative" Levinas) is already problematic. Totality seems to be a philosophic error, one that is presumably relatively easy to avoid. But what is its source? Is it found in Western thought, as opposed to Middle Eastern? Peperzak suggests this, but also tells us that Plato was not a totalizer. Is it found in modern thought, as opposed to ancient thought? Peperzak suggests this as well, but also tells us that some modern thought does not totalize, and some ancient thought does. And Peperzak complicates the problem further as he continues. He explains next that Levinas links totality with the same or assimilation, and infinity with the other or what cannot be assimilated, and also that "whereas the category of totality summarizes the way in which the Ego inhabits the world — its worldly economy — the infinite names the other's ungraspable or incomprehensible character."[7] Suddenly totality is not an avoidable error, but rather a condition of our being in the world.

The difficulties that arise from Peperzak's undifferentiated definition can be resolved into a critical distinction. Samenesses or totalities can be classed into two types: avoidable errors (for instance, Heideggerian ontology, or pre-Socratic monism) and conditions endemic to human life (for instance, politics and thematization). Neither type can be pinned down or given precise boundaries; as an avoidable error, totality appears in all sorts of varieties and traditions, and as a "worldly economy" it also takes many forms. But the distinction between avoidable and endemic remains clear, at least theoretically, and useful.

What about infinity? By definition, infinity cannot be categorized, but I have already begun to suggest that it too appears in two different aspects in Levinas's thought, or functions in two 'times'. On the one hand, the other's alterity or infinite difference exists as what cannot be contained by totality. It overflows all attempts to categorize it, and at the same time as totality is trying to make it same, it breaks totality. On the other hand, infinity is what Levinas thinks back to: infinite alterity is the origin and motivation of politics as the infinite saying is the origin and motivation of the said. Thus infinity seems both to follow totality and also to precede it[8] — and we have here a double-nature that corresponds, roughly, to the double-nature of totality. The tension between totality's two meanings — as a condition of human life or an error in life that can be avoided — is analogous to the tension in infinity — which also appears as a prior condition of existence, and as something one encounters at a particular time, in the face of another human being.

Each doubling — but especially the doubling of infinity — is intended to create confusion. One can best sort the matter out by seeing that Levinas sometimes chooses to describe reality in a theoretical 'order in which it is', and, at other times — more often — to describe it in a phenomenological order, the order as it occurs to human beings or as it 'happens'.[9] Infinity, as it is, is prior; it has always already come to pass, or passed. But infinity occurs or happens insofar as it intrudes on and breaks sameness. Ethics is first philosophy, but one must think out of experience back towards it. Once one does, one can speak of a theoretical ordering; one can put one's thoughts in an order that is not the order one thought them in, not the order of experience. Levinas's theoretical ordering, offered in *Totality and Infinity*, moves from the human being alone, to the human being in relation, to the human being in society, that is, from the one, to the two, to the three. I will only sketch its outlines here.[10]

First, there is the primary or primal anarchy, which is to say, an infinite number of different things, beings, aspects, and qualities. A human being cannot, however, see these things as separate until she herself is separated from the chaos; until this point they appear to her as a formless mass, or as Levinas describes it, the *il y a*, the throb of undifferentiated being. From this, a human being wrenches herself, separating herself as a particular, a consciousness, an autonomous being, (what I will call 'the one'). Thus she becomes able to see others as others, or to experience exteriority. But at the same time, and before she meets any others, she finds that in separating herself from the *il y a*, she becomes her own sameness, which is to say, a being who is the same as herself, a being who understands herself to be herself, a being, who, qua that being, is consistent with herself despite the possible existence of conflicts in the soul. Moreover, in order to preserve her realm of the same, she must continually be assimilating to herself the things she finds in the world: eating, breathing, knowing, taking, and making. She becomes the sole possessor of her world, an 'atheist' engaged in use of the good things that come to hand. This position — or, as Edith Wyschogrod says, 'ontic level' — is not evil but profoundly innocent; Levinas describes it in an early text as 'salvific' (TO 62, see EE 92) and in *Totality and Infinity* as 'enjoyment' or 'living from . . .' or 'good soup' (TI 110–15). However, it is not yet enough; the subject here is not a yet a true human being. Now she meets the other ('the two'), and the face to face encounter takes place. Her realm of the same is put into question by the other, and, as a result, her abilities to take, to own, and to make are put to the service of the other; even her very bread and breath are his for the asking. She gives herself, and in doing so, she becomes a true self: no longer an autonomous locus of sameness but a human being in relation or in dialogue. But in the eyes of the other, she also sees the other's other ('the three'); indeed, she sees the whole world and thus an infinite number of infinitely different things. Now, despite and because of this awareness she finds herself called to impose various kinds of sameness: those of the said and conceptual thought and coherence and symmetry and politics and justice and equality. But she is free to impose these samenesses in a great many different ways. Her speech, though it must employ a said, can employ the said of French or English, of Hebrew or Greek; though it must be coherent, it can utilize the coherencies of a logician or a novelist. Likewise, her political understanding or her philosophy may take a host of different forms. Her impositions of sameness at this level are better or worse depending on whether or not she remembers, in them or through them, that they were called for not by any ultimate ascendancy or priority of sameness, but by the other's rupture of all samenesses.

Infinity's two functions or 'times' find narrative places in the scheme. The command to respect alterity is already inscribed in the initial anarchy, the myriad of differences at the beginning of things or at the heart of reality, but it is discovered only in the encounter with another person. Totality's two functions also find their places here. Endemic totalities arise at the level of the 'one' and the level of the 'three'; the subject's autonomous or atheistic same-making is necessary, and so are the samenesses she is called to impose by the other's other or the rest of the world. Avoidable totalities are simply the versions of these totalities that are less responsive to difference, the versions that claim that there never was an anarchy (either primal or introduced by the 'two'), that they never have been broken, that they can explain or describe everything; in short, those that forget that they themselves are always already ruptured, are conditioned by rupture, and were called forth by rupture. Egologies, participations, and wars are at times endemic totalities and at times avoidable totalities. One might chart the typology of totality with which I began this chapter onto the typology of endemic and avoidable as follows. As endemic, egology is consciousness, participation is justice, and war is just war, or — a phenomenon we will take up in the next section — intertotality critique. As avoidable, egology is possession or egoism, participation is ontology, and war is unjust war or dialectical philosophy. But this double-typology is hardly comprehensive, for these are just a few of the many terms that might be adduced here, and almost all of the terms in Levinas shift about in meaning. 'Ontology' for instance, is almost always used for avoidable totalities (of any variety), but I have already cited a passage where it is applied to endemic totalities (RK 28, cited in section I of this chapter). What may be said with certainty is that all of the avoidable totalities Levinas criticizes are perverse versions of endemic ones. The bad egologies and some of the bad participatory structures are perverse varieties of the necessary egology of getting a self or attaining consciousness, and the monisms or ontologies and most of the bad participatory structures are perverse varieties of the necessary political, philosophical, conceptual or linguistic structures. It may be said, in short, that endemic totality is an exigency of finitude while avoidable totality is the belief that all is finite, the misunderstanding of a finite construction as infinity.[11]

Levinas would, I think, not be averse to another illustration of the scheme, one drawn from Genesis chapters 1 to 11. The tower of Babel, the first attempt at third-level totalization recorded in the Hebrew Scriptures, must be broken by the introduction of alterity or diversity in the confusion of languages. But the very attempt at totalization would not have been possible without the prior alterity or diversity that is described in the creation account in Genesis 1. Infinity — otherness or diversity — is the primal precondition for thought and action. Once it is established, totality and infinity each appear in various manifestations, intertwined with one another, answering or breaking one another. Some of the totalities that subsequently appear are towers built with the intention of obfuscating difference; these are avoidable totalities. Most, though, are simply the huts we need to live in; these are endemic. This illustration also makes it clear — though perhaps it is clear already — that the notion of totality itself is flawed or in the deepest sense false. Robert Bernasconi, commenting on Levinas's statement that "we can proceed from the experience of totality back to a situation where the totality breaks up, a situation that conditions the totality itself" (TI 24), writes that "it might be said in consequence that the conditions for the possibility of the experience of totality are at the same time the conditions for the impossibility of the experience of totality, in the sense that the rupture of totality shows that there never was a totality."[12] Bernasconi is quite correct. Because all totalities are always already broken, totality never was; totalities are shams; or, as another commentator puts it, the same 'hallucinates' its sameness.[13] But in most cases they are relatively virtuous shams, made up of good intentions and leading to good results.

The reason I did not begin this chapter with the narrative scheme I have just outlined is because, useful as it is to understand certain things about Levinas's thinking, it is not really a good reflection of his understanding of reality. No one actually begins alone, or with the experience of the *il y a*; no one takes or makes for herself before ever having met another human being. The scheme is not an account of the development of a child, nor of the development of civilization, nor of any actual temporal development. It should be recalled that the comparable scheme in Genesis appears in what is sometimes called the "primeval history," which may be understood as a nontemporal 'history' before the beginning of history, an account of all the elements of reality — cosmos, God, love, sin, the family, the political unit — laid out in an order governed by significance rather than chronology. Levinas's scheme is similar. All of us can recognize each of its movements without necessarily placing them in a particular sequence. The terrifying pulse of being as an undifferentiated synthesis that constitutes the experience of the *il y a* is something we all sense; the dread that it brings, the fear of the absolute indifference which is nondifference, is recognizable as a common variety of angst. So too the need to declare oneself autonomous, the impossibility of such a declaration, the ethical arrest, the conflicts between politics and ethics. Both Levinas and the authors of Genesis 1–11 offer narrative progressions explaining how the human being comes to be as she is or live as she does. But the truth lies in the narrative and not in the progression; the critical thing is not that we came to be what we are in this order, but rather that these stories explain the parts of what we are.

The most artificial aspect of the Levinasian theoretical scheme — and it is a fault shared by much of my own discourse up to this point — is the way it represents totality's and infinity's various functions or movements as happening at different times. The misrepresentation is less serious with respect to totality: while totality on the level of the one need not precede totality on the level of the three, they are, at any rate, two distinguishable movements; and endemic totality always precedes avoidable totality, even if they are sometimes hard to distinguish. But infinity's movements cannot be distinguished from one another except on the level of theory; in experienced reality, there is no prior infinity as opposed to a rupturing infinity. Let me lay the matter out more gradually, at the same time extending the understanding of infinity. It might be said that, in Levinas's thought, infinity actually has four theoretical functions. Infinity is (1) the primal precondition, the basic diversity of things and their differences one from the other; (2) the command in the face of the other that accuses me and breaks my totalities; (3) the awareness or acknowledgment of that command, the transformation of that accusation to infinite responsibility; and (4) what follows the totalities that are engendered by the encounter and rebreaks them or reminds them of their origin in brokenness. None of these functions can properly be expressed in speech, for any words that would express them would nullify them: the word 'difference', for instance, renders all differences the same difference, and thus the same per se. Levinas does, however, offer certain phrases that can provisionally describe the third function, and we can follow him by according all four functions provisional words or phrases: for the primal precondition, 'difference'; for the command, 'I am accused'; for the acknowledgment, 'here I am' or 'after you'; and for the unsaying or the reminder of brokenness, 'interrupt me'.[14] The critical point, however, is that to say one of these things is already to have said them all. They are the same moment: they constitute the face to face. As I have said, the confusion between them is deliberate.

I believe this point to be at the core of many of the problems that arise as one reads Levinas, and so would like to dwell on it a while, offering three examples of the coincidence of two or more of infinity's functions. We begin with the command and the response to the command (numbers 2 and 3). These 'two' events — the command and the response, the order to serve and the service — are one in Levinas's thinking, since as he understands it the only way one knows that the command exists is through the graciousness of one's initial response. To be sure, when a reader of Levinas considers her own experience it may seem to her less problematic to say that one is charged with responsibility before all thought, and rather more problematic to say that one responds to the command, initially, positively, that one's first response is generosity, hospitality, welcome. But phenomenologically, the two must be there at once; one's acceptance of responsibility is the way the accusation appears in consciousness. Without the acceptance, one would not be able to speak of the command — or, rather, if one were to speak of a command without recalling the experience of its acceptance, one would be making a dogmatic statement, based on nothing in reality.

Thus when Levinas describes the face to face, he refers not only to a great primal laying on of the yoke, but also to great primal shouldering of responsibility. Certainly one can refuse the command and murder the other; this is a commonplace event. In such a case, "the impossibility of declining responsibility is reflected only in the scruple or remorse that precedes or follows the refusal" (OB 6). But the existence of that scruple or remorse is enough to show that the refusal is secondary to the experience in which one is commanded, in which one *feels oneself* to be commanded, and in which one's awareness of being commanded is translated into an awareness of being responsible. "Violence can only aim at a face" (TI 225). All attempts to make the other same occur after one has seen the other as ultimately different, even if this 'seeing' does not rise to the level of what might be called conscious awareness; all dealings one has with the other occur after one has been shown that the other cannot be made same. We will not obscure the fact that this claim is radical. Although there is certainly a prescriptive or hortative aspect of Levinas's account of ethics — a call not to forget the ethical encounter — it is in the main descriptive; the ethical encounter is, for him, built into the nature of reality and the responsibility he describes is something we all know. Levinas's extraordinary descriptions of responsibility — I am in the other's debt, I am accused, I am persecuted, I am martyred, I am responsible for the other's responsibility, I am responsible "for the very outrage that the other, who qua other excludes me, inflicts on me, for the very persecution with which, before any intention, he persecutes me" (OB 166) — these descriptions are not spoken for himself alone, or even for himself and then as a call to his readers, but as the conclusion of his thinking back. Were the experience not a shared one, we should not have ethical behaviour at all; "it is through the condition of being hostage that there can be in the world pity, compassion, pardon, proximity — even the little there is" (OB 117). And, indeed, were the experience not a shared one, we should not have murder; for what would motivate us to kill the other if not the urge to rid ourselves of this persecuting assignation, this awful responsibility?

The second example involves the prior infinity and the infinity discovered in the face to face (number 1 and what we can now call number 2/3). Robert Bernasconi postulates, at one point, a distinction between these two things, though he classifies both of them as part of the face to face, speaking therefore about a 'transcendental' face to face and an 'empirical' face to face. "The question," he writes, "is: what status is to be accorded the face to face relation? Here interpretations diverge. Some interpreters understand it as a concrete experience that we can recognize in our lives. Other commentators have understood the face to face relation to be the condition for the possibility of ethics and indeed all economic existence and knowledge. If the first interpretation arises from what might be called an empirical reading, the second might be referred to as the transcendental reading. The puzzle is that Levinas himself seems unable to decide between these rival interpretations."[15] The problem is not insoluble. The face to face is always a concrete experience and nothing but a concrete experience. The transcendence it inscribes appears only in the concrete, and the possibility for ethics — which is also the possibility for the subsequent totalities of "economic existence and knowledge" — also appears only in the concrete. There is no direct experience of the infinity that precedes everything and conditions everything; infinity is discovered in the face — and its pastness or precedence, its already-there-ness, is discovered in the face.

The matter is recomplicated by the fact that Levinas writes at length in *Totality and Infinity* of Descartes's "idea of the infinite" in which the thinking subject finds that she contains more than she can contain, or finds in herself an infinity that overflows her. This suggests that there is an access to infinity that is not the face, and that can be found by the human alone prior to an encounter with the face. But ultimately, for Levinas if not for Descartes, one does not have the idea of the infinite outside of or before the encounter with the other. "To approach the other in conversation is to welcome his expression, in which at each instant he overflows the idea a thought would carry away from it. It is therefore to receive from the other beyond the capacity of the I, which means exactly, to have the idea of infinity. . . . The idea of infinity, the infinitely more contained in the less, is concretely produced in the form of a relation with the face" (TI 51, 196). Thus Levinas can describe his thought as "a transcendentalism which begins with ethics" (GCM 90): the transcendent is met only in the empirical; the trace of what is not in the world is met only in the world. And one cannot ask why we need to have an empirical face-to face if plurality, and thus the ethical assignation, is transcendentally always already there. This is the sort of question one could only ask if one had taken the temporality of *Totality and Infinity*'s narrative scheme too literally. By offering us an apparently temporal scheme, Levinas intends only to offer a way back to ethics or infinity from all our starting points, not to restrict himself to the scheme's chronology.

The third example is constituted by all of the many passages in which Levinas says that infinity does not precede totality, but occurs only after it as what breaks it (number 1/2/3 and number 4). "[T]he idea of infinity is the mode of being, the infinition of infinity. Infinity does not first exist, and then reveal itself. Its infinition is produced [*se produit*] as revelation, as a positing of its idea in me. . . . [It is] produced by withstanding the invasion of a totality" (TI 26, 104). Levinas uses the term '*se produire*' frequently with reference to infinity's movements. It is possible that he intends to play with the passive/reflexive nature of the French verb, wanting both the sense of 'is produced' (which is the translation Lingis prefers) and also 'produces itself'. But he clarifies his use of the term with reference to a different tension: 'is accomplished' versus 'is revealed'. "The term production indicates both the effectuation of a being (an event 'is produced', a car 'is produced') and its being brought to light or its exposition (an argument 'is produced', an actor 'is produced'). The ambiguity of the verb translates the essential ambiguity of the operation by which, at the same time, a being is accomplished and revealed" (TI 26). This ambiguity is significant. The mode of being proper to infinity is not the mode of an objectivity that simply exists as accomplished and of which one can say "it exists first." Rather, infinity's mode of being, its accomplishment, is its revelation. The passage about the 'infinition of infinity' stands, then, not only as a crystalline expression of the problem of narrative order in Levinas, but also as its solution. In the passage, all the functions of infinity seem to come together: the revelation (as a rupturing force) is the accomplishment (infinity itself); the empirical is the form of the transcendental. Infinity is always experienced as a breaking; it is "produced [made/revealed] by withstanding the invasion of a totality" (TI 104). It is only after the fact that we can say that this withstanding refers to a responsibility, this responsibility to a rupturing command, and this command to an always prior diversity.

Levinas's desire to restrict his speech to the level of experienced reality has another result, a result that recomplicates the entire issue. In order to express the nature of infinity, in which what appear to be several times come to pass, as it were, at once, in the face to face, he describes relation itself as a temporal phenomenon. This kind of description forms the theme of his earliest philosophical works, in which time, rather than the space of *Totality and Infinity* or the language of *Otherwise Than Being*, is the substrate of relation. And in the later works, the idea (or metaphor) of time persists in descriptions of the face (which however are more spatial in form) and descriptions of the response or the saying (which however are more linguistic). Let me now run quickly through the evolution of Levinas's understanding of time.[16]

In the early works, Levinas (very much at this time in dialogue with Husserl, Heidegger, and Bergson) argues against a notion of time in which instants are strung together in a timeline to form an eternity. That vision of time, he suggests in *Existence and Existents* (1947) is a feature of what we have called the level of the one, where the instant is the point at which one wrenches oneself from the *il y a* and eternity is the time one subsequently makes for oneself, a projection of a past and future made up of a theoretical string of instants of me-ness, a 'postponement' or 'extension' of immature subjectivity, a contemporaneousness or simultaneity. In *Time and the Other* (1948), he speaks of how the other brings to me another instant, irreconcilable with my instant, and thus introduces to me the real dimensions of past and future: a past in which the other existed before meeting me and a future in which novelty is possible. The critical idea is that the dimensions of pastness and futurity brought to me or imposed on me by the other cannot exist, for me, as parts of my timeline, and cannot be assumed into a new timeline, but exist rather as a rupturing of the timeline with which I have been bolstering my security. Thus the conflict that occurs in the encounter is not between two instants or between two timelines, but between a an instant-made-eternity and the rupturing of that eternity. My timeline is a re-presentation of the instant *as* time, and the other ruptures it by showing me time *as* rupture. The use of time-talk, therefore, allows Levinas to raise and at least partly address a potentially destructive problem in his thinking, namely, that if the other is different from me, and I am different from him (which follows), then we are simply two differences, equally different and therefore equal in difference, and therefore, in a sense, comparable, reciprocal, two halves of a whole, or in short, a totality. Levinas is always at pains to stress that his understanding "breaks the dialectical model of unity in difference" and the use of time-talk is one of the ways he goes about it. As Richard Cohen explains, Levinas's time is not difference in contrast to difference — his *other* time in contrast to *my* time — for this would imply identity or in-difference. Rather it can be described as the difference between (his) difference and (my) contemporaneousness — his other and my same — and thus as non-in-difference, that is, my nonindifference to the other.[17] In effect, time is ethics.[18]

In *Totality and Infinity* (1961), this understanding, while not the focus of the text, is nevertheless reiterated and even intensified. The time of nonreturn, the time that is my going out of myself or having my timeline put into question, is identified as positive ethics. Here synthesis becomes more obviously connected with the spatio-temporal present of the immature subjectivity or egology, the present of presence or the present of representation, and pastness and futurity become more obviously connected with the other or others, with the one who is there before me, awaiting the ethical encounter, and with the one who is not yet, to whom I dedicate my life and my work. Presence or the present is always mine; any other way of thinking of it — for instance, the postulation of a present in the life of someone else long dead and past or someone not yet born and future — is merely a projection disguising the presence/present of my thinking. But the other ruptures the present by revealing to me the existence of a past that was never (my) present and a future that will never be (my) present.

One of the problematic narrative structures we have identified — that an already-there infinity only appears or 'comes to be' in the face — can now be seen as the only possible mode of relation. It is not that several times come to pass, in the face to face, at once — but, as it were, that the face to face comes to pass in several times. There must be a temporal gap or lapse between me and the other if his alterity is to be maintained, a gap such that he both arrives on the scene first and also remains on the scene afterwards, presenting to me a past and future that repudiate my 'past' and 'future'. If he is to become my first priority, my 'before-me' — if the reversal of priorities that constitutes ethics is to take place — then he must be temporally beyond and the source of a temporality that ruptures my temporality. His height (to use the spatial term from *Totality and Infinity*) must be a non-simultaneity with simultaneous time.

In *Otherwise Than Being* (1974), the philosophy of time is reinscribed, once again, into the linguistic forms that mark that text. Thus the saying, which bears reference to a past insofar as it is constituted by exposure and to a future insofar as it exists as an unsaying, becomes "the impossibility of the dispersion of time to assemble itself in the present, the insurmountable diachrony of time" (OB 38). From this text on, 'diachrony' becomes Levinas's term for his conception of relation as time. In "Diachrony and Representation" (1985), diachrony is connected to alterity, but it is not equivalent to alterity. It refers to the whole ethical structure, to the nonsynchronic existence together of sameness and alterity; or, to be more precise, the nonsynchronic existence together of synchrony and nonsynchrony. Diachrony is the tension between a tension and a harmony; it is not a time, but the coexistence of two kinds of times. Were diachrony merely alterity as opposed to synchrony, the two terms would exist as opposites, that is, on the same plane; they could be synchronized. But "time and ethics effect a curvature."[19] Diachrony and synchrony cannot be synchronized; the attempt to synchronize them is one way of describing avoidable totality.

Temporal speech is better than spatial speech in large part simply because it is less familiar. Spatial speech fails most obviously in the idea of transcendence. For Levinas, what might be called the transcendent happens here in the immanent and *is not* — but the very word transcendent seems to imply that it happens elsewhere and *is*. The neologism 'diachrony' replaces the transcendent/immanent paradigm and avoids its errors, at the necessary cost of clarity. Diachrony is otherwise than being; it wrenches events out of their time in a history in a way more profound than any talk about transcendence can wrench them out of their place in a space. To be sure, the things engaged in a diachronous relation are not themselves outside of history, nor are they outside of ontology: they are existents; they exist in locales. What is outside of, or past, or otherwise than temporality or history, and otherwise than 'my space' or 'your space' or 'somewhere in between' or 'somewhere out there' is their relation. The relation happens in a nontime or a nonspace; it is diachronous.

It is enough, for now, to draw from these abstruse analyses some insight into the extraordinary boundaries that Levinas draws around infinity or alterity, boundaries that protect it from being subsumed into a contemporaneousness, a synchrony, a simultaneity — in spatial terms, into a presence. Infinity remains never-present even when it is manifest in experience in the face of the other. It is thus preserved, so that as well as standing always at the beginning of things (although never as a starting point) it also stands always at the end. Or rather, it stands as the lack of an end, the destruction of all *teloi* on which one might come to rest. All totalities have the tendency to claim finality, even those that are endemic; which is to say that all totalities lean toward their perverse versions. It is relatively easy to forget the saying in one's said, or the other in one's politics. Most people, most of the time, are armed against the face to face; we do not see the eyes of the other because we are busy looking at whether they are blue,[20] whether the other has a higher social standing, whether he is carrying a knife, or any of a hundred considerations that have nothing to do with his alterity. Conceptual totalities — categorizations and closed structures — appear to be most important to us as we make our way through the world. And they seem, too, to be capable of structuring infinity; indeed, the very interchangeability of the two terms in the common parlance — by which the term infinity is understood to mean totality and thus rendered closed, or finished — suggests that totality is a concept greater than infinity, or that infinity is a part of totality. It is very difficult to shake the conviction that the diachrony can be rendered a synchrony, especially given the fact that Levinas's writing itself — like all speech and all writing — synchronizes, representing diachrony as there, on the page, in the moment of writing or the moment of reading. But since infinity is unencompassable, it must render totality or synchrony open. Levinas writes that after the ethical encounter "I simply cannot anymore" by which he means that I cannot ontologize or thematize or synchronize the other. My structures remain broken.

And yet it is not so. As we have seen, not only am I perfectly capable after the ethical encounter of ontologizing, synchronizing and thematizing, I do these things of necessity; I *must* do them. I must do what I "simply cannot anymore" do. How is this to be unraveled? The answer, broadly, is that to create totality infinitely or history diachronously or sameness ethically, I must do it badly. And 'doing it badly' is the beginning of the answer to the problem we are about to take up.

Ethics and politics

I can make sameness ethically, but I cannot make sameness ethical; I can totalize ethically by totalizing badly or 'untotally', but I cannot make an ethical totality. That this is so, for Levinas, and the reasons why it must be so, will form the subject of this section. I will restrict the discussion to politics, but at the same time will note that this is hardly a restriction at all. There are many ways in which one might lay out the relations that exist between an individual, her other, their society, various societies, 'society' as a phenomenon, their state, various states, the 'state' as a phenomenon, groups or allegiances that exist within the society or state, and groups or allegiances (such as religious communities) that cross the boundaries of societies or states. All of these things exist concretely, all of them are related one to another, and most of us have opinions about how they ought best to relate. Levinas, however, is in general interested only in a single aspect of these relations, an aspect that arises from his basic structure, namely, the transition between the two and the three, or the face to face and 'politics'. Politics, in his usage, inscribes all group relations, all relations that include more than me and the other who stands in proximity to me; all third-level totalities, including the said, are politics.

The relation of two, for Levinas, is the realm of the ethical. The entry of the third always means the ethical will be compromised. But as we have seen, the third is already there in the eyes of the other. Why, then, can relations of three not be ethical? When Levinas is pressed in an interview with Richard Kearney on this point, he admits readily that third level structures — those of the said, or of institutions, or of society, or in short of politics — can be 'moral', but refuses to accord them the status of the 'ethical'.

> This distinction between the ethical and the moral is very important here. By morality I mean a series of rules relating to social behaviour and civic duty. But while morality thus operates in the socio-political order of organizing and improving our human survival, it is ultimately founded on an ethical responsibility toward the other. As *prima philosophia*, ethics cannot itself legislate for society or produce rules of conduct whereby society might be revolutionized or transformed. . . . When I talk of ethics as a 'disinter-estedness', I do not mean that it is indifference; I simply mean that it is a form of vigilant passivity to the call of the other which precedes our interest in being, our inter-est, as a being-in-the-world attached to property and appropriating what is other than itself to itself. Morality is what governs the world of political 'inter-estedness,' the social interchanges between citizens in a society. Ethics, as the extreme exposure and sensitivity of one subjectivity to another, becomes morality and hardens its skin as soon as we move into the political world of the impersonal 'third' — the world of government, institutions, tribunals, prisons, schools, committees, and so on. (RK 29–30)[21]

For Levinas, a grouping of two cannot provide 'rules of conduct' for society, and a grouping of three cannot be ethical. He insists on the distinction, reserving the word 'ethics' for a second-level movement, referring to salutary third-level movements here as 'morality' and, much more often, as 'justice'.[22]

What is the distinction's status? What does it mean to say that politics or justice cannot be ethical? In actuality, there are two competing thrusts in Levinas's thought. The dominant thrust, expressed for instance in the Kearney interview, is an insistence on the tension between ethics and political justice; it stresses the part of the basic structure where the same and the other vie with one another, where the entry of the third compromises the relation with the second. The less-dominant thrust allows for a blurring of the two terms; it stresses the part of the basic structure where the other calls for the same, where the relation with the second already implies the presence of the third.

A passage from *Totality and Infinity* will serve to illustrate the dominant thrust. Here Levinas first mounts a defense of institutions, and then follows it up with a scathing denunciation. "Freedom," he begins, "is not realized outside of social and political institutions, which open to it the access to fresh air necessary for its expansion, its respiration, and even, perhaps, its spontaneous generation. . . . An existence that is free, and not a velleity for freedom, presupposes a certain organization of nature and society." But then he explains that the objective judgment of these institutions kills the will of the individual as subjectivity. Having released it from a "brutish tyranny," their objectivity delivers it to a new tyranny, to the totality of "the universal and of the impersonal, an order that is inhuman, though distinct from the brutish." He continues, explaining that human beings assert themselves against this violent reduction only by subsequent experiences of the ethical encounter with the other (TI 241). In an interview with Raoul Mortley, he calls these subsequent manifestations of the two, in and yet outside or beyond the world of the three, "charity." And, to this, he adds one of his clearest suggestions of a tension between ethics and justice: "I always say that justice is the primary violence" (RM 18).

The less-dominant thrust tends to emerge when Levinas uses terms other than 'ethics' and 'justice': for instance, 'responsibility'. Can three be responsible? Levinas vacillates on the question. In the discussion of politics in chapter five of *Otherwise Than Being*, he writes first that the symmetry required by justice is "a betrayal of my anarchic relation with illeity [i.e. a betrayal of anarchic responsibility]"[23] (OB 158), but then seems to retract this idea, writing that "*in no way is justice* a degradation of obsession, a degeneration of the for-the-other, a diminution, *a limitation of anarchic responsibility*, a neutralization of the glory of the infinite, a degeneration that would be produced in the measure that for empirical reasons the initial duo would become a trio" (OB 159, my emphasis). The first statement, which seems to suggest a tension between ethical responsibility and justice, is corrected in the second statement. And it is the thrust of the second that is sustained in the discourse that follows. Levinas defines the just society as the society that allows ethics to exist within justice; in other words, he argues that the preservation of ethics in society is necessary not only because of the demands of ethics as something distinct from justice but is also the fundamental requirement for justice itself, or, to put it bluntly, that justice, to be justice, must allow its justice to be ruptured by ethics. Justice suddenly seems to have a double-meaning: it appears as the element of thirdness that is ruptured by the ethical relation between two, and also as that rupture. The second meaning — justice as rupture — begins effectively to conflate justice and ethics.

Of course, this creates difficulties for Levinas. He continues, writing that because "the contemporaneousness of the multiple is tied about the diachrony of two, justice remains justice only in a society where there is no distinction between those closest and those far off, but in which there also remains the impossibility of passing by the closest" (OB 159). There is to be "no distinction" between the other who stands before me and the thousand other others in my society (or indeed, the billions of other others in the world). What does

Levinas mean? If there is truly no distinction between the other and the other's other, then ethics is justice, and justice ethics. If it is only that the just society does not distinguish between the one near and the one far off then proximity — the forum of the ethical encounter — is lost in society, and the alterity of the other lost in the equal claims of the other others, in which case the just society is unethical and therefore unjust. The fact is that Levinas does wish to maintain the distinction between the two and the three, or the one near and the ones far off; for the one closest has the distinct honor of being impossible to pass by. But he also wishes to blur that distinction, to suggest the possibility of a continuity between ethics and justice, or, in other words, the possibility of an ethical politics. He sums the tension up in an interview conducted in 1975, explaining that the distinction between the two terms is true "at the same time that the proximity between [them] is true" (GCM 82).

Robert Gibbs devotes much of his chapter on Levinas and Marx to an argument for a socially responsible Levinas. His main concern is to show that Levinas's ethics is not only a matter of two individuals alone, or not a 'private' matter. This he draws from Levinas's delineation of the involvement of two people utterly wrapped up in one another as a realm of the same, a delineation that generally occurs in critiques of Martin Buber and his I-Thou relation. The exclusive involvement of two, or, as Gibbs puts it, the 'honeymoon', is not the meaning of the Levinasian face to face, and thus the face to face "is not exclusive, is not a withdrawal from others." Gibbs's point is well taken. The fact that the face to face is not withdrawn suggests a continuity between it and social relations, or at least, the depolarization of the distinction. Moreover, as Gibbs points out, there are responsibilities in both the ethical and the political arenas: as much as I am called to feed the other with bread from my own mouth, *we* are called together in such a way that "we give each other commands, we do work, all for the sake of social justice."[24] But, again, while the distinction is blurred, it is not abandoned entirely. It remains the case for Levinas that ethics *only* occurs in the relation with the other — even if it does not occur in everything that might, in common parlance, be designated as a 'relation' between two, and even if something that looks very much like ethics takes place in social relations. The shouldering of the symmetrical responsibility proper to justice depends on and is conditioned by the asymmetrical face to face that precedes it. "The poor one, the stranger presents himself as equal. His equality in this essential poverty consists in referring to the third, thus present at the encounter and whom, in the midst of his destitution, the other already serves. He joins himself to me. . . . [But] the *you* is posited before a *we*" (TI 188). Ethics and justice — the *you* and the *we* — appear more and more to be continuous one with the other but remain distinct. And the *you* remains prior to the *we*.

Gibbs also points to the transitional role of the family in between the realms of two and three. Levinas's analyses of the family are extended and complex; here I will say only enough about them to make it clear that they are another forum in which ethics and justice are blurred. The love relation, for Levinas (and despite his critique of Buber), is at once a relation with an other and also a social phenomenon; the lover stands as paradigmatic for the aspect of every relation that commands ethically and requires justice at the same time. And reproduction — or, to use Levinas's technical term, 'fecundity' — inscribes the ambiguity even more clearly than the relation with the lover. My child is 'me' before he is 'not-me'; to be precise, he is me though I am not him. Therefore my relation with my child — or with lover and child at once — is a forum in which the one, two and three meet each other; the unit they form may thus provide a model of society in which ethics and justice occur together. Gibbs writes that there is, in Levinas, "a social programme of sorts, based on the discontinuity and separation of selves in the family, which can stand as an alternative institutionalization of the responsibility demanded by the face."[25]

What would such a society look like? The matter is clarified somewhat by the fact that Levinas connects fecundity to religion, thinking surely of Judaism which can be understood, despite the number of centuries that have passed since Abraham, as an extended family. But a Jewish society, or a society based on the model of Judaism, does not in the end turn out to be a society in which ethics and justice merge. Rather, such a society turns out to have, as its defining characteristic, what I have called, 'making totality badly', or ensuring that justice understands itself to be a broken totality and remains open to further breaks accomplished in the name of ethics. Structures are found in Judaism, and especially perhaps in rabbinic Judaism, which, while they remain totalities, mitigate the betrayal of ethics necessary to totality. In rabbinic law, for instance, justice is structured so as always to recall the ethical. This is accomplished most notably by the partial erasure of the distinction between legislative and juridical functions. Rather than having a single fixed law that must be interpreted according to particular cases, the law itself changes and grows with every case that is brought before it. There is, thus, no set of principles by which all cases are measured symmetrically or equally; instead we find the constant subordination of the general rule to the particular case. In other words, rabbinic law, like rabbinic hermeneutics, is grounded in a refusal of closure. Just as one turns and turns the Torah ceaselessly, because there is no end to what can be drawn out of it, so the volumes of Responsa pile up over the centuries with no end in sight to the modifications that can be made to *halachah* as new particulars arise. Just as the Talmud preserves entire debates, including dissenting or even 'heretical' opinions, so the *halachah* contained

within the Talmud and the subsequent texts is expressed
and formed from a plurality of voices, each of which dissents
or differs in its own way. In a society founded on these books
and this law, ethics — the respect for difference — becomes
the mode of justice. Certainly then the fecundity of Judaism
is the best example of a continuity between ethics and justice in Levinas's thinking.

But even rabbinic law — for all that it hesitates over a
judgment, subsumes the general to the particular, and preserves its breaks or its openness — is law, and therefore to
some extent works with the idea of the precedent or the rule,
an idea that imposes symmetry. Perhaps this is the beginning of the explanation of the fact that, in later works like
Otherwise Than Being, Levinas reasserts the tension in the
basic structure, speaking less about fecundity and religion
and more about the way ethical service to the other is betrayed in the institutions of the 'state'. Even before *Otherwise Than Being*, the state was probably the most dubious of
totalities in Levinas's understanding. Gibbs follows up his
argument that "Levinas devotes much of *Totality and Infinity* to discovering a sociality that will preserve responsibility" with the qualification that such responsibility is hardly
ever connected to the secular sociality of the state. Indeed,
for Levinas, "the state, as an institution of reason and of
universality, is always drawn toward totalitarianism" since
from its viewpoint "my obsession with the other and my
infinizing responsibility for the other are impossible." And
while in *Totality and Infinity* other totalities or varieties of
politics, such as those of institutional religion, need not necessarily lead to the inception of the state, in *Otherwise Than
Being* religion more or less disappears and "any full social
responsibility has become impossible. . . . Social institutions
are now limited to political ones. . . . Liberation becomes . . .
a praxis [that] can never be established or instituted."[26] Thus,
for all the blurring in the writings of Levinas's middle period,

the distinction between ethics and justice remains clear enough that a profound tension between them can eventually be reasserted.

What is the significance of the distinction to Levinas? Why does he never entirely allow it to drop? There are, I think, two reasons. First, there is a reason for the less-dominant thrust in which the continuity between ethics and justice is emphasized; this involves the necessity of preserving the two in separate spheres because of their separate functions. Then, there is a reason for the dominant thrust in which the tension is emphasized; this involves the idea of politics remaining open to ethical critique. I will take up the former first.

Levinas is neither an 'essentialist' nor a 'conventionalist'; to the best of my knowledge he never makes use of the terms 'nature' and 'convention' except to dismiss them. When John Caputo describes the position of Derrida's deconstruction on this question, his words apply equally (and first) to Levinas's ethics. "Everything in deconstruction," writes Caputo, "is organized around . . . the incoming of the other. . . . Indeed . . . deconstruction is best thought of as a certain *inventionalism*. For if Derrida is anything but an essentialist, someone who hangs everything on the hook of unchanging essences, that does not mean he is a conventionalist, which is but an alternative way to hang things up (or tie them down). . . . The business of deconstruction is to open and loosen things up."[27] The ethics/justice distinction is — at least in part, and in its continuous aspect — intended to supplant the nature/convention distinction, to categorize the same phenomena in a new way, replacing 'nature' with the idea of the for-the-other and 'convention' with the idea of a social justice arising directly from the for-the-other though compromising it as well. This is to say, in short, that one of the functions of the ethics/justice distinction is to provide a critique of the idea, proffered by thinkers from Hobbes to Freud and expressed generally with some form of the nature/convention distinction, that ethics is unnatural, that the state of nature or the condition of the presocial human being is nonethical, and that ethics is the result of the stabilizing structures necessary for us to live in society. Levinas's new distinction allows him to retain any truth there might be in the old one — for instance, the fact that certain of our political, economic, social, and religious institutions (including certainly most 'schools' and 'committees', see RK 29–30 cited above) exist for the purpose of curbing violence, and, more generally, of making social life easier and smoother or of making their members 'good citizens' — while also ridding himself of the idea that the difficulties that these institutions exist to smooth over or solve represent the last word on the 'nature' of the human being or the human being in 'the state of nature', or that these difficulties are the decisive factor in the formation of polities. Levinas puts the matter, typically, in the form of a rhetorical question: One must know "if the egalitarian and just State in which man is fulfilled . . . proceeds from a war of all against all, or from the irreducible responsibility of the one for all, and if it can do without friendships and faces" (OB 159–60). The answer Levinas seeks cannot be stated using the Hobbesian distinction, but can be stated in terms of ethics and justice: for while convention cannot be natural, justice can be ethical.[28]

This substitution — the supplanting of nature/convention by the continuous-but-distinct structure of ethics/politics — can be understood as a Judaicization. For, ultimately, the ethics/politics distinction in its continuous form is the distinction between ethics and *halachah*. From a Levinasian perspective, *halachah* cannot be ethics; it cannot be the epiphany of absolute rupture that is the service of the other. But it can come from this rupture, and recall or inscribe this rupture, standing as a structured set of normative rules on the basis of which a society can function but that nevertheless exists in some measure to rerupture the conceptions or consciousness of the one who practices it, to take her, as it were, by surprise and ask of her something that could not have come from within her. Levinas does not wish, like Buber, to reject the *halachah* as nonethical, nor does he wish, like other thinkers, to reinterpret the *halachah* until it is merely a manifestation of the ethical impulses of the human heart. *Halachah*, for him, is neither ethics nor nonethical; it is the translation of the ethical encounter into the structures that will maintain a stable and just society; it is ethics with a 'hard skin' (see RK 29–30 cited above). The main reason, then, for the maintenance of the continuity between ethics and politics in Levinas's thinking is to avoid, on the one hand, Buber's error, in which everything legal or political (everything that is not love) is conventional and inferior, and on the other hand, Hobbes's error, in which everything legal or political (everything that is not nasty and brutish) is conventional and superior. Against both, he supports the structures of traditional rabbinic Judaism, offering an understanding that makes space for responsible *halachah* without reducing it either to ethics or to convention.

The second reason — the reason for the dominant emphasis on the tension in the distinction — rests, very broadly, on Levinas's profound uneasiness about the hegemonic, irresponsible and violent tendencies of societies, states and communities (I will use community as the general term). What is interesting here is that Levinas is not particularly concerned about the violence done in or by involuntary communities — communities into which one is born or finds oneself thrust — but is deeply concerned about the violence of the voluntary community — the neighborhood in which one chooses to live, the church one attends, the state to which one gives one's willing allegiance. The ultimate voluntary community is the ideology (or avoidable totality) to which one devotes oneself and in which one is lost. The ultimate involuntary community is the human race, where it is possible to be found by the other.

The beginning of the problem is simply that voluntary communities are exclusive. Donna Jowett, speaking of her own experience, writes that "it is proximity and not community which produces the relation with the neighbor I have not chosen . . . If I regard my occupation of space, my being . . . as a matter of entitlement I may, through altruism, be moved to behave benevolently or charitably, but this comes from my sense of fortification and authority; it does not put that fortification and authority into question. . . . I may be prepared to give up some surplus . . . [b]ut I do not give up my life, my presence in being, my occupation of this and other spaces."[29] In Jowett's experience it is not possible to be called into question by a community one has decided to become a member of; this can only happen through the unchosen face, the face that *chooses me*, or, in Levinas's terms, 'elects' me. Jowett draws support for her argument from Levinas's assertion that "it is as if the other established a relationship or a relationship were established whose whole intensity consisted in *not presupposing the idea of community. A responsibility stemming from a time before my freedom*. . . . Responsibility for my neighbor, for the stranger or sojourner, to which nothing in the rigorously ontological order binds me — nothing in the order of the thing, of the something, of number, or causality" (LR 83, my emphasis).

Levinas strikes a chord with this idea of a responsibility that is not based in voluntary community and that stands against all communal allegiances; the idea is picked up again and again in the thought of continental philosophers who describe a community of responsibility as one that is involuntary and incomplete, one whose boundaries remain open and whose principles remain unfixed — a community that, in fact, insofar as it can be called a community at all, must 'not yet' exist. Jean-Luc Nancy speaks of an "inoperative community," a community of lovers where community is communion with the divine and thus is always to be understood as not yet achieved;

Maurice Blanchot speaks of a "negative community," a community of writers "in which the aesthetic articulation of writing signifies as a doomed effort at ecstatic communication, but which nevertheless points to a ghostly absence of community";[30] Alphonso Lingis speaks of a "community of those who have nothing in common," a community of the dying to which everyone belongs; Georges Bataille speaks of an "absence of community," a community of the passionate, again encompassing all human beings; and Jacques Derrida speaks of a "community of the question," a community of "those who can still be called philosophers."[31] All of these thinkers take off from the same experience, the experience of the closedness and violence of the voluntary or 'present' or manifest community — the community that knows what it is and what it stands for — as opposed to the nonviolent absent community, the community of desire or of a 'trace' that cannot be realized. The position is basic anti-idealism or anti-utopianism, at least if idealism and utopianism are to be understood as representing the impulse to realize an ideal society or to build perfect institutions.[32] The political idealist conceives of his own understanding as encompassing both justice and ethics, that is, as a realization of the ethical on the level of the third.

It is, according to Levinas, the societies or regimes founded on this understanding that are the most destructive. Marxism, for instance, is, an attempt to found a society on the relation that can only be ethical, to found a society on charity.[33] And once a society believes itself to have such a foundation, nothing holds it back from violence. The only way to preserve the openness of a community is to preserve a conception of an ethics that operates in its own sphere and calls all communities into question, an ethics that calls everything into question, an ethics the very nature of which is a calling into question, that is to say, the ethics of the involuntary encounter with the other. The maintenance of a firm distinction between ethics and justice means that we are able

to criticize or revise justice (including *halachah*, which, as I
have said, remains to a degree open to such revision) from a
ground that is prior and more solid than any ground that
might be provided by a different third-level institution. This
is, I think, the main reason Levinas generally stresses the
tension in the distinction.

This is not to say that institutions cannot legitimately criticize one another. Canada can legitimately criticize America
for cultural hegemony; Palestine can in certain cases legitimately criticize Israel, and in other cases Israel Palestine;
the church can legitimately criticize the doings of the state
or the condition of modern society; the state can blow the
whistle legitimately on certain doings in the church. Moreover, institutions can legitimately criticize certain interactions (we cannot call them relations) between two: abusive
interactions, irresponsible interactions, and perhaps even
honeymoon interactions which are constituted by a withdrawal from society; a religious congregation that intercedes
in a marriage, for instance, seeking to make that marriage
better or to bring the couple into the community, is in all
likelihood acting in a way that is unexceptionably praise-
worthy. However, all of these interventions or critiques exist,
for Levinas, on the level of the third, or the level of justice —
they refer to the level of the second for their existence, but
they are not, themselves, of that level. The difference between the two levels must be maintained precisely so that
the second level can continue to ground, fuel and renew the
third.[34] Moreover, to Levinas's way of thinking, all communities without exception depend on the second level for this
fuel or renewal. For, although the need for the ethics/justice
distinction is particularly apparent in the case of the state,
it remains the case that all institutions must modify or compromise their acceptance of the infinite and extraordinary
demands of ethics simply in order to act in the world; politics
must operate in ways that are not absolutely ethical, even

though they may be just. This is why they must remain open to the critique that arises from the face to face, the critique raised on behalf of the other. The ultimate purpose of the face to face may well be social critique, but the face to face cannot be equivalent to social critique if it is to continue to fulfill this purpose.[35]

Surely, then, Levinas's insistence that space be reserved outside of the moral for the ethical has a great deal to with the dismal failure of third-level institutions in the twentieth century to act either ethically or morally. Why, at the time of the Holocaust did the political bodies of the world show so badly? Why did the religious bodies do so little? This is not to say that collectivities and politics are always or even usually evil. It is to say that Levinas seeks a moment or a point that is noncompromisable, and that this point, for him, is the ethical point. The relation between two people is itself no guarantee against murder, but in it and only in it is found something that is not clothed in the slight falsehoods necessary to social interaction, something that is not tainted by demanding to be believed or accepted or conformed to — a willingness, an exposure, a gift.[36]

There remains a problem with Levinas's description of the relation between ethics and politics, or the two and the three. He never adequately explains how it is that we move from the ethical encounter into third-level institutions. He is much more interested in tracing all good third-level institutions and the critiques they can provide of other third-level institutions *back* to their origin in second-level ethics than he is in painstakingly describing the movement *forward*. Parts of the transition are sketched in the account of the development of economics in *Totality and Infinity*: I require a variety of things to give to the other; gift requires not only labor but also exchange and therefore rules of exchange; presumably, then, the rules of justice that grow up around society emerge from these initial rules. But the account is not fleshed out. If it were, it would be possible for us to determine the point where, according to Levinas, ethics gets lost in the symmetrical structurings that follow — or at any rate the degrees by which it is compromised, covered over, and finally at times forgotten. And we might also have a better of idea why, according to Levinas, the ethical encounter is at one time hardened into the *halachah* and at another time into the laws of the liberal state. But Levinas is not a political theorist. He does not take these matters up.

Ethics and Judaism

The ultimate source of the command to serve the other is God. However, in Levinas's understanding, God does not appear to human beings; he is not present to us. Only what might be called his back — that is, his absence — can be glimpsed, and it is glimpsed only in the interaction with other human beings, ethical and social. The glimpse of God in the social realm, or the thirdness of God, is a topic I will take up in chapter two. For now, I will say that what we have of God arises only in the ethical encounter, in a form Levinas calls 'the trace'.

The question of why Levinas's God cannot be described as present is critical to this book. In chapter two, I will sketch Levinas's phenomenological explanation for God's absence; later, in chapter five, I will offer a historical or circumstantial explanation. Suffice it to say now that the idea of a present God is problematic to Levinas in at least three ways. First, the idea will almost always operate to mitigate earthly responsibility, if only slightly; a present God generally suggests a God who takes care of ethics and justice or forgives in his mercy, and thus to claim God as present is already to make possible the thought that one might do less than everything for the other, or that one might perhaps not be always accused. Second, the idea may operate, deliberately or otherwise, as a justification of evil or violence; to say that God is present may also be to say that one knows God or understands God's will and that one is determined to act on it, regardless of the consequences for the other or the others. To claim that God is present in this sense is analogous to the claim that one's politics inscribes an ethics; it is the claim of the absolutist who cannot be criticized. Third, the idea operates to provide an absolutely other that, in its absolute otherness, may relativize the differences between beings in the world; the presence of this absolutely other may allow us to say that 'we are all equal under God', thus losing the sense of the asymmetry or nonreciprocity of the relation with the other, who is always unequal to me — higher spiritually and lower economically — before he becomes equal in the presence of the third.

In *Totality and Infinity*, Levinas begins his description of how God is concealed in the revelation of the face by offering a phenomenology of need and desire. Need, according to Levinas, is the everyday experience of lack; it leads to seeking, finding, grasping, assimilating, same-making, totalizing. The paradigm for need is the need for food: we know about food; if we are hungry, we know we lack food; we can absorb food. But need can also apply to objects we can intellectually absorb, things we can mentally assimilate or make part of our consciousness. I may have need of things like "the land in which I dwell, the landscape I contemplate. . . . I can 'feed' on these realities and to a very great extent satisfy myself." In distinction, desire is the persistent human experience of wanting something that we do not know and cannot name, something we have never had, cannot picture, and cannot absorb. Because of the element of unknowing, Levinas calls desire "desire for the absolutely other" and also "desire for the invisible," where the word invisible "implies relations with what is not given, of which there is no idea." Desire, writes

Levinas, is "metaphysical desire"; it is desire for what is not in the world; it is, in short, desire for God (TI 33–34).

But desire cannot lead one directly to God. Instead it leads one to the other (for all that a particular other may be personally undesirable). While need is the basic drive that characterizes the first ontic level or state of 'enjoyment', desire is what pulls us out of enjoyment's egology toward novelty and alterity. Thus desire "has a meaning. It is understood as the alterity of the other and of the Most High" (TI 34). "[T]he dimension of the divine opens forth from the human face. A relation with the Transcendent is a social relation . . . There can be no 'knowledge' of God separated from the relationship with men. The other is the very locus of metaphysical truth. . . . He does not play the role of a mediator. The other is not the incarnation of God, but . . . is the manifestation of the height in which God is revealed" (TI 78–79). It is one of Levinas's seminal claims that the other and what we have of God coincide, that ethics is revelation, that in meeting the other we experience the desire for God, and that in the desire for God we reach out to the other. What we reach to in the other is the aspect of his alterity that reveals an infinity; this is the trace of the absence of God.

Need is linked to the totality of egology and desire to the infinity of alterity; thus God is linked to infinity. But the precise relation between God and infinity is immensely difficult to thematize. Peperzak stresses those passages in which Levinas seems to make a distinction between God and the other — to speak, for instance, as we have seen, of "the other *and* the Most High" (TI 34) — and on this basis he argues that while the other is infinite, God is The Infinite, and that the distinction between God and the other is always maintained, even in all of the many passages where Levinas speaks of their co-incidence in human experience.[37] Peperzak is undoubtedly correct: Levinas goes so far as to refer, at one point, to the other and the other's others as "intermediaries" between the subject and God (OB 128),[38] and writes in "God and Philosophy" that "God is not simply the 'first other', or the 'other par excellence', or the 'absolutely other', but other than the other, other otherwise, and other with an alterity prior to the alterity of the other, prior to the ethical obligation to the other and different from every neighbor" (GCM 69). It seems then that God in himself, is, for Levinas, an Infinite different from the infinite experienced by human beings in the face.

But, for all that, it is critical that Levinas almost never speaks of God in himself. Instead, he speaks of the experience of infinity, and in this context, speaks of God as a word given to certain aspects of ethical relation as opposed to totalizing interaction. To recomplicate the issue, we can look again at a line previously cited: "the idea of infinity is the mode of being, the infinition of infinity. Infinity does not first exist, and then reveal itself. Its infinition is produced as revelation, as a positing of its idea in me" (TI 26). Infinity *does* seem to "first exist," for its infinition is its positing of its idea, the idea of the infinite, in me — and yet Levinas insists that "infinity does *not* first exist." What the passage reveals is Levinas unwillingness to discuss the Infinite or God in himself, which is of course a facet of his unwillingness to discuss anything at all in itself. He speaks almost always of relation rather than essence, and relation is a matter of overflow or boundlessness — that is infinity — and not a matter of different 'infinites' — or infinite things — that can be compared as more or less infinite than one another. Thus the quotation from "God and Philosophy" cited above, which treats God in himself, closes — must close — with Levinas's statement that God is "transcendent to the point of absence" (GCM 69). Whatever may be said about the essential difference between the infinite and the Infinite is said about them as they are concealed; as phenomena, they appear together. What we have of God phenomenologically is an absence, and it is experienced as the trace and desire; in other words, the infinite divine is experienced in the functions of infinity delineated in the second section of this chapter, as a diversity, a command, a critique, a hospitality, a responsibility. This is why, in the temporal scheme offered in the second section of this chapter, I did not include God at all. That scheme was an artificial laying-out of the theoretical ordering in which the elements of experienced reality occur in themselves. God, as he occurs in himself, is not, for Levinas, an element of experienced reality but the absent ground and source of all of the movements of the infinite.

Since the meeting with the other is the arena for the meeting with God, Levinas's conception of ethics and his conception of how we understand God must coincide at an original point. What, then, about ethics and Levinas's own religion, or Levinas's ethical *philosophy* and his Judaism? Are they compatible, or is he torn? It is commonly argued that Levinas's philosophy and his Judaism chafe against one another, but how so? Is there a tension in his thought between philosophy and theology, or reason and revelation, or Judaism and universal humanity, or 'Greek' and 'Hebrew'? Let us take up these pairings one by one.

In the preface to *Totality and Infinity*, Levinas sketches a certain relation between theology and philosophy, but his meaning takes work to uncover. We can begin by looking at a passage made up of the excerpts in which he speaks about what he calls 'prophetic eschatology'.

> Philosophers distrust it. . . . [F]or them eschatology — a subjective and arbitrary divination of the future, the result of revelation without evidences, tributary of faith — belongs naturally to opinion. . . . However, the extraordinary phenomenon of prophetic eschatology certainly does not intend to win its civic rights within the domain of thought by being

assimilated to philosophical evidence. To be sure, in religions and even in theologies eschatology, like an oracle, does seem to 'complete' philosophical evidences; its beliefs-conjectures want to be more certain than evidences — as though eschatology added information about the future by revealing the finality of being. But . . . its real import lies elsewhere. It does not introduce a teleological system into the totality; it does not consist in teaching the orientation of history. Eschatology institutes a relation with being *beyond the totality* or history. . . . The first 'vision' of eschatology (hereby distinguished from the revealed opinions of positive religions) arrives at the very possibility of eschatology, that is, the breach of the totality, the possibility of *signification without a context*. . . . (TI 22–23)

Two definitions of eschatology are offered here. Philosophers and theologians both understand eschatology with reference to evidence or information, specifically, information about the future. The argument between them is only that the philosophers mistrust this so-called information, while the theologians hold it to be 'more certain' than any information that can be arrived at philosophically. But their definition is quickly called into question, and at the end of the passage Levinas provides an alternative conception in which eschatology is synonymous with the breach of totality, or in short, with the ethics that ruptures or calls into question all systems supported by information. Evidences or pieces of information, he further suggests, are the weapons in a type of war; this is to say that they are brought forth to battle one another within a totality in which certainty or factuality is the key to living and that they do not admit of the novelty or the infinity of the face. Prophetic eschatology, in distinction, is peace (TI 24); it is novelty; it is ethics; it is the rupture of totalities. We should note here Levinas's remarkable understanding of peace as related to rupture and as opposed to coherence or wholeness. Coherence or wholeness cannot be

peace for Levinas, for they are false impositions of factuality
or sameness; if they come in the guise of peace, it is a peace
of provisional ceasefire, not a true peace. True peace, in distinction, is an anarchic and epiphanic phenomenon; it is not
a stasis but a movement, not a factuality but the critique of
factuality. In any case, the important opposition being erected
here is not the one between philosophy and theology, but the
one between same-making, static philosophy/theology, with
its objective determinations about the future or warlike
rejections of those determinations, and difference-oriented,
dynamic Levinasian ethics, here called prophetic eschatology, and often simply called prophecy.

Two kinds of God-talk, two theo-logies, have been offered
to us here: theology, which is an avoidable totality linked to
war, and prophecy, which ruptures totality and is linked to
peace. What about philo-sophies? Are we offered a correlative doubling? Not immediately. On the page following the
excerpted passage above, Levinas recomplicates the issue,
writing that "ever since eschatology has opposed peace to
war the evidence of war has been maintained in an essentially hypocritical civilization, that is, attached to both the
True and the Good, henceforth antagonistic. It is perhaps
time to see in the hypocrisy not only a base contingent defect
of man, but the underlying rending of a world attached to
both the philosophers and the prophets" (TI 24). The hypocrisy involves a tension between what Levinas here calls the
True, by which he means the factual that totalizes, and the
Good by which he means the ethical that breaks totality.
Ethics, the Good, and prophecy — these are linked with one
another and contrasted with factuality, the True, and philosophy. However, shortly afterwards, we are indeed offered
a description of a second, different kind of philosophy, one
that no more originates in factuality than does prophecy. "Is
not philosophy . . . defined as an endeavor to live a life beginning with evidence . . .? . . . Unless philosophical evidence

refers from itself to a situation that can no longer be stated in terms of 'totality'. . . . Unless the non-knowing with which philosophical knowing begins coincides not with pure nothingness but only with a nothingness of objects" (TI 24). One philosophy, like theology, is concerned with information and equivalent to ontology. Another philosophy, like prophecy, begins in unknowing or a nonontological 'nothingness of objects', and perhaps also seeks "signification without a context" or meaning without totality. Thus when Levinas speaks of the 'underlying rending of the world' he is contrasting a certain kind of philosophy, ontological philosophy, to the nonontological philosophy or theo-logy that is prophecy. He is not contrasting all philosophy to prophecy any more than he is contrasting philosophy with theology.

In order to explain the complications here, I should backtrack for a moment, keeping in mind that in this preface Levinas speaks of all his words as 'unsayings' and maintains that the words given out here are "not a word of honor" (TI 30). In the first paragraph of the preface, Levinas links 'philosophy' and 'being' under the general rubric of the same or totality; later, in the paragraph on the True and the Good, he adds 'truth' to this list of samenesses. But before the end of the preface all these links are undone; each of these terms is wrenched out of its place as a term of sameness and offered a place as an expression of otherness; which is to say that Levinas effects his own, small-scale rupture of the same, in literary form, by reaching into the totalizing structures he has erected and pulling away their foundational terms. As it turns out, it is not being itself that is warlike and objectifying, but rather the relation with being Levinas characterizes as ontology, and so it is possible for Levinas to speak of peace as "a primordial relation with being" (TI 22). Similarly, philosophy — or at any rate nonontological philosophy — is reinscribed or redeemed in the passage cited above, where it is disassociated from evidence. And, finally, by the end of the

preface, Levinas is speaking of a "truth" that is constituted
by the "aspiration to radical exteriority" (TI 29). It is possible, then, to hold that a certain relation with being, a certain
kind of philosophy, and a certain understanding of truth are
properly connected to prophecy, to ethics, to peace, and to
the Good. (It is also worth noting that in at least one of
Levinas's later essays, 'the Good' itself takes a beating; in
that essay the Good is understood as an ideology perpetu-
ated by a collectivity, and thus as a totality.[39] What persists
always in Levinas's esteem is the Good Beyond Being, and
this cannot be understood as anything other than a philosophical concept, the culmination of a philosophy conducted
face to face.)[40] There is thus a higher philosophical truth than
ontology. And the world that is rent in its attachment to philosophy and prophecy is a world that may have a glimpse of
the meaning of prophecy, but does not understand higher
philosophy, seeing philosophy only as objectifying analytics
or ontology. So while the 'hypocrisy' of the attachment to the
'True' and the 'Good' is Levinas's own hypocrisy insofar as he
refers to prophecy vs. ontology, he does not think of true philosophy as standing in tension with prophecy.[41]

And in the essay "God and Philosophy" we find a similar
movement of thought with respect to reason and revelation. When Levinas writes that "if, for the benefit of religion,
[rational theology] pulls out some domain over which the su-
pervision of philosophy is not exercised, then this domain
shall have been, on good grounds, recognized as philosophically unverifiable" (GCM 55), it sounds as if he is erecting a
reason/revelation distinction, or indeed erecting the very distinction between philosophy and theology he rejects in the
preface to *Totality and Infinity*. However, he immediately
proposes a rational discourse, or a 'reason', that would be
based neither on verification nor on the unverifiable, but on
the experience of desire. "To ask oneself, as we are attempting to do here, whether God cannot be uttered in a reasonable

discourse that would be neither ontology nor faith is implicitly to doubt the formal opposition, established by Yehuda
Halevy and taken up by Pascal, between, on the one hand,
the God of Abraham, Isaac and Jacob involved without philosophy in faith, and on the other the god of the philosophers.
It is to doubt that this opposition constitutes an alternative"
(GCM 57). Here we find a doubling of reason, analogous to
the doubling of theo-logy and philosophy. First there is the
'rational theology' of the theologians, concerned with (unverifiable) information. Then there is the 'reasonable discourse'
of Levinas's own thought, which is concerned neither with
the verifiable nor the unverifiable.

This is already enough in the way of evidence to dismiss
the idea that a distinction between philosophy and theology
or reason and revelation is in any way critical to Levinas's
thinking. Let me, therefore, speak more generally for a
moment about how and why the distinction is broken down.
As I see it, a philosophy of alterity *must* break down the distinction between reason and revelation as it is usually understood. For Levinas, no primacy can be accorded the
distinction between what comes from 'within me' and what
comes from 'without' or 'beyond', since my very foundations
come from without and beyond. To be sure, this is not incompatible with what philosophers and theologians have always
said about the relation between reason and revelation, but
in Levinas it is evidently a more radical position. Everything
I see is shown me by the other (and proceeds ultimately from
God) and in this sense all reason is revealed. Every experience takes place in human consciousness and in this sense
all revelation is reasoned. Unreasonable revelation is either
the folly Levinas calls 'mysticism' (the participatory fantasies
of the beautiful soul), or the folly he calls 'theology' (dogma);
he would refuse such experiences the name of revelation.
Unrevelatory reason is the folly he sometimes calls knowledge, or intentionality, or egology; only occasionally does he

call this reason. It may be that, for Levinas, the degeneration in the terms reason and revelation, by which they vie
with one another over the source and authority of their information, results largely from their division one from the
other, for this division leads almost inevitably to competing
claims based on evidence. If reason and revelation are not
divided one from the other, then an understanding of both as
arising from the ethical encounter may be taken up more
easily. What is needed is a different starting place, one from
which the two terms appear as aspects of the same movement.
Levinas's starting place, the other, does not refer to a present
God, that shibboleth of 'revelation' that offends the devotees
of 'reason', nor does it assume that God is not real, that
shibboleth of 'reason' that offends the devotees of 'revelation'.
To speak first of the other allows for a discourse that can say
the word God, as reason and as revelation, and yet does not
take that word to signify as a theme, that is to say, a discourse
that does not denominate and therefore does not dominate.
This is the beginning of higher philosophy, of that philosophy
Levinas refers to in *Otherwise Than Being* as "the wisdom of
love in the service of love" (OB 162). It is also the beginning
of non-theological religion; the encounter with the other is
"the latent birth, in the other, of religion; prior to the emotions
and to the voice, prior to 'religious experience' that speaks of
revelation in terms of the disclosure of being, when it is a
question of the unusual access, at the heart of my responsibility, to an unusual derangement of being" (GCM 72).

The categories by which philosophy and theology vie with
one another — verifiable, unverifiable, reason, revelation —
do not concern Levinas. What is good — i.e. what is ethical
or moral — has reference to the God, and reference to the
God is made only through what is good. There is no special
or irrational or nonverifiable revelation to be believed outside of the ethical, but neither is the ethical understood
reductively as including only those concepts that can be

subjected to analytical tests to prove their rationality. The reason and the revelation of evidences are totalities; moreover, they are avoidable totalities, totalities that have all but forgotten the ethical encounter. Both constitute ontologies; both restrict meaning; neither pays attention to the novelty of the encounter with the other. The pattern that emerges in Levinas's treatment of philosophy and theology or reason and revelation occurs quite often in his writings. He takes a distinction that is a commonplace of thought, allows the two sides of the distinction to merge with one another, and then confronts the resulting synthesis with something entirely new, something that cannot be merged or synthesized. Philosophy, theology, reason and revelation all look the same when put up against ethics; they all appear as totalities when faced with what breaks totality and cannot itself become totality. The mode of alterity that is contrasted with them — by the light of which they merge, and their arguments appear in their true shape as the internalized war or dialectic that marks totality — is given several names. Sometimes Levinas simply uses the term ethics to fulfill this function, sometimes religion (distinguished from theology or "the revealed opinions of positive religions" and also from ecstasy, religious experience, or mysticism), sometimes philosophy (distinguished from ontology) and, in at least one notable discussion, scepticism. But the term that Levinas most often uses to show up the totalizing nature of the synthesis is prophecy. More of this in chapter two — and more in chapter four of the structure that has just emerged: the introduction of a distinction, the merging of the two sides, and the contrast to what cannot be synthesized. I leave these things behind for the moment. For in the distinction between 'Hebrew' and 'Greek', which more generally is the distinction between Jewish and universal, we return to the basic structure that I have spent much of this chapter tracing.

It is quite easy to think of Levinas as a rather dubious sort of Jew, either on the basis of an antinomian thrust in his thought, or an ahistoricist thrust, or a universalist thrust, or perhaps especially on the basis of the suggestion, foundational to his thought, that one should, as it were, turn the other cheek. But to drum Levinas out of the fold for these things would be to drum him out on the basis of a definition of Judaism formed in antagonistic response to Christianity, that is, to Christian claims to antinomianism, or ahistoricism, or universalism, or compassion. Such negative definitions of Judaism are only a small range among a great many. Levinas's own definition is quite different. He thinks of Judaism as having some fundamental insight into plurality, diversity, alterity, infinity — into the fact that each human being is unique. In short, Judaism is for him a mode — or at times *the* mode — of relation or ethics. To be sure, in various contexts and for various reasons, he speaks of the Jews as a collectivity like other collectivities. But he is more likely to use Judaism as a symbol for the ethical impulse. "Jewishness stands for giving the other bread from one's lips, bread that some non-Jews would describe as a wafer. It stands for a certain universality that transcends Judaism. Don't be shocked! The authentically human is everyone's Jewishness and its echo in the singular and the particular" (ITN 8). As John Llewelyn puts it, Israel (or Jew, or Hebrew) in Levinas's thought refers at times to the particularity of a people, and at other times — more often, I believe — to the particularity of each person, the particularity that is experienced in relation.[42]

The term that stands as Judaism's foil is 'Greek'. Greek is the universality to the Hebrew particularity, the symmetry to the Hebrew asymmetry, the presence to the Hebrew absence, the ontology to the Hebrew rupture. Greek, in short, is what the Hebrew looks like after the entry of the third, and Greek/Jew or Greek/Hebrew are more or less synonymous with politics/ethics, said/saying, totality/infinity, and the other pairings I have mentioned.[43] More particularly,

'Greek' is a "sub-textual . . . way of thinking and speaking" that seeks to describe the whole, using terms like *"morphe* (form), *ousia* (being), *nous* (reason), *logos* (conceptual thought), or *telos* (goal)"; its distinguishing mark is the equation of truth with "an intelligibility of presence," which is to say that it is essentially equivalent to ontology (RK 18–19). 'Hebrew' thought or speech, in distinction, is polyphonic or dialogical; it hesitates or stutters; it is never complete; it evokes the concealed, preserves dissent, and asks to be interrupted. As with all the pairings that describe the basic structure, both terms or modes are necessary and also basically good. Indeed, Levinas thinks of himself as, on the one hand, 'finding the Hebrew in the Greek' (moving from Greek to Hebrew, rupturing structures of thought by reminding us of their origins in ethical rupture), and also, on the other hand, "translating Hebrew into Greek" (moving from Hebrew to Greek, conveying infinity or rupture in a said; GCM 85).

The Hebrew/Greek distinction, then, does represent a tension basic to Levinas thinking, but it is not the tension between reason and revelation, or Judaism and philosophy — at least not as those terms are commonly understood. Rather, it is the tension inherent in the basic structure: the problem of how to make an ontology badly, or of how to speak a saying in a said without destroying the saying. And this is a problem for *anyone* who thinks or speaks; if it is more of a problem for Levinas than for the rest of us, it is only because his project involves not only thematizing, but thematizing the saying itself. There is no doubt that Levinas understands both Jews and Greeks, prophets and philosophers, to live in this tension and to have this problem, and also to be able to overcome it or at least mitigate it; thinking otherwise than ontologically does not require a voluntary allegiance, and the involuntary allegiance it inscribes is experienced every day by almost everyone. The labels "Hebrew" and "Greek" — which suggest a connection between infinity and institutional

Judaism, totality and what is not institutional Judaism —
can obscure this truth, and thus perhaps should not be taken
as definitive for Levinas's thought.

Two difficulties arise, both soluble. The first begins in fact
that Levinas occasionally uses the terms 'Hebrew' and 'Greek'
in quite another sense: to divide his own writings into two
groups, that is, to divide his talmudic works from the rest.
This is not say that he regards the two as in any sense incompatible; on the contrary, "they may ultimately have the
same source of inspiration" (RK 18). It is only to say that he
knows that his talmudic works will be read as confessional
and unprofessional and does not want his other works tainted
by similar accusations. But this second use of the Hebrew/
Greek distinction, in comparison with the first, may lead a
commentator onto tricky ground. She may for instance, be
led to conclude that Levinas is somehow more Greekish (that
is, more totalizing) in the philosophical works, and more Jewish (more rupturing) in the talmudic works. In fact, all of
Levinas's works involve thematization, *logos*, and *telos*, not
to mention having their own *morphe* and proposing (to
reapply a line from the preface to *Totality and Infinity*), 'a
certain relation with *ousia*'— and, correspondingly, attempts
are made in all the works to undercut these tendencies.[44]
The second difficulty emerges from the main use of the
Hebrew/Greek rubric. If the Jew is paradigmatic for the particularity of *every* person met in relation, do we not have in
Levinas's conception of Judaism a resurgence of the universal,
or the symmetrical, or equality, or synchrony, or totality —
and is the Hebrew not therefore a new Greek? Or, to put it
more bluntly, how is it even possible to speak of Judaism as
distinct from universal humanity, if everyone is at some level
Jewish? The answer is that Judaism does refer to a kind of
universal, but it is not the universal of 'the all', or the totalizing universal of the collective. Rather, Judaism refers to
the universal of 'the each', which is the universal of infinity

or of ethics. Indeed, the distinction between each and all is one of the quickest and dirtiest ways of describing the whole basic structure: all the pairings Levinas uses to denote the structure, including Hebrew and Greek, describe a situation in which the each is prior to the all, calls for the all, and conditions the all; in which, in addition, the all poses a threat to the each, but the each persists and ruptures the all.[45] If we did not feel commanded to feed *each* other who faces us, we would not have any conception of social justice, or justice for *all*. Social justice or justice for *all* by its nature overrides individuality, but is called into question by *each* other we meet. Each and all of us can be seen as an each or as part of the all, as other or as same; the way in which one is seen depends on whether the person doing the seeing is playing the Jew or playing the Greek.

Thus, although a certain amount of play can be made with the Hebrew/Greek rubric, some of it quite fertile, the critical distinction in Levinas always remains same and other; or, to be more specific, the other, the same that remembers the other, and the same that forgets the other. The various uses of the terms 'Hebrew' and 'Greek' can be understood most fruitfully in terms of how they fit into this pattern. 'Hebrew' either represents the other or the same that remembers the other; Judaism is Levinas's philosophical ethics; it is, for him, the conscience of the world. 'Greek', in distinction, runs the gamut; it may refer to Plato's otherwise than being in which case it represents the other, or to the language necessary to communication, in which case it is a same that remembers the other, or to ontology, in which case it is a same that forgets the other. The best Greek thought, true philosophy, is like the best Judaism — both are breaks in complacency, disallowings of what is allowed by totality.

What is most interesting about the addition of the terms Hebrew and Greek to the rest of the pairings is that they are true to Levinas's experience and his understanding of the experience of the Jews in history — so much so, in fact, that this experience and history suggest a source for the whole of the basic structure. Judaism inscribes the respect for the particular, but it also calls for the universal; the Hebrew Scriptures present an ethics and a *halachah* of particularity, but also an ethics, a halachah and a cosmology that are to be taught to everyone; moreover the latter universalizing tendency is intensified in later Scripture and in subsequent historical attempts to define the nature of Judaism, which suggests the idea that the rupture cannot remain a rupture but tends in time always more and more toward a totalizing wholeness. Judaism is, of course, threatened by the universal, in ways that need no explanation. But it also asserts itself against the universal, surprising the universal or reminding the universal of its ruptures, and in order to be able to do this it preserves for itself certain duties and rituals that it guards jealously from adoption by universal humanity. The whole of the basic structure is here.

To be sure, this is a loose analysis. But there is no doubt that for Levinas the history of the relation between the Jews and the world has been paradigmatic for the relation between ethics and politics, infinity and totality. Judaism, like any collectivity, can support fixed social structures, class interests, ideologies, ontologies and theologies, but in general it has not done so to the same extent as other collectivities have, in part because of an innate or textual unwillingness and in part simply because it has not had a chance. Levinas has learned from history that Judaism is the religion of a people with no security or fixed structures; as he points out, although there were hierarchies within the ghetto, everyone was oppressed (BTV 3). And he has learned from Rosenzweig's account of history that the Jews stand outside the world-historical; as he puts it, they are a diachrony breaking the Western timeline.[46] The concrete history of the Jewish people is what allows him to use the term Judaism for ethical rupture, for uncertainty, for the experience of being called into question on which his philosophy rests.

I do not quibble here with the fact that Levinas seems to be projecting the history of his nation into the cosmos at large and making it the basis for a metaphysics.[47] This sort of projection — perhaps what Levinas means when he says that it is "as if the history of Israel were the 'divine comedy' or the 'divine ontology' itself" (BTV 6)[48] — is not without precedent. But I should mention that he seems at times to sense a hubris in his links between Israel and ethics, and Greece and totality. In some late works he seems to have rethought the matter through Derrida, and to move in the direction of new links, links between Israel and writing, and Greece and speaking-thinking.[49] Moreover he never looses sight of the fact that the same experiences recorded in the sources of Judaism are also present in other great works of literature, not just Plato and Descartes but also Shakespeare and Dostoyevsky and others.[50] But he remains, despite all qualifications, always convinced that Judaism, in its worldly doings and sufferings, represents fundamental truths about the human being.

Why Levinas thinks of Judaism in the way or ways described above is the subject matter of this book. Here I may extend the question by pointing out that he wishes to retain many of the words common in the Jewish tradition but also to qualify their meanings rather severely (though he would perhaps regard this as clarification rather than qualification); moreover there are certain terms used by some Jews that he simply abandons. Let me briefly take up two cases. In the preface to *Totality and Infinity*, Levinas writes that "historically, morality will oppose politics and will have gone beyond the functions of prudence or the canons of the beautiful to claim itself unconditional and universal when the eschatology of messianic peace comes to superimpose itself upon the ontology of war" (TI 22). We have already seen that, despite the use here of the future perfect tense, eschatology as it is explained in this preface has nothing to do with knowledge of the future; I should now add that it also has nothing to do with an end of time or an eternity that destroys time, and, moreover, that these disassociations are equally true of Levinasian messianism. However, eschatology and messianism are commonly understood with reference to knowledge of the future or a cessation of duration; for this reason, in later years, Levinas abandons one of the terms and takes great pains to give the other a different nuance. When Richard Kearney asks him in 1984 if it is possible to have an eschatology in which man does not ultimately fuse with God — a question almost certainly, and quite reasonably, suggested by the passage above and by other statements about eschatology in *Totality and Infinity* — Levinas replies:

> But why eschatology? Why should we wish to reduce time to eternity? Time is the most profound relation man can have with God, precisely as a going towards God. There is an excellence in time that would be lost in eternity. . . . The term *eschaton* implies that there might exist a finality, an end to the historical relation of difference between man and the absolutely other, a reduction of the gap that safeguards the alterity of the transcendent to a totality of sameness. To realize the *eschaton* would therefore mean that we could seize or appropriate God as a telos and degrade infinite relation with the other to a finite fusion. (RK 23, 30)

Kearney presses him, and after Levinas again expresses "reservations" about the term eschatology (RK 30), Kearney switches to the term messianism. This term Levinas does not repudiate, but he insists that it be understood in a particular way, namely, "according to the talmudic maxim that 'the doctors of the law will never have peace, neither in this world or the next; they go from meeting to meeting, discussing always — for there is always more to be discussed'" (RK 31).

Why does Levinas rid his discourse of the one term and only redefine the other? Because the first term, *eschatology*, is derived from the Greek, while the second term, *messianism*, is derived from the Hebrew. Levinas feels he must use the Hebrew terms; indeed, the term messianism comes to stand in Levinas's writings for ideas at the center of his thought. He insists, however, this term, and the other Hebrew terms he feels it necessary to retain, are to be understood in a certain way. He wrests them away from their theological or institutional significances, a process that requires them to be 'deontologized' and 'dehistoricized'. But all of this remains to be shown. Levinas's way of reading the source texts and what he finds in them are the subjects to be taken up.

Two

The Bible and Prophecy

Take away from me the noise of your songs;
to the melody of your harps I will not listen.
But let justice roll down like waters,
and righteousness like an ever-flowing stream.
— *Amos 5.23–24*

Here I am — is saying with inspiration,
which is not a gift for fine words or songs.
There is constraint to give with full hands . . .
— *Levinas*, Otherwise Than Being

The many ideas expressed in the final chapter of *Otherwise Than Being or Beyond Essence* are incited and unified by Levinas's thematization of a single phenomenon: that the word of God appears only in the mouth of the human subject. This phenomenon, which in its basic or paradigmatic form Levinas calls witnessing, is manifest, he argues, in varying degrees in the entire range of human expression, from the saying that underlies all speech through to specific forms of speech such as scepticism, poetry, prophesy, or prayer. Levinas focuses, for the most part, not on prophesy or prayer per se, but on the more difficult topic of the apparently secular manifestations of witnessing. However, in order to illustrate his theme, he fills the chapter with biblical references, so many that they form a subtext of midrash almost complete unto itself; this subtext implicitly addresses the question of how a sacred text, in which human authors ascribe words directly to God, bears witness. In their succession, the biblical references illuminate the line of Levinas's thought; as an aggregate, they suggest that the Bible is one of his sources. But while Levinas has vast regard for the biblical text, his description of the phenomenon of witnessing implies that he does not understand the authority of Scripture in a conventional or static sense. "Authority," he writes, "is not somewhere, where a look could go seek it, like an idol, or assume it, like a logos" (OB 150). On the contrary, the subject's verbally or textually expressed relation with the divine — her witnessing — is 'contestation'.

The first half of this chapter gives an account of some of the content of chapter five of *Otherwise Than Being* including the idea of contestation; the ideas described here complete the discussion begun in the preceding chapter of the Levinasian interplay between totality and infinity. The second half takes up the biblical references that underlie Levinas's chapter, this is to say, Levinas's own contestation in practice; it forms the first of the four accounts of how Levinas reads and reflects that comprise the argument of this book.

Illeity and Levinas's book

Perhaps the most memorable idea presented in the last chapter of *Otherwise Than Being* is the withdrawn God, the ungraspable infinite that Levinas calls 'illeity'. But this idea is not the point from which the chapter springs. Levinas's starting point is his phenomenological insight about the relation between our relation to God and God's relation to us, between the movement up from below and the movement down from above.[1] His insight is that the two movements are indistinguishable in human experience. What God does to or for me is present to me only as what I do for God; what God tells me to do is present only in my spoken answer; "the command is stated by the mouth of him it commands" (OB 147); I have "received, one knows not from where, that of which I am the author" (OB 148–49); "I find the order in my response itself" (OB 150): Levinas repeats again and again the structure of the phenomenon he calls 'witnessing'. The phenomenon is the most central and critical piece of the play with narrative order that we examined in the last chapter. Witnessing is my coming upon and producing or having produced for me what was always already (not) there; it is the infinizing or the becoming infinite of the infinite, in the infinity of the infinitude of others;[2] it is, as Levinas puts it here, the glory and the glorification of the Glory.

The insight that God is present only in the response or the mouth of the subject is lost as soon as God is objectified, or placed in a locus. If this is done — or rather, *once* this is done, for the objective, located God has become a fundamental tenet of Western theology or the philosophy of the divine — the single relation that Levinas designates as witnessing must be differentiated into two movements: the 'from God' and the 'to God'. In order to preserve his insight, then, Levinas must correct the idea of God as object in locus. He does so by speaking of a God who is utterly withdrawn, who does not appear in 'the present of representation'. What we have of God is a trace, seen in the face of the other, but that trace is not left by something that is present, or by something that was once present and has moved on; it "comes from a past that has never been represented, has never been present"

(OB 144). The trace is — must be — the trace of something that is not and never was 'there' spatially or temporally, for it is the trace of something that is not a being. If the something had been there, its trace would merely be a feature of one of my past instants, and thus one of my (past) presents; if it were there now it would be a feature of my present. In neither case could it shake me up, breaking my timeline. But to shake me up is the fundamental function, the identifying mark, of the trace. The trace is a diachrony; it is the sign of an unbridgeable temporal gap.

Thus God is pushed past the point where he can be made present in speech or thought, and is kept there by Levinas's vigilance over the patterns of his own speech. Levinas takes great pains disassociate the word 'God' from God; moreover, he coins his own term to describe an aspect of this disassociation, namely, 'illeity'. Neither 'illeity' nor 'God' is a word 'for God' in the sense of a signifier pointing to a signified. Both terms, at their best, express a 'for God' in the sense of a pledge or a direction, in other words, a 'for God' in the sense of a *to God*, an *à-Dieu*, indistinguishable from a *from God*, or an upheaval in the subject. But the two terms are somewhat different in nuance or usage. Illeity — which might perhaps be rendered more clearly in English as 'he-ness' — refers to the state or event of being a pronoun: pronounness or pronouneity. It is, in grammatical form, a noun or a proper name, but one that achieves the function of a pronoun by pointing, not to an object, but to another word — and the word to which it points, *il*, is itself a pronoun. Insofar as it points at another word, illeity is a placeholder; insofar as the word being pointed at is a pronoun, illeity points at the holding of place. In effect it is an apophasis that points only at apophasis, a placeholder that holds the place of holding place; the term thus sets God inside a double fence, protecting him from being represented or objectified. God, experienced as illeity, is the absolutely other who cannot be addressed easily in the second person, who cannot be coopted into a personal present or a philosophical assembly. Now, the word 'God' carries all the nuances of the word 'illeity', and also has a further function. While the word 'illeity' expresses, not God, but God's withdrawness, the word 'God' expresses, not God, but the enigma by which he enters human consciousness; in other words, the word 'God' expresses God's entry into consciousness while the word illeity expresses the consciousness of God's *non*-entry into consciousness. Thus the word illeity inscribes that aspect of our experience of the infinite that is constituted by the ambiguity between the face of the other and the trace — the *il* of illeity points to the 'he' of the face because it cannot point to any 'he' of the withdrawn God per se — while the word 'God' points to the fact that God is and remains otherwise than the other of the face. In effect, 'illeity' points to a blurring between the other and the-otherwise-than-the-other, while 'God' inscribes a greater tension, the tension between this blurring and the impossibility of such a blurring. If illeity means — and this is the simplest way of defining the term — that God cannot be pointed to with a word, then the word 'God' must inscribe a tremendous tension; it is a powder keg of a word; it is, perhaps, a blasphemy.

Illeity or the withdrawn God is the source of a command, a command that, while it is given prior to time, coming from an infinite past, is experienced, in time, as the response to the face of the other. Levinas explains that the nature of one's witness, the response that is all one has of the command, is part of one's address to another human being; it is the saying that lies under a given said. Earlier, in chapter one, I discussed the way the relation between saying and said is another manifestation of the dynamic that accrues between infinity and totality, or ethics and politics. The moment of saying, the moment of address at the inception of speech, is, in *Otherwise Than Being* much more than in any earlier text, the ethical moment itself, and Levinas's descriptions of that

moment are as extraordinary as any of his descriptions of
ethics. In her saying, the subject gives herself, utterly and
completely, to the other. She not only announces her openness, her sincerity, her willingness to engage, and her acknowledgment of the other's height. She takes on, moreover,
an extreme obedience, an unimpeachable assignation. Her
subjectivity emerges as "being subject to everything" (OB
146). She is entirely 'for-the-other'; she gives herself as hostage to the other. Thus, in *Otherwise Than Being*, Levinas
offers not only — as he has before — an account of the morality inherent in human speech, a linguistic ethics, but — in
addition — a speech-based account of all human thought and
action, an ethical linguistics; perhaps strangely, the latter
seems to be the more concrete and liberating account. Here
the face largely drops away to be replaced by discourse, and,
moreover, the focus is placed particularly on the part of discourse that is *my* saying. No longer does Levinas speak of
the other and I looking into one another's eyes and revealing
glimpses of our alterity; now he is curious only about what *I*
give in *my* subjectivity that arises from *my* response. It is in
Otherwise Than Being that Levinas designates the saying
with the phrase: 'here I am'.

'Here I am' inscribes the structure of witnessing much
more obviously in French, where it is *me voici*. Unlike the
English, *me voici* does not use the copula verb, the verb of
equivalences that is the root of all thematization (OB 167).
The French does not imply that the subject *is* something,
but simply that she offers herself. Moreover, as Levinas points
out, the subject or the 'I' of *me voici* appears in the accusative; the speaker of the phrase is therefore, grammatically,
the 'author of an exposure that originates she knows not
where' (see OB 148–49). Insofar as *me voici* implies an ambiguity between the authorial and accusative voices, it
expresses, better than the English, the ambiguity or ambivalence of witnessing, in which responsibility is both "a claim

laid on the same by the other in the core of myself" and also an "exposure of me to the other" (OB 141): a command and an offering. With the *me voici*, Levinas continues to direct our attention to the always-prior moment in which I am commanded or accused, and in which this command or accusation is indistinguishable from my assumption of responsibility, responsibility for everyone if not for everything. In this moment, as described in *Otherwise Than Being*, I am 'passive', and my passivity is signification; my passivity carries the meaning of responsibility, expressed with the words 'here I am'.

The term 'passivity' is not intended to indicate that the subject is not the agent of her actions. Obviously to maintain the integrity of the witnessing structure it is necessary that Levinas never clarify the agent of the movement, and so he explains that passivity includes an active element and is also beyond activity and inactivity. He expresses this lack of clarification — the heart of the witnessing structure itself — by saying that the structure is an 'enigma', or an 'ambivalence', or a diachrony. Diachrony, we recall, is opposed both to chronology and synchrony; it is not an ordered line of instants, nor is it the occurrence of many instants at once. Rather, it is, as it were, the occurrence of one instant in two or more times; it is the rupture of the instant; it is the meeting of the instant with what breaks it. To say that the witnessing structure is diachronous is to say that the saying, which refers to the beyond, and the said, which attempts to assemble and synchronize everything in the present, cannot themselves be synchronized on the same temporal plane: diachrony refers specifically to a tension between tension and harmony, that is, to the non-synchronic occurrence 'together' of the synchronic element of human thought and the anarchic element of illeity which upsets synchrony. A theologian might try to synchronize synchrony and anarchy — to bring together on the same plane the substance of the (no longer anarchic) infinite command and the (always synchronic) expression in a said of the response to that command — but this, according to Levinas, would be a betrayal of the anarchy of illeity, a betrayal of the tension inherent in the witnessing structure, "the extreme tension of the command exercised by the other in me over me" (OB 141). Such a move immediately results in the degeneration of illeity into a being, the saying into a saying-less said, and the enigma into a dilemma, a contradiction that can and must be 'thought out'. To make this move, to betray anarchic illeity, is to risk "the idolatry of worshipping knowledge at the expense of the responsibility toward others."[3]

What can be done to lessen the risk of such a betrayal? Levinas admits that it is impossible to speak of the witnessing structure without creating a synchrony, and impossible to say the word 'God' without betraying anarchy. It is, in fact, not only the theologian, but any 'theo-logian' — anyone who uses the word 'God' — who implies, in the word, an attempt to contain illeity by making it into a theme: to say the word 'God' is to betray God. But, as Levinas has it, the word 'God' is not just a word; it is also an "overwhelming semantic event," in which the betrayal inherent in saying the word is undone, in which the word is rendered ruptured, in which, in fact, the word acquires the meaning: rupture (OB 151). This is to say that the word itself does not allow the theo-logical idolatry; it breaks the betrayal; even as the infinite is done up in a said, it undoes itself; even as it is said, it is unsaid. In effect, the word 'God' expresses Descartes's idea of the infinite; it assembles the unassemblable, and thus is both a said (an assembly) and an unsaying (because what is said cannot be assembled).[4] Thus the word has a double structure: it betrays the beyond and also conveys it. This betraying/conveying is 'contestation'.

To witness is to acknowledge a God who is not, or who is not in locus. And to acknowledge this is to admit that I cannot call upon God, for a God who can be supplicated is a God in locus. To witness is to acknowledge that I am responsible to do everything. And to acknowledge this is once again to admit that I cannot call upon God, for to call upon him would compromise my responsibility. In short, my witness or responsibility, stemming from an awareness of God's withdrawness, is fundamentally "not counting on any God" (OB 154), and this "not counting" is so extreme a movement as to be describable as negating God. But what does the negation negate? It negates only the theological God, God understood as a being or a presence. It negates the statement of the word 'God' as if it could be a synchronic event. By saying the word 'God', the subject vies with the infinite; she attempts to negate it, to make the withdrawn present and thus to shed her responsibility in the very act of speaking. But if she also states the word as a semantic event, she acknowledges her own absolute responsibility, her witness to a God who cannot be brought into the present. Contestation appears as a structure of consciousness, or as Levinas puts it a 'psychism', a tension in the soul or split in the subject, in which the acknowledgment of the higher status of the commander chafes against the fact that the responsibility devolves onto the commanded one. The word God is 'the other in the same' — alternatively, the 'same' which is the word is at the same time a forgetting *and* a remembering of the other behind, within, and beyond it. Contestation preserves the enigma by holding the beyond and the being in tension; it refers to the fact that they can be inscribed in the single word God, and yet not be synchronized or made compatible.

I will return later in the chapter to the question of how to reduce the risk of betraying illeity, and, still later, to the question of whether the theologian (as opposed to the theo-logian) can engage in a reduction of the betrayal. But now I want to stress the importance of witnessing in Levinas's thought in general. The fact that, in the witnessing structure, Levinas thematizes and brings together an account of the response to the trace of the withdrawn God and the relation to the human other means that this discussion in *Otherwise Than Being* fills several gaps that appeared in my last chapter. There I said that God was only present in the trace of his absence in the face of the other. Here the thought behind that assertion is fleshed out. The way one knows that the true God is not a phenomenon is also the way one knows God, that is, by witnessing, by the response that sounds in one's own mouth before the commanding other. Levinas can speak of the withdrawness of God, not present to human experience, because that withdrawness follows in human awareness from the witnessing structure, which is present to human experience. Responsibility precedes theo-logy. In addition, the phenomenon of witnessing helps to clarify what I called the question of narrative order, the problem of how the ethical command can be always prior to thought and action, while it is at the same time encountered, in time, in the face of the other. In the speech-based account of *Otherwise Than Being* it is much easier to see that while the "substantial nucleus of the ego that is formed in the same" (OB 141) is always already undone by the assignation that one expresses every time one opens one's mouth, one must nevertheless encounter a human other in order to express that assignation. The infinite source of the undoing of the ego is not, as one might think, 'ever-present' but, in contradistinction, 'never-present'. And the command coming from that source is neither ever-present nor never-present; it *becomes* present in the ethical encounter. "That the glory of the Infinite is glorified only by the signification of the-one-for-the-other, as sincerity, that in my sincerity the Infinite passes the finite, that the Infinite comes to pass there, is what makes the plot of ethics primary, and what makes language irreducible to an act among acts" (OB 150). God is absent, but the trace of his absence is present as the positive movement toward another human being. The positive movement is first in experience; the negative movement — the passing or going away of God — is primordial. Ethics, which takes place as sincerity in language, as the here I am of saying, is also the point from which all speculation and action follows.

The discussion of illeity here can also add substantially to our analysis of ethics and politics. For the word illeity is not the only coinage that a pronoun-for-a-pronoun might take. The fact that Levinas does not speak of *tu*-eity or *vous*-eity is significant. The word is in the third person, and suggests therefore a connection of some kind between God and the third. I have spoken up until now as if God appeared only in the ethical relation — the relation between two — but I have left open the possibility that there may be a further manifestation of God in the social sphere created by the entry of the third. Levinas speaks in both ways, sometimes emphasizing the trace that can only be produced in the face of the other to whom I stand in proximity, and sometimes speaking of a God who passes in justice. God does not appear with his own face, but he may appear either in the face, or in the aggregate of faces.

The two appearances of illeity are different — as ethics and politics are different. When illeity appears in the face, it ruptures and destroys my conceptual structures; it is anarchic; it destroys my ability to make demands of the other. When illeity appears in society, it commands the building up of conceptual structures; it is a principle of order; moreover, it commands me to make demands of the other.

> The relation with the third is an incessant correction of the asymmetry of the proximity where the face is faced. There is weighing, thought, objectification, and, by that, an order which betrays my anarchic relation to illeity but where my relation is translated before us. *Betrayal of my anarchic relation with illeity, but also a new relation with it*: it is only thanks to God that I am a subject incomparable to the other, that I am

approached as other among the others, which is to say "for myself." . . . The "passing" of God of whom I speak only by reference to this help or to this grace, is precisely the reverting of the incomparable subject into a member of society. (OB 158, my emphasis)

We have seen that on the level of the three I myself become an other to the other, that I am commanded to call for a justice based in equality — justice for the other, justice for all the others, and even justice for myself. We now see in addition that this movement of justice, like the ethical movement, is directed to or from the withdrawn God; it takes place "thanks to God." "The realization of the just society is *ipso facto* an elevation of man to the company of God" (DL 197).

The fact that God passes in both the ethical and the political spheres by no means functions to collapse the distinction between ethics and politics. My politics, in which I am commanded to command, must still be subjected to the critique of my ethics, in which my ability to command is called into question. The insecurity that is imposed on me by the trace in the face persists in the social sphere, as what might be called the 'trace of the trace'. And the trace of the trace grounds social action — grounds my commanding of others — and at times warns me away from certain social actions — disallowing my commanding of others. The ethics/politics distinction as I have drawn it is maintained. What is added here is the idea that God passes both in the rupturing encounter with the other, and in the normative laws and rules of social conduct — including perhaps especially the *halachah*. The *halachah* takes up the pieces of the conceptions broken by the encounter with the trace, and, in the shadow of the trace of the trace, builds from them a justice that remains just insofar as it refuses to become a closed system. It is true that, by the ambiguity of the witnessing structure, it is strictly impossible from a Levinasian perspective to say that the *halachah* was 'written by God'. But nor would he say that the *halachah* was merely written by human beings. It arises from God as God passes in the social realm, just as ethics arises from God as God passes in the face of the other.

What does Levinas's linguistic ethics mean for his own language, as it appears in the book at hand, or, as he puts it, 'at this very moment' (OB 155, 170)? Part way through the chapter Levinas turns to the subject of how his own book can be understood in the terms he has been describing, and most of the rest of the chapter consists in essence of an apology for his book, a defense of his philosophic discourse. The lines that the apology follows are recognizably a re-presentation of what I am calling the basic structure of his thought. Levinas raises the question of the status of his book at the same time as he raises the question, which I have already examined, of the status of the state. The two questions are actually one. As asymmetrical proximity is hardened in the symmetrical state, so "the very discussion which we are at this moment elaborating about signification, diachrony and the transcendence of the approach beyond being, a discussion that means to be philosophy, is a thematizing, a synchronizing of terms, a recourse to systematic language, a constant use of the verb being, a bringing back into the bosom of being all signification allegedly conceived beyond being" (OB 155). Levinas is party to a betrayal. He synchronizes the diachronic beyond, thereby sacrificing its diachrony. He makes a critique of thematization his theme, thereby contradicting himself and, it might be thought, rendering his argument absurd. These are, he writes, "familiar objections" (OB 155). His subsequent apology falls into two parts. First he explains briefly how it is that all speech, and especially philosophy, must betray the saying. Then he explains how the betrayal can be reduced.

The explanation of why philosophy's betrayal is necessary

involves the entry of the third. Along with universality, uni-
vocality, equality, and symmetry, the other's other makes a
specific demand for books in which "the saying is fixed in a
said" (OB 159). So despite the fact that "the unnarratable
other loses his face in narration" (OB 166), Levinas must
narrate. Since he cannot speak to each of us as an other, he
must cast his discourse in the language of universality; he
must make his speech a theme or system; he must inscribe
his saying in a series of dead saids, thereby sacrificing the
particularity that would mark any discourse he had with the
single other who stood before him. A betrayal is necessary in
all speech that seeks to describe, for "everything is shown by
indeed betraying its meaning"; and philosophy, which seeks
to describe essential reality, is therefore particularly called
to betray. However, in addition, "philosophy is called upon to
reduce that betrayal" (OB 156).

Levinas's account of how the reduction is accomplished
has three layers. He begins with a description of 'abusive'
discourse, which is followed and clarified somewhat by a description of prophetic or poetic discourse, and then by a
description of scepticism. None of these discussions is very
well sketched; obviously Levinas cannot offer systematic
instructions for the reduction of systematization. Nevertheless, he manages to point gradually at an answer to the question of how the betrayal might be reduced, and provides, I
think, a sufficient apology for his book — given, of course,
the fact that the command disqualifies apology, and that the
Levinasian subject is never justified.

Abusive discourse is discourse that affirms universality
and undercuts that affirmation at the same time; it is broken language. To explain it, Levinas turns back to the idea
of contestation, the saying of the word God that encompasses
the tension in witnessing. Insofar as signification is contestation, there must be a meaning being contested. Contestation tries to negate, but, in doing so, it first admits the force,

or indeed the reality, of what is to be negated. Thus the contestation that is the saying of the word 'God' admits the beyond being even as it contests it. In this way, contestation is abusive speech. In reflection, the contestation will appear to be a contradiction: to say 'beyond being' will appear to be in contradiction with the conditions for making statements. But before reflection, in the immediacy of the saying of the word God, the contestation is not yet a contradiction but an abuse, holding beyond and being in tension. "God," he explains, is "nothing but an abusive word" (OB 156). As such, it both betrays and conveys the infinite; it both betrays and reduces the betrayal.

The account of prophetic or poetic[5] discourse is complementary; it extends the account of abusive discourse by suggesting that all language, insofar as it carries within it a saying, bears the marks of abuse. To understand this it is necessary to see, first, that prophecy is linked, throughout Levinas's chapter, to saying — in other words, prophecy, for Levinas, is a characteristic of all good speech. Indeed, not only are prophecy and saying linked to one another, the two are also linked to witnessing and to other terms such as 'inspiration' and 'glorification' (which is the glorification of the infinite, and also, following the structure of witnessing, the glory of the infinite).[6] It might be argued that a number of levels should be identified in this concatenation of terms. Saying, which is implicit even in the most mundane sentences, might be thought of as distinct from saying-as-witnessing or saying-as-inspiration, in which the subject is aware of the assignation she acknowledges in her saying; and both might be thought of as distinct from prophesy or prayer or glorification, which suggest a further intensification of the awareness of assignation by giving a single name to its source. However, such distinctions are far from explicit in Levinas's chapter. It is probable that he blurs the terms because any attempt to distinguish them, even a distinction based on degrees of intensity, would tend to slip towards a distinction between the relation to the human other and the relation to God-as-other. To speak of a relation with God outside of the relation with the trace would precisely put God in locus as an object and undermine the witnessing phenomenon, while to refuse to accord prophecy a status categorically separate from that of quotidian saying prevents this kind of idolatry. Levinas emphasizes that all saying, witnessing, prophecy, inspiration and glorification refers to God precisely insofar as it contains the promise to love the neighbor, to feed him with the bread from one's own mouth. "Prophecy," writes Levinas early in the chapter, "[is] the very psyche in the soul, the other in the same, and all of man's spirituality [is] prophetic" (149).[7] More particularly, prophecy stands for the fact that the said conveys the saying while betraying it; the continued presence of saying within the said is thus "the resonance of every language 'in the name of God', the inspiration or prophecy of all language" (OB 152). Thus it is that the account of prophecy can function here to extend the definition of abusive language from the word God to all language. All speech, insofar as it is prophetic, insofar as it is internally broken, inscribes a contestation; all speech both betrays and reduces the betrayal.

This extension allows Levinas to begin his apology-proper. Insofar as discourse, qua prophetic discourse, appears as a said, it appears as information, as a record of something that can be thought. But it is not just a said; it inscribes, in addition, an attempt to preserve the sincerity of the saying by always pointing beyond information, beyond what can be thought, beyond its own said. Levinas is not tremendously concerned about the relation of signifier to signified being; he is not concerned, for instance, that when I say 'table' the word is different from the thing. The problem that concerns him is that when I say the name of a human being, or describe him, I can only re-present his being — his locus, time,

history, ontology, what he has disclosed or made known —
but I cannot re-present his otherwise than being — the trace
in his face of the passing of God that arises in our relation
and always escapes re-presentation by not being present.
When I say the name 'God' — when I try to encompass the
trace itself in a word — the problem with all naming or describing is there at once, in an intense way. But the name
'God' is, in this respect, paradigmatic for all speech; and more
than this, it is a part of all speech, since every human being
addressed in speech shows me the trace of the otherwise than
being. The trace in the other gives all my words the structure of assembling the unassemblable, that is to say: assem-
bling/finding unassembled, or constructing/deconstructing,
or saying/unsaying. Levinas applies this linguistic conception to the writing of his own philosophic works. Prophetic
discourse can "exceed the limits of what is thought, by suggesting, letting be understood without ever making understandable, an implication of a meaning distinct from that
which comes to signs from the simultaneity of systems or
the logical definition of concepts" (OB 169–70).

This quality of pointing beyond the said or beyond what
can be thought: what is it pointing toward? Toward the
pastness and futurity of the trace to which it is a response.
In particular, Levinas's books point towards and exist as a
response to the past of books — tradition — and the future of
books — interpretation. Levinas makes the call for interpretation ad infinitum explicitly in *Totality and Infinity*, which,
as he has it, can break its own thematization into "fragments"
because it is incomplete, a philo-sophy rather than a wisdom, a discourse rather than a teaching, "told to the other, to
the reader who appears anew behind my discourse" (TI 295).
And he makes it again in *Otherwise Than Being* where "I
still interrupt the ultimate discourse in which all the dis-
courses are stated, in saying it to one that listens to it, and
who is situated outside the said that the discourse says,

outside all it includes. That is true of the discussion I am elaborating at this very moment" (OB 170). Levinas calls, with his own books, to other books not yet written. He speaks to someone who is 'not yet'. The fact that his book is written at all — for whom, after all? — points outside of its own system to an unknown, an unpredicted. In the same way, every author compromises her claim to coherence; all books point outside of totality. "In totalizing being, discourse qua discourse thus belies the very claim to totalize" (OB 171). Coherent discourse requires a certain incoherence, and that incoherence is a matter of a diachronous occurrence in two times, in a past and in a future. This, above all, is the prophetic quality of discourse.

The final part of Levinas's apology is the discussion of scepticism that closes the main body of *Otherwise Than Being*. Scepticism, writes Levinas, is "a refusal to synchronize the implicit affirmation contained in saying and the negation which this affirmation states in the said" (OB 167). By refusing to accept the truth in a given assembly of being, scepticism makes a distinction between the speaker's presentation of herself in truth and her content or theme; in short, scepticism does not allow the saying to be lost or negated in the said. Philosophy refutes scepticism in two ways. First, it applies the old logic trick: if, as you say, there is no truth then it cannot be true that there is no truth. In this refutation, writes Levinas, philosophy "puts [scepticism's] thesis into contradiction with the conditions for any thesis" (OB 171). But philosophy also refutes by means of a grander use of logic whereby it absorbs scepticism into its system as an antithesis and thus grows historically and territorially. Both refutations are, in effect, attempts on the part of philosophy to destroy scepticism by absorbing it into the said, by forcing it into coherence or synchrony with itself and with philosophy's logos. (I will note briefly that 'philosophy' is here playing the role of those who pose the 'familiar objections' to Levinas's thought, accusing him of incoherence or self-contradiction, or attempting to subsume him into a larger — probably Hegelian — rubric, while the sceptic here is Levinas. I will take this issue up again in chapter four.)

Levinas admits the strength of philosophy's case, but notes as well that philosophy is never able to destroy scepticism entirely. "Does not the last word belong to philosophy? Yes, in a certain sense, since for Western philosophy the saying is exhausted in things said. But scepticism in fact makes a difference, and puts an interval between saying and said. Scepticism is refutable, but it returns" (OB 168). In effect, scepticism refuses to be synchronized into philosophy's impersonal logos, for "to contest the possibility of truth is precisely to contest this uniqueness of order and level" (OB 168). Scepticism contests the very ground of philosophy; it contests coherence.[8]

In explaining scepticism's contestation, Levinas offers the marvelously clear metaphor of the knots. Philosophy attempts to conceal the incoherencies of reality by knotting together the breaks in the thread of its discourse; the knots allow it to claim that its discourse remains always coherent and unbroken. But philosophy does not in this way get rid of the breaks; it only conceals them. And concealing them, paradoxically, makes them apparent. "The interruptions of discourse found again and recounted in the immanence of the said are conserved like knots in a thread tied again, the trace of a diachrony that does not enter into the present, that refuses simultaneity" (OB 170). Scepticism is aware that there are things that cannot be synchronized, that do not appear on the common plane of philosophic knowing, that cannot be made intelligible. This awareness is enshrined forever in the knots, and the sceptic always finds them and points to them. With the discussion of knots, Levinas closes the defense of his discourse and the account of how the betrayal inherent in language is reduced. As the infinite is both betrayed and

conveyed by the abusive word, and as the saying is both betrayed and conveyed by the prophetic said, (and as ethics is
both betrayed and conveyed, albeit with its 'skin hardened',
by the state), so anarchy or incoherence or scepticism is both
betrayed and conveyed by philosophy.

So much for the three layers of apology. We must now confront a problem. The apology so far has implied that all
language betrays and reduces the betrayal: all language is
abusive insofar as it is prophetic, and Levinas says explicitly
that "[all] language is already scepticism" (OB 170). Why,
then, does Levinas insist that it is the role of philosophy in
particular to reduce the betrayal?

Levinas's only explanation seems to be that "philosophy is
called upon to conceive ambivalence, to conceive it in several
times" (OB 162). The phrase, 'in several times' has at least
two meanings here. First, Levinas suggests, as he has before, that the philosopher must allow the enigma to remain
diachronous, and not attempt to synchronize it. The philosopher is called on to understand that the harmonious said
and the tension-full or anarchic saying/unsaying take place
in different times — the said referring always to an assembly in the present or a re-presentation, the saying referring
always to a past that was never present, and the unsaying to
a future that will never be present; thus, also, the conveying
always prior to and after the betraying, the tension or anarchy always prior to and after the harmony. Thus, when
Levinas says that philosophy must think in 'several times',
he means in large part that philosophy can reduce the betrayal of concepts and language by remembering that there
is a brokenness or a deconstruction inherent in its conceptions, a deconstruction that comes from the other's rupture
of my constructed or postulated eternity; in other words,
philosophy reduces the betrayal by ensuring that its conceptions are not governed by an attempt at synchrony. But the
phrase 'in several times' also has another meaning, for this

very movement — the very remembering of brokenness — takes place on two levels or at two times, a less reflective level or time and a more reflective level or time. To be precise: it is not entirely clear from Levinas's descriptions of abusive language whether philosophy is commanded to say, less reflectively, the word God — that is, to pray — or, in distinction, to recollect, on a more reflective level, the less reflective saying of the word — that is, to remember that all speech is prayer. The phrase 'in several times' suggests both. Prephilosophical language already betrays as soon as it transforms the call, the cry, and the groan into words like 'God'; philosophical language betrays further by reifying God as word or concept and therefore forgetting the call, cry, or groan that lies beneath it. Thus the possibility of betrayal is actually the possibility of a double betrayal — not merely the betrayal that is part of all speech, the endemic totality that is there even in the truest philosophy, but also the further betrayal that forgets, or refuses to admit, that speech is a betrayal. The enemy here is not the one who betrays, but the one who refuses to admit that the betrayal can be reduced; this one is the perpetrator of the second betrayal, the treacherous betrayal, the betrayal of the avoidable totality, or, as Levinas says here, "Western philosophy" which has "issued out of proximity" but "nonetheless "refute[s] it in discourse absorbed in the said and in being, in ontology" (OB 169).

This second betrayal cannot be reduced, since it is comprised of the refutation of proximity. But the first betrayal can be reduced, and not only by the abuse or prophecy or scepticism inherent in all language, but also, very simply, by a refusal to commit the second betrayal. This is to say that, in order to reduce the first betrayal, philosophical abusive language must appear not only as what might be called "simple contestation" — saying God — but also as a kind of meta-contestation — a fight against the tendency to forget the contestation when saying God. And if we allow that both contestation and meta-contestation can be called prayer or prophecy, then the many passages in which Levinas castigates or deconstructs the history of Western thought appear as a kind of philosophical prayer or prophecy. The job of philosophy — the job of Levinas's philosophy in particular — is to prophesy, which now can be seen to mean: (1) to reduce the first betrayal by preserving the saying in the said, (2) to do this precisely by refusing to commit the second betrayal, which forgets the saying in the said, and therefore (3) to do it by promulgating the fact that first betrayal is a betrayal, i.e. to call out, for all to hear the fact that language and philosophy constitute betrayals. In short, to reduce the betrayal is, very simply, to recollect the betrayal. Since this is a difficult movement of thought or discourse, it can best — or only — be done by philosophy. Because it can only be done by philosophy, it is philosophy's job.

We see here a recurrence of the problem I defined in chapter one. Totality is endemic in human existence; indeed, it is commanded by infinity. But it is not necessary for us to slip into the many further deformations that consist in forgetting the infinity that commanded us to totalize. The structure of contestation, necessary upon the entry of the third, means that speech and philosophy must thematize; paradoxically, before philosophy is called upon to reduce the betrayal, it is called upon to betray. But if it can preserve the memory of what commanded it to betray it will have reduced the betrayal. Economy, war, politics, and justice, like philosophy and thematization, appear in various forms — sometimes as part of the structure of contestation necessary upon the entry of the third, sometimes as a degeneration of the contestation. The denial or atheism inherent in contestation is always a duty of the subject under God, but it is also always possible for it to grow until it swamps the admission that is the other side of contestation; the withdrawal of God can turn to forgetting. The first totalities that the preoriginal

encounter with infinity calls us to create are already compromises, and must be watched lest they degenerate further.

The tendency toward such degeneration becomes amply
clear in the way Levinas's description of philosophy changes
during the chapter. In segment three of the chapter, in which
Levinas describes the entry of the third and the totalization
she demands, he appears hopeful of philosophy's ability to
reduce the betrayal. He suggests that while the totality that
is the political state cannot reduce the betrayal on its own, it
can be advised by philosophy to this effect. Philosophy can
do this because, even while it is part of what the third party
calls for — "control, a search for justice, society and the State,
comparison and possession, thought and science, commerce
and philosophy" — it is at the same time "this measure
brought to the infinity of the being-for-the-other of proximity, and it is like the wisdom of love" (OB 161). Thus, "[e]ven
if [philosophy] is called to thought by justice, it . . . remains
the servant of the saying that signifies the difference between
the one and the other as the one for the other, as non-indifference to the other. Philosophy is the wisdom of love at the
service of love" (OB 162). However, in the discussion of scepticism and the refutation of scepticism in segment five of the
chapter, philosophy takes as its main role the deliberate forgetting of proximity and the absorption of the saying into
the said. "Western philosophy," writes Levinas, "has been . . .
the refutation of transcendence" (OB 169), and, in the same
vein, towards the end of the chapter, he postulates a Foucaul-
dian alliance between the state, philosophy and medicine
which conspire to destroy proximity (OB 170). At this point,
he attributes the abusive language that stands against the
alliance not to any form of philosophy, but to scepticism, and
also to prophecy and religion (as distinguished from faith
and theology, and linked instead to the witnessing structure).
Certainly, the two accounts — that of segment three and that
of segment five — are ultimately more or less compatible.

Levinas calls in both for a resurgence of proximity within totality; he only varies in the degree to which he sees philosophy and the state as able to initiate or accept this resurgence. But this variation is interesting: the word 'philosophy' at one moment names an endemic totality and at the next moment names a totality that can and must be avoided. We have here a fairly clear example of the way a totalization called for by the third can at any moment slip into one or a number of degenerate forms, denying its own origin.

Let me summarize. Before philosophy is called upon to reduce the betrayal, it is called upon to betray. But the trace of the infinite that appears in proximity also calls upon it not to betray too much — to remember that the other it betrays is also the source of its call to betray. If primal, prephilosophical language is abusive, then philosophy, which must take that abuse and reflect on it — making it nonabusive by squeezing its asymmetry into a 'corrective' symmetry — must at all costs squeeze gently. In taking all the responsibility — to universalize, and to respect the particular — philosophy bears witness to the withdrawn God. Bearing witness can only be done by feeding the other with bread from one's mouth. Levinas's book, written as a theme, expressed in universal terms, is at the same time bread for the mouth of one who is 'not yet'. Along the way, others, if they are at all sceptics, can examine the knots in Levinas's discourse and find in them the moments where the diachrony is hinted at without being made intelligible.

The midrash

Levinas on theology

Clearly the witnessing phenomenon, with its withdrawn God, points to a critique of Western theology. Such a critique is explicitly alluded to at various points in the chapter, but is

never explained in detail. As I understand it, Levinas sees
Western theology as the perpetrator of attempts to define
God, to objectify and locate him. Following this location, theology distinguishes — must distinguish — the movement
from below and the movement from above, calling them reason and revelation, or, in other aspects, faith and grace, or
nature and providence. All of these distinctions collapse in
Levinas, since all of the experiences to which these words
refer are found to happen within the face to face, understood
as taking place under God or 'in God's name', that is, understood as witnessing. Levinas describes witnessing so often
in so many different ways because he sees it as a radical
critique of the way the human relation to God is most often
understood. "One is tempted," he writes, "to call this plot
[i.e. witnessing] religious; [but] it . . . does not rest on any
positive theology" (OB 147). Nor indeed does it rest on a negative theology, for the unknowing of negative theology is effectively equivalent to the knowing of positive theology: "the
not-known and the unknowable would still refer to a present,
would form a structure in it, would belong to order" (OB 154),
while witnessing, in distinction, is beyond knowing and unknowing, anarchic. In fact, Levinas does not want his philosophy of the divine connected to the negative at all; the
subject's 'negation' of God follows from a fundamentally positive movement, the ethical obligation to the other (OB 151).[9]
But leaving aside the question of whether or to what extent
witnessing is positive or negative or neither or both, we can
be certain that it is not theology. Levinas writes of the structure: "what a deception for the friends of the truth that
thematizes being, and of the subject that effaces itself before
Being!" (OB 149) — referring to the theologians who totalize
God by the very movement with which they bow before him.

The problem with theology, more specifically, seems to be
that its totalization is never undermined. Theology is like
philosophy insofar as it is called to betray meaning by the

entry of the third, but, unlike philosophy, theology never reduces the betrayal. Thus while philosophy may appear sometimes as truth and sometimes as ontology, theology is always
the same; theology is always ontotheology. A degeneration
has taken place rendering it not merely one of the endemic
totalities demanded by the third, but an avoidable totality. A
fixity has set into its categories that precludes the possibility of a theological expression of the witnessing structure.

What then is this theology? What is Levinas referring to
with the word? Levinas draws extensively on the Hebrew
Bible throughout the chapter; his references are, as I said,
so thick on the ground as to form a subtext of midrash or
biblical commentary. Perhaps, then, he is criticizing all post-
biblical theology from a biblical perspective. But this cannot
quite be the case, for though the witnessing structure and
the notion of the withdrawn God are certainly present in
Hebrew Scripture — in the image of God's back and in the
passages to which Levinas refers in this chapter — it must
be admitted that Scripture often points to a God in locus;
moreover the idea of bearing witness to the withdrawn God
is expressed in rabbinic and kabbalistic texts as well as in
the Bible. Perhaps, then, he presents a Jewish critique of
Christian theology. But this too cannot quite be the case, for
though it might be argued that Christianity insists more
adamantly on locating God and distinguishing between the
movement from above and the movement from below, such
tendencies are also undercut in Christian thought — just as
they are insisted on and undercut in Jewish thought.[10] Probably it can only be said that Levinas believes that the phenomenon of witnessing is somehow preserved in the Hebrew
Scriptures — to the extent that his thought on the matter is
illuminated at every turn with biblical reference — and later
lost to theology. Despite the fact that linguistic descriptions
of God must thematize him, and despite the more pertinent
existence of many Scriptural passages that do not in any

obvious way allow for contestation or the idea of a withdrawn God, the Hebrew Scriptures retain something later forgotten, forgotten by degrees but in the end forgotten to the extent that Levinas, writing in the modern period, feels no need to qualify his dismissals of theology at large. It is, I believe, because Levinas holds the idea of bearing witness to be almost irretrievably lost, that he argues so strongly for it, and for the idea that follows from it and forms its ground, the withdrawn God.

While Levinas does not describe the gradual process by which witnessing is forgotten, he does hint at some of the effects of the forgetting on our hermeneutics. I think it likely that Levinas sees himself in almost complete accord with the Scriptural understanding of God, and that at the same time he sees that the nuances of this understanding cannot be thematized today using the same images. Levinas's Isaiah, for instance, manages to express the idea that the order is present only in the response while at the same time speaking metaphorically of a God in locus. But in an age when theology is caught either in the stranglehold of ontology, with its differentiation of the from-God and the to-God, or in the subsequent stranglehold of a 'psychologism' that reduces all movement to mental operation, it may be impossible to express the witnessing structure without describing God somewhat less metaphorically and more metaphysically as otherwise than being or beyond being. People in our era tend to read all words literally — that is, as having referents that can be pointed at. These referents, in general, are understood to take two forms, physical or psychological; in short, words are understood to point either at beings or at ideas. For such readers, the word 'God' must refer either to a Something existing Somewhere or to a function of the human mind, human emotions, human needs, or human social circumstances. When a reader comes to the Bible with the literalist hermeneutic, it will certainly seem to her that its authors understood God in the former sense, but it will also appear that she has a choice; she may adopt what she thinks of as their conception of God as a being, or may 'look through' that conception towards the state of mind of its authors, a state of mind that represents either psychological truths about the human being, certain contingent political and social circumstances of the period of authorship, or both. Neither way does the Bible appear meaningless: God-as-being is obviously meaningful, and God (or God-talk) understood as representing ideas may, likewise, provide us with information, or even insight. Nevertheless, neither of these literalist hermeneutic modes makes room for the way Levinas understands God, or the way he thinks the biblical authors understood God. For these modes deal exclusively with the two totalizing levels of existence, that is, the level of the one (the locus of ideas) and the level of the three (the locus where beings coexist) at the expense of the level of the two where infinity is produced. Thought at the level of the one, as an idea, God appears as part of the subject or as a function of an egology. Thought at the level of the three, as a being, God appears as part of a whole or as a function — albeit the highest function — of an ontology. As a reader, Levinas differs from ontological or third level readers in that although he, like them, holds God to be a reality, he repudiates the treatment of God as a being. He differs from ideational or first-level readers in that although he, like them, is interested in what the biblical words mean about an earthly movement or affectivity, he repudiates the treatment of this movement as a facet of the individual or the society, and thus makes a space for passivity, for reception, for teaching — and for God's reality.[11]

Ultimately, for Levinas, the third-level and first-level readings coincide. Like all totalizing conceptions, they overlap or spill into one another; perhaps it may even be said that they *are* one another seen from different perspectives. Ideas are ideas of things; God as a being can just as easily be called

'God as the idea of a being'. So too ideas take on substance and have effects in the world; God as an idea becomes 'the thing that is the idea of God'. Ideology is ontology, and vice versa. But though the hybrid of thing and idea has effects, it does not have the effect of shaking up the human subject to the core, of calling her right to exist into question. One can only be shaken up by something that is neither a being nor an idea, something that comes from outside being and ruptures all ideas. As Levinas puts it in the chapter under consideration: "Neither realism nor idealism, twin brothers, have the birthright. It is justice signified by signification, by the one-for-the-other that requires phenomenality" (OB 163). No ontology will give us ethics; the existence of ethics thus points beyond ontology to another source. Justice is not revealed in beings or ideas, but is concealed in the phenomenality of the trace in the face.

It should be said, though, that once infinity is produced in the encounter with the face it may be possible to speak meaningfully of God as both being and idea. In this case one will not be using ideational speech after the manner of the idealist or being-speech after the manner of the realist; one's speech will not be superscribed by the 'twin brothers' of the literalist hermeneutic and thus the reduction of God-as-idea to *mere* thing and God-as-thing to *mere* idea will not take place. After and from the face to face, to speak of God as a Somebody existing Somewhere or as experienced within the soul are both legitimate ways to bear witness; the former is, in fact, the way of speaking of God most common in the Bible, and the latter is relatively common in Levinas, as, for instance, in his discussions of the Cartesian idea of the infinite. Indeed, such ways of speech are unavoidable, since speech always operates at the level of thematization. This is why the great temptation for those who feel religious stirrings is to think of God at the third level. The first, in which God appears as an idea, can be dismissed; the second can be overlooked since God does not appear before us as a dialogical partner; but the third, where God seems to take on substantial existence is compelling. In short, if God is real but cannot be talked to, it seems that he must be talked about; language itself conspires to treat God on the third level. But language can be subverted. The reinscription in language of the call, the cry, the offering, the prayer, the poem — these and other such abusive speech-acts allow us to express God from within the ethical. This is how Levinas 'thinks' God, and how he thinks the authors of the Bible thought God. The key, once again, is broken speech, speech that uses the categories of being without being a slave to those categories, speech that says 'God is here' without locating God in a particular place.

This is to say that the literalist error is not simply a function of language, but a function of avoidable totality, a forgetting of the ground of language in nonspatial ethics. While, for the authors of the Bible, being-talk was a necessity of linguistic communication, a betrayal committed in awareness of its status as betrayal, for us it is simply ontology, a betrayal without awareness. Whether we are theists or atheists all of us believe that the God in whom we believe or disbelieve is either a located God or the idea of a located God — and we believe that the authors of the Bible believed this too. We have forgotten that these images stand as the only linguistic possibilities of describing the witnessing structure in language and, instead, have taken the words literally. Levinas, I believe, assumes that his readers are generally not capable of reading biblical images of a God in locus metaphorically, as the Bible's intended audience perhaps was. Idolatrous reading, always a possibility, has become the prevailing hermeneutic. And this idolatry — the basis of his critique of theology — obviously did not become widespread with an original entry of the third. What Levinas calls theology is the witnessing structure destroyed by the second betrayal at some point long after the writing of the Hebrew Scriptures. He does not define that point.[12]

The beginning of the midrash

I count 12 Scriptural references in the chapter in question, most of which are from segment two of the chapter. In succession they are: *hineni* (from many passages including Genesis 22.1 and 11, and Exodus 3.4), Song of Songs 5.8, Genesis 3.12, Isaiah 50.6, *hineni* (from Isaiah 6.8–10), Isaiah 57.18–19, Ezekiel 8.3, 1 Samuel 17.45, Job 4.12, Exodus 24.7, Isaiah 65.24, and Genesis 1.2.

The first two biblical references appear together, as they must.[13] The command can only be answered, writes Levinas, with a 'here I am' "where the pronoun I is in the accusative, declined before any declension, possessed by the other, sick . . ." (OB 142). The word 'sick' is footnoted to Song of Songs 5.8, "I am sick with love."[14] In the biblical context, the speaker has opened herself to her lover. She reaches for him, but he is gone. She cannot feel his embrace; she is sick for him; she desires him; what she has of him is precisely a reaching, a sickness, a desire. Thus, though he is withdrawn, he is present in the trace that is her sickness and is also the trace of his absence. It is *her* sickness, but it comes from without; it is hers but hers in passivity; hers but imposed on her. Just as in the witnessing structure where "I have received, one knows not whence, that of which I am the author" (OB 148–49), she has received, she knows not whence, a sickness that is in her, belonging to her, made by her. Two Levinasian experiences are illustrated here: first, the trace understood as the presence of an absence, and second, the 'I' of the 'here I am' understood as inscribing a confusion between what is within me or mine and what is imposed on me from without, the 'I' of the approach as a sick 'I', an 'I' formed not only *in* the absence of the one desired, but *constituted out of* the absence of the one desired.

Just before the image of the withdrawn God, but in the same breath, Levinas gives us the word of witness, the 'here I am'. 'Here I am' is the common English translation of the Hebrew *hineni*, but there is no doubt that a better translation could be desired. The Hebrew word *hineni* shares the two grammatical characteristics we noted in its common French translation *me voici*. First, it is not a form of the copula verb, but rather a form of the verb meaning "to behold," and second, the speaker of the word refers to herself in the accusative (which in Hebrew appears in the form of a verb-suffix), rather than with the nominative of the English.[15] *Hineni* appears a number of times in the Bible, but since later in the chapter Levinas cites a specific biblical passage in connection with the term, we will reserve any extended discussion of it for a moment. Now, though, we should note something about its context in Levinas's midrash, namely, that 'here I am' occurs *before* the sickness that illustrates the withdrawn God. We may recall here the discussion of narrative order in chapter one. The ethical structure of witnessing in all its immediacy precedes, in consciousness, any determinations that may follow from it about the nature of God, even if those determinations ultimately 'place' God as prior. Levinas has been accused, most notably by Derrida, of disguising a theology as an ethics, of beginning with a religious story or scheme and cooking up an ethics to fit.[16] Levinas insists, however, that his thought is "a transcendentalism that begins with ethics" (GCM 90). Ultimately it is true that the withdrawn God makes way for responsibility by the fact of his withdrawness, but Levinas, and human beings in general according to Levinas, do not begin with a knowledge of God's withdrawness and then act ethically; they discover God's withdrawness through their own ethical action. Thus in his ordering of these first two biblical references, Levinas represents the order of his own thinking. He also suggests that the Hebrew Bible is based on similar existential phenomena.

The scriptural re-presentation of God, re-re-presented by Levinas, is undogmatic. It allows one to understand that the *hineni* is all we have, and that only in saying *hineni* does it become clear that one is sick with love for something that is not there.

The next reference comes in Levinas's account of the phrase 'as-for-me,' with which a speaker asserts her ego in a denial of proximity. Levinas describes the as-for-me as "like the thickets of paradise in which Adam hid himself upon hearing the voice of the eternal God traversing the garden from the side from which the day comes, [thickets which] offered a hiding place from the assignation" (OB 144). Adam's is the paradigmatic expression of the deliberate avoidance of responsibility.[17] "The woman You put at my side — she gave me of the tree, and I ate" (Gen. 3.12) — with these words Adam throws the blame for his sin onto the woman and onto God, that is, onto everybody present besides himself, indeed everybody *presently existing* besides himself. The assignation is upon Adam, as it is upon all of us, but Adam refuses, in the most complete way possible, to bear witness; he is not present in his speech; he is not sincere; there is no saying in his said. The correction of that refusal, the saying in the said, the *hineni*, occurs first in the mouth of Abraham, expressing his unshakable commitment to God at the time of the binding of Isaac (Gen. 22.1, 11), and then in the mouth of Moses, expressing his openness before the burning bush (Ex. 3.4).[18] But, as I mentioned, Levinas will footnote it more specifically in a later use, where he reads it as emerging from the mouth of Isaiah.

This later use is foreshadowed by the next reference in the sequence, where Levinas is already thinking of Isaiah as the quintessential sayer of the saying, the sayer of *hineni.* "The exposure," he writes, "without anything held back, . . . a cheek already offered to the smiter, is sincerity as saying, witnessing to the glory of the Infinite" (OB 145). This is a reference to Isaiah 50.6, "I offered my back to the smiters, and my cheeks to those who tore out my hair. I did not hide my face from insult and spittle."[19] Here the sayer of *hineni*, Isaiah, comes up against someone who refuses the saying, someone like Adam or worse. Now the word of witness is put to the test. If one cannot say 'here I am' to the smiter, one cannot say it with complete frankness to anyone. If one approaches the other with questions about the other's intentions, one can hardly allow the other to call one's own intentions into question. One is compelled, therefore, to give even to the one who does not give back, the one who has already raised a hand to strike. Levinasian responsibility, like Isaianic responsibility, does not pick and choose its others. The subject is responsible for, or hostage to, any other she comes across.

It is shortly after this that *hineni* is footnoted for the first time (OB 146). Levinas writes that he refers to Isaiah 6.8, "here I am, send me," and he also explains that in that text, " 'here I am' *means* 'send me'" (OB 199 n. 11). So *hineni* is not only a record of Abrahamic faith or Mosaic sincerity; it is also a record of Isaiah's acceptance of a mission, and thus the expression of the connection, in the saying, between the response to a divine command and the ethical movement toward a fellow human being. And, too, it is a part of Levinas's self-understanding. The longer passage from which the quotation is drawn is very famous.

> Then I heard the voice of my Lord saying, "Whom shall I send? Who will go for us?" And I said, "Here I am, send me." And he said, "Go, say to that people:
> 'Hear and hear but do not understand; see and see but do not perceive'.
> Make the heart of that people fat, stop its ears and shut its eyes — lest seeing with its eyes and hearing with its ears and understanding with its heart it repent and heal itself."
> (Isa. 6.8–10)

Levinas takes the role of Isaiah, confusing us, not allowing us to see, hear, and understand. I suspect that the meaning of these three words is very specific for Levinas; they mean that, like Isaiah, Levinas is not allowing us to understand in the objective or ontological terms connected to sense perception, to seeing and hearing.[20] For to do that would be to take up the literalist understanding in which God is located and appears as a being, and to lose the insight that obedience to the assignation is the way the divine comes to pass, to lose the understanding expressed in this passage from Isaiah, where precisely the command sounds in the mouth of the commanded one. Isaiah, who writes down the words "God said" and then writes down the words that God said — Isaiah, who engages in his own contestation, saying the word God, being broken open by it, and nevertheless conveying the ethical truths that he has received he knows not whence — attempts here to prevent the kind of misunderstanding that would sap the movement of his experience, rendering it a theme devoid of a saying.

In order to preserve his understanding and prevent misunderstanding, Isaiah hides or veils God from the eyes and ears of the people; he develops, evidently, a kind of negative theology. But since Isaiah's time, reading has changed and, so therefore must writing. Veiling is not enough for Levinas: "the refusal that infinity opposes to assembling . . . does not come to pass in the form of a veiling and does not exhaust its meaning in terms of consciousness, clarity or obscurity, or distinctness and confusion, known or unknown" (OB 154). Negative theology now functions merely as the flipside of a positive construction, the postulation of nonbeing that is the counterpart to being, a postulation that speaks, despite its negativity, of an "ideal essence" (TI 66). As scepticism is continuously absorbed into the discourse of philosophy, so 'veiling' or negative theology has been absorbed, much more definitively, into theological ontology. Isaiah's insight — expressed in the statement about making heavy and fat, and expressed again in the very fact that God's words are relayed entirely through Isaiah's response, the text at hand — must now be expressed with an even more figurative and shocking image: Levinas's new 'negative theology' involves speaking of a God who never was. This kind of God cannot be understood as a being, and cannot come to be understood as an idea. Levinas attempts, as best he can, to subvert the tendency inherent in language to ontologize or literalize experience. The Bible as a whole, read without the kind of interpretive help offered by Isaiah and offered in an intensified form by Levinas will appear to be a fundamentally ontological document. Levinas intensifies Isaiah's hermeneutic in an attempt to preclude a reading of the text that ignores the ethical turn that underlies the images of a located divine.

A reader may leave this quotation from Isaiah somewhat depressed. "Make the heart of this people fat," says God, sounding in the mouth of Isaiah, "lest . . . it repent and heal itself." But are we never to repent and heal ourselves? or be healed? or — by the ambivalence of the witnessing structure — heal one another? Levinas's next reference, once again to Isaiah, takes up this concern. He writes, "Glorification is saying, that is, a sign given to the other, peace announced to the other, responsibility for the other, to the extent of substitution" (OB 148), and cites in a footnote, Isaiah 57.19: "Peace, peace to the far and to the near, says the Lord; and I will heal him" (OB 199 n. 15, see OB 157).[21] We return here to the themes of my first chapter, for we looked there at this quotation in the context of the discussion of justice and ethics. In the just society, there is no distinction between the one near and the one far off, although it remains impossible to pass by the one near. There *is* healing; in fact, there are two healings, the healing of the ethical encounter with the one near and the healing of social justice in which there is no distinction between the one near and the one far off. Healing is not to come from words about God that give us the sense that we might hear God or see God — our hearts must be made fat to prevent this false kind of healing. But it does come from the interactions between human beings, both on the level of the two and on the level of the three. Moreover, this healing is connected to peace, which is another word for the infinite, or for God-as-experienced. Peace is outside of and prior to history, which is always the history of war, ensuring that war is not the explanation of all human doings; but peace is also attainable in history, not in the form of the provisional ceasefire that emerges out of war, but as proximity. This peace, the peace within history that is the trace of the peace outside of history, is the responsibility of the subject, is the saying. Levinas stresses that God's "I will heal him" appears only in the mouth of the prophet by prefacing his quotation of Isaiah 57.19 with the final line of 57.18: *"producing as an utterance of the lips*, 'Peace, peace . . .'" (OB 199 n. 15, my emphasis). Later in the body of the text he writes: "Peace is incumbent on me in proximity, the neighbor cannot relieve me of it. Peace then is my responsibility" (OB 166– 67). Peace is my responsibility — which is to say that I already have peace, for the sentence is an invertible equation: my responsibility is peace.

Levinas on prophecy

Before I discuss the remaining references, I want to take an extended look at what Levinas means by prophecy. I suggested earlier that a number of the terms thematized in *Otherwise Than Being* chapter five cannot easily be distinguished one from the other; saying, witnessing, inspiration, glorification, and prophecy tend to blend together, all referring to the exposure of the subject in discourse, to her acknowledgment of the other's alterity, and to her obedience to the other's command. But while the terms are not distinct, it may nevertheless be the case that prophecy takes on casts of meaning that do not *usually* accrue to saying. Prophecy comes to stand not only for the subject's exposure, acknowledgment, and obedience; but in addition, at times, for the aspect of ethics that allows it to appear on the level of the third as the ground of social critique, the aspect of ethics that commands me to command the other.

John Llewelyn is probably the best expositor of prophecy insofar as it resembles the saying, insofar as it has no special meaning of its own. He begins with what I have called the question of narrative order, that the command from the other grounds everything I do and so precedes, and also ruptures everything I do and so follows: he refers to the command as an "apriori aposteriority." This he links (as I have done) to the witnessing structure, in which the command appears in my response. He then recomplicates the issue by adding to the temporal structures a quasi-spatial structure: the business of "minding the other before having him or her in mind" is taking place "both inside and outside my mind" since it comes to me from exteriority. Finally, he argues that prophecy occurs as an aspect of these links or betweens; it is the point where the prior command becomes the response in the now, and the outside is internalized.[22] Llewelyn does not, however, take up the idea that the internalization of the prophetic command means that a further turnaround may be produced whereby prophecy entails that the commanded subject commands.

Indeed most commentators on Levinas tend to emphasize prophecy's relation to the saying, to exposure, and to obedience.[23] It is Robert Gibbs, again overwhelmingly concerned with the socially responsible Levinas, who insists on a distinction between saying and prophecy, emphasizing prophecy's role as command rather than obedience, and thus drawing a link between prophecy and social justice. "If we reason [i.e. assemble, compare, think in symmetries or categories] for the sake of justice, we can also discern a responsibility to reason about responsibility. That is, reasoning produces a said, and there is a *said* about *saying*, a thematics that is ethics itself. . . . Levinas's most important use of the term *prophecy* is as the speech that discusses my own responsibility. But discuss is not the right word. For prophecy commands my responsibility, most of all for justice; . . . prophecy is the commanding of myself to judge, to judge matters of justice; to command a responsibility for general justice."[24] So Levinasian prophecy occurs when, without ceasing to be the commanded one, I turn and command others. Moreover, Gibbs goes on to suggest that since the term prophecy must necessarily denote a particular relation with God, my commanding of others is its own relation, over and above the ethical relation in which I am commanded. This is a relation with the God thanks to whom I am an other for the others (OB 158), with God as the third, or God in the third.

I said in chapter one that one of the reasons Levinas rejects the idea of a present God is so that we do not appear as equals under the presence of this absolutely other, thereby losing sight of the otherness of the others who stand before us. Later, in this chapter, I qualified that statement, arguing that although it remains true that Levinas's absent God functions, by his absence, to allow a space for differences among individuals, his absence is still the absence of an absolutely other — and thus, even in his absence, *after* he makes a space for difference in the ethical, he also makes a space for symmetry in the social. This latter movement of God is God's thirdness; it is illeity with emphasis on the fact that *il* is not *tu*.[25] This aspect or movement of God is part of what Levinas refers to when he speaks of prophecy. Prophecy is "sermon [and] exhortation," because "by essence the prophetic word responds to the epiphany of the face . . . inasmuch as [the face] attests the presence of a third party, the whole of humanity, in the eyes that look at me. Like a shunt every social relation leads back to the presentation of the other to the same without the intermediary of any image or sign, solely by the expression of the face. . . . Monotheism signifies . . . human kinship, [i.e., the] idea of a human race that refers back to the approach of the other in the face, in a dimension of height, in responsibility for oneself and for the other" (TI 213–14). The prophetic word refers back to the epiphanic encounter with the other, but is itself a word spoken in the presence of the entire human race; indeed, it is *addressed to* the entire human race in kinship, for the purpose of instituting justice. In the prophetic word there is a third level symmetry to match the second level asymmetry; there is responsibility for the all, for oneself as well as the other.

The link between prophecy and the third emerges most clearly in the fact that Levinas almost always employs the term prophecy to criticize social institutions. In the preface to *Totality and Infinity,* for instance, theological eschatology — a historically based monism that Levinas explicitly compares with Hegelian conceptions — is called 'speechless', and the prophetic eschatology that is placed up against it as its opposite becomes the source of speech: "the [prophetic] eschatological vision breaks with the totality of war and empires in which one does not speak" (TI 23). Prophecy thus remains linked to the saying; it is the saying's source and meaning insofar as the saying is directed to the individual outside the totality. But prophecy's function here is distinct from the function of the saying per se; it is the critique of religious structures; it is the saying as critique in the social sphere. A similar dynamic crops up in the final section of "God and Philosophy," where prophecy is what allows us to criticize philosophy. "In our time — is this its very modernity? — a presumption of ideology weighs upon philosophy. This presumption cannot appeal to philosophy, where the critical spirit would not rest content with suspicions, but owes it to itself to provide proofs. Yet the presumption, irrecusable, draws its force from elsewhere. It begins in a cry of ethical revolt, a bearing witness to responsibility. The presumption begins in prophecy" (GCM 77). Here prophecy reveals philosophy to be ideology; in other words, prophecy functions as scepticism. And finally, in the last paragraphs of "Freedom of Speech" (DF 205–07), Levinas employs prophecy against the ontologies of psychoanalysis and sociology which, again, are destroying our ability to speak:

> We can no longer speak. . . . Psychoanalysis and sociology lie in wait for the speaker. Words are symptoms or superstructures. . . . We are powerless to break out of [the] infinity of falsehood. Political totalitarianism rests on an ontological totalitarianism. Being is all, a Being in which nothing finishes and nothing begins. Nothing stands opposed to it and no one judges it. . . . We can no longer speak, for how can we guarantee the value of a proposition, if not by offering another proposition which, however, no one can answer for?
>
> The only believable word is the one that can lift itself out of its eternal contest . . . the word of a discourse that begins *absolutely* in the person in possession of it, and moves toward another who is *absolutely* separate. It is a masterful word that Europe can no longer hear. . . .
>
> And in a precise sense, one that contains not a whiff of saintliness, it is a prophetic word. (DF 206–07)

Here prophecy stands, quite simply, against all the things Levinas stands against. The belief that everything is an idea (here 'psychoanalysis') and the belief that everything is contingent (here 'sociology') come together under the rubric of ontology. The whole gamut of errors Levinas blames on theology and philosophy — not only the twins mentioned here, psychoanalysis and sociology, but also those other twins, idealism and realism — all these "swarming insinuations" (DF 254) or "multiplicity of allergic egoisms" (OB 4) are corrected or undone in the prophetic word. Levinas's critique of the dominant understandings of our society is his prophecy. Prophecy is the epiphany of the encounter with the other, given to the third as demand or command.

As the command to command, prophecy is also exegesis. In the giving of commands, one steps (carefully, hesitantly) into the shoes of the withdrawn God, one responds to the command from the Most High not just by saying 'here I am' *to* the Most High, but by relaying one's response to others in the form of a new command, by inscribing one's 'here I am' in a new said, a said which, if it is to remain an open address, must necessarily now pay heed to the particular circumstances of the ones being newly addressed. This requires interpretation; indeed, it is, according to Levinas, the work of interpretation. In the forward to *Beyond the Verse*, Levinas describes the finite and infinite qualities of the word. The Hebrew Scripture, he says, lends itself to infinite interpretation; the word itself, through the history of interpretation, represents the infinite. But the Talmud says 18 times that "the Torah speaks with the language of men" — and while this is usually taken to imply simply that one should not allow oneself to be carried away with abstruse interpretations, it also means what it literally says, that the word of God exists only in human language. The word is the infinite within the finite; each word inscribes the structure of Descartes's idea of the infinite, except that instead of thinking more than one can think, the word says more than it can say. Levinas calls Scripture's ability to say more than it says "the prophetic dignity of language" (BTV x). Prophecy is *dignified*; human words and divine words do not meet each other in an ecstasy of inspiration; on the contrary, the words of God, including the commands, have to be sought carefully and soberly by human beings through interpretation of the saying in the said.

Here we see another tentatively drawn distinction between prophecy and saying, for Levinas speaks here not of an aspect of the speech act, but particularly of writing. Scripture is not, according to Levinas, the written record of thoughts or of speech; it is quintessentially, or primally writing. It was, he explains, writing even before it was written down; it was "a literature before the letter" (BTV xi). And it is because it is writing — and not speaking — that it allows for infinite interpretation. Writing makes more room for interpretation, since however many times I may *say* to the other 'interrupt me', the other is constrained by my presence, while if I walk away and leave my word in text, he is no longer constrained. This is a twist in the basic structure we have not as yet come across. The level of the third, the level of writing, the level in which I do not address an other directly but address all the others — this level is in certain ways more liberating than the level of the second. The same can be said of the other manifestations of the third: justice may be understood as more liberating than ethics, since in justice I am not pressuring the other with my constant gifts — to put the matter colloquially, I am not constantly shoving towards him my already-chewed bread. There is a real freedom to be found in being left alone, in being touched only as a part of collective, in being called on only when one becomes relevant to the needs of the all. And we may take a further step. It is possible that a command — coming from the other to me or me to the other — can likewise be liberating. With a command one knows where one stands; one can dispute it or debate it or refuse it or interpret it. Thus the symmetries of the state, like writing, form a prophetic realm in which the freedom under God takes shape.

The rest of the midrash

In the next reference, Levinas writes that, in my saying, I am "taken up by the hair" (OB 149),[26] referring to Ezekiel 8.3, in which the prophet is called to prophesy. In part his meaning is evident on the surface: Catherine Chalier explains that Levinas uses the passage to illustrate that "man is invested with responsibility even when he does not want to be. . . . Passivity lies at the core of [responsibility]; yet passivity does not mean inertia or apathy but man's ability to be moved by what happens to his neighbor."[27] But an understanding of Levinas's meaning is deepened by an examination of the biblical context. Ezekiel is called to responsibility, yes, but to do what exactly? How does Levinas understand Ezekiel's mission?

Two of the five epigraphs to *Otherwise Than Being* are drawn from Ezekiel. They are as follows:

> Or if a righteous man turn from his righteousness and do what is wrong, and I make that the occasion for bringing about his downfall, he shall die; because you did not warn him he shall die for his sin, and the righteous deeds which he has done shall not be remembered, but his blood will I require at your hand. (Ezekiel 3.20)

> Then he . . . said to him, "Pass through the city — through Jerusalem — and set a mark upon the foreheads of the men who sigh and cry for all the abominations that are done in the midst of it." And to the others he said in my hearing, "Pass through the city after him, and slay without mercy or pity. Old men, young men, maidens, little children and women — strike them all dead! But touch no one on whom is the mark. And begin at my sanctuary. (Ezekiel 9.4–6)

In the second passage, the prophet is called upon to witness the judgment of God, and a dreadful bloody judgment it is. In the first passage he himself is called upon to judge, or at least to execute judgment. He is to warn others away from wrongdoing, but if he does not do so, or does not succeed in turning them from evil, he is to kill them. The harshness of the passages is emphasized or intensified by Levinas's third epigraph, Rashi's comment on Ezekiel 9.6:

> The sages have said, "Do not read 'begin at my sanctuary',
> but 'begin with those that sanctify me'," . . . as teaches the
> talmudic treatise Sabbath, 55a.

It is the pious who are to be put to death by the prophet.

And yet, it is Ezekiel of all the prophets who understands responsibility in the extreme way Levinas does; Levinas writes in another text that "we are all familiar with the admirable passages from Ezekiel in which man's responsibility extends to the actions of his neighbor" (DF 21). How can one condemn or kill those for whom one is responsible, those whose very responsibility one bears? This is the harsh side of prophecy, prophecy as the commanding of others and the punishment of others, prophecy as the gritty exigency of social justice. Killing the other is sometimes necessitated by the 'thou shalt not kill'.

Shortly below this, we have another reference. "The 'here I am'," Levinas writes, "signifies me in the name of God, at the service of men that look at me," citing in a footnote Isaiah 6.8 again — "here I am, send me" — and also 1 Samuel 17.45 — "in the name of God" (OB 149, 199 n. 17). The citation from 1 Samuel is drawn from a passage in which David seems to be wielding the name of God as a weapon, suggesting that because he comes in God's name, he will be able to destroy his enemies the Philistines. And yet Levinas takes David's "in the name of God" to mean that he is "at the service of men" that look at him! Again the superficial point is clear. The saying of 'here I am' is directed to God only through the other; it is said under God or in God's name. We thus return here to the idea of the withdrawn God that has lain under all of these analyses: one is sick with love for the God who is absent, but one cannot approach him; rather, one approaches the other in his name, which is to say, service of the other is concretely in the name, inscribed by the name, the meaning of the name. But again there is another implication suggested by the biblical context: serving men (men plural = 'others', the third, the social unit, the world) may at times mean putting the particular others to death. To say not only 'here I am' but also — within the 'here I am' — 'send me', is to shoulder the prophetic burden of commanding, and of enforcing the command by executing judgment.

Such judgment is, to be sure, perilous. One of the places where *hineni* occurs in the biblical text is as Abraham's response to the God who will immediately afterwards tell him that he must sacrifice his son. If Derrida's analysis of this text is correct, then Abraham is the subject, God the other, and Isaac the other's other or all-the-others.[28] This means that 'here I am' inscribes a willingness to sacrifice all-the-others for the one other, to sacrifice justice for ethics. If, however, Derrida is incorrect, and we read Abraham as the subject, Isaac as the other, and God as the third or all-the-others, then the text, like the one from 1 Samuel, suggests a sacrifice of the other for all-the-others, ethics for justice. The latter, I think, is a more Levinasian reading, for God cannot be an other from Levinas's point of view. But either way, the text undercuts its own initial meaning when Isaac is redeemed. No one is to be sacrificed; no judgment is to be executed. One of the points of the story, as Kierkegaard and others have seen, is that one must be careful about listening to the voice of God when the voice is suggesting execution. But, as Kierkegaard also points out, this care is secondary to the demand for obedience, an obedience that may involve the relaying, the interpretation, the giving anew, of the command.[29]

Some paragraphs after this, Levinas writes that the non-phenomenality of illeity comes "slipping into me like a thief," and cites in a footnote Job 4.12, a verse from the speech of Job's friend Eliphaz (OB 150, 199 n. 19). In fact, Levinas has quoted Job 4.12 twice before — without, however, citing the source — both times in connection with the trauma that the command causes in the subject, a trauma caused by the surprise of the sudden occurrence, in her mouth, of that to which she has always been exposed (OB 145, 148). Again the biblical context is illuminating. The 'word' that has slipped into Eliphaz's ear like a thief is, "Can mortals be acquitted by God? Can man be cleared by his Maker?" (4.17). Being commanded from one's own mouth is traumatic enough; being commanded to convey that command to others, or enforce it on others, is far more traumatic; it seems to bind one in an inescapable web of sin. Levinas alludes to the preoriginal accusation, the accusation by which the subject is always accused, the accusation from which, in this world at least, she is never acquitted; and perhaps he also refers to the extra guilt carried by the commanders and the judges. Responsibility persists infinitely; it commands one to command, but also places a control on the command to command, forcing one continuously to recall that the subject who commands is included in the general description of humanity that follows in the biblical text: "those who dwell in houses of clay, whose origin is dust . . . [are] shattered between daybreak and evening. . . . Their cord is pulled up and they die, and not with wisdom" (Job 4.19–21). With this reference we thus begin to shift away from the tenuous territory of the command to command or the command to kill, back onto the more familiar ground in which justice is kept in check by the accusation that takes its place in the ethical encounter, in the subject's discourse with the other, like, for instance, the discourse of Job and Eliphaz.

The next two references are a pair. Levinas writes:

> An obedience preceding the hearing of the order, the anachronism of inspiration or of prophecy is, for the recouperable time of reminiscence, more paradoxical than the prediction of the future by an oracle. "Before they call I will answer," the formula is to be understood literally. In approaching the other I am always late for the meeting. But this singular obedience

to the order to go, without understanding the order, this obedience prior to all representation, this allegiance before any oath,
this responsibility prior to commitment, is precisely the other
in the same, inspiration and prophecy, the *passing itself* of
the infinite. (OB 150)

"An obedience preceding the hearing of the order" is a reference to Exodus 24.7, in which the people of Israel say they
will 'obey and hear' God's commandments, suggesting to some
commentators that they pledge themselves to obey *before* they
hear.[30] "Before they call, I will answer" is Isaiah 65.24. Obedience before hearing; answering before calling. Obedience
(ours) and answering (God's/the other's) are prior; hearing
(ours) and calling/speaking (ours) follow. What is primary is
a certain relation between the world and God, a relation of
obedience to an answer. The answer and the obedience are
there before I approach the other; thus I 'come late to the
meeting'. Hearing or understanding, and calling or speaking; these occur later as the way the prior realities are manifest. Here, certainly, we return to the familiar ground of the
earlier references. Prophecy is no longer a matter of commanding as much as it is a matter of obeying, a matter of
approaching the other in humility, ready to give him anything he asks. The 'other in the same' here seems to have
nothing to do with the third, but to refer instead to the
shakeup of my egology, a shakeup imposed upon me in the
ethical encounter.

Still, there is something about this pair of references that
should give us pause. The first of them refers to the beginning of Judaism, the giving of the law. The second refers not
only to the end of Judaism, but to the end of the world; it is
drawn from Isaiah's description of the messianic era, an era
in which (in the verse that follows the one cited) the 'wolf
and the lamb graze together' (Isaiah 65.25). The two references can be understood, therefore, to evoke infinity and
prophecy in a pure form, a form that does not occur in the

in-between of history. The obedience at the beginning, equivalent to the answer at the end — both of which are at the
beginning as motivation and at the end as an eternal breaking of categories, an antitelos — are compromised in the middle by the command that the commanded one command the
other. The middle is a broken middle, broken by the beginning and the end; nevertheless and unfortunately, it requires
certain fixed structures of judgment and punishment. These
structures are kept in check by our awareness that we were
born in dependence and will all eventually die, but they remain the prophetic work of the moment.

This brings us almost to the end of Levinas's midrash; we
turn now to the final reference. "The-one-for-the-other of responsibility" he writes, can "'float above the waters' of ontology in its irreducible diachrony" (OB 167). As it happens,
this same idea, expressed in almost the same words, occurs
also much earlier (OB 141), though only in the later passage
are the biblical words enclosed in quotation marks; the idea
thus opens the chapter's string of biblical references as well
as closing it, a common feature of homiletical midrash.
Levinas refers to Genesis 1.2, in which the *ruach* — wind,
breath or spirit — of God floats above the waters of the
unformed earth. The point is clear and rich. As God, beyond
or 'over' being, persists despite or because of being, so responsibility, beyond or over ontology, persists despite or because
of ontology. The God, who remains beyond being, nevertheless enters being in two forms: first, as a trace, an anarchic
wind taking one out of oneself and directing one to the other
in responsibility, and second as the nonanarchic organizing
principle governing the division of things into types that
marks Genesis 1; in other words, God enters as difference
and as the categorization of difference, as ethics and as justice.
Responsibility, likewise, is both ethical and just, both a rupture and a structure, both an anarchy and a symmetry —
and in both forms, it is the aspect of the world that points to

the beyond. Infinity, having called for the creation of totality, cannot be negated by it, but floats over it; it is not nonbeing but otherwise than being.

Let me say, in conclusion, a few general words about Levinas's method. First, he uses an enormous number of different terms to describe what is essentially the same movement, over and over. None of the many terms is superfluous. Each has its own meaning, or at least its own nuances. But they do not form a network of connected meanings, a system in which it would be necessary to grasp the precise meanings of and links between all the terms in order to understand the content of the argument. Rather, the proliferation of terms describing a single structure has as its purpose to point out how common that structure is in human experience, and also to appeal to readers of various types. Some of Levinas's descriptions may not mean anything to some readers. They need not. Levinas defines each term with reference to the others in order to bring any and all readers into the awareness of the structure he is describing. From any starting point, one is invited to see the nature and effects of relation.

Not only is Levinas's writing repetitive, it is also provisional. Distressingly, but perhaps necessarily, one of the ways he breaks down his readers' preconceptions is by using his terms inconsistently. For instance, while consciousness is introduced in the preface to *Totality and Infinity* as a route to infinity (TI 27) it is later linked with totality (TI 204). To be sure, this particular problem, like many others, is resolved when Levinas reveals that he is using the term in two different ways — thus we eventually read that "the consciousness of obligation [the consciousness of the preface] is no longer a consciousness [qua totality], since it tears consciousness up from its center, submitting it to the other" (TI 207). Nevertheless, it can be confusing to find words shifting around in meaning as one reads. All of the occurrences of terminological displacement are examples of a single device: they are a way of preventing a systematizer from laying the work out in a flow chart, of preventing the work's insights from degenerating into a set of technical terms to be memorized in the correct order or pattern — for this way the works could be read as empty abstraction, void of contact with the engendering insight.

I have already mentioned provisionality with reference to the lines that close the preface of *Totality and Infinity*, but those lines are worth looking at in full.

> The word by way of preface which seeks to break through the screen stretched between the author and the reader by the book itself does not give itself out as a word of honor. But it belongs to the very essence of language, which consists in continually undoing its phrase by the forward or exegesis, in unsaying the said, in attempting to restate without ceremonies what has already been ill understood in the inevitable ceremonial in which the said delights. (TI 30)

Levinas reaches out to us with his preface. But the preface is not his word of honor, nor is it his first word or his last word. Like all speech, Levinas's words unsay themselves, and they do it by means of what comes before — the preface — and of what comes after — the exegesis or reading. Perhaps the symbolization does not entirely work; perhaps, for the symbolization to work, the preface would also have to have a preface, and that preface another preface, and so on; perhaps only then would the unsaying, and thus the saying, gain a kind of ascendancy over the said, the without-beginning an ascendancy over the beginning. But perhaps this is, in a way, the truth of writing; perhaps the preface always *does* have a preface. In any case, the process of exegesis or reading is certainly potentially endless; the commentaries pile up in heaps, disregarding death. The continuity of discontinuity is thus ensured at least on one end; the finality of nonfinality, itself a delightful ceremony, defeats the said's delight in ceremony.

Derrida describes Levinas's writing as proceeding "with the insistence of waves on a beach, return and repetition of the same wave against the same shore."[31] Handelman takes this up and argues that its repetition, in combination with what I have called its provisionality, renders the writing "less 'art' than a kind of 'prophetic appeal'. . . . His prose embodies [a] sense of otherness . . . as a grave call . . . as the summons to inescapable responsibility . . . [His] circling around . . . [his] repetitive prose style is . . . not 'disclosure' but the constant 'exposure' and re-exposure of philosophical language to the intrusions of the other." Because the form changes slightly with each repetition, the repetitive form stands as a kind of openness, as well as a kind of obsession. In these respects, Handelman concludes, the style is comparable to that of the biblical prophets.[32]

Levinas plays a prophetic role in several senses. First, he preserves contestation in his speech, persistently using language that is deliberately confusing. Despite his necessarily ontological critique of ontology and his thematization of the idea that the otherwise than being cannot be thematized, he tries insofar as is possible to ensure by means of repetitions, hesitations, and deviations — by means even of contradictions or logical impossibilities — that his saying is not swamped by his said. Second, his work calls for infinite interpretation. His writing, directed to a not yet, calls for responses that themselves will call for other responses, and this call too is there in the repetitive style that allows him to break down the monolithic block of his readership and to address various others in various ways. Third, he calls for others also to use abusive language and write to a not yet. Or rather, he conveys a call; in this book, he is precisely the author of a call that comes he knows not whence. Thus when he tells us that philosophy at large is called upon to reduce the betrayal of language and when he tells us that we have always already offered our cheeks to the smiter, he is not only responding to the withdrawn God — as he says we all do — but reporting what he understands of that God's commands so that others may follow them; he is expressing the saying in a said or the two in a third level structure. Fourth, he extends and interprets the command he is conveying and in this sense is a commander in his own right (though a commander whose command is constantly undermined by the command imposed upon him). When he 'updates' or 'corrects' the passages in Scripture that would give way too easily to ontological interpretation, that is, when he calls Isaiah's God 'illeity', the God who is not 'there', he is following a prophetic call to address himself to those around him 'at this very moment', to play a commanding role before his others, in short, to teach. In this sense, as in others, the midrash compliments the main body of Levinas's text; this is to say that not only does it illuminate his ideas in sequence, it provides a fourth defense of his discourse, an argument from authority, as it were — but the meaning of this common phrase now wrenched from its usual contexts is immeasurably deepened. The prophet breaks down ontological thought; the prophet draws from the past the words and images that can be used to address the future; the prophet conveys a command; the prophet obeys a command to command, and in obeying it, commands.

THREE

The Kabbalah and Deconstruction

*The worlds change each and every hour, and there is no hour
which is similar to another. And whoever contemplates the
movement of the planets and stars, and the changes of their
position and constellation and how their stand changes in a
moment, and [how] whoever is born in this moment will
undergo different things from those which happen to one who
was born in the preceding moment . . . will understand the
changes of the constellation and the position of the worlds
which are the garments of En Sof; these changes are taking
place at each and every moment, and in accordance with
these changes are the aspects of the sayings of the book
of the Zohar changing, and all are words of the living God.*
— Isaac Luria, quoted by Hayim Vital

The last chapter's consideration of the ambivalence or
contestation in his relation to Scripture and God provides an
introduction to the question of whether Levinas's thought
bears any affinity to Jewish mysticism or Kabbalah.[1]

139

Kabbalistic writers tend, like Levinas, to position themselves in an ambivalent or contesting relation to Scripture and perhaps to God; moreover, many take up what Levinas calls the sceptical attitude towards ontology. But before embarking on any search for proximity between Levinas's thought and mysticism, one must ask whether the possibility of such a thing should be ruled out on the basis of Levinas's critique of the idea of mystical union.

In the first section of *Totality and Infinity*, Levinas distinguishes his own thought about transcendence from the "transcendence of religions" that grounds "all ecstatic behaviour," claiming that the latter involves a desire for the *unio mystica* that ignores the radical separation between human and divine. One of Plato's great insights, he explains, was his refusal of "the false spiritualism of the pure and simple and immediate union with the divine [that he] characterized as desertion." In the wake of Plato's insight, he continues, it is possible to speak of a "philosophical transcendence" that "differs from the transcendence of religions (in the current thaumaturgic and generally lived sense of this term), . . . the transcendence that is already (or still) participation, submergence in the being toward which it goes, which holds the transcending being in its invisible meshes, as to do it violence" (TI 48). Later in section 1, the "invisible meshes" appear again. Levinas explains that the Infinite, as it presents itself to the mature, autonomous human being "does not have the mythical format that . . . would hold the I in its invisible meshes. [The Infinite] is not the numinous: the I who approaches him is neither *annihilated on contact* nor *transported outside of itself*, but remains separated and *keeps its as-for-me*" (TI 77, my emphasis). Levinas's objection to the numinous God and the attempt to reach it in a participatory union begins in the concern shared by other critics of mysticism: such a desire cannot ground an ethics for it takes the mystic away from her fellows in an attempt at lone ascent.

But Levinas also fits the criticism into his broader understanding: the desire for mystical union is a desire for violence, an attempt to make a totality encompassing God or to throw oneself into a totality made by God. In addition to amounting to desertion, then, the desire implies an understanding disposed or habituated to totalization; the mystic will focus always on what is common or participatory and ignore difference.

Does this position rule out the possibility of an affinity with mysticism? It might seem possible to answer by citing an opinion commonly held about Jewish mysticism, originating with Gershom Scholem. Scholem has stressed in all his work that what distinguishes Jewish mysticism from that of other traditions is that the Jewish mystic seldom strives after mystical union. "If the term [mysticism]," he writes, "is restricted to the profound yearning for direct human communion with God through annihilation of individuality . . . then only a few manifestations of Kabbalah can be designated as such, because few kabbalists sought this goal. . . . However, Kabbalah may be considered mysticism insofar as it seeks an apprehension of God and creation whose intrinsic elements are beyond the grasp of the intellect."[2] The debate about whether or not there is mystical union in Jewish thought is complex and revolves around the meaning of two words: *devekut* (usually translated 'cleaving') and *yichud* (usually translated 'identity' or 'union'). The first of these terms is fairly common in all kabbalistic texts; the second more common in Hasidic texts — where it does indeed seem to imply 'direct human communion with God through annihilation of individuality' — and less common in pre-Hasidic Kabbalah. The existence of two words implies the existence of a distinction; thus, according to Scholem, *devekut* is not quite or not always *yichud*, and in general pre-Hasidic Jewish mystics try to follow, know, or cleave to God, but not to become one with God. In this light, Levinas's critique of the mysticism of unity begins to appear not only compatible with a pre-Hasidic Jewish mystical outlook, but possibly the direct result of a familiarity with that position, and his objection to mysticism is all but fully explained by Edward Caird's words: "The Jew was always defended against the extreme of Mysticism by his strong sense of the separate personality of God and man, and, as a consequence, his vivid consciousness of moral obligation as involved in the worship of God."[3]

Some support for this idea as an answer to our question can be drawn from a cursory analysis of one of the oldest Jewish mystical stories, that of the four who entered the *pardes*, or orchard: "Four men entered the pardes, namely, Ben Azzai, Ben Zoma, Aher, and Rabbi Akiva. . . . Ben Azzai cast a look and died. . . . Ben Zoma looked and was stricken. . . . Aher cut the shoots. Rabbi Akiva departed unhurt."[4] This story — one of many texts on which Scholem's theory is based — is close in meaning to the second passage cited from Levinas above. The talmudic tradition is evidently critical of an approach to the Infinite in which the I is, in Levinas's words, "annihilated on contact," like Ben Azzai, or "transported outside of itself," like Ben Zoma. Rabbi Akiva, the hero of the story, is the only one of the four who leaves in the same way he came in; clearly he "remains separated and keeps [his] as-for-me."[5] Moreover, Akiva is iconic within the rabbinic tradition for his fierce devotion to ethics. If he can be understood as a mystic — and the story of the *pardes* suggests that he can — his mystical experience in no way reduces his concern for social justice nor does it amount to desertion. Levinas's critique of the mysticism of union appears, then, to be compatible with the nonannihilative Akivan style of mysticism lauded in the Talmud and the many subsequent texts that retell the story of the four who entered the *pardes*.

Still, without entirely dismissing such considerations, I think it necessary, for two reasons, to take a different approach to the question at hand. First, in the past two decades,

Moshe Idel has produced much evidence, contra Scholem, that the desire for mystical union is a fundamental element of kabbalistic thought, that "far from being absent, unitive descriptions recur in kabbalistic literature no less frequently that in non-Jewish mystical writings and the images used by the kabbalists do not fall short of the most extreme forms of other types of mysticism."[6] Once such an argument has been made, it is impossible to maintain without qualification that a distaste for union is compatible with an affinity with Jewish mysticism. Second, the insistence on the necessity of the 'as-for-me' that grounds Levinas's critique of mysticism is hardly his last word on ethical behaviour. In the section of *Totality and Infinity* where the passage about the 'as-for-me' cited above is found, Levinas is overwhelmingly concerned to establish *separation* as the ground of relation; he is concerned to establish the subject as something apart from the participation with the world that is 'enjoyment' and thus as a being ready for nonparticipatory relation with other beings — and therefore, in this section and others like it, his rhetoric is bent to the support of autonomy even to the point of atheism. It is not until later in *Totality and Infinity*, and then again in and throughout *Otherwise Than Being*, that it becomes quite clear that autonomy, for Levinas, is a good thing only if it exists as the ground for relation with others, atheism a good thing only as the ground for relation with illeity, and, most pertinently, 'as-for-me' a good thing only as the ground for *hineni*. And *hineni*, far from 'as-for-me', is 'I am you': at one point Levinas suggests that the *hineni* can be described with the extraordinary line from Paul Celan, "I am you if I am I."[7] All of this seems to open the possibility of a different kind of affinity between Levinas and Jewish mysticism. Maybe the Jewish mystical tradition desires and venerates union more than Scholem admits. Maybe, too, Levinas desires and venerates a certain kind of union.[8] In short, the flux of experience as Levinas sees it is complex, involving an

'I am you' that retains within it a prior as-for-me — and the Jewish mystical pattern may be equally complex, perhaps even in the story of the pardes. Akiva's retention of his 'as-for-me' does not necessarily preclude his having experienced union of some kind.

These two points should direct our attention to the nature of the desire for union itself. What, after all, is it? Levinas links it to desertion, and above all to the craving for totality or sameness evinced in the attempt to define a single ontology encompassing the mystic and God, equivalent, for him, to a desire for self-annihilation or the annihilation of the other. Since, as he holds, there is no contact with God except through the other, unitive mysticism must involve the postulation of a second reality, a reality in which there *is* direct contact and in which, perhaps, the mystic is able to believe himself a god or invested with God's powers. But one may ask whether this is an entirely adequate description of mystical union as it is understood by any Western tradition. We noted earlier that Robert Bernasconi casts some doubt on whether the description of Western philosophy that Levinas erects for the purpose of critique is anything but a straw man.[9] Perhaps Levinas's general critique of mysticism is equally weak, and, like the critique of philosophy and philosophers, would not withstand even his own closer examination. Adriaan Peperzak writes that "a careful reading of Plotinus, St. Augustine, Pseudo-Dionysius [and] Bonaventure . . . — to name only a few pillars of our spirituality — shows that the Transcendent has never been seen by them as the highest of all beings. If the name 'ontotheology' is applicable at all to their thoughts, it should not be forgotten nor left unsaid that they dedicated the utmost of their thinking energy to the attempt to show that the *'theon'* could not be seized by the patterns of ontology and that there was infinitely more difference between God and phenomenal being than between a highest being and the rest."[10] Christian mystics who speak of a mystical union do not, according to Peperzak, attempt to totalize humankind and God, but on the contrary agree with Levinas that such totalization is impossible. It appears, then, that the mystic Levinas criticizes in *Totality and Infinity* may not actually have a counterpart in reality. On the contrary, as Peperzak begins to suggest, actual mystics may be closer to expressing what Levinas calls "philosophical transcendence" (TI 48) — that is, the encounter with the height of the other and, in that height, the Most High or the Good Beyond Being — than they are to expressing what Levinas terms 'religious' or 'ecstatic' or 'thaumaturgic' or 'mythical' transcendence (TI 48,77), that is, the postulation of the invisible meshes. In other words, it may be that mystical union as described in mystical texts is in many ways comparable to Levinasian relation.

But does Levinas not know this? Does he not at least know that it is possible? Has he read no mystical texts? Has he read them thoughtlessly? David Tracy argues that if Levinas is familiar with any mystical writings, he has not given them careful consideration. "I am, Tracy writes, "unpersuaded by Levinas's consistent polemic against the religious phenomena he variously names mysticism, the violence of the sacred, and paganism. I realize that the latter are difficult, subtle, and often anagogical categories in Levinas's thought. Nevertheless, if I may presume to say so, Levinas nowhere, to my knowledge, phenomenologically studies these categories with the care and subtlety he accords other phenomena in his rich thought."[11] But I believe that Tracy is mistaken and that Levinas does study the mystical categories, or at any rate certain mystical texts, phenomenologically and with care and subtlety. Just as his abuse of philosophy and theology does not imply an unfamiliarity with philosophy and theology, so any abuse he heaps on mysticism does not rule out a profound familiarity with mystical writings. As we will see, a large number of the images and ideas most central to Levinas

echo kabbalistic images and ideas. If he is critical of the
Kabbalah or mysticism in general, it is, I think, because he
is aware of how easily and frequently mystical images may
be misused or misunderstood. There are reasons for the fact
that the Kabbalah is an esoteric tradition; these reasons guide
Levinas to occult the kabbalistic images in his own text and
to protect them under a layer of antimystical argument.

Let us try out a preliminary sketch of the parallels between
Levinasian relation and mystical union using the widest possible conception of union, the conception generally known as
shamanism. In the introduction to his seminal study, *Shamanism*, Eliade dismisses the theories of structuralists and
diffusionists, offering instead an existential or phenomenological account of mystical union as the basic structure of
speech, poetry or ritual by which human beings express their
craving for what is not in the world.[12] He describes a simple
pattern: (1) an ascent, which brings one into contact with
something higher than oneself, (2) an epiphany, in which the
multitude of considerations that infect one in one's day-to-
day life are wiped away and things come clear, and (3) a de-
scent back from the height into the mundane world. The point
of the experience, as he understands it, is to enable the mystic to lead and to heal the community; because of her experience on the 'vertical' she becomes a wise woman, a doctor, a
prophet, or a ruler — invested with knowledge of how justice
is to be meted out on the 'horizontal'. By this understanding,
Levinasian relation is unquestionably an example of unitive
mysticism. Impelled by a desire for what is not in the world
(see TI 33), the Levinasian subject (1) seeks out and encounters a 'height', (2) experiences an epiphany in which the structures of her mundane thinking are ruptured, and then (3)
reenters or reerects those ruptured structures on the social
and political level — a level of symmetry or horizontal equality — in ways that inscribe and recall the experience of height
for the purpose of bringing communal justice. Levinas's

description of the ethical relation with the other and the subsequent imposition of ruptured justice on the level of the three stands parallel to unitive mysticism — at least at the 'primitive' or predogmatic levels Eliade's research treats.

If, however, we are to push the parallel further, we must make certain assertions that are more difficult to defend. If Levinasian relation is precisely parallel with mystical union, then mystical union must be ethical in precisely a Levinasian sense, which is to say, (1) that in its epiphany it must provide access not to an ultimate coherence but to an ultimate incoherence, i.e. that it must not merely wipe away mundane considerations but exist as an anarchy destroying all categories or samenesses; (2) that the difference or incoherence or anarchy implied in the epiphany must be understood not as arbitrary but as ethical; and (3) that the ontological or historical elements of the experience must be understood as secondary to its existential import; in other words, the 'vertical' must be understood as happening in the world, in the 'horizontal', in the face or the speech of the other. If we can find these three marks — ultimate rupture, ethical rupture, and an aontological conception in which mystical images refer not to other places or times but to human experience in relation — if we can find these in the traditional mystical texts of Judaism, then we are closer to being able to claim that Levinas has absorbed the insights of these texts.[13]

Little has been written on the subject of whether Levinas's thought bears affinities to Jewish mysticism. In what is perhaps the most widely circulated article on the subject, Charles Mopsik argues that while Levinas culled the writings of the Lurianic kabbalists for some of his central terms, images and ideas — "the infinite, the trace, the *il y a*, shame, the feminine, the masculine, the enigma" — he used them improperly, without due regard for the Kabbalistic understanding of the human relation to God and the human mission on earth.[14]

Others, however, have begun to lay the ground for a counter-case. Shira Wolosky, in an article devoted mainly to Derrida, mentions that "Levinas adheres to rabbinical and kabbalistic traditions," basing this claim partly on the fact that he speaks of a God who is "nothing" but is nevertheless represented as a creative force.[15] In addition, Richard Cohen and Susan Handelman both describe a limited proximity between Levinas and mysticism, though both are tentative in their argumentation.[16] Before beginning his argument for a 'resonance' between Levinas and Kabbalah (and also Rosenzweig and Kabbalah) Cohen hesitates and then hesitates about his hesitations, offering, first, four disclaimers — that he is not revealing Levinas's or Rosenzweig's hidden intentions; that he does not know how much Kabbalah they knew; that he is not attempting to prove that they drew on Jewish mysticism; and that he is not calling them mystics — and, on top of this and in contradistinction to it, two qualifying statements — that "their written words show beyond a shadow of a doubt that both Rosenzweig and Levinas are not merely aware in some vague way of a Jewish mystical tradition, but diversely refer and allude to Jewish mystical sources," and that although "both thinkers explicitly deny the label 'mystic' . . . in these matters, affirmative or negative avowals are of little account. Such is the freedom or mystery of mystical thought."[17] Mopsik's critique, Wolosky's and Handelman's reticence, and Cohen's qualified set of disclaimers remind us of the slippery status of the endeavor on which we are embarking. We will keep this in mind in the comparison that follows. The proximities we will find between Levinas and the kabbalists are limited; as we will see, he may reject as many elements of their thought as he takes up.

In the first half of this chapter, I shall argue for an affinity between the ideas Levinas expresses in the last chapter of *Otherwise Than Being* and certain statements made by

Abraham Abulafia, a thirteenth century mystic. In the second half, I shall move from *Otherwise Than Being* back to *Totality and Infinity* and from Abulafia in the thirteenth century forward to Isaac Luria in the sixteenth, and look at Levinas's proximity to the more 'mainstream' Lurianic ideas. I use Abulafia — and, I should add, almost exclusively Moshe Idel's Abulafia — because Abulafia as interpreted by Idel is the first great kabbalist of rupture. It is Abulafia, more than any other kabbalist, who holds that the route to God is the breaking of the divine name rather than its reconstitution; and insofar as such breakings are found in the writings of later kabbalists, they are, according to Idel, very often signs of Abulafian influence. My argument is not, however, intended to lend support to a certain interpretation of Kabbalah, nor even to present an analysis of Abulafia's thought. In distinction, it is best understood as a speculative exercise in what might be called 'Comparative Judaism', an exercise that uses several Abulafian motifs playfully to flesh out the Levinasian understanding of Judaism as the religion of rupture. What we will find in Abulafia are two of the three 'marks' we are seeking. Not only is union, for him, profoundly a matter of rupture, but in addition, it happens on the horizontal plane as an infusion of desire for a height. However, his interest in ethics (the 'second' mark as I have defined them above, but also a critical part of all three) is an ambiguous matter. Hints of an ethics appear in Abulafia, but they are inchoate. For ethical Kabbalah, we turn to Luria. And while my argument treating Abulafia — my exercise in Comparative Judaism — does not depend on Levinas's having read Abulafia or having heard his ides from Chouchani, my argument treating Luria depends on the unquestionable fact that Levinas is familiar with Luria's teachings and has considered them closely.

Levinas and Abulafia

Moshe Idel has been most influential in recent decades in raising the work of Abraham Abulafia out of relative obscurity.[18] In several studies, Idel promotes and extends a distinction made by the kabbalists themselves between, on the one hand, the theoretical, magical tradition represented primarily by the Zohar and the many Zoharic commentaries, and, on the other hand, Abulafia's school of 'prophetic' or 'ecstatic' Kabbalah. Abulafia (1240–1292) was, above all, a practical mystic, the author of a large number of manuals explaining how mystical illumination could be achieved. He was influenced most profoundly by Maimonides, whom he understood to be a kabbalist. Among other concepts, he adopted from Maimonides a psychology centered on the relation between the intellect and the imagination and an explanation of mystical experience as involving the relation of the intellect to the Active Intellect; in addition, he learned from Maimonides to regard prophecy as the highest form of mystical experience. He exercised, moreover, some influence on later kabbalistic strains or trends, including those of the Lurianic school.

Levinas and Abulafia coincide both in certain ideas, and in the images they use to express them. We will look at these ideas and images in three sections. In the first section (which corresponds to the first mark, absolute rupture) we will describe Abulafia on the breaking of the name of God and the brokenness inherent in Scriptural language or language in general; we will compare these Abulafian ideas to the corresponding Levinasian ones discussed in the last chapter and will also look briefly at the attempts of Abulafia and Levinas to make their own discourse broken or abusive. We find on these matters great proximity between the two thinkers. The second section (which corresponds to the second and third marks, ethics and the locus of the vertical in the horizontal) treats Abulafia's blend of 'inside' and 'outside' as comparable to the ambiguity of the exterior and interior in Levinas's witnessing structure. Here we begin almost to find hints of an Abulafian *face*, and certainly here we find Abulafia the mystical phenomenologist, reaching out to the divine with an internal, immanent, or horizontal ascent. The third section treats Abulafia more generally on the question of union, and re-asks the question with which we began, whether there might not be an affinity between Levinas's relation and some conceptions of mystical union.

Deconstruction and knots: rupture from the height

Abulafia uses two phrases to refer to his mystical approach: *Kabbalat ha-Shemot*, the Kabbalah of the [Divine] Names, and *Kabbalah Nevu'it*, Prophetic Kabbalah. His mystical practice consists, for the most part, in meditating upon and reciting the divine names, the letters in those names, and those letters in various new combinations.[19] In a representative manuscript, he first instructs the disciple to study the Torah and the Oral Torah with understanding while keeping himself "far from all sin and transgression and clean from all guilt, iniquity and wickedness"; then he begins to speak of the letters.

> Now the time has come to elevate you in the stages of love so that you become beloved on high and delightful here on earth. First begin by combining the letters of the name YHVH. Gaze at all its combinations. Elevate it. Turn it over like a wheel which goes round and round, backwards and forwards like a scroll. . . . For the initial letters and the final letters . . . the combinations of letters and their permutations, their accents and the forms they assume, the knowledge of their names and the grasping of their ideas, the changing of many words into one and one into many, all these belong to the authentic tradition of the prophets. . . . We know by a prophetic tradition

of the Torah that when the sage who is an adept combines
[the letters of the Divine Name] one with the other, the holy
spirit flows into him.[20]

In other manuscripts, Abulafia lists at length the precise letter patterns to be used, and includes instructions for movements of the head and breathing patterns to be performed
during the exercise. All the exercises of "combination" are to
be understood as stemming from "a prophetic tradition of
the Torah"; they represent, according to Abulafia, the true
technique of breaking names and recombining letters as received from the biblical prophets. Moreover, Abulafia applies
the practice of letter recombination to Scripture, breaking
down and recombining the letters of various words or verses.
Applied to Scripture, the practice becomes a hermeneutic that
"enables the mystic to penetrate the most recondite strata"
of the text. Abulafia interprets Scripture allegorically, but
"what is . . . characteristic of Abulafian hermeneutics is not
only this allegorical drift . . . but rather the superimposition
of the combination of letters upon the allegorical method. . . .
Abulafia points the way to a method of returning the text to
its hylic form as a conglomerate of letters to be combined
and new meanings being infused in the new 'text'."[21] In short,
Abulafia holds that the beginning of the deepest understanding of the Bible is the linguistic deconstruction of the
scriptural text.

It is difficult to determine the intentions or self-understanding behind Abulafia's meditative practice, but fairly easy to
discern several affinities with Levinas's understanding of
language. In Abulafia's exercise, the unbroken form of the
name exists as a vessel for the broken name within it, a vessel that is unable to contain that powerful anarchy and is
ruptured by it again and again. This stands in proximity to
Levinas's understanding of the word God, the 'abusive word'
in which "the glory of the Infinite shuts itself up in a word . . .

[b]ut already undoes its dwelling and unsays itself without vanishing into nothingness" (OB 151). For Levinas, the word God, as an unbroken said, betrays the meaning of the infinite, sapping its power, but at the same as it is said it also stands as the 'overwhelming semantic event', unsaying its own saidness, rupturing or deconstructing its own form — and this unsaying or brokenness or deconstruction is what conveys the power of the infinite. The word's "signification has let itself be betrayed in the logos, only to convey itself before us" in the brokenness behind the said (OB 151): this statement expresses Abulafia's understanding of the divine name as well as it expresses that of Levinas. For both, the powerful form of the name is the broken form. For both, the unbroken name pushes toward or conveys this brokenness; the unbroken name inscribes a momentum towards its own rupture.

The fact that Abulafia extends his exercise from the divine name to scriptural language in general presents another parallel, for in the final pages of *Otherwise Than Being* we find a similar extension. As we saw in the last chapter, Levinas moves from his discussion of abusive language, which is the saying of the word God, into a discussion of the prophetic or poetic nature of all language. Ultimately, all language — insofar as it has any spiritual content at all, which is to say, insofar as it has a saying/said structure — shares the nature of the abusive word as said and unsaid, because every saying "always seeks to unsay [the] dissimulation" of the said (OB 152). The saying vies with the said for the reason that the meaning of the saying — 'here I am in the name of God' — is the same as the meaning of the abusive word, 'God'. Thus Levinas can speak of "the resonance of every language 'in the name of God', the inspiration or prophecy of all language" (OB 152), or say elsewhere, that "every sign is a trace" (TrO 357). The identity of the name of God and language in general is an ancient idea. Nachmanides mentions "a mystic tradition that the whole Torah is comprised of

Names of the Holy One," and the Zohar goes further, describing not just the Torah but the whole of creation as "graven with 42 letters, all of which are the ornamentation of the Holy Name."[22] Abulafia stands in the tradition mentioned by Nachmanides; he understands that if his model word/broken word applies to the divine name it applies likewise to all Scripture, all prophetic language. Levinas, like the Zohar, goes further; for him all language is prophetic, all language is broken, in short, all language "resonates in the name of God" (OB 152).

This parallel can be taken one step further. Neither Abulafia nor Levinas can stop at word/broken word; both are forced into a threefold exercise — word/broken word/word, or text/deconstruction/reconstruction — in which they reassert the coherence of the unbroken form, allowing totality, in a sense, to triumph. Levinas writes books that, while they deal with incoherence, are themselves coherent (or relatively so). And Abulafia ultimately offers a coherent interpretation of Scripture expressed, in fact, in the logical formulations of Maimonidean philosophy. But the important point is that both retain, even in their reconstruction, the desire to stop in deconstruction. Levinas's desire not to reconstruct the word but to remain in rupture is manifest most strongly in the discussion of philosophy and scepticism that closes the fifth chapter of *Otherwise Than Being*. There he says, we recall, that there exist in reality incoherencies, othernesses, uniquenesses and that these break the coherent thread of philosophy. The philosophers ignore them, knotting up the thread of their discourse and then averting their eyes from the knots. But the sceptic points to the knots and in so doing reasserts the incoherencies. Philosophy tries to refute scepticism, and in its own terms succeeds, but it cannot keep scepticism down since scepticism contests the very imposition of coherence by means of which it is refuted. The sceptic always rises again, and points again to the knots. What is more, this pointing and pointing again is, for Levinas, already ethical behaviour. There is no way to mitigate philosophy's betrayal of reality except to proclaim that it is a betrayal. One cannot come up with a new nonphilosophical philosophy; this would merely be a new coherence. One only points to the breaks, notes the incoherencies, preserves the differences; one finds the points where the discourse stutters and then one stutters them out. Thus Levinas, as sceptic, wants to stop at the broken word, or at broken discourse. And Abulafia's analogous desire is equally clear. One of his students relates that his teacher told him: "it is not the intention that you come to a halt with some finite or fixed form, even though it be of the highest order. . . . And he produced books for me made up of [combinations of] letters and names and mystic numbers of which nobody will ever be able to understand anything, for they are not composed in a manner meant to be understood. He said to me: This is the [undefiled] path of the names."[23] Though in the end Abulafia does not only produce 'undefiled' unintelligible texts, but rather (relatively) coherent interpretations of Scriptural passages, he would, if it were possible, follow the undefiled path exclusively.

Obviously this threefold structure of text/deconstruction/ reconstruction is a pattern of totality/infinity/totality. This suggests that there is a political motive for the construction of textual coherencies, that they exist for the purpose of social justice, and that the same can be said of the *re*construction of textual coherencies. The work of the sceptic is to point to the knots and perhaps also to untie them, bringing some incoherence back into the false coherence perpetrated by philosophy — but it is not to descend into gibberish or silence. Far from reveling in nonsense, the sceptic reveals to us the non-sense that underlies philosophic sense. Sceptical coherencies, coherencies that understand themselves or are understood as imposed on incoherencies, coherencies that are the making coherent of incoherence itself — these are necessary in the world of the three, the world in which we live; sceptical philosophy is necessary for justice. Certainly this is the case for Levinas, and it may be the case for Abulafia too. The idea cannot be drawn easily from his writings, but Moshe Idel does speculate at one point that "at least as [Abulafia's] later writings testify, it seems that the return of the focus to the inherent forces of [deconstructed] language in themselves, in comparison to their function in the traditional texts, bears evidence of a certain alienation to the ordered linguistic, social and religious universes of medieval Judaism."[24] Thus Abulafia may appear as a medieval sceptic, pointing out the knots of the dominant discourse, and so perhaps for both men deconstruction lays the ground for a social criticism — or at least a fertile social alienation — that insofar as it is presented must be coherent, but that can only do its job because it arises from the incoherence of the deconstruction of the divine name and language in general. In any case, whether the purpose of their enterprises is social justice or not, it remains clear that, for both, any discourse presented coherently would have to be open itself to the critique inherent in the deconstructed form. The important thing, in Levinas's terms, is to retain the saying in the said or the ethical in the political, or, in Abulafia's terms, to continue to subject the word to the turning and breaking of the undefiled path.

Levinas describes a part of the movement in question with the metaphor of the knots, and Abulafia does so too, using the phrase a 'loosening of the knots' or 'an untying of the knots' to describe a critical step in his mystical praxis. Scholem's explanation of the Abulafian concept is sensitive, since it assumes that when Abulafia speaks of untying oneself from the things in the world he is not expressing a crude rejection of nature or a body-hatred, nor does he wish to float off into the ether never to return. Rather, Scholem writes,

Abulafia suggests that as the mind perceives the "sensible world," it creates for itself "a certain mode of existence that bears the stamp of finiteness" and that this "natural" understanding must be "transformed in such a way as to render it transparent for the inner spiritual reality, whose contours will then become perceptible through the customary shell of natural things."[25] This interpretation, in which the loosening or untying of the knots is a metaphor for the movement of the mind away from the search for finitude towards the search for spirit, provides a good ground from which to look closely at a passage in which Abulafia describes the concept. In *Ozar Eden Ganuz* he writes:

> And the cosmic axis is none other than the knot of the spheres, and there is no doubt that this [knot] is the subject of their existence, like . . . the connections of the limbs within man . . . which are suspended in the bones at the beginning are also called the axis in man as well. And [the axis's] secret is that a magician bring this knot of desire and renew it in order to preserve the existence of this compound for a certain amount of time. And when the knot is undone, the matter of the testimony of the knot becomes clear, and one who cleaves to these knots cleaves to falsehoods, for as they are going in the future to be undone . . . nothing will remain with him anymore. [A]nd therefore, before he loosens these, he must tie and cleave [with] ropes of love those who have not loosened the knots of his love and the cleaving of his desire; and that is God, may He be exalted, and no other in any sense.[26]

The parallels with Levinas are remarkable (at least until the Abulafian mystic begins to tie up his second set of knots). The knots to be untied are those that form the "cosmic axis" or order of being, and those that form the microcosmic axis of the "limbs within man," which axis connects the human being to the order of being. The Abulafian knots, then, comprise or hold together the thread of what Levinas would call ontology, the postulated cosmic and microcosmic order in which beings are bound and by which their behaviour is determined. Abulafia's suggestion that the adept must untie the threads of the cosmos is certainly radical; like Levinas he rejects entirely the finality of any ontological order. In fact, ontological order proves to be a fiction in Abulafia quite as much as in Levinas. The Abulafian knots are protected or preserved by a "magician" and, once untied by the mystic, their meaning becomes apparent, revealing the sayings of the magician as spells that perpetuate "falsehoods." The description of untying in Levinas is precisely analogous: the Levinasian knots are protected or preserved by a philosopher and, once untied by the sceptic, their meaning becomes apparent, revealing the sayings of the philosopher as false totalities.

For both men, the loosening of or pointing to the knots performed by the mystical or sceptical practitioner is accomplished through meditation on the broken divine name. Abulafia explains that the mystic "must link and change a name with a name and renew a matter to tie the loosened and to loosen the tied."[27] Similarly, the Levinasian sceptic is able to loosen the knots of philosophic discourse because she grasps the incoherence that enters into coherence from infinity, the incoherence that underlies the assembly that constitutes the word God, or the said of all speech. Thus the loosening/pointing is, for both thinkers, the same movement as linguistic deconstruction, the movement of the revelation of the in-finite, or the differences between things, or the brokenness of things that are no longer bound together by magical, philosophical ropes. The image of the knots, then, deepens the parallel between Abulafian rupture and Levinasian rupture. Although, for both, rupture may stand ultimately as the ground of a kind of social criticism, it can only do so because it represents the true incoherent nature of things — linguistic things and being-things — an incoherence discovered in an ascent or an encounter with a height in which all coherencies come undone.

But we must now confront a possible difference between the two thinkers. In the passage cited above, Abulafia writes that when the knots are undone "nothing will remain with [the mystic] anymore. [A]nd therefore, before he loosens these, he must tie and cleave [with] ropes of love . . . God, may He be exalted, and no other in any sense." In other words, before untying the knots of the cosmic axis, Abulafia's practitioner ties or tightens the knots that connect him to God. The issue here can be treated in two parts. First, there is the question of the number of movements necessary for the ascent, or the number of knots to be dealt with: in Abulafia, there seem to be two movements, an untying of one set of knots and a tying of another, while in Levinas the two movements occur as one. Second, there is the question of whether Abulafia's second set of knots takes the mystic out of the horizontal or phenomenological world in a nonethical ascent.

For Levinas, the discovery of ontology's incoherencies is already the discovery that one is hostage to the other; to 'otherwise than be' is immediately to be for-the-other. Or, to turn the matter around, one only discovers ontology's incoherencies in the face to face; to be for-the-other is immediately to 'otherwise than be'. In any case, the Levinasian sceptic connects herself to illeity *by* untying the knots of the philosophic discourse; she stands in relation to illeity *by* standing in a relation, understood to be a relation of difference or rupture, to her fellow human beings. However, Levinas does speak, at one point at least, of a second knot.

> The knot tied in subjectivity — which, when subjectivity becomes a consciousness of being, is still attested to in questioning — signifies an allegiance of the same to the other, imposed before any exhibition of the other, preliminary to all consciousness — or a being affected by another whom I do not know and who could not justify himself with any identity, who as other will not identify himself with anything. This

allegiance will be described as a responsibility of the same for the other, as a response to his proximity before any question. (OB 25–26)

Here we find a knot that is never to be untied, a knot that "signifies an allegiance of the same to the other"; in short, a knot that connects the subject to illeity. Moreover, this knot, like Abulafia's second set of knots, is prior to the first set: Levinas writes that this knot is *"preliminary* to all consciousness" and Abulafia that *"before* he loosens the knots" of ontology, he must "tie and cleave" the ropes of love. There is room, therefore, to read Abulafia in Levinasian terms once again. It is possible that the tying of Abulafia's second set of knots is not distinct from the untying of the first set, and that, for Abulafia as for Levinas, the untying of the one and tying of the other are the same experience. But the second question remains and sheds some doubt on our answer to the first question. Are the tying and untying connected in the same way for the two thinkers? Levinas can conflate the rupture of ontology and the meeting with illeity because, for him, illeity is met in the world in the face of the other. Is this true for Abulafia as well? Or is it rather the case that his second set of knots cannot be conflated with the first set because the second set implies a lone ascent, a movement beyond rupture into a new kind of wholeness and oneness with God? Is there a vertical in Abulafia that is distinct from the horizontal and that would direct the attention of the Abulafian practitioner away from ethics? Does Abulafia's second set of knots carry him away from his fellows and erect an ontology on a cosmic or supra-cosmic scale?

Unless the Abulafian knots-to-God can possibly be understood as an ethical phenomenon, we have here a profound difference between the two thinkers, to the point where Abulafia represents everything that Levinas scorns about mysticism. But some hints of an Abulafian ethics are indeed to be found in his description of prophecy. And, in connection with these ethical hints, we find in the description of prophecy, in a fully articulated form, the third mark, the horizontal in the vertical.

Prophesy, witness and glory: union on the horizontal

The fact that one of the two names by which he refers to his mystical approach is *Kabbalah Nevu'it*, or Prophetic Kabbalah, underlines the fact that Abulafia understands his entire oeuvre to comprise in some way a prophetic mission. When he comes to speak directly of prophecy his descriptions are complex, including several types and levels; they can, however, be presented fairly accurately by applying four distinctions. First, the lower prophetic levels involve light or seeing, while the higher levels involve speech.[28] Second, the lower levels can be reached by those seeking personal experience, while the higher levels are reached only by the prophet-messenger whose endeavor has a social as well as a personal element. Third, the lower levels are active and are reached by striving, while the mystic who has risen spiritually is the passive recipient of something he could not hace anticipated or striven toward. Finally, the fourth distinction involves an Abulafian polemic I shall discuss later: the lower forms of prophecy are connected to the Kabbalah of the *sefirot*, the Kabbalah of the divine emanations, while the higher forms are connected to the *Kabbalat ha-Shemot*, the Kabbalah of the names.

The first two distinctions are linked in Abulafia's thought: while light may provide personal illumination, "true prophecy — that is prophecy that is directed both to the prophet himself and to his fellow man" must derive from speech.[29] The proximity with Levinas could not be clearer, for not only does he too regard the sensory modes of conception or interpretation — and particularly the visual mode — as 'lower' than discourse, he also links the ontological perspective that sensory evidence supports to personal knowledge or egology.

Indeed, in *his* link, Abulafia seems to take up a very Levinasian position, suggesting that all forms of thought based on
disclosure are the tools of a solipsistic consciousness bent on
knowing, and thus possessing or consuming. The higher form
for both thinkers is speech — at least, Abulafia calls it the
higher form of prophecy or 'true prophecy', and Levinas would
simply call it prophecy, as opposed to the other nonprophetic
modes of consciousness or existence. Speech is higher because
it implies a relation with human beings under God, a relation in which the word of God is communicated, a relation of
gift. Prophecy, for both thinkers, then, must involve a relation with one's fellows, and we begin to find a hint of an
Abulafian ethics.

The third distinction is semantically tricky, since what
Abulafia means by passivity is not what Levinas means by
passivity. When Abulafia speaks of passivity, he refers to the
reluctance of the true prophet seized by divine inspiration
and forced to speak or to write. "Know you," he writes, "that
every one of the early prophets was forced to speak what
they spoke and to write what they wrote, so that one finds
many of them who say that their intention is not to speak at
all before the multitude of the people of the earth, who are
lost in the darkness of temporality, but that the divine influx
which flowed upon them forces them to speak, and that they
are even subjected to shame, as in the saying of the prophet,
'I gave my back to the smiters and my cheek to those that
plucked; I hid not my face from shame and spitting.'"[30] When
Levinas speaks of passivity, in distinction, he means an assignation prior to thought or deed, prior even to freedom and
non-freedom. However, the experiences Abulafia expresses
with the word passivity — reluctance, succeeded by inspiration, succeeded by shame — do appear in Levinas, in the
temporal sphere that follows upon the Levinasian assignation and in which the assignation makes its appearance. In
the order of the events in the book of Genesis, which Levinas

uses to illustrate his meaning in the final chapter of *Otherwise Than Being*, the first free speech after the assignation is Adam's reluctant as-for-me, and the second is the *hineni* — a structure that parallels the experience of many biblical prophets, for instance Jonah, whose unwillingness to go to Ninevah is followed by his eventual compliance. As we have seen, Adam's as-for-me is not merely the mark of reluctance but also of essential autonomy; certainly, then, it remains the first impulse for human beings in time, and Levinasian prophesy appears as fundamentally reluctant. There is still, however, a difference between Abulafian passivity and Levinasian reluctance/inspiration/shame, namely that the Levinasian movement is experienced by all human beings. Levinas would say of the human being in general what Abulafia says above about the few chosen to be prophets: each of us, for Levinas, is "lost in the darkness of temporality"; each of us is seized by inspiration or assignation and forced reluctantly to speak, breaking the hold of that temporality; each of us is exposed or exposes herself thenceforth to shame and spitting. For Levinas, everyone is a prophet.

So Abulafian passivity has a parallel in Levinas's description of the human experiences connected to the encounter with the other: reluctance, inspiration, and shame. What about Levinasian passivity? Does it have a parallel in Abulafia? Levinasian passivity, we recall, is also described as 'before passivity' and is the witnessing structure, in which before all choice the subject is surprised by the occurrence of the word of God in her mouth. It is called 'passive' because it is not a matter of choice — and it is 'before passivity', as that term is usually used, because, though not a matter of choice it is also not simply suffered passively but in addition assumed or taken on; it is already — in-itself and thus in-us — an acceptance of the command and a welcoming of the other. In short, the witnessing structure is called a passivity before passivity because it refers to a time before the distinction between that which comes from without and is received passively and that which comes from within and constitutes action. Levinasian passivity is a blending of the from-without-to-within and the from-within-to-without, a blending of the exterior command and the interior command, a blending that has nothing to do with the categories of active and passive as they are usually understood, but that is constituted, rather, by an action in-the-subject-done-to-the-subject, a desire that is hers and comes she knows not whence. All of this I have called the phenomenological insight motivating *Otherwise Than Being*, chapter five.

A similar structure emerges in Abulafia beginning with the fact that he gives the same name — prophecy — to the lower levels, which are driven by human striving, and the higher levels, in which the human being is seized from without. For Abulafia, as for Levinas, it is evidently difficult to distinguish the movements of God from those of men; they are separated, in the meditative exercise, by level or degree but not by kind. In fact, awareness of this difficulty — the difficulty of separating the to-God and the from-God — arises not only in Abulafia but also in the kabbalistic writers who preceded him. The issue crystallizes, as Idel points out, in consideration of the nature or source of the words of God, and particularly in rabbinic and mystical interpretations of the biblical verse: "Moses spoke, and God answered him with a voice" (Exodus 19.19b). "With the emergence of Jewish philosophy, which developed the doctrine of the incorporeality of the Divine, those thinkers who saw God as a spiritual entity found it difficult to interpret this verse literally."[31] Rabbi Abraham ibn Ezra was one of the first to reinterpret the verse, writing: "The one speaking is man, and the one hearing is man." Many other mystics subsequently adopted this way of thinking, Abulafia being one. He writes: "And behold, the voice of the living God speaks from within the fire, and it dwells within the heart, and thus is the speech there."[32]

Moreover, Abulafia applies this understanding of the way God's speech is heard not only to Moses, but to himself and his own disciples. In the instructions for an exercise in which the mystic says a letter and listens for it to be repeated back to him, Abulafia writes: "And consider his reply, answering as though you yourself had answered," and elsewhere: "[G]o back as if the one standing opposite you is answering you, and you yourself answer, changing your voice so that the answer will not be similar to the question."[33] The conversation is between the prophet or mystic and an aspect of the divine, but the words are the words of the prophet. For Abulafia, as for Levinas, we have only our own mouths or pens; God's command, though its source is the infinite, takes its form in the response expressed with these worldly instruments. There is, then, a version of the witnessing structure, and Levinasian passivity, in Abulafia.

In order to clarify the problem we are describing, Abulafia develops the symbol of the glory or *kavod* as a dialogic partner. The glory exists within the human heart, but it is also worshipped. Though a correlative for the symbol is difficult to determine — it may be angelic, or the human intellect linked, after Maimonides, to the Active Intellect — its function in Abulafia's thought is relatively clear. As Idel explains, its purpose "is to give witness that the source of the speech is not inside man but outside of him."[34] Levinas uses the concept of the glory of God, or "the glory of infinity," in a similar way; it appears early in the last chapter of *Otherwise Than Being* as a way of connecting the infinite to the passivity of the subject. Glory, he writes, is "the infinition of infinity." It does not become a phenomenon; it remains outside the totality and ruptures it; and yet it is "but the other face of the passivity of the subject." "Glory is glorified in . . . responsibility." It "is the ego led to sincerity, making signs to the other to whom and before whom I am responsible, that is, of this responsibility: 'here I am'" (OB 144–45).

In addition to the glory, other symbols occur in the writings of both thinkers to express the blending of inside and outside. Abulafia speaks at times, of an angel. "We . . . know in truth," he writes, "that God, may he be praised, is neither a body nor will he ever be corporealized. But at the time when the prophet prophesies, his abundance creates a corporeal intermediary, which is the angel."[35] Here, prophetic speech reaches out and without pretending to compromise God's unreachability, makes the human being more than he was. This moreness — superfluity, abundance, overflow — represented in Abulafia sometimes as the glory but here as an angel — brings the outside and inside together; it is the outside on the inside exploding again to the outside. It appears, in Levinas's thought, as the sickness of the lover in the Song of Songs, the word of God in the mouth of the prophet, the word God that unsays its assembly, and the idea of the infinite that similarly undoes itself and that strikes us whenever we meet another human being. In all these relations, for Levinas as well as for Abulafia, God remains at an infinite distance; he is not made like us or totalized; he is "neither a body nor will he ever be corporealized," neither a thing nor will he ever be ontologized. However, he is met in the corporeal realm in the angel in the prophet, or the glory in the saying, or the sickness in the lover, or the idea of the infinite.

With this blend of inside and outside we begin to see our third mark in Abulafia. Abulafian union, while it expresses a desire for what is not in the world, takes place in the world, in a 'more' that inscribes the beyond in the mundane. But in order to complete our understanding of the Abulafian desire in the world — or God-in-the-subject, or the other-in-the-same, or the vertical-in-the-horizontal — we will have to look at the fourth distinction he applies to the levels of the prophecy, that the lower levels involve the *sefirot* while the higher levels involve the name. We will, however, leave this matter to the second half of the chapter, where a fuller discussion of *sefirotic* Kabbalah can be provided.

Mystical Union

> If . . . he has felt the divine touch and perceived its nature, it seems right and proper to me and to every perfected man that he should be called 'Master', because his name is like the Name of his Master, be it only in one, or in many, or in all of His names. For now he is no longer separated from his Master, and behold he is his Master and his Master is he; for he is so intimately adhering to Him that he cannot by any means be separated from him, for he is He.[36]

Here, one would certainly think, we have mystical union. And yet this passage is the source of a debate between Scholem and Idel on this very question. At one point in his most extensive description of Abulafia's thought, Scholem suggests that Abulafia does speak of union with an aspect of God or with a guide, but that it is a controlled rational union rather than a passive ecstasy. Later, he clarifies this opinion somewhat, saying with reference to the passage cited above that although "to a certain extent, as we have seen, the visionary identifies with his Master, complete identification is neither achieved nor intended."[37] Idel argues, in distinction, that the passage describes complete union intended and achieved, and that, indeed, "the passage even in Scholem's rendering is sufficient to refute [Scholem's] interpretation."[38]

I think it fairly obvious that Idel is correct: "he is He" expresses union definitively. But it may be that Scholem is also correct, given that he, like Levinas in *Totality and Infinity*, understands union to be self-annihilation. For "he is He" does not necessarily mean that the two are destroyed in one another, or that they merge ontologically, or even that they form together a whole or a totality. On the contrary, it may imply a different kind of union, one in which the knot in the 'rope of love' is made fast, and the mystic is finally free of the hindrances to a relation with illeity that appear in the forms of the ontological structures of the cosmic axis and the conceptual structures of unbroken words and texts. And this kind of union would not suggest annihilation, nor would it preclude an ethics; on the contrary, it would be the ground of the for-the-other. I believe that Scholem maintains that no complete unity is intended here because of the existence, in Abulafia's work, of other passages that seem to speak of a relation with God quite different from union understood as self-annihilation, other passages in light of which the passage above can be interpreted and the meaning of "he is He" clarified. Take, for instance, this passage from *Ozar Eden Ganuz*.

> For all things which exist are intermediaries between God, may He be blessed, and man. And if you say: how can this be, for if so it would require that man be at the greatest distance from God, I say to you that you certainly speak the truth, for thus it is. For he and the reality of Torah are witnesses to this . . . and the abundance of *mitsvot* which exist exist in order to bring near he that was distant, in the utmost distance from God, to bring him near in the epitome of closeness to Him. And all this [is] to remove all the intermediaries which are tied in the knots of falseness and to free him from beneath them.[39]

If this is another description of mystical union, then Abulafia's union begins to look much less like the construction of invisible meshes and much more like Levinasian relation. God, in this passage, as in the passage about the angel cited above, remains beyond; moreover in this passage human beings relate to him by means of ethics or "the abundance of *mitsvot*."[40] Passages like this one may lead Scholem to understand the previous passage as referring to an experience somewhat different from self-annihilation, and he expresses this discovery by claiming that there is no complete union intended.

This is not incompatible with Idel's claim that the passage refers to union. It does not refer to union if union is understood to rule out ethics; it refers to union if union is otherwise understood.

In fact, this second passage bears remarkable affinity to Levinas. The infinite separation of the prophet and God is expressed by Abulafia in the image of the whole world standing between them. The world, Abulafia suggests, is at times a hindrance to the mystic. But Abulafia is no ascetic or world-despiser. We may perhaps then put his meaning in Levinasian terms, following Scholem's interpretation of the loosening of the knots: the world is a hindrance to the relation with infinity when it is seen as a finitude, as a self-supporting totality.

It must be said however that there are very few passages in Abulafia that speak of the infinitely separated God and quite a number that, despite the attractive train of thought I have just attributed to Scholem, seem to speak of a union that comes close to annihilating the individual. Moreover, we do not often find attention to the 'abundance of *mitsvot*' or to any sort of ethical action in Abulafia's corpus. From a Levinasian perspective, Abulafia is a mixed bag. I have stressed his Levinasian elements, but even in my analysis there have been times when the two have been at odds. Abulafia seems at times to speak of rupture as the most profound truth and at other times to tie knots that connect him to God and perhaps take him away from his fellow human beings. He seems at times to laud a speech-based prophetic mysticism that is directed outward at others, and at other times to wrap himself up in himself, playing, in his mystical discourse, both the part of the subject and the part of the other. Without doubt, he understands ascent to be a movement that takes place in the world and the divine word to appear in the mouth of the subject, but his world is not Levinas's world, populated by other human beings, but rather the world of his own heart, and his divine word is not spoken in response to a face, but arises in a solo communion. Idel is, I think, in large measure correct to suggest that Abulafia's overwhelming concern is an "escapist" groping for personal illumination (despite Abulafia's own placement of personal illumination on the lower level), a concern that comes at the cost of reflection on the *halachah* and brings about a "retreat from collective worship as the central and highest form of religious experience."[41] We will have a little more to say about Abulafia in the second half of the chapter, but now let us turn to the hyper-ethical Lurianists.

Levinas and Luria

Charles Mopsik is not wrong to address the question of Levinas and the Kabbalah in general as the question of Levinas and Lurianic thought. The teachings of Isaac Luria (1534–1572) have been enormously influential on subsequent developments in Judaism. His Kabbalah can be understood today, for practical purposes, to be synonymous with Jewish mysticism, and indeed, his ideas are often taught to Reform and Conservative children in Sunday Schools as an introduction to the study of Jewish life properly lived. Luria's thought is influenced by the school of Abulafia as well as the larger tradition of theosophical Kabbalah; his teachings bring together a large number of previously existing mystical strands. But a concern for ethics is at the heart of his thinking. The centrality of ethics to Luria makes a comparison with Levinas immediately attractive, and to Mopsik's list of motifs that Levinas borrows from the Lurianic Kabbalah — of which I would like to emphasize here only the infinite and the trace — there must be added the ethical face to face that we missed to some extent in Abulafia.[42]

Lurianic mysticism is of a different order than Abulafian mysticism. Its scope is grander, and it is presented mainly in the form of a cosmogony rather than a praxis. In this half of the chapter, therefore, we will not focus on the three marks we sought in Abulafia, but will discuss more general parallels in structure. We can, however, say a few words about the three marks here. With reference to the first and second marks, we should note that there is less emphasis in Luria than in Abulafia on rupture. As I will argue, the basic 'breaking' critical to Luria (*shevirah*) is not the anarchy of the epiphanic encounter with the divine trace but rather, a reverse-breaking, a breaking of difference, or, in short, a same-making. The thrust of Luria's cosmogony stands against this 'breaking', and in favor of difference, and in this sense Luria is compatible with Levinas. Still, it seems to be that case that Luria stands in favor of an ordered division of difference rather than an anarchic one, and, moreover, that his ethics is connected to this ordered particularity rather than to an absolute rupture. The questions surrounding the third mark are more complex and a discussion of them requires a distinction between the Lurianic imagery and the experience that imagery expresses and is intended to evoke. In Luria's account of reality, the vertical seems to be utterly distinct from the horizontal, the transcendent distinct from the immanent. While the Lurianic epiphany does, in a sense, take place in a face, the face is not in the world but in a supernal realm; moreover, the desire for what is not in the world seems, in Luria's account, to be a desire to blend with this supernal realm or to bring it down to earth, effecting a new ontological dispensation, a transformation of nature in history. All of this imagery is outside the scope of Levinasian thought. If it is definitive for Luria's meaning, it follows that from a Levinasian perspective Luria's understanding is less radical and less true than Abulafia's praxis. For where Abulafia tries to describe the affections of *each* human being or mystic — to reveal the truth of the human experiences of language, of the divine voice, and of the aspiration for the divine — Luria

encompasses *all* human beings in a grand vision similar in
scope to other cosmogonies, cosmologies and, indeed,
ontologies. However, it may be the case that Luria's images
are intended to be read aontologically, as mythologized expressions of the face to face. Insofar as Levinas uses them —
and use them he does — this is the way he reads them. He
ignores any tendency toward a movement out of the world or
a replacement of the world — or he transforms it, deontologizing and dehistoricizing it until it stands as the mythic
expression of a phenomenological insight. Deontologization and dehistoricization will be discussed further in the
next chapter where, as we will see, Levinas suggests that
his aontological hermeneutic is borrowed from the Talmud.
For the purposes of this chapter, though, it is sufficient to
draw some justification for the hermeneutic from Abulafia.
We will lay these matters out more gradually and clearly in
what follows.

Luria borrows from earlier theosophical kabbalistic cosmogonies a certain understanding of God and a vision of creation
involving ten supernal emanations, or *sefirot*, that emerge
from God in succession at the beginning of time and contain
the archetypes for all existing beings.[43] But on this foundation he builds a great new cosmogony that in some ways con-
tradicts the spirit of the earlier *sefirotic* theory. We must begin
with a few words about the pre-Lurianic cosmogony.

Most kabbalistic cosmogonies begin with the *En Sof*, literally the "without end," the infinite. Scholem explains that
"in the popular Kabbalah which finds expression in ethical
writings and Hasidic literature, *En Sof* is merely a synonym
for the traditional God of religion," however, in the classical
Kabbalah the term has special connotations. He quotes the
explanation offered by the kabbalist Baruch Kosover: "*En
Sof* is not His proper name, but a word which signifies His
complete concealment, and our sacred tongue has no word
like these two to signify His concealment. And it is not right

to say '*En Sof*, blessed be He' or 'may He be blessed' because He cannot be blessed by our lips."[44] Thus, in its technical meaning, the term *En Sof* points not to God but to God's concealment. The pre-Lurianic Kabbalah affirms a God who is like Levinas's illeity: infinite, and also so holy or withdrawn that he cannot be caught in a word or even pointed to with a word, and must be referred to with a word that points to his absence.

As this stab at the meaning of *En Sof* attests, the central concern of the entire Kabbalah is, in Richard Cohen's words, to solve "on the symbolic plane . . . a religious-metaphysical problem — namely, the problem of making sense, in a finite world, of God's absolute transcendence,"[45] or, in other words, the problem of determining the extent to which and ways in which human beings are separate from and connected to God. The codification and exposition of the ancient theory of the *sefirot*, which was the great work of Luria's teacher Cordovero, was in large measure an attempt to resolve this question. By Cordovero's account, the *sefirot* stand between God and the world, thus the separation between God and world is firm and unblurred. But the status of the *sefirot* themselves — the question of whether they are more firmly linked to us or to heaven — then becomes ambiguous. In effect, Cordovero wants to have his connection and his separation too; he "wants to preserve, on the one hand, the concept of the simple and immutable God, and on the other hand to maintain God's providence in the world."[46] He thus resolves the longstanding question of connection and separation by contracting the question until it is contained in the *sefirot*. One of the ways Cordovero preserves the ambiguity of his *sefirot* is by describing a paradoxical relation between revealing and concealing: "Revealing is the cause of concealing and concealing is the cause of revealing." Scholem explains these words: "The process of emanation of the *sefirot* is described by Cordovero as dialectical. In order to be revealed, God has to conceal himself. This concealment is in itself the coming into being of the *sefirot*."[47] Cordovero's God is thus in the *sefirot* by a process involving a dialectical reversal. Mysteriously, he is manifest in them because he is concealed from them; one could perhaps even say that he was in them because he was not in them. This idea — which bears obvious affinities to Levinas's notion of the God who is only manifest in the world insofar as he is withdrawn from it, and the word God, which conveys the concealed by betraying or revealing — appears significantly at beginning of the Lurianic cosmogony.

Luria's cosmogony has three main movements: *tsimtsum, shevirah* and *tikkun*.[48] *Tsimtsum* ('contraction' or 'withdrawal') begins the cosmic drama. At the beginning, the *En Sof* fills the entire cosmos; it must thus contract or withdraw itself in order to make the *tehiru*, an 'empty space' in its midst in which finite creation can take place. This idea, in which a negative movement or limitation precedes any positive movement or growth, seems to stand in opposition to a theory of emanation in which the first movement is positive, and is usually understood to be Luria's main break with previous Kabbalistic cosmogonies. Clearly, though, Luria's notion was in some way prepared for by Cordovero's notion of a dialectic of concealment and revelation, of which it is a more extreme version. Luria's idea that there can be no creation unless the Infinite withdraws is the narrative correlative of Cordovero's idea that there can be no revelation of God unless he is hidden: concealment is mythologized or made narrative as contraction.

The *En Sof* effects *tsimtsum* by means of the power of *din* or 'judgment', for judgment is also the power of limitation or boundary. Prior to *tsimtsum, din*, like all of what we call aspects of God, is part of the undifferentiated harmony that makes up the *En Sof*. But in *tsimtsum, din* is separated out and becomes a quasi-independent power; moreover, some of its power or 'fires' seem to take up residence in the *tehiru*.

And this is not all that is left in the empty space. When the *En Sof* pulls back, it leaves some residue of divine light, like drops left in a jar of oil. These drops are the *reshimu* (the 'trace'). Scholem notes that the ideas of *tsimtsum* and *reshimu* together form a denial of pantheism, suggesting instead that particularity or differentiation are inherently good: "there is a residue of divine manifestation in every being, [and yet] under the aspect of *tsimtsum* it also acquires a reality of its own that guards it against the danger of dissolution into the non-individual being of the divine all-in-all."[49]

Once *tsimtsum* is established (though it is never completed, and is maintained only by a constant effort on the part of the *En Sof*), there follow certain direct emanations into the *tehiru*: the *yod*, which is the first letter of the Tetragrammaton, and with it, or in its form, a divine ray of light. From the ray is formed the primal man, the *Adam Kadmon*, and from his eyes then streams the light that will effect the creation of everything else. Vessels form from the *reshimu* to catch the new light; vessels of light to contain light. These vessels, animated by the new light, will be the *sefirot*, the archetypes of all beings to come; they will ensure that the particularity that is characteristic of the realm of finitude is effected correctly, that the proper divisions are made. But the structure is in some way unstable. Perhaps the new lights conflict with the trace; perhaps the direct emanations from the *En Sof* are in tension with the continuous process of contraction; or perhaps the powers of *din*, existing in the *tehiru*, imply the existence of evil there, causing instability. In any case, it is certain that the vessels formed of the trace are not strong enough to hold the light of the new ray. They break, and this break, or *shevirah*, is the cosmic disaster that begins the second movement of Luria's account. Shards of the vessels fall. With them fall sparks of the holy light or the powers of *din*. The sparks give life to the shards, which become the *kelipot* (the 'shells', i.e. the husks of the sparks), the demonic powers that exist in the *Sitra Ahra* ('Other Side') and try continuously to tear down the world. Good things are intermingled, and mingled with evil things. What should have been differentiated merges.

Once the *kelipot* have fallen away, *tikkun* or 'restoration', the third movement, can begin. New gentle lights are issued forth from the forehead of *Adam Kadmon* and the world as we know it takes shape. But whatever would have been its purpose in the original plan, it now has as its mission the correction of the chaotic state that followed from the breaking of the vessels. The *kelipot* must be held at bay, or better, disempowered. The sparks that animate them must be transformed from sparks of judgment into sparks of mercy, at which point they will be liberated and the *kelipot* will no longer be alive. In the writings of the Lurianists, the traditional *halachah* in its entirety is reinterpreted, or given theological justification, as intending *tikkun*; all *mitsvot* are directed towards the goal of finishing the process of creation correctly. And human beings are fully responsible for this act; the messiah appears only after *tikkun* is completed. Indeed, the amount of responsibility given to human beings in the Lurianic scheme is extraordinary, for their task — to finish creation and thus effect redemption — is also described as the task of making God God or perfecting God.[50]

The main symbols that express the way *tikkun* is effected are the five *partsufim*, or faces. The *partsufim* are a new way of describing the ten *sefirot*. In pre-Lurianic Kabbalah each of the ten *sefirotic* archetypes represents a different quality or virtue, for instance wisdom or kindness. The Lurianic account speaks instead of five personalities: *'Arich* ('long suffering'); *Abba* ('father'); *Imma* ('mother'); their son, *Ze'ir anpin* ('impatient'); and *Nukba* who is the female corresponding to *Ze'ir anpin*. What happens in the world of the *partsufim* also happens below, and what happens below can affect the doings of the *partsufim*. There are several narrative descriptions of the way human beings can bring about *tikkun* through the *partsufim*. One of them says that when the sparks reascend, they go up to the *sefirah* of *Binah* ('intelligence') who has become, in the symbolism of the *partsufim, Imma*. The sparks render her fertile and allow her to couple with the *sefirah Hochma* ('wisdom'), symbolized as the *partsuf Abba*. This coupling, which is the whole symbolic function of these two *partsufim*, is called 'looking face to face' (*histakkelut panim-ve-fanim*). Scholem describes their turning towards one another as "metaphorically . . . the common root of all intellectual and erotic unions."[51]

The story continues; the cosmogony moves into history; Luria describes the failures and successes of various biblical figures in bringing about *tikkun*. But what we have sketched so far is sufficient to begin a comparison to Levinas. There can be no doubt that Levinas has borrowed certain motifs from the Lurianic cosmogony; it may be recalled that even Mopsik, who denies any similarity between kabbalistic and Levinasian conceptions, allows that Levinas makes frequent and free use of the Lurianic symbols. Even without reference to any specific passage in Levinas, we can recall that Levinas's God is withdrawn from the world; that he must be so in order to leave room for separate beings; that he leaves a trace of himself in the world, a trace that it is humankind's mission to see or realize; and that this realization is accomplished by means of ethical action, which is also describable as a meeting of faces or a setting face to face. In addition, though it is perhaps coincidental, it is worth noting that there are five archetypal *partsufim* in the Lurianic cosmogony, and also five primary archetypal others encountered in *Totality and Infinity*; moreover in both accounts the first figure is male and higher than the other four, the other four comprising two female figures and two male figures.[52] It might be possible to compare at some length the various Levinasian couples — the father and the lover of *Totality and Infinity*,

the ego and the homemaker of the same text, or the father of
Totality and Infinity and the mother of *Otherwise Than Being* — with the various Kabbalistic couples — *Tiferet* and
Malchut ('beauty' and 'kingdom') of the *Zohar, Hochmah* and
Binah ('wisdom' and 'understanding') of the same text, or
Abba and *Imma* ('father' and 'mother') in the Lurianic version. But I shall not make this a focus here. Instead, I shall
turn to the larger parallels between Levinas and Luria in
image and meaning.

Let us begin by looking at an extended passage from *Totality and Infinity*, section 1. Mopsik also cites this passage,
pointing out that it appears strongly Lurianic.

> Infinity is produced by withstanding the invasion of a total-
> ity, in a contraction that leaves a place for separated being.
> Thus are delineated relationships that open up a way outside
> being. An infinity that does not close in upon itself in a circle
> but withdraws from the ontological extension so as to leave a
> place for separated being exists divinely. Over and beyond
> totality it inaugurates a society. The relations that are estab-
> lished between the separated being and infinity redeem what
> diminution there was in the contraction creative of Infinity.
> Man redeems creation. Society with God is not an addition to
> God nor an interval that separates God from the creature. By
> contrast with totalization we have called it religion. Multi-
> plicity and the limitation of the creative Infinite are compat-
> ible with the perfection of the Infinite; they articulate the
> meaning of this perfection. (TI 104)

A number of Lurianic themes here emerge: First, infinity
contracts to leave place for separated being. This is Luria's
tsimtsum. Second, cryptically or paradoxically, only by means
of this contraction is infinity produced, that is, only an infinity that stands in relation to separated beings 'exists divinely'.
This is the Lurianic understanding Mopsik describes by
saying: "Man is the way in which the Infinite achieves its

constitution as God. It is by the action of man that the Infinite is made God."[53] Third, separated beings relate to the divine, and these relations constitute a redemption of the diminution of contraction, and a redemption of creation. This is the Lurianic *tikkun*. Finally, we may note in the Levinasian passage a kind of interplay — almost a blending — of divine and human realms, cosmos and society. This interplay is characteristic of Levinas and lends many of his works rich ambiguities. The fact that one often cannot tell whether the word 'other' in a given passage in Levinas refers to God or some human being is precisely an expression of the witnessing structure in literary form (or lack of it). Levinas's point in all such passages is to suggest that it is precisely in society that the cosmic drama is continuously played out, a point that can be understood, with reference to the passage above, to be an interpretation of the meaning of Luria's cosmic account, a deontologization or a pulling of the Lurianic vertical onto the horizontal.

This quick sketch of parallels in image and meaning allows us to begin to map Levinas's understanding onto the Lurianic scheme in more detail. We must, however, begin with a slight discrepancy — or perhaps it is an argument. The only parallel in Levinas to the idea that the *En Sof* exists before creation and fills all is the *il y a*, which is not divine but rather represents a totality that encompasses and therefore consumes all being, an infinite totality, an oxymoron that can only exist as an idea or an anxiety. The Lurianic notion of a being that is all being may sound totalizing to Levinas; it may well be, however, the origin of his *il y a*, and what leads him to place the *il y a* at the beginning of the theoretical *ordo essendi* at which we looked in chapter one. In any case, once *tsimtsum* takes place, we are on shared ground. *Tsimtsum*, as we have noted, is paralleled by Levinas's idea of the withdrawn God,[54] and the residue left by *tsimtsum*, the *reshimu*, is equivalent to the Levinasian trace. Now, *tsimtsum* creates the *tehiru*. But though the *tehiru* is the realm of finite creation, it is not yet what Levinas would call totality. For, although finitude is the precondition for totality, totality is not merely finitude. Totality is the imposition, in and on the finite realm, of sameness; moreover, avoidable totality — the kind of totality Levinas criticizes — is the misunderstanding of this sameness as encompassing everything, that is, the misunderstanding of the same as infinite rather than finite. Totality is, in fact, closer in concept to the second movement of the Lurianic cosmogony: *shevirah*.

There is an old kabbalistic dictum that says that there are two kinds of evils: the separation of what should have been joined and the joining of what should have been separate. The former is the nature of all everyday crime — a murder or a theft separates what should have been joined. The latter is the crime of magic, and the more serious matter. The disaster of *shevirah* involves both sorts of evils to a degree, but primarily the latter sort: the particularity intended in the division of the *sefirotic* lights into vessels is violated and the interior of the *tehiru* becomes characterized by a dangerous blend. This joining of what should have been separate is precisely the character of Levinasian totality. When totality appears as philosophy, it appears most often in the form of a monism. When it appears as a characteristic of everyday life, it is once again a blending, a (sometimes necessary) attempt to impose a unidirectional coherence on speech, thought, and action. Levinasian totalities link together everything in the world or *tehiru*, blending them and imposing a false order onto them. *Shevirah*, then, is not Levinasian breaking, but its opposite, Levinasian merging or participation. The definitive condition of life in the world, for both Luria and Levinas, is not an anarchy that tears things apart and reveals them in all their difference, but a blending that pushes things together under mistaken categories, obscuring their proper differences.

Shevirah or totality manages to engulf or subsume the *reshimu* or trace. But it does not destroy it. And it is the job of individuals, both in the Levinasian and the Lurianic scheme, to seek out the trace and liberate it from the position to which the *shevirah* or totality has relegated it. This process, the process of *tikkun*, is described in both schemes as having as its goal the establishment of proper differentiation and proper relation, that is, as redeeming or finishing creation. The goal can also be described in a way that makes it appear twofold, first as ethics or *halachah*, and second, as the making of God, or, as Levinas has it, "the production of infinity."

Let us take up the latter of these two first. The Lurianists say that *Infinity* withdrew and that *God* is produced by a realization of alterity in totality (or in the state that follows *shevirah*). At times Levinas speaks the same way — "an infinity that . . . withdraws from the ontological extension so as to leave a place for separated being exists divinely" (TI 104) — but at other times he reverses the terms, suggesting that *God* is withdrawn and that *Infinity* is produced by a realization of alterity in totality. Is there any substantive difference here? I tend to think not. Levinas and the Lurianists are equally interested in preserving the differences between created beings; Levinas, however, is more careful about the kind of language that describes difference as a phenomenon of existence in the world, and thus generally reserves the word infinity to describe illeity as it is encountered *here*. The discrepancy may call for further exploration, but for us it is sufficient to note that kabbalists and other Jewish thinkers do not generally regard infinity as an undifferentiated entity, that the link between infinity and difference is well established. One of the critical premises of *halachah* that Kabbalah justifies or gives reason for is its attention to things in their particularity, to the small as well as the great, each in its uniqueness. The exaltation of the particular is the point of a philosophy based on the infinite: only in the realm of finitude is the worth of things quantifiable, while when each particular refers to an infinity, there is no more calculation or gradation.[55] This is precisely the position for which Levinas stands, against ontology. In both the Lurianic and the Levinasian understanding, the being that withdraws (which the kabbalists call infinity and Levinas sometimes calls God) withdraws to make a space for unique being, the only kind of being that can be treated with infinite care, and the entity that is produced (which the kabbalists call God and Levinas usually calls infinity) can be produced only out of that uniqueness, in the infinite ethical concern separated being shows for beings different from itself.

With respect to the former point, the goal of *tikkun* understood as ethics, the parallels are more straightforward. Luria's ethics, like that of Levinas, is extraordinary. Since the ethical actions of each human being help to bring about redemption, each of us is responsible for every other; in Levinasian terms, the fate of every other rests on 'my' actions. And because each is tied to each other, each bears an extreme responsibility. Joseph Dan describes Luria's ethics as an understanding in which "there is no neutral ground, there are no thoughts and deeds which do not contribute to one side or another in this mythological strife. If a man is idle for an hour, he has missed an opportunity to uplift a spark. Idleness and idle thoughts certainly strengthen evil. . . . A person who accepts . . . the ethical and religious consequences of the idea of the *tikkun* must always be under enormous pressure. Every mundane or apparently unimportant deed may carry endless cosmic meaning."[56]

So much, then, for an initial comparison of the three Lurianic movements with the conceptions of Levinas. We can now move on to the broader issue of the hermeneutic with which Levinas approaches the Lurianic motifs. The Lurianic notion that, in Dan's words, actions have "cosmic meaning" does not seem entirely to fit Levinas. For Levinas, as we have said and stressed, there is no special or 'other' sphere in which a cosmic drama is played out; actions have consequences in the here and now in the relations between human beings. This brings to the fore the question of the deontologization of the Lurianic scheme. In order to explore the question further, let us turn back for a moment to Abulafia.

Prior to Luria, the great symbolization by which the central question of Kabbalah — that of separation and connection — is expressed and partly resolved is the symbolization of the *sefirot*. As we have seen, Cordovero attempts to resolve the question of separation and connection by defining a dialectical status for the *sefirot*; in addition, he makes use of a complex scheme of *behinot* or figures by which each of the ten *sefirot* contains an internal dialectic of separation and connection such that the ambiguity characteristic of the *sefirot* as a whole reappears within each *sefirah*.[57] But in the centuries before Cordovero's exposition, there are other attempts to deal with the question of the status of the *sefirot*. One school sees them as consubstantial with God, another as God's instruments, and a third as an immanent manifestation of God's ten attributes in the world.[58] A fourth school, however, that of Abulafia and his followers, does something categorically different: Abulafia simply places the *sefirotic* Kabbalah lower than the Kabbalah of names in his prophetic hierarchy, in a place shared by the visual, the personal, and the active — or, in Levinas's terms, the ontological and the egological. Abulafia has distaste for the symbolization because he rejects "the esoteric aura surrounding the *sefirot* viewed as pointing to a mysterious divine structure"[59] — in other words, he rejects the symbolization insofar as it is understood as an ontology, one that can become, as we see in Cordovero, a supernal *deus ex machina*, solving the problem of connection and separation logically without necessarily bearing reference to human experience. However, he accepts it as

long as it is 'properly' understood; as Idel has shown, Abulafia
is content with the *sefirotic* symbols understood as expressions of the actions and experiences of the human psyche.[60]
Handelman calls this interpretation an 'internalization' and
suggests that it is because Abulafia has internalized the *sefirot*
that he can bridge the human-divine gap by means of mystical union understood as a movement within.[61]

Like Abulafia, Levinas has little use for the *sefirotic* symbolization so prone to being (mis)understood as an ontology.
But his rejection can *also* be described as a reinterpretation,
such that if the *sefirot* appear at all in his work it is in the
form of earthly *partsufim*, the face of the *partsuf* appearing
as the phenomenological the face of the other, and the face to
face of *Abba* and *Imma* appearing as the face to face of the
subject and the other. This is quite not an internalization,
since it involves another human being, but it can perhaps be
described as an immanentization, and Levinas does, at one
point, come close to describing the witnessing structure as
an interiorization (OB 147). Levinas bridges the human-
divine gap by a movement within that is also a movement to
the other; this may be understood as a kind of ethical or relational mystical union analogous to the one Abulafia experiences within himself, and, concomitantly, as implying an
Abulafianesque reinterpretation of the *sefirot*.

Levinas generally seems to hold that to regard a symbolization as an ontology is to take it literally and to assume it
describes beings or ideas, that is, fixed things. But although
this is certainly the danger Abulafia was responding to by
refusing to use the *sefirotic* symbols, there is little doubt that
the greatest kabbalists neither took their symbols literally
nor understood them to point at eternal unwavering verities.
How, then, did they understand them? Joseph Dan, in an
examination of the loose play with which the kabbalists manipulate their symbols argues not only that the kabbalist
"does not know the truth behind these symbols," but also

goes so far as to suggest that there was, for them, no truth behind the symbols at all.[62] Handelman, however, draws a conflicting argument from Idel: "the plurality of meaning . . . comes not from any inherent fragmentary nature of language [though it may be expressed as one] nor from its ultimate emptiness, nor from its symbolic nature, but from the infinitely changing dynamic process of the divine life and the human active relation to it."[63] Whether or not Handelman is right about the majority of kabbalists, she is almost certainly expressing an opinion shared by Abulafia and Levinas. It is precisely the fact that there is no single static truth signified by the kabbalistic symbols that enables them to point to the truths of existence in reality. In this light, Joseph Dan's argument appears as a small but perfect example of why Levinas cannot use the symbolization of the *sefirot*. We live in an age in which symbols are most frequently understood either to have an objective literal referent, or no referent at all: the *sefirot* must be seen either as (the idea of) a primitive series of God's aspects, or as a symbol-structure with no meaning. To avoid the former, Dan feels he must choose the latter. It seems fairly clear that anyone who wishes to convey the experiential meaning of a medieval symbolization today must abandon the symbol entirely and describe its meaning in other terms, terms like the witnessing structure which translates the ambiguity in the status of the *sefirot* into an existential ambiguity in which the immanent speaks always of a beyond. Therefore Levinas, like Abulafia, abandons the symbolization of the *sefirot* and immanentizes its meaning.

But what he does with the Lurianic symbolization is more complex. We will look at the question in three aspects. In one, the symbolization is relatively easy to read aontologically and Levinas can do so without radical reinterpretation; in a second, the symbolization presents difficulties that may nevertheless be overcome; in a third, the symbolization is recalcitrant to an aontological Levinasian reading. The first aspect is the *partsufim*. These are already in themselves more amenable to a nonontological interpretation than are the *sefirot*. Cordovero's *sefirot*, as he makes clear in his major ethical work, *The Palm Tree of Devorah*, are to be imitated. This argument accords the *sefirot* a kind of ontological being; it reifies them as supernal existents. In distinction, Luria's *partsufim* imitate human behaviour. Thus they lend themselves more obviously to being understood as representations or expressions of human ethical experiences. It is possible that Levinas sees the partsufim as deontologized *sefirot* — as revelations of the ethical or phenomenological meaning behind the old symbolization — and that this is why he makes use of the *partsufim* rather than the *sefirot*.

The second aspect appears in the fact that the motifs are presented as part of a historical plan, a plan that seems to reveal the meaning of history. Before embarking on a discussion of the historicism of Luria's thought, we should sketch the outlines of Levinas's understanding of history, outlines which I will not, however, fill in until chapter four. In Levinas's understanding, history or historicism is one of the fundamental forms of ontology. Things that are accorded a place in history or time take up a kind of ontological reality greater even than that of ever-present supernal entities and more difficult to reinscribe in a phenomenology. The problem of reification is compounded in historical schemes, since those schemes form the most effective sacred groves, allowing for an abdication of responsibility in the understanding that history will take care of justice, or, in short, that everything will come out right in the end. Levinasian responsibility requires the repudiation of historical schemes: "when I maintain an ethical relation I refuse to recognize the role I would play in a drama of which I would not be the author or whose outcome another would know before me; I refuse to figure in a drama of salvation or of damnation that would be enacted in spite of me. . . . Everything that cannot be reduced to an interhuman relation represents not the superior form but the forever primitive form of religion" (TI 79).

Levinas's repudiation of historical schemes requires a re-interpretation of a conception basic to Judaism, that human existence is governed by the historical, exterior, objective pattern of creation, revelation, and redemption. In my intro-duction, I described briefly how Levinas reinterprets these ideas as movements or expressions of experience, denying them the kind of eventness that would allow them to be misunderstood as merely 'what happened' or 'what will hap-pen', and thus as irrelevant to ethics in the here and now. Bracketing the questions of what happened and what will happen — questions about which Levinas cannot speak, and perhaps finds too removed from existence to be interest-ing — Levinas interprets creation as an expression of the experience of a dependence that is at the same time an inde-pendence, a freedom-that-did-not-make-itself; revelation as the ever-accessible testing ground of that experience through a calling of freedom into question; and messianism as the development of this questioning into ethical responsibility. Redemption he seldom speaks of, and when he does he re-fers to a desire and not to a future occurrence. All of these interpretive moves are intended to preclude the abdication of responsibility implied in the acceptance of a drama of sal-vation. They do not mean that there was no creation, no Sinai and will be no messiah. Beings and things are not themselves outside of history and ontology: they are existents and can-not escape the temporality and locales that accrue to ex-istents. But the relations between them are outside history and ontology, in a time that is not a temporality or a history and that cannot therefore be pinned down; relations exist in a non-time; they are diachronous. Robert Gibbs argues, with respect to the redefinition of creation, that Levinas is erect-ing a correlation between ethics and theology. When "a term usually taken as theological is claimed for ethics," there is some "retraction of the theological term," but the exercise serves a critical purpose: it shows us that theo-logy is founded in ethics and that ethics refers to God.[64]

It is not immediately obvious that Luria's scheme is intended to be read as a description of diachrony; it appears, rather, to present a grand vision of history that acts, precisely, as a drama of salvation. But this impression is undercut by certain features of Lurianic thought. For one thing, the history of creation Luria offers is not intended to supplant the biblical account of creation but to complement it. This already implies that Luria's account is not a description of 'what happened', and that we must look for another meaning here. For Levinas, this other meaning must be a prior meaning, a meaning that arises out of the ethical experience that is the core of illeity, and the experience of illeity that is the core of ethics. That the purpose of the Lurianic scheme is to describe and exhort an extraordinary ethics suggests that the Lurianic 'prior meaning' may be the same. For another thing, we find in Luria, despite the detailed cosmogony, a reluctance to speak of first things similar to Levinas's reluctance. Readers of Levinas are always stymied in their attempts to discover what was *there* originally, or what was there *first*. Not much answer is given these questions in the Levinasian corpus; in fact, his formulations are fairly clearly designed not to answer the question but to avoid giving an answer. When Levinas speaks, for instance, of 'a past that was never present', he offers nothing more (or less) than a refusal to offer a time or a thing; in other words, he implies that he cannot answer because any answer would have to stand in temporal and ontological terms. The kabbalists seem, in distinction, to give an answer — and yet it too is ambiguous and suggests uneasiness with the question. For the *En Sof*, the infinite, can also be referred to as *ayin*, meaning 'nothing'. Bloom notes that when the Kabbalah links the *En Sof* to *ayin*, it "thinks in ways not permitted by Western metaphysics, since its God is at once . . . total presence and total absence, and all its interiors contain exteriors."[65] The Kabbalah, like Levinas, not only refuses to be tied down by any conception of ontological logic in its descriptions of God, but flaunts its own refusal.

These two points suggest that the historical cast of Luria's thought is not definitive, or not intended as a presentation of ontological fact. Insofar as the kabbalists are describing the human condition, they are, as we have seen, more or less compatible with Levinas. Their scheme, in temporalized form, maps onto a temporalized version of Levinas: both begin with the withdrawal of the divine; both continue with a kind of totality formed in the finite realm that is left by the withdrawal; and both speak, next, of a restorative ethics. Thus, if in the Lurianic scheme, like in the Levinasian scheme, the temporalization is understood to be a narrative device rather than the laying out of an ontological-historical timeline, they are more or less analogous to one another in thinking. If any discrepancy still remains on this point — if Luria still seems more likely than Levinas to speculate about ontological transformations at the beginning and the end of history, if Luria still seems to offer a theological eschatology that stands in distinction to Levinas's prophetic eschatology, if Luria still seems to speak of *this* time and *that* time rather than an experienced nonsimultaneity — it may be nevertheless possible to redeem the proximity between the two by saying of Levinas something like what Luria said of his teacher Cordovero: that Cordovero's thought dealt with the *olam ha-tohu*, 'the world of confusion', while his own teaching was about *olam ha-tikkun* 'the world of restitution.'[66] According to Luria, there is no conflict here; reality is being examined from two different angles. Levinas does not speak of the world before *tsimtsum* or after *tikkun*. Rather he speaks, in ways that still echo those of Luria, of our world of confusion.

The third aspect of the Lurianic symbolization relevant to

a consideration of deontologization involves the fact that Luria is, in general, more friendly than Levinas to the idea of an order of being. For both Luria and Levinas, the withdrawal of the *En Sof* or God implies that a certain kind of wholeness is inappropriate to human beings. For both, the transcendence that exists in the world — God or infinity — is not the same as the wholeness that withdrew. Transcendence in the immanent realm or in human experience is dynamic, and is misrepresented or betrayed by the same-making that the Lurianists call *shevirah* and Levinas calls totality. However, the Lurianists connect *shevirah*/totality to a breaking — a breaking which, I have argued, is a same-making — while Levinas connects *shevirah*/totality to same-making pure and simple, and reserves the term 'breaking' for ethics. A discrepancy emerges here despite the great proximity. Levinas's analysis of wholeness as inappropriate for human beings involves the idea of rupture as the human good. Luria's analysis of wholeness as inappropriate involves the idea of ordered differentiation as the human good, and may therefore, from a Levinasian perspective, be suspected of harbouring a nostalgia for wholeness.

This is not to say that the goal of the kabbalists is to reattain or recreate the pre-*tsimtsum* state, although this *is* the Hasidic interpretation of Luria. For the Hasidim, *tikkun* involves a striving for a personal union from which ultimately arises a cosmic union. *Yichud*, the Hasidic goal, "refers to the reuniting of all things, transcending their particularity and separation and achieving the universal relatedness that is the true nature of existence; it also refers to reunion with God, overcoming the isolation and estrangement of creation from its Creator."[67] Moreover, the Hasidim also strive for *ayin*, nothingness, self-annihilation or the annihilation of one's worldly existence in the transcendent *ayin*. In short, the Hasidim have a unitive interpretation of Luria, and their union is the kind of union that Levinas regards as inauthentic and totalizing: they strive for the annihilation of alterity and autonomy in the oneness of everything with God. But the interpretations of Luria that predate the Hasidic movement are different. Hayim Vital, for instance, suggests that *tsimtsum* was an act of love on the part of the *En Sof* who wanted to create free beings outside of himself. For Vital, the human goal is not to return to primal unity, but to finish creation as it was meant to be, that is by means of the study of Torah "to attain the restoration of the supernal anthropos, which is the ultimate intention of the creation of man . . . [and] to perfect the supernal tree [of *sefirot*]."[68] Idel notes that if there is an annihilative mystical union here, it is not the desired end but a stepping stone on the way to a further goal. And it is clear that the further goal involves not unity but proper differentiation. To repair the anthropos and the *sefirot* is to repair the vessels of particularity; the Lurianic goal is right differentiation and right relation.

In short, though Luria does not seem to be guilty of the extremes of the ontological position, he may be an ontologist of sorts. He seems to wish to put things in their proper places, i.e. to put them in places that are objectively rather than relationally determined; and this may bespeak the weaving of invisible meshes. Two more points can be added. The first is that the kind of union desired in Luria's thought, unlike Abulafian union, is communal and universal; it is for the all, rather than, as in Abulafia, for each mystical practitioner. The second is that Luria, again unlike Abulafia, wants not to break down the divine name but to restore it: "the *tikkun* restores the unity of God's name that was destroyed by the original defect — Luria speaks of the letters YH as being torn away from VH in the name YHVH — and every true religious act is directed toward the same aim."[69] The connection between the two points is clear: Abulafia's breaking of words facilitates the kind of mystical ascent proper to the individual or the individual in relation, where Luria's objective vision of the redemption of the whole world and its historical transformation necessarily involves communication, and therefore whole language. Though the Lurianists may not go all the way towards a gnostic alliance of God with the self or with the world, their thought, insofar as it remains recalcitrant to deontologization, is, from a Levinasian perspective, inadequate.

That Abulafia internalizes the *sefirotic* theory, that he advocates a deconstructive letter-patterning, that he speaks of 'loosening the knots', and that he describes an ambiguity of voice — all these are indications of a rejection of the primacy of ontology. His account of the knots could be read as an ontological account of human ascent, but such a reading would be in error; his abandonment of the *axis mundi* in that passage precludes such a reading. The Lurianists are less likely to reject ontology; they, however, stand in extraordinary proximity to Levinas when they describe ethical action as the way to put right the blending of things characteristic of the world after *shevirah*. Both Abulafia and the Lurianists speak of a mystical union, desired or achieved. But I have argued that they mean by this something like the metaphysical desire Levinas speaks of in *Totality and Infinity*, the desire for what is not in the world (Abulafia) which directs us to humble ourselves in extreme responsibility before the other (Luria). Even Abulafia seems to speak of something like a trace, in us, of the withdrawn, unreachable God, and of ethics as our link to this God — and the Lurianists are certainly working with these (proto-)Levinasian concepts or motifs. These proximities allow us to speculate that Levinas comes close to describing a *unio mystica* himself, especially perhaps in chapter five of *Otherwise Than Being*. The fact that he is unwilling to clarify the agent of the movement, that heteronomy appears in and as autonomy, that the infinite comes to pass in my witness to the infinite, that the "saying belongs to the very glory of which it bears witness" (OB 150) — is this not a mystical union, a union that does not, as a union need not, abandon the radical separation between human and divine or postulate an ontology? But the gist of my argument is not really that Levinas is a mystic; I contend only that he draws on the mystical tradition while rejecting what he calls mysticism, just as he draws on the theological tradition while rejecting what he calls theology and on the philosophical tradition while rejecting what he often calls philosophy.

The question that remains to be asked is: why? It should be asked with reference to all three forms — mysticism, theology, and philosophy — but in the present context can only be asked with reference to the former. Given that Levinas draws on kabbalistic sources, why does he adopt an antimystical stance? Given his own tendency toward the *unio mystica*, why does he reserve the word 'mysticism' for the planting of sacred groves? Why does he say repeatedly that Judaism is a 'religion without myths'?

I think some credence can be given to the argument Susan Handelman attributes to Gershom Scholem.

> Scholem . . . would make the same objection to Levinas's position as he made to Hermann Cohen's — that his rationalism was hostile to myth and mysticism, still too tied to an Enlightenment ideal of reason. In fact, Scholem is purported to have once said of Levinas, "He is more of a Litvak than he thinks." This is a reference to the highly intellectual character of the Lithuanian Jewish culture from which Levinas came, which intensely cultivated talmudic learning, gave birth to the ethical sobriety of the *mussar* movement, and was a bastion of resistance to Hasidism.[70]

But Scholem's statement is ambiguous. When he says that Levinas is 'more of a Litvak than he thinks' he either means that Levinas is a Maskil, a follower of the nineteenth century

Eastern European Jewish Enlightenment, or that Levinas is a Mitnagid, a follower of the nineteenth century Lithuanian school of opposition to Hasidism. Handelman speaks as if the two were compatible or even equivalent — as if being 'tied to an Enlightenment ideal of reason' were more or less the same thing as being part of the contemporary 'bastion of resistance to Hasidism' — but in fact they are not. The relation between the Maskilim and the Mitnagdim in Lithuanian Jewish history is complex and remains under debate, but certainly the two movements, which were often at odds with one another, should not be conflated.[71]

Is Levinas a Maskil? Handelman rightly defends him from this charge, pointing out that he always seeks an 'other reason'— or a one-for-the-other reason — distinct from the classical reason of Enlightenment philosophy.[72] And yet there may indeed be a kind of knee-jerk rationalism operating in the recesses of Levinas's thought. I see such a rationalism in the various passages in his work that periodicize the emergence of the mature human being using the threefold scheme discussed earlier: enjoyment or oneness with the world, ethical relation, and the solidification of ethics in social relation. The Levinasian structure parallels a structure common in nineteenth century European thought, especially German thought, by which the development of the human being from infant to adult and the development of civilization are assumed to be analogous and periodicized with a single scheme: a childish or 'pagan' consciousness of oneness with nature; the emergence of the idea of God as separate from humanity; and finally the consciousness of full human autonomy that allows social and individual relations with God and under God.[73] While Levinas does not adopt such an understanding wholesale, there are signs that he is, at times, working unreflectively with a version of it, for instance when he labels the first of his own developmental stages 'pagan' (TI 142, 160), or when he distinguishes Judaism from pagan conceptions by calling it a 'religion for adults' (DF 11). It may be that one of the things that sticks in his thought from this historicist intellectual inheritance is the idea of 'myth' as paradigmatic for totality. Myth can be dismissed as primitive ontology: myth offers a complete explanation of human beings, the world and God or the gods, cushioning one from the discomfort of surprising encounters with the unexpected in the form of alterity.[74] In short, Levinas adopts a stereotype about myth. This is perhaps excusable, since he is not in the business of reading, say, Hesiod — but it appears less excusable when one remembers that he has at his disposal a deontologizing hermeneutic that allows him to do justice to the myths of the Jewish tradition and that might also be fruitfully applied to those of the Greeks or other cultures.

So much for myth. What about mysticism? Here, the suggestion that Levinas is a Mitnagid bears fruit. According to the scholar Allan Nadler, the argument between the Hasidim and Mitnagdim boils down to a straightforward and familiar paradigm: the Hasidim were essentially egalitarians, and the Mitnagdim were essentially concerned with how egalitarianism might water down Jewish learning and practice.[75] As Nadler explains it, the argument over prayer is representative of the entire debate. The Hasidim sought a way for everyone, even those ignorant of the minutiae of Torah and *halachah*, to feel the presence of the divine, and to this effect professed a shift in emphasis from study to prayer, and from praying *halachically* to having the right feelings while praying, or being in the right spiritual state ('*kavana*'). The Mitnagdim were not against prayer and *kavana*, but they saw the Hasidic shift in emphasis as coming at too high a cost: they argued that while certainly prayer was important, if it were seen as all-important, study would suffer; and that while kavana was certainly important, if it were seen as all-important, prayer would suffer. The Hasidim saw the Mitnagdic complaint as petty; the Mitnagdim seized on stories of the Hasidim coming late to services or disregarding certain tenets of the law and called them apostates, sometimes even Sabbateans.

Levinas comes very close to identifying himself as a Mitnagid.[76] I have chosen not to treat the subject of his writings on Hayim of Volozhin in this book in favor of more radical areas of exploration. But it is worth recalling that all of Levinas's articles that explicitly take up the subject of the Kabbalah deal with Hayim, and that Hayim was one of the founders of the Mitnagdic movement. It is also worth noting that a Mitnagdic stance is entirely compatible with an anti-Enlightenment stance. Though the argument could be made that the Mitnagdim and the Maskilim had a certain amount in common — both were rationalists, sceptical of faith and feeling, and advocates of rigorous education — the Mitnagdim themselves saw the matter quite differently. To them, the Maskilim and the Hasidim were on the same side. Maskil and Hasid both stood for liberation (though of different kinds) and downplayed Talmud-Torah and praxis (though in favor of different things). Both movements arose from the middle class and explicitly attacked the rabbinic aristocracy; both were likely to lead to a lessening of *halachic* practice and a general waning of self-control. And, to this Mitnagdic insight, we may add the Levinasian insight that ecstasy and ideology have essentially the same structure. Levinas's critique of modern thought as a form of the sacred grove may well have at least one root in the Mitnagdic understanding that Hasidism and Enlightenment thinking were much the same error.

The argument between the Hasidim and the Mitnagdim on the subject of the Kabbalah was similar to their argument over prayer. Both groups saw the Zohar and the Lurianic teachings as divinely inspired revelations of the secrets of the universe. But while the Mitnagdim did not believe the books could be understood by anyone except masters of the oral and written Torah who had painstakingly rendered themselves

ethically worthy, the Hasidim proclaimed kabbalistic teachings to anyone who would listen. The argument is encapsu-
lated neatly in Nadler's discussion of *tsimtsum*. According to
Nadler, both groups saw *tsimtsum* (literally withdrawal) as
a paradoxical metaphor for God's immanence in the world.
But, as the Mitnagdim had it, the Hasidim spoke too openly
about this immanence. Hayim complains that "it has become
the doctrine of all common men, and it has even become a
parable in the mouths of fools to proclaim, 'behold, in every
place and every thing there is total divinity.'" Their eyes and
hearts contemplate this deeply all their days to the point
that even the hearts of youngsters are inclined to base all
their deeds and actions upon this awareness [of God's imma-
nence]."[77] The meaning of Hayim's reference to Isaiah 6:10 is
relatively clear. The untrained knowledge of divine immanence is a vehicle for hubris. If one becomes aware of divine
immanence but remains ignorant in other ways, one will almost certainly begin to regard the Torah and the *halachah*
as excess baggage. Nadler's discussion of union reveals a similar dynamic. For Hayim, Torah study was mystical union:
the highest spiritual goal was Torah study for its own sake
or *Torah Lishmah*: this study, which was neither more nor
less than study for the purpose of comprehension, was a cleaving to God, a *devekut*. But Hayim was uneasy about the
Hasidic idea of union without study; too easy union is, as he
saw it, a dangerous delusion; like too easy immanence, it leads
at best to the relativization of the *halachah* and at worst to
immorality. Thus it was that at a certain point, argues Nadler,
the Mitnagdim stopped writing about immanence and union
almost entirely; indeed, they effectively gave up the Kabbalah
to the Hasidim and began publicly to preach against its teaching. But they continued privately to respect it and to teach it
to those they thought were ready. It is, I believe, this complex and sophisticated stance that underlies Levinas's use of
kabbalistic ideas and images, as I have sketched it.

My point here is not that Levinas reveals some unwitting residue of a Lithuanian Mitnagdic upbringing when he speaks against mysticism overtly while at the same time teaching it covertly. The Mitnagdim had reasons for taking their Kabbalah underground, and so does Levinas. It is as true today as it was in the nineteenth century that the open promulgation of kabbalistic doctrines seems to offer a healing or a cleaving that is too easy and that will undermine *halachah* and Torah study, not to mention the use of one's rational faculties and one's understanding of ethics. And it is also as true today as it was in the nineteenth century that kabbalistic doctrines are being openly promulgated. I do not refer only to the idea of Kabbalah as self-help, or to those of the general population who conceive of mysticism as ecstasy or bliss (although, despite my defense of mystics at the beginning of this chapter, this is a widespread conception). Levinas has more respectable — even illustrious — opponents in the persons of Buber and Scholem. Buber is the quintessence of the Mitnagdic fear: his philosophy is based on the idea of ethics as arising from a form of ecstatic union, and, as might be expected, he praises Hasidism and denigrates the teachings of the rabbis. And the case of Scholem is only slightly more complex.

Scholem sees the Kabbalah as fundamentally antinomian. For Scholem, ordered conceptions of thought come in several varieties — mythic orders, Enlightenment orders and *halachic* orders among them — and Kabbalah stands against all of them; it is an 'anarchic breeze' that reempowers an atrophying religion by importing therein a creative force, or, in effect, by subverting the legal structures that form the basis of the rabbinic tradition.[78] Now Levinas would probably agree with all of this; for him, the Kabbalah is about the ethics that calls structures into question. But Scholem does not see the anarchic and the antinomian as equivalent to the ethical — indeed, he does not even suggest that they are compatible — and, what is more, he often praises the Kabbalah at the expense of what he sees as rabbinic legalism. And Scholem's understanding is generally accepted in the scholarly and philosophical world. This is unfortunate, but perhaps not surprising. To read the Kabbalah as fundamentally ethical is not an entirely easy thing — at least not until one has absorbed either Levinas's philosophy or the ideas in the traditional Jewish texts that give rise to Levinas's thought, that is to say, not until one has come to the understanding that rupture is ethics, and that rupture is therefore tied to *halachah*.[79]

In short, to disseminate the kabbalistic doctrines too openly is not at all to widen the scope of their acceptance; rather it is fundamentally to misrepresent them. The Mitnagdim saw this in the Hasidic deemphasis of *halachah*; Levinas sees it in Buber's dismissal of *halachah* and in Scholem's claim that the Kabbalah is anarchic and anomian, which sounds to the untrained ear as if it means antiethical and anti*halachic*. Therefore, although in one sense Scholem may be correct in saying that Levinas is more of a Litvak than he thinks (since he may cherish some residual Enlightenment notions about myth), in the more important sense Levinas is fully aware of the extent to which he is a Litvak, and, moreover, the extent to which Scholem is not. Levinas allies himself at every turn with the rabbis of the classical era and the inheritors of their tradition in Lithuania.

So Levinas's Kabbalah remains underground, where, perhaps, it has always belonged. A student of Abulafia cites a conversation with his teacher in which he asks: "Why do you, Sir, compose books in which the methods of the natural sciences are coupled with the instruction in the Holy Names?" Abulafia replies: "For you and the likes of you among the followers of philosophy, to allure your human intellect through natural means, so that perhaps this attraction may cause you to arrive at the knowledge of the Holy Name."[80]

FOUR

The Talmud
and History

What does the end of history matter? says the Lord.
I judge each person for what he is,
not for what he will become.
— *Levinas*, Difficult Freedom

The first Colloquium of French Jewish Intellectuals was held in the spring of 1957.[1] Levinas did not give a paper but was in attendance and participated in the roundtable discussions. His first intervention — his first public statement to the group of learned Jews to whom he was in later years to present his 30 talmudic lectures — makes a controversial claim which, moreover, sets the philosophical agenda for his contributions to the Colloquium for the next three years.[2] He announces that Judaism is not a religion; rather it is a way of comprehending reality such that the interpersonal relation is valued above all else. He then offers two illustrations from the Talmud of this Jewish way of comprehending.

The first is an account of a talmudic commentary on Cain's

words, "my sin is too great to be borne." The rabbis, Levinas says, twist the grammar and read the sentence as a question — "is my sin really too great to be borne?" — by which, as they explain, Cain means: "you, who will pardon the 600,000 Jews who make the golden calf, cannot pardon me?" Once the sentence is read as a question one must ask why God did not answer it. Could it be that God had no answer? No, continues Levinas, it is only that he did not wish to answer. If he had, the response would have been simple, since the two cases are different. The 600,000 Jews sin against God, while Cain sins against a man. Levinas states the moral succinctly: "The only way to respect God is to respect the neighbor."[3]

The second illustration is a story drawn from elsewhere in the Talmud. Levinas tells it as follows.

> Different peoples present themselves before the Eternal in order to receive their place in history. We affirm in passing that there is not at all a radical superiority of the Jews. A pagan who has studied Torah is as great as a High Priest. But everything acquires its meaning through Torah. The enemies of Israel [are aware of this and] ready to accept the law. They want to enter election. . . .
>
> God lets the people take their chances. There is one commandment which is easy to accomplish: the Succah. Everyone applies himself to building a Succah. But God sends a torrid heat wave. Everyone leaves his hut and kicks it to pieces. They cannot withstand the test. But do the Jews resist the torrid heat? No, they also leave their provisional dwellings, but they do not destroy them. And God laughs. . . .[4]

Again Levinas draws out the moral: "To reserve to themselves the possibility of residing outside the solid dwellings of the sedentary historical peoples — to keep the Succah — is the privilege of the Jewish people. What is essential originates in interpersonal relation and not in the splendors of architects. The Jews too protect themselves from the heat and install themselves in houses, but they do not forget the Succah. The Jew does not situate his humanity in enrootedness."

Levinas calls the first illustration an example of the "desacralization" of the Bible in the Talmud. It is an immensely useful and expressive word. By it, Levinas refers to the hermeneutical phenomenon I described in the last chapter as immanentization or deontologization, that is, to the representation of the significant human ethical experiences that underlie and give rise to images of a supernal realm or a divine. The act of desacralizing is an element of what Levinas sees as the rabbinic Jewish antimystical[5] comprehension: just before he offers the first illustration he says, "ethics is an optics towards God; all the rest is suspect, and in this sense, is the mystical temptation and decadence," by which he means that to employ the image of a relation with God that is *not* an expression of a relation with the trace of the infinite in the face of the other is the dangerous postulation of 'invisible meshes' and a sign that she who employs the image has succumbed to the mystical temptation, the desire to make a totality encompassing God.[6] The application of the concept of desacralization to the first illustration is clear: whereas in the Bible the ultimate measure of virtue and sin might seem to be one's relation to God understood literally as direct or participatory, in the Talmud, the measure of one's relation to God, and thus also of virtue and sin, is revealed as one's relation to one's fellows. The biblical account is brought down to earth by the Talmud; it is not altered but its meaning is clarified; the ethical impulse behind its sacral images is made manifest.

Levinasian desacralization is what I have called his discovery of the horizontal in the vertical, diachrony in synchrony, or the other in the same. More simply, it is his phenomenological reduction, his looking back to see what is

behind the same or the system or the 'invisible meshes' or
the 'sacred grove'. This looking back is his philosophical work
and his prophetic work; it is, to put it plainly, his message to
the era. In the last two chapters I have touched, here and
there, on the subject of how Levinas's reinterpretations of
the Jewish sources are intended to address a certain contemporary problem, namely, the reification of images that
express our relation with the divine and a subsequent inability to read the old texts in any way but literally. But this
is not, as Levinas sees it, the main degeneracy of the contemporary understanding; it is merely a symptom. Our inability to read existentially or phenomenologically bolsters,
justifies, and arises from the real problem: a way of standing
before the other that places him into a system where he becomes an aspect of 'what is' and has an identifiable, classifi-
able, 'correct' relation to all the other things that are — in
short, a way of being in the world that subsumes difference
into the same. In other words, the reification of images is
merely a form or a sign of sacralization of experience, for to
reify an image, to read it as representing an idea or thing, is
necessarily make a sacred grove, to place the idea or thing
into a plan or pattern — and thus to commit an idolatry in
which the plan or pattern itself is regarded as paramount, or
even worshipped, at the expense of any understanding of the
experience that gave rise to the image.

These sacral systems take two basic forms for Levinas, both
of which can be called ontologies. In the first, space becomes
a synchrony and spatial differences are understood to be the
coordinates of the system; this involves theorizing about a
hierarchical 'order of being' and might be called 'ontology-
proper'. In the second, time becomes a synchrony and moments
in time are understood to be the coordinates of the system;
this involves theorizing about a progressive 'order of history'
and can be called historicism. Both systems flatten out the
gaps and diachronies of reality by seeing them under an
all-encompassing rubric, a rubric under which reality can

theoretically be seen 'in one place', or 'all at once'. Thus while
at first glance the link between the two illustrations Levinas
offers of the talmudic comprehension is not obvious, in actuality the link is part of Levinas's philosophical point, for the
second illustration, like the first, is an example of the
desacralized talmudic comprehension. Placing one's faith or
hope in the course of rooted history is equivalent to placing
one's faith or hope in a spatially located and reachable God;
both are signs of succumbing to the seductive grandeur of a
scheme or realm that overarches the interpersonal, to which
the inter-personal becomes secondary. The connection between the high value the Talmud puts on the interpersonal
relation and its ahistorical or antihistorical stance is dependent on the logically prior connection — or spiritual equiv-
alence — between participating wholeheartedly in world
history and totalizing the divine. Once the logically prior
connection is seen, it becomes clear that one can only stand
in relation to the extent that one stands, as it were, outside
world history. Desacralization — the removal of mystical
elements in a text by uncovering the ethics that lies behind
them — involves the reinterpretation both of images that
might be misunderstood as suggesting an order of being and
of images that might be misunderstood as suggesting an
order of history.

The question of deontologization (and that aspect of
deontologization that is dehistoricization) arises again — but
with a difference. I have been speaking in the last two chapters about Levinas deontologizing the sources of Judaism —
or, to put it in the new jargon, desacralizing them. Now we
find that Levinas himself speaks of one Jewish source desacralizing another, of the Talmud desacralizing the Bible.
I suggested in chapters two and three that, according to
Levinas, the Bible and the Kabbalah, read without interpretive help, will appear to be fundamentally ontological texts,
full of sacral imagery, imagery that reifies and locates the
divine. It now becomes clear that, in Levinas's view, the

necessary interpretive help is found mainly in the Talmud. To be sure, the Bible and the Kabbalah offer their own hermeneutical keys to desacralization, for instance the negative theology of Isaiah, or the internalization and deconstruction of Abulafia. Nevertheless, it is the Talmud that stands, for Levinas, as the main source of the deontologizing and dehistoricizing hermeneutic, the hermeneutic that refuses to place beings, things, events and ideas into a 'worldview' and reads them instead as representations of the ethical urge, that is, as what they originally were. We may ask, however, whether and to what extent Levinas is correct to say that the Talmud desacralizes the Bible. As we have seen, it is at least partly Levinas himself who desacralizes the Bible and the Kabbalah; it is possible, then, that he desacralizes the Talmud as well, and reads the desacralizing hermeneutic into it. In fact, both notions are to some degree true. Robert Gibbs lends some support to the second when he describes Levinas's hermeneutic for reading the sources of Judaism by saying not only that Levinas "makes a strong claim that biblical texts can be approached only through the Midrash and the Talmud" but also that "he designs *his own style* of reading in such a way as to avoid both a historical-philological reading and a pietistic, *halachic* reading of the rabbinic texts."[7] By this account, Levinas's ahistorical hermeneutic is his own; he himself desacralizes the Jewish sources. And the second notion receives further support from the circumstances under which Levinas continues to illustrate the concept of desacralization. His contributions to the first four Colloquia comprise a fullscale battle with Hegel, a battle in which the ahistorical or antihistorical aspect of the desacralized rabbinic comprehension becomes the vanguard. We may wonder, on this basis, whether Levinas does not overemphasize the lack of historicity or historicism in the rabbinic comprehension in order to gain anti-Hegelian ammunition. And yet the first notion can also be supported: with his first intervention, Levinas has begun to show that the Talmud does indeed desacralize the Bible. It is likely, therefore, that when Levinas applies his own technique of desacralization to the old books, he understands himself to be working in the talmudic tradition; in short, he applies to the Bible, the Kabbalah, and the Talmud itself the hermeneutic that the Talmud, at least sometimes, applies to the Bible.[8]

Levinas's first intervention receives no response. The discussion moves on to other issues; it appears that he has made little impact on the participants. But he does not let the matter drop. Almost everything he says in the next three Colloquia is an attempt to clarify and defend the initial intervention. He continues to argue that Judaism is a way of comprehending. He continues to maintain that sacral images are essentially anathema to Judaism, and that insofar as they are used they are always meant to be understood in light of the nonsacral, ethical (or just) experiences that underlie them. And though he does not take up the argument against ontology in his favorite form — that is, Heideggerianism — he does explicitly address Hegelian historicism, repudiating all structures that accord significance to world history and representing such structures as sacral and immoral. Finally, he offers, in support of all this, a desacralized interpretation of talmudic messianism by which messianism has nothing to do with ontological transformation in a historical future, and everything to do with ethical transformation in the diachronous here and now.

Levinas's argument against Hegelianism has two basic aspects, one of which is fairly narrow and the other of which is wider in scope. The narrow aspect touches less on Hegel himself than on the interpretation of Hegel offered by his great French disciple, Alexandre Kojève. Levinas does not explicitly address Kojève, but the concepts he draws from Hegel in the second and third lectures to the Colloquium and especially his use of the phrase 'universal and homogeneous state' suggest more than a mere familiarity with Kojève's interpretation of Hegel's thought. I believe that Levinas's Hegel is largely Kojève's Hegel, and I am not alone. Peperzak writes that "as far as Hegel is concerned, we must be aware of the Parisian scene of the years during which Levinas prepared his opus magnum. In the fifties and sixties, it was still dominated by Alexandre Kojève's interpretation of the *Phenomenology of Spirit*" and it is "this Hegel" that looms so powerfully in Levinas's thought.[9] In any case, when Levinas's critique of Hegel is read as a critique of Kojève's Hegel, interesting nuances emerge. We begin to see a Levinas who, for all he praises the liberal West as a place where political and religious freedom is possible, is also uneasy about certain aspects of liberalism. And we begin to see that liberalism (taken up below) and totalitarianism (taken up in the next chapter) have, from a Levinasian perspective, certain features in common: both are historicist ontologies; both are monisms; both are progressivist ideologies that seek to subsume difference into the same; both see world history as marching toward a time when human beings will be fulfilled because they have everything in common. In the main body of this chapter we will trace Levinas's argument that the Hegelian-Kojèvian historicist ontology dominates our thinking and our politics, and also his argument that this ontology can be corrected only by the phenomenon he defines as Judaism, a phenomenon that is in some sense universally accessible, but that is best expressed in the sources of Judaism, for instance in the openness of a Rosenzweig or, especially, in the inconclusiveness of the rabbinic give-and-take, an inconclusiveness intended to preclude the fixed structures of the sacred grove.

This first aspect of Levinas's argument against Hegelianism will be fleshed out further as the chapter progresses. But it is necessary now to speak at some length about the second more general aspect. This begins with Levinas's admission of what is perhaps the central Hegelian point: dialectics is totality, or dialectics is ontology. This understanding is already relatively clearly drawn in the preface to *Totality and Infinity*, where Levinas links 'war' and 'being', meaning by 'war' all actions and understanding that pit two or more sides against one another, and by 'being' ontology. The two are very nearly identified: the intended result of war, he argues, is participation, order, subsuming of the other into a structure of the same, identity, egology, totality, ontology. The discussion seems simple and straightforward, but it has far-reaching significance, for with it Levinas repudiates utterly a standard paradigm for the understanding of human nature, human society and human thought: the paradigm of 'agon vs. the end of agon', in which beings either come together in a participatory order or whole or else struggle constantly with one another to maintain their autonomy and ascendancy. For Levinas, these two things are one: a struggle of autonomies exists for the purpose of creating a stable synthesis or harmony; moreover, a synthesis or harmony already exists in the struggle insofar as the two parties struggling can already be seen as mutually dependent, mutually defined, two parts of the whole that is the struggle. Levinas allows struggle and harmony — part and whole, war and ontology — to merge. And the resulting hybrid of war-ontology or struggle-harmony is, he tells us in the preface to *Totality and Infinity*, the nature of politics, the nature of "harsh reality," and the nature of history (TI 21).

The insight is borrowed from Hegel. Depending on how one interprets Hegel, one will either stress his synthetic telos, the achievement of Absolute Knowledge or political utopia — in which case the distinction between struggle and synthesis is all part of a greater synthesis — or one will stress the way in which his account illuminates the continuing course of world history and the history of ideas — in which case the distinction between struggle and synthesis is all part of a greater and ongoing struggle. In either case it is clear that the two are effectively two sides of the same coin. Struggle leads to synthesis; struggle has synthesis as its purpose; struggle *is* synthesis and synthesis a temporary ceasefire that covers over struggle — Hegel already knows all this. In Levinas, it becomes the insight that, just as war (or dialectics) can be seen from above as a kind of ontology and thus linked to the act of theorizing about an order of being, so ontology — any ontology — can be seen as a war. For in war two structures dominate: first, the structure within an army, in which is established "an order from which no one can henceforth keep his distance" (T1 21) analogous to an order of being, and, second, the structure between armies, in which we find "a mobilization of absolutes" (TI 22) analogous to the war of all against all. In both "the meaning of individuals is derived from the totality" (TI 22). The two are one action or event or phenomenon, seen from different perspectives.

The question is where one goes from here. Is the hybrid of struggle-harmony an explanation of all human doings, or is there ground outside of the hybrid from which it can be criticized? Levinas's break from Hegel comes in the form of an argument that such a ground exists. The break is best seen in his rewriting of the Hegelian master-slave story. In Hegel's version, two men (a subject and an other, to use Levinasian terms) meet and fight for mastery until it is clear to both that one is the master and the other the slave. The differences between the two men — and indeed all differences between all human beings — are defined as antagonisms; difference is violence. The master can, however, achieve the temporary appearance of harmony or nonviolence — which lasts until a new struggle begins — by subsuming the slave's possessions into his own and the slave into his way of life. History, for Hegel, is the story of such temporary struggles and temporary harmonies, and the course of history is predetermined. In Levinas's version the story begins in the same way: two people meet with the intention of struggling for mastery. But the subject is arrested by the command in the face of the other — that is, in his very difference from her — the command that orders her not to kill, not to master, not to make same. Henceforth the subject who would have mastered subjugates herself willingly to the other. She offers herself to him, but she does not become his slave; she does not become part of him but remains separate and keeps her as-for-me. This separation is not autonomy, for she has seen in the moment of approach that she is fundamentally indebted to the other. But the separation does support a freedom, a freedom with which she can kill the other if she likes, or serve him. So Levinas transforms the story completely. Instead of the differences between people giving rise to antagonism, they give rise to ethics. Instead of the merging of two into one, the subsuming of the slave into the master, there is asymmetrical relation, relation in which the *you* remains higher spiritually and lower economically than the *I*, relation that bespeaks the desire for an ever-absent and infinitely higher God. Moreover, the Levinasian encounter, far from being predetermined, is utterly indeterminate. Although the subject is responsible to preserve the freedom of the other, she is not bound or conditioned to do so. Each encounter is new, each surprising, each in its own way serendipitous or unfortunate; no encounter can be understood as part of a grand scheme of being or history. Thus, while history, for Levinas, may be Hegelian history — at least this is what we read in the preface to *Totality and Infinity* — the motivations for human action, and thus the originating impulses of history, are not Hegelian; these motivations or impulses stand, in this sense, outside of history.

It is critical to see that Levinas's transformation of the story is not a matter, as it were, of 'lopping the end off' the Hegelian dialectic. It is true that in the standard interpretation of Hegel with which Levinas generally works the entire history of struggle-harmony is finally revealed as part of a greater harmony that relativizes all previous stages, subordinating them to the system, making it evident that in the same way that all previous harmonies were merely disguised struggles, so all previous struggles were merely disguised manifestations of the ultimate harmony. And certainly it is precisely this vision of an 'end of history' that Levinas both accepts as the logical outcome of history and is horrified by, and this vision that leads him to seek a nonhistorical ground for history. But his deeper insight is that the end of history is already there *in* history if history is understood as dialectical. "Thesis and antithesis," he writes, "in repelling one another, call for one another. They appear in opposition to the synoptic gaze that encompasses them; they already form a totality" (TI 53). Thus even a revisionist Hegel, for whom history was a progression of endless struggle, would already have sacrificed real difference to a paradigm, effectively proffering a telos of history; the fact that that telos may be temporally extended to the point of virtual endlessness makes no difference. Were the Levinasian subject and other to struggle with one another, or stand against one another, they would already form a whole, a whole that could be seen from the outside and would, from that perspective, appear as a totality or a participation or a synthesis or a harmony. Only insofar as the two remain separate, giving and speaking to one another, are they engaged in something that cannot be seen from outside, something that cannot be classified in a pattern.

In sum, Levinas finds his non-Hegelian ground in relation, and can thus reject the idea that human nature, society and thought is based in any primary way not only on struggle as opposed to harmony or harmony as opposed to struggle, but also on the hybrid of struggle-harmony that governs Hegelian history, whether one understands that hybrid ultimately as a manifestation of an overarching harmony or as a manifestation of a ceaseless struggle. Moreover, once the non-Hegelian ground is laid, Levinas can erect a wider critique of dialectical-ontological structures, or wars. His argument against the apparently harmonious intra-army structure is his general critique of ontological philosophy, especially the kind of philosophy based in a certain religious understanding that seeks to establish an order in which each being has its place or function and from which each derives its meaning. His argument against the apparently agonistic interarmy structure is his critique of those philosophies that base themselves on oppositions, most notably for him, Hobbes. When he writes that "the visage of being that shows itself in war is fixed in the concept of totality that dominates Western philosophy" (TI 21), he is speaking of both ways of thinking. Harmonious systems in which "the ultimate meaning alone counts" are effectively equivalent to agonistic systems in which "the last act alone changes beings into themselves" (TI 22).

Thus Levinas accepts a certain Hegelian insight and repudiates a certain Hegelian error. But let us lay the matter out more clearly. The links between war or dialectics or ontology and politics, between war and history, and between war and "harsh reality" — all the links that are borrowed from Hegel and presented in the preface to *Totality and Infinity* — are not inflammatory rhetoric; on the contrary they must be taken completely seriously. Levinas holds that Hegel understands the nature of totality better than any other single thinker, and that insofar as history and 'reality' (as well as the less controversial politics) are totalities, they can be best explained using Hegelian logic. However, Levinas does not conceive totality as the fundamental nature or ultimate meaning of reality or history or indeed politics; in fact it may be said that he does not even conceive totality to be the fundamental nature of totality, since totalities are themselves always already ruptured by infinity or responsibility. Thus, for Levinas, where Hegel goes wrong is not so much in his description of totality as in his notion that the totality he describes is total; in other words, he makes the error of postulating an avoidable totality. The matter can be described in plainer terms as follows. Levinas accepts Hegel's description of most of the features of historical political reality. He accepts Hegel's description of most of the course of historical political reality. But he does not accept Hegel's description of the origin or end of historical political reality. Hegel, according to Levinas, is correct to suggest that political history tends toward a universal synthetic regime that is already all but completely established, correct to suggest that the regime attempts (and to a great extent succeeds) in putting an end to movement and debate or history and philosophy, correct to suggest that political historical particularities are nothing more than inchoate syntheses or that struggles are nothing more than inchoate harmonies, and correct to suggest that action in any 'present' tends to be conditioned by an idea of a future telos. But Hegel is incorrect to suggest that the universal regime would be utterly synthetic, incorrect to suggest that the regime would succeed completely in putting an end to critique or philosophy or history, incorrect to suggest that all particulars are the kind of particulars that tend toward totality, and incorrect to suggest that action in any present is not also conditioned by a nonteleological future inscribed in desire for the 'not yet' and, jut as importantly, by a past encounter with a divine trace. And no matter how critical the points on which Hegel is correct, the points on which he is incorrect are decisive. For although Hegel may describe much of our present, past, and future condition accurately, when he mistakes the origin and end of that condition he mistakes its meaning, conceiving a wholeness where none exists.

What Levinas begins to do in the rewriting of the master-slave story is to offer a way to move back out of the Hegelian understanding towards meaning. The turning away is accomplished by the awareness that, despite the evidence of war, politics, and history, human experience is founded on something that cannot be subsumed into a synthesis, something that is not struggle but rather ultimate rupture. Dialectical structures present themselves implicitly as rupturing and as judging one another, but the presentation is false. Wars present themselves as great clashes or breakings that shake up and call into question everything in their path, but this is no true break, no true shaking up, a calling into question of nothing. Dialectical structures and wars — all antagonistic struggles — are closed, fixed, boundaried, and, because of this, essentially at rest. Any movement that seems to be taking place within them is a mere mimicry of the true dynamism of ethics, by which human beings *are* called into question; under this mimicry there is only a realm of the same, in which individuals are sacrificed to the war machine, in which incoherencies are made to play their part in a pattern, or in which the event of the subject's encounter with the other has no meaning unless it furthers the postulated course of world history. *Shevirah* appears under the guise of rupture but it is, in fact, totality. *Tikkun* therefore must be true movement. Levinas seeks to step back out of the totalities of war, dialectics, politics, and history — with their false breakings — into dynamism, into real rupture.

This second and wider aspect of Levinas's argument against Hegelianism returns us to a structure of Levinas's thinking we took up briefly in section four of chapter one, a structure in which a common distinction — for instance reason and revelation or theology and philosophy or, as we now see, war and harmony or struggle and synthesis — is taken up, merged until there is no distinction left, and then set up against an element of experience that cannot be merged into the resulting identity, an unsubsumable element. In chapter one we called the unsubsumable element prophecy or ethics;

in the anti-Hegelian texts taken up in this chapter it is more often called religion, or love, or messianism. In Levinas's first lecture to the Colloquium, he shows us that Franz Rosenzweig agrees with Hegel that history (supposedly active, dynamic agon) tends toward or merges into indifference (passive, synthetic), but sets up against this synthesis the unmergeable thing called religion or love. In the second and third lectures, he shows us the rabbis anachronistically agreeing with four Hegelian-like syntheses — the present merges into the future, acting 'for one's own time' into acting 'for all times', inside into outside, and particular into universal — but all the hybrids are then put up against an unsubsumable 'here' and a 'now' and an 'each-for-each other'. All of this is the overcoming of a the Hegelian sacred grove, an overcoming by means of moving back. Levinas does not fight Hegel on Hegel's ground, for he knows Hegel to be correct in his claim that to fight him is already to admit that life and thought are a matter of agon and harmony, and thus to lose the battle. Instead Levinas simply turns away from Hegel, and, moreover, shows us Rosenzweig and the rabbis turning away as well. Levinas's Rosenzweig and Levinas's rabbis make play with the truth of the Hegelian account of reality. They set antitheses against theses and conflate them into syntheses — but out of this discover ethical elements of experience that cannot be made to play roles in the Hegelian drama. They anticipate Hegel, but finally make light of him. They never lose sight of nonagonistic, nonsynthetic ethical difference; it remains for them the root of the richness of a created world that can never stand as an unbroken totality.

Only a few more introductory words need to be said about Levinas's critique of Hegelian thinking as it emerges in the lectures that form the focus of this chapter. Levinas's rhetoric in these lectures runs rather high. In order to set up a foil for the critique of Hegel that eventually arises, he argues strongly for the truth of the Hegelian account. Part of his subsequent counterargument then consists of the suggestion that, although true, the Hegelian account is grotesque. The complete counterargument, that the Hegelian account is at bottom incorrect, then depends in part on the grotesqueness of the account, which in turn depends on the assertion of the account's partial truth. This is a complex and at times confusing movement of thought. Moreover, Levinas's manner of expression is (as always) unsystematic. For the most part, he uses the term 'history' as equivalent to Hegelian history, thus suggesting that Hegel has analyzed history correctly and that history (and the history of philosophy) is a totality that moves inevitably toward its end and fulfillment in the universal and homogeneous state. At these times he speaks of 'standing outside of history' as the way to overcome or step out of the bonds of Hegelian logic. But once he has completed this part of the critique, once he is, as it were, standing outside of history himself, he begins to criticize any notion that history has a telos. At this point it becomes possible for him to speak again of action in history or historical action without the idea that such action must be part of a historical plan or a historicism. The second of these two ways of speaking expresses Levinas's bottom line: while there may be meaning *in* history, there is no meaning *of* history; history is not going anywhere. But he seldom speaks from the bottom line. In order to present the strength of the Hegelian threat he must show that Hegelianism, and especially Kojèvian Hegelianism, gives a compelling if appalling account of most of what has happened in the course of history, and of modern society; he thus speaks throughout much of the three lectures like a disaffected Kojèvian. It should be kept in mind, during the account that follows, that 'standing outside of history' is equivalent to standing within a history that has no overarching meaning; and we should be accommodating to Levinas's movements back and forth between the claim that history is fulfilled in universality and homogeneity and the claim that history has no fulfillment.

This introduction has jumped from the rabbis to Kojève

and Hegel, for these thinkers are the poles that govern Levinas's participation in the first four Colloquia. They are approached and connected by means of three implicit questions and answers. First, what are the particular sacred groves that shape contemporary thought and action? Levinas describes a Kojèvian end of history in which indifference is the dominant characteristic. Second, what is the way out of such sacralization? Levinas describes an antisacral way of comprehending that he calls Judaism, a way of comprehending focused on ethical experience; when pressed, he says that this kind of Judaism is found above all in the Talmud. Third — and here we have a series of connected questions — if Judaism is a way of comprehending, and if that way of comprehending is based on desacralization, and if desacralization is the way to stand apart from a Kojèvian historicism in relation, then shouldn't everyone be Jew? Or, indeed, given that this sort of standing-apart-from-history-in-relation is foundational for human experience, is everyone not already a Jew? And, if everyone *is* already a Jew, how can Hegelian history have come about at all? To these questions Levinas does not offer a clear answer. Part of the problem is already implicit in the analysis above, where Levinas both finds an ethics prior to Hegel and also accepts the Hegelian vision of the course of history; this part of the problem can perhaps be solved with the application of the (albeit sketchy) account I have offered in previous chapters of how endemic totalities become avoidable totalities. But in the course of the lectures to the Colloquium the problem remains entwined with Levinas's analysis of the nature of Judaism's relation to other religions, and is, I believe, at least in part left unresolved.

The three questions arise in his first lecture to the Colloquium, and we will treat them in order in the three sections that form the first half of this chapter. In the second half, we will turn to his second and third lectures to the Colloquium, published together as "Messianic Texts." Here he narrows his focus to the all-important second question, seeking a proto-anti-Kojèvian-Hegelianism in certain rabbinic teachings about messianism.

Between Two Worlds

"Between Two Worlds" is a lecture on the life and thought of Franz Rosenzweig. I offer here an interpretation of the lecture, into which I interpolate some passages from Levinas's other writings and an account of some parts of the roundtable discussion that followed the lecture's presentation.[10] I should mention that I occasionally employ my own neologism, 'Levinas-Rosenzweig' in place of the cumbersome phrase, 'Levinas, speaking in the name of Rosenzweig'. I offer as justification the fact that part way through the roundtable discussion, Dr. E. Minkowski notes that Levinas effaces himself behind Rosenzweig during the lecture, effectively becoming Rosenzweig, and that Levinas expresses gratitude for the insight (EDM 141, 147). It must, however, be kept in mind that Rosenzweig and Levinas differ in certain respects at least semantically. For instance, the setting of Rosenzweig's discourse is the cosmos (understood as a macroanthropos or 'relation writ large') while Levinas prefers to restrict himself to the anthropos and the relation per se; for another instance, Rosenzweig speaks of 'love' while Levinas prefers the terms 'relation' or 'ethics'; and for a third, Rosenzweig speaks of 'eternity' as what breaks linear history while Levinas understands eternity precisely as the extension of linear history. In this analysis, I use for the most part Rosenzweig's way of speaking.

The problem

Levinas opens the paper with the beginnings of a biography of Rosenzweig, in which he explains that Rosenzweig came to Judaism gradually in the course of his life from his study of humanity in general and that his thought moves similarly "to Judaism from the universal and the human." (EDM 122/256/183). His lecture, he says, is intended to reveal the way this movement is accomplished, that is, to trace the route from the contemporary manifestations of universalism — modern doubt, and participation in the modern State — towards Judaism. Already Levinas has begun to address Hegel. According to Hegel, history (and philosophy, which is equivalent to the history of philosophy) are to be understood as the progressive unfolding of spirit. As I have suggested, the unfolding takes the form of the struggle between masters and slaves, or between master-moralities and slave-moralities, in the effort to gain freedom and recognition. In each historical stage the ideas of the previous stage are synthesized and transcended until the achievement of absolute freedom and recognition for all heralds the arrival of the universal synthesis and the end of history and philosophy. The process is predetermined and the end inevitable; that history appears while it takes place as an unintelligible series of events merely reveals 'the cunning of reason', which has dissembled the ultimate plan, hiding its existence from all thinkers prior to Hegel. Hegel can see the plan because, as he understands it, the end has arrived; history has reached its final stage in the ideas of the French Revolution being spread throughout Europe by Napoleon — liberty, or absolute freedom, and equality, or absolute recognition. There can be no further historical stage; these ideals will nevermore be challenged. All that remains is their further spread and implementation, which are mere technical problems.

In short, then, Hegel's philosophy and history moves from

the particular to the universal, while, in contradistinction, Rosenzweig, in life and thought, moves from the universal to the particular; which is to say that Rosenzweig moves in a direction Hegel would call backwards. And it is all the more perverse, from a Hegelian perspective, that the particular toward which Rosenzweig moves is Judaism. According to Hegel, Judaism was in its early years a historically necessary phenomenon, providing the antithesis to the Greek comprehension of the divine that allowed the two to be subsumed into the superior philosophy of Christianity. But it continues to exist in post-Christian centuries only as a sort of hangover, and in the present era of universality as a blind anachronism. Levinas's opening account of Rosenzweig's path thus attacks Hegel implicitly from two fronts.

But the attack does not take the form of a claim that Hegel was wrong in any simple sense. It is true that Levinas-Rosenzweig has suggested, contra Hegel, that genetic, credal or territorial particularities (like Judaism) need not merely be inchoate forms of syntheses ("the universal and the human"), and that it is possible to move temporally through life and thought against the flow of Hegelian history. He has, moreover, sketched the beginning of a logical argument supporting this anti-Hegelian stance: he has labeled the notion that history culminates in the universal a "modern" notion, and thus, perhaps, temporally contingent and vulnerable to refutation. But he has also allowed us to perceive the difficulty of arguing against Hegel. For to label universalist conceptions "modern" merely highlights the fact that the conceptions are in a sense self-proving. That history has had universalism as its goal and end is surely manifest beyond doubt by the fact that moderns are fundamentally and profoundly universalists. If Rosenzweig swims against the Hegelian stream, he also swims against the prevailing stream. Levinas intends us to perceive this; he intends, in short, to begin the paper with what is at least a partial admission of the triumph of Hegel. So far, therefore, his attack only exists in the form of a question: by what means does Rosenzweig (and might we, with him) move outside and beyond this triumph? This is, in fact, the critical question; it is what Levinas means when he says, at the end of the lecture, that the question Rosenzweig raises is "the first question a Jew today should raise" (EDM 137/280/201). It is also a way of describing the general question of the relation between Hegel and the Talmud that governs Levinas's first three lectures to the colloquium, for, as gradually emerges, to move beyond the triumph of Hegel is to stand outside of history and within the Jewish way of comprehending that Levinas has referred to in his first intervention.

That Levinas-Rosenzweig gives a good deal of credence to the Hegelian conception of history becomes clearer as he begins to define contemporary universalism. "Rosenzweig knows," says Levinas, "that Hegel spoke the truth when he affirmed that this was 'the end of philosophy and that philosophers have become superfluous'" (EDM 125/260/186).[11] The end of philosophy, he continues, is equivalent to the ubiquity of philosophy. In the contemporary world, everyone has become a philosopher, and thus there is no longer any distinction between philosophers and those to whom they philosophize, and no longer a distinct thing called philosophy. The end of philosophy means, in effect, that everyone today experiences an unprecedented intimacy between life and thought, and that no one needs to be taught. It should not, says Levinas, be confused with an 'age of philosophy' in which many or most human beings *choose* to philosophize. At the end of philosophy, everyone *must* philosophize. The necessity enters the consciousness of each individual through "the anguished certainty of the inexorable march of history towards goals that surpass the intentions of human beings" (EDM, 125/259/185). Hegel is right: we have attained absolute freedom. But by its very nature as an absolute, this

freedom is manifest as tyranny and enslavement. "The movement that led to the liberation of man . . . [results in] the
experience of the necessity of philosophical totality known
as totalitarian tyranny" (EDM 125/259–60/186).

This sketchy description of the end of philosophy from the
beginning of the lecture may be fleshed out somewhat with a
further description of the malaise of the contemporary age
from the lecture's final paragraphs. Levinas illustrates the
initial description by referring to a Marxist poem,[12] but in
the final description suggests that we face a further degeneration of understanding, beyond the Hegelian or Marxist
forms. "Alongside [history's] Hegelian and Marxist interpretation, in which it seems to be ineluctably directed toward
a goal, there is an interpretation that offers to go nowhere:
all civilizations would be equal. Modern atheism is not the
negation of God, it is the absolute indifferentism of *Tristes
Tropiques*. I think that this is the most atheist book that has
been written in our day, the most absolutely disoriented and
disorienting book. It threatens Judaism as much as the
Hegelian and sociological vision of history does" (EDM 136/
279–80/200–01). It is perhaps not necessary to speculate on
Levinas's objections to Lévi-Strauss in great detail. Lévi-
Strauss holds that the perceived differences between things
are not given in reality but are a product of the structure-
creating capability of the human mind, and that social or
cultural structures are created in accordance with the structures perceived in reality, that is, in accordance with the
shared human mental structures. A Levinasian critique of
this understanding is not difficult to formulate. That Lévi-
Strauss finds the essence of the human being in cultural or
social structure means that the other, for him, does not remain other but can be made intelligible through a comparison of those structures. And it could be further argued that
Lévi-Strauss's other is not a true other at all, for he sees
each individual as, to all intents and purposes, composed of

the same structure-creating mental material as each other.

I think it likely that Levinas conceives the structuralist understanding as fundamentally Hegelian and Lévi-Strauss's contention that all difference occurs within the given human mental material as a failed attempt to claim or internalize the Hegelian dialectic. The reason Levinas does not place Lévi-Strauss himself into the Hegelian camp in "Between Two Worlds" but instead labels *Tristes Tropiques* evidence of a further degeneration is that Lévi-Strauss himself argues against Hegel, dismissing the importance of history. Dialectical progressive history, according to Lévi-Strauss, is one of the structures by means of which *our* society perceives reality; it is not a given, but a myth, and in privileging it, Hegel (or, more often in Lévi-Strauss's analyses, Sartre) illegitimately privileges our society over others. But his argument with Hegel does not preclude the possibility that his philosophy, as expressed in *Tristes Tropiques*, may be an expression of the ultimate triumph of identity over difference, and thus itself Hegelian. It may, therefore, be the beginning of an indication of what Levinas refers to when he adopts Hegel's claim that we have reached the end of philosophy.

The matter may be further clarified by a different text: Levinas's essay, "The Trace of the Other." Here, as at the end of "Between Two Worlds," Levinas suggests that a new degeneration has succeeded Hegelianism or Marxism. Eric Weil expresses the old form: he is convinced that "every attitude of the rational being is directed into a category" and that "the outcome is a category reabsorbing all standpoints." But in this comprehension, Weil is "in conformity with philosophical tradition," tradition that has been abandoned by an "anti-intellectualist" contemporary thought. Contemporary thought is quite comfortable, even complacent, with a "multiplicity of cultural significations and . . . games of art," and by this complacency, it "lightens being of its alterity." Thus it remains "indifferent to the other and to others, refusing every movement which does not return" (TrO 347). In effect, while Weil sought a category incorporating all standpoints, contemporary thought employs a vast number of categories without questioning their nature or putting them into contention. The attempt to subsume difference into synthesis has given way to mere indifference to difference. And again, while this most modern stance is perhaps not strictly Hegelian, it may be understood as the ultimate result of the Hegelian search for identity, for indifference is without doubt the most effective form of nondifference. Lévi-Strauss's argument against Hegelian dialectics — his unwillingness to privilege one society over another — is precisely an example of this indifference to difference. Indeed, Levinas suggests that Lévi-Strauss's indifference is indifference par excellence by honoring it with the ubiquitous suffix of modern totalizing comprehensions, that is, the 'ism' (EDM 136/279–80/200–01). It may be then that Lévi-Straussian 'indifferentism', which appears to stand contra-Hegel, is an expression of the Hegelian triumph of identity, and may likewise precisely represent the 'philosophy' of people living at the end of philosophy, when everyone is a philosopher, when everyone is satisfied with her own thought, and when no one needs to be taught by an other.

That Levinas sees contemporary indifference as a direct descendant of Hegelianism becomes clearer in "Messianic Texts," where he begins to refer implicitly to Kojève. Writing a century and a half after Hegel, Kojève documents the post-Hegelian spread and implementation of the ideals of the French Revolution. Liberty and equality have increasingly been achieved in what he calls 'the universal and homogeneous state', the political entity in which each citizen accords recognition to each other and the freedom of each is ensured. And if we have not quite as yet achieved the practical implementation of the universal and homogeneous state, we are very close to having achieved the practical implementation of the universal and homogeneous state of mind. As a student of Kojève's thought, Barry Cooper, puts it: "Hegel's political teaching, as interpreted by Kojève and summarized by the phrase 'the end of history', expresses the purposes and ideals of modern civilization for both bourgeois capitalists and bourgeois socialists (including that aspect of modernity identified as totalitarianism) with an unequaled depth, coherence, clarity and exhaustiveness."[13]

Cooper draws from Kojève's thought a link between liberalism and totalitarianism. Certainly, the differences between the two are critical, but, according to Cooper's Kojève, they are not different in all respects. For while it is true that liberalism founds its self-understanding on the idea that it has escaped totality by means of its pluralism or its respect for the individual, in practice it appears, like totalitarianism, to be a political version of what Levinas calls the realm of the same. Liberalism has as its goal the Hegelian ideal of the self-actualization of all citizens; its pluralism and individualism mean, to all intents and purposes, that each citizen respects each other's chosen method of self-actualization. But because self-actualization is the goal of all, there is little need for philosophical debate; any method of self-actualization is as good as any other; we are, in fact, complacent with a multitude of categories or cultural significations. Meaningful arguments in which human beings throw political, ethical or philosophical concepts or principles into contention are superfluous, and any strong belief that might suggest the existence of fundamental differences between people, for instance religion, tends to remold itself until it is compatible with liberal goals or becomes a strictly private affair. Everyone is a philosopher; there is no need for discourse; effectively or in practice, there are no meaningful differences between people. This, at least, is Kojève's Hegelian understanding of liberalism as interpreted by Cooper.

Levinas's criteria for the justice of a regime, we recall, is twofold. First, with respect to the other's other or the ones 'far off', the just regime will in one way or another make laws that arise from ethics and represent 'ethics with a hard skin'. What these laws might look like we are never told; thus it remains quite possible that Levinas sees liberalism as just in this respect. Second, with respect to the other or the 'one near', the just regime will allow for difference and thus encourage ethics. Again the criterion is unclear — this time necessarily so — and yet it is clear enough to make us wonder if Levinas sees liberalism as entirely just in this respect. For the differences allowed for and encouraged by liberalism, as they are described by Kojève, have little to do with Levinasian alterity. On the contrary, they constitute a plethora of affectations and affiliations — chosen rather than endemic, superficial rather deep, and, above all, arbitrary rather than ethical — which together form nothing less than the illusion of fulfillment without the necessity of an encounter with an other; they are, in short, a distraction from infinite difference.[14] Kojèvian liberalism is not Levinasian liberality, for its live-and-let-live does not require encounter, and therefore does not engender the self-questioning that is manifest as the gift to the other. Kojèvian pluralism is not Levinasian plurality, for in the 'ism' lurks the egological assumption that I need not change my chosen affiliations and attitudes on the basis of the other's needs any more than I would expect the other to conform to my affiliations and attitudes. Thus, with respect to the possibility of a true encounter with the other or the 'one near', a liberal pluralistic regime is perhaps as unjust as a totalitarian one — and the Kojèvian link between liberalism and totalitarianism through indifference is quite probably the source of Levinas's claim that the modern movement of liberation is a movement toward a 'totalitarian tyranny'. The description of the end of philosophy from the beginning of "Between Two Worlds" is a description of a Kojèvian end, one in which we have moved beyond the Hegelianism of a Weil into the Hegelianism of a Lévi-Strauss, that is, into indifferentism. But empirically verifiable as this end may be, Levinas will turn away from it.

Incidentally, because this turning away is not only a rejection of the more straightforward Hegelianism of Weil but also of the ideas of the structuralists and contemporary philosophers who, despite their claim to be anti-Hegelian or antimodern, merely take the Hegelian comprehension to its logical conclusion — because of this, Levinas cannot be called postmodern without clarification or qualification. The definition of postmodernism by which it refuses closure — by which it recomplicates, ruptures, or breaks open each issue or question as soon an answer threatens to emerge — is merely a form of indifferentism. Though Levinas appears at times to be a philosopher of ultimate rupture — finding a different in every same, a many in every one, and an incoherence in every coherence — he is in actuality a philosopher of structure. For the difference or openness to which he points is not arbitrary. It is an openness with a direction, a direction neither spatial nor temporal — neither ontological nor historical — but ethical. Thus the point of Levinas's argument against Hegel and Kojève is not merely that the progressive augmentation of Identity in History is broken *somehow — anyhow*, by spontaneity or an adirectional openness[15] — for this would only be an assertion of the sameness that is indifferentism, and thus ultimately a vindication of Hegel and Kojève. The point, rather, is the nature of the meaning that does the breaking open, namely ethics. What emerges in Levinas's rewriting of the master-slave story is that to say, in the language of Levinas, that identity or the same is ruptured by the other or difference, is to say, in plainer speech, that identity or the same is ruptured by *service to* the other, by *responsibility for* difference. From a Levinasian perspective, Hegel and Kojève's argument is immoral: Hegelian-Kojèvian 'relation' is a denial of true relation that is not mutual or reversible, but elevates the other. His argument against their understanding can be simply put: pluralism is always already ruptured by a prior plurality, liberalism by a prior liberality.

Levinas's account of Rosenzweig's movement from universal to particular must be understood in this context. It is a movement away from universalism understood as the end of philosophy, as the fulfillment of the Hegelian plan in complacency. When Levinas describes Rosenzweig's path as a movement away from the modern idea that one's "participation in the State [is] the accomplishment of one's very vocation to be a human being" (EDM 123/257/184), he implies that it is a movement away from the Kojèvian universal and homogeneous state, away from the state of indifference that characterizes the contemporary thought of moderns and postmoderns. The problem Levinas-Rosenzweig treats is a concrete one: the triumph of Hegel is evident in the ideals of our own society, which is Hegelian as well as liberal. We are the proof of the truth of Hegel's claim that history marches under the banner of the progressive augmentation of the realm of the same. But, as the remainder of the lecture shows, Levinas-Rosenzweig can back out of the Hegelian triumph.

Religion and love

It is not possible, according to Rosenzweig, to avoid the inevitability of philosophy simply by refusing to philosophize and subsisting in spontaneity or asserting one's individuality. The only way one can live outside the tyranny of philosophy is by religion. Here we have a slight semantic irregularity, for what Rosenzweig means by religion turns out to be precisely what Levinas was referring to when he said, in the previous year's intervention, that Judaism was *not* a religion; in other words, religion, for Rosenzweig, means a way of comprehending reality such that the interpersonal is valued above all else. In fact, Rosenzweig, in order not to confuse his conception of religion with a human institution, a form of culture, a collection of beliefs or opinions that run parallel to rational truths, or, for that matter, anything "unctuous, mystical, pious, homiletical, or clerical," avoids the word religion entirely in his great work, *The Star of Redemption*, just as Levinas tried to avoid or deny the word in his intervention (EDM 126/262/187). But Rosenzweig does use the word in other works and letters, and in "Between Two Worlds" Levinas chooses to use it also. Religion, in "Between Two Worlds," then, refers to an ethics that involves no abdication of either action or reason and that "has to do with questions that are put to every man." (EDM 125/260–61/186–87). Religion, understood as service to the other, provides the only adequate way of life after the end of philosophy.

The decision to use the word religion creates difficulties for Levinas. During the question period, Robert Misrahi asks: "why does it have to be religion that takes over at the end of philosophy? Why can there not be some true philosophical and nonreligious life that rises to the challenge?" (EDM 139). Later, a slightly different objection is made by E. Minkowski, who asks, "Does what Rosenzweig calls religion really still merit the name religion? For one word was not spoken, that is faith, and in the end, a religion without faith is nothing but a contestation of fact" (EDM 141). Levinas responds by clarifying his definition, in a way incidentally that may remind us that in 1959 he is in the process of writing *Totality and Infinity*.

> The original concept of religion — the condition for all positive religion — signifies, for [Rosenzweig], the very life where God, Man and World are rejoined, God, Man and World which were affirmed in their irreducible distinction and had ruptured the totality where philosophy had united them. Philosophy has come to an end not because it is arrived at the point where all has been thought and it is necessary to realize this thought; it is finished precisely because it has already

descended into the events of the street, and, since Hegel, humanity knows it. What comes after this end is Kierkegaard and the Kierkegaardians, the protestation against the imprisonment of life in the system or in history. Rosenzweig remains Hegelian on one point. For him, the subjective protestation is powerless against historical necessity. Religion and the religious community represent a mode of being which opens to the individual an existence which is neither his overlapping in a totality nor the vanity of his personal protestation. In this sense, religion is the event which follows the end of philosophy. It is determined in a manner anterior to concepts of belief and faith. (EDM, 148)

Misrahi and Minkowski both define religion in a way that Levinas-Rosenzweig rejects, as belief or faith. Misrahi, like Rosenzweig, rejects this conception of religion, but in favor of philosophy rather than in favor of a different conception of religion. Minkowski, in distinction, embraces the conception of religion as faith and defends it against Rosenzweig's rejection. Levinas's answer reveals some frustration: it is difficult to speak of religion without evoking notions of faith. He defends his use of the word *religion* as opposed to the word *philosophy*, which may suggest either objective conceptions like Hegel's or subjective conceptions like Kierkegaard's. Rosenzweig's religion is neither a participatory exercise (in the sense of an invisible mesh) nor the work of the human being in solitude; rather, it is communal. It is based, both cosmically and socially, on the coming into relation of beings who retain their autonomy.

Misrahi and Minkowski have a point. Levinas-Rosenzweig uses the term religion to disassociate his ethics from what is usually called philosophy, but he might just as well have used the term philosophy to disassociate his ethics from what is usually called religion. As we have seen, Levinas vacillates in his use of the term philosophy. It is partly his assertion in "Between Two Worlds" that at the end of history or philosophy everyone must philosophize which prompts Derrida, turning to Aristotle to push the Hegelian envelope, to say to Levinas that 'not to philosophize is still to philosophize'.[16] In a later essay, "God and Philosophy," Levinas corrects Derrida, saying that, no, not to philosophize is *not* still to philosophize but rather to engage in prophecy (GCM 77). However, at other times Levinas is quite willing to speak of a philosophy that comes after the end of philosophy, a philosophy beyond Hegel, a philosophy that remains broken or that is in question at all times, a philosophy that is equivalent to Levinasian prophecy or Rosenzweigian religion (see RK 33). So Levinas might well have returned here to the usage of the previous year's intervention and called his way of comprehending a philosophy rather than a religion. But while in the previous year's intervention, Levinas *was* interested in disassociating his thought from religion, here he has a special interest in drawing a firm line dividing himself from philosophy, namely, his battle with Hegel. In fact, it might be argued that he draws his very definition of religion on the basis of the demands of this battle. Although Levinas defends the Rosenzweigian conception of cosmic relation not as something new but as the "original" religion or the "condition" for religion, he also suggests, with a twist of time, that this original religion comes about only *after* philosophy, in response to philosophy's having united God, Man and World in a totality. Such twists of time are, of course, characteristic of Levinas. But what is interesting about this particular twist is its slant: religion's status as 'original' is clearly of less interest to Levinas here than is its status as the postphilosophic answer to Hegel. Indeed he goes so far as to say that in a sense "religion is the event that follows the end of philosophy"; echoing the even balder statement made in the body of the lecture that religion "does not precede philosophy, it follows it" (EDM 125/260/186). At the beginning of his response to the roundtable discussion Levinas says that of everything he has presented to them in the name of Rosenzweig, the anti-Hegelianism is dearest to him (EDM 147). It might be truer to say that everything he has presented to them in the name of Rosenzweig is anti-Hegelianism, beginning from the definition of Rosenzweig's religion.

But, once again, this is not anti-Hegelianism in the simple sense of a claim that Hegel was wrong. "Rosenzweig remains Hegelian," says Levinas, "on one point," — only *one* point, but one that happens to be the *central* point of Hegel's philosophy — that "the subjective protestation is powerless against historical necessity." In other words, Rosenzweig accepts the idea that autonomy becomes participation in history, that the part exists only by virtue of its relation to the whole. And it is in fact *because* Rosenzweig accepts the basic Hegelian insight that Levinas-Rosenzweig's definition of Judaism becomes, in effect, *that of which Hegel knows nothing*. The heart of Judaism is now presented as an antidote to Hegelianism, an antidote further clarified as love. The core of "Between Two Worlds" is a summary of *The Star of Redemption*, focusing on the structure of the Star and the love that generates it and holds it in place. We watch Levinas move, with Rosenzweig, out of universalism into religion: from the consciousness of the experience of death, to which philosophy cannot give meaning despite its evident universality, through the experience of a profusion of beings in their essences — divine, human and natural — to arrive finally at the awareness of the relations between beings, relations not of theory but of love, relations that cannot be described but are experienced, relations that have nothing to do with the category of relation but are always particular. And the critical or initial form of relation, for human beings, is the relation with other human beings. The love between man and God is neighbor love, for "the love of God for Man is the fact that Man loves his neighbor" (EDM 129/267/191) and "the response of man to God's love is the love of the neighbor"

(EDM 129/268/192). The Jewish law is love, for only love can command, and love always commands love. But love, though it commands, does not force or bind lovers into a totality; it is an infinite possibility, the possibility of a *me* learning to say *you* to a *him*. All of this is, according to Levinas-Rosenzweig, outside of Hegel's comprehension. Hegel reduces the individual to a movement in the historical system, and a movement in the system is not capable of love. That human beings love is equivalent to their standing outside of the Hegelian framework, and is also equivalent to their Judaism.

The question of love, like the question of the nature of religion, is taken up by Misrahi in the debates. In response to Levinas-Rosenzweig's claim that Judaism is the religion of love, Misrahi argues that Judaism is one of the least loving of religions; on the contrary, it is contractual. In support of this claim, he alludes to several biblical passages on the covenant, and, when prodded by Levinas, who suggests to him that the texts he has chosen are innocuous compared to some he might have chosen, he extends his claim, stating: "I said contract, but I was thinking extortion" (EDM 140, 149). Levinas's response treats the relation between the Bible and the Talmud. "Judaism," he explains, "reads the Bible only through the Talmud." This allows the Jewish reader, he continues, to take in the Bible, not as a diverse collection of stories or sayings, but as an entirety, since "each page of the Talmud thinks the whole of the Bible at once." What the Talmud adds to the Bible is the "spirit" of the stories, which is to say, the ethics that underlies them. And it offers the spirit by means of a hermeneutic that sounds shocking to those trained in modern schools of biblical criticism; in effect, the Talmud takes what does not fit and reinterprets it until it does. "We claim," Levinas says, "that the primary evidence is that the Torah is a law of absolute goodness and justice. Consequently, particular texts must be treated in the light of what is essential and not the inverse. It is the tradition that gives to these obscure [biblical] texts, closed, and often more scandalous than you think, their meaning, and that restores order." Then, having explained the talmudic hermeneutic, he turns to "the problem of love."

> I have been, for my part, very embarrassed by the frequency of this word in my exposition; it falls heavily from the mouth of a Jew because the Jew is not habituated to naming the absolute without reserve, and the prohibition against pronouncing the name of God in all letters expresses to him a congenital delicacy. There is, certainly, in Rosenzweig, a great familiarity with this word, as in the Western Jews who cite the Gospel in an absolutely spontaneous manner.[17] But the Jewish Bible speaks of absolute love when it seems to speak of other things, and this is not only out of reserve. Judaism is true because it doesn't preach in the ether but in the concrete of the real. Recall the book of Jonah — it is a book where there is a question of all other things besides love. But it is a book on the love of the neighbor, and above all on the love one must have for enemies. Jonah refuses the message that must save Ninevah. Why? asks the Talmud. Because Ninevah will destroy Israel and Jonah, the prophet, knows it. The love of enemies that God teaches to Jonah and to us is hard; it is mortally difficult. It is our way to teach it and believe it. (EDM 149)

Thus is Judaism defended as the religion of what Levinas-Rosenzweig calls love, and Levinas speaking on his own would call ethics. And if we recall the previous year's intervention, we are not surprised to find that it is in the Talmud's reading of the Bible, rather than in the Bible itself, that one discovers a conception of Judaism in which it becomes equivalent to love or ethics. The proto-anti-Hegelian thrust which, as we just saw, is the defining core of Levinas-Rosenzweig's religion, is found, first and foremost, in the Talmud, or in other texts read with talmudically trained eyes. Talmudic desacralization is here, for the first time, mobilized as part of the argument against Hegel that drives the lecture as whole, a phenomenon that emerges more strongly in "Messianic Texts."

But we should be slightly wary of this particular example of desacralization. Does the Talmud really reveal that love is the subject and content of the Bible? Perhaps to some extent it does. But surely Levinas's reticence about using the word love is *also* talmudically grounded — and this suggests that to some extent the Talmud does *not* reveal that love is the subject and content of the Bible, that to some extent it is not desacralizing the Bible, or that it continues to contain sacral elements. To the extent that the Talmud is not desacralizing the Bible, Levinas must be understood in his response to Misrahi to be desacralizing the Talmud.[18] And this is a process he has already begun during the lecture proper, for, as we will see, he concludes his argument there by asserting that Judaism — and not merely Rosenzweig's post-Hegelian Judaism but Judaism in general, meaning rabbinic Judaism — is ahistorical and thus anti-Hegelian. He is hotly challenged on the point.

Standing outside of history

Levinas closes the central portion of the lecture by taking up Rosenzweig's description of the interdependent relation of Christianity and Judaism. I will not summarize this now famous conception except to recall what is perhaps its central point, that Christians participate in history while Jews do not. "The Jews," says Levinas-Rosenzweig, "are strangers to the history that has no hold on them. The Jewish community already has Eternity" (EDM 131/270/194). By this understanding, instead of according significance to events on the basis of their placement in the progress of linear history, Jews bring an eternal significance out of each temporal event, a singular significance that is expressed by the pattern of the ritual structure according to which the community lives. The yearly repetition of fasts and feasts is a reenactment of the natural structure of the day — morning, noon, and evening — and also of the three movements of the Star — Creation, Revelation, and Redemption. The cyclical nature of the ritual year operates as a desacralization: it reveals the brokenness of linear history and offers an alternative basis for life and thought. The Jewish ritual year stands apart from history and inaugurates eternity.

The command to resist historical necessity is the idea with which Levinas concludes the lecture. Once he has spoken about Rosenzweig's life, proceeded to a description of some of the key elements of his thought, and then returned to finish the biography by describing Rosenzweig's death, the lecture would appear to be finished. In fact, though, it has not yet reached its culmination. All of the philosophy he has expounded, he now says, was necessary primarily in order to raise the critical question: "does Judaism still exist?" And, here, finally, Levinas begins to discuss Hegel by name. Judaism is threatened today, he says, by a new opponent — not Christianity, or atheism, or philosophical science, but Hegelianism. Hegelianism attacks Judaism's "most ancient claim," the claim to a stand apart from the political history of the world and freely to judge its events without regard to their apparent internal logic. Hegelianism, "the exaltation of the judgment of history as the ultimate jurisdiction of every being, and the affirmation that history is the measure of all things" undermines any claim to eternity in an event or an other, or indeed, in a people like the Jews. According to Hegel, "what is eternal is the universal history itself which inherits the heritage of dead peoples," and thus, for him, "the particularity of a people is equivalent to its finitude" (EDM 135/ 278/199). The reason the Hegelian attack is so strong today, Levinas suggests, is because it is only recently that the extraordinary benefits of modern universalism have become evident. How can Jews stand apart from the contemporary history that has provided us with freedom and comfort? Why would we want to? We are being assimilated — and our erst-while desire to stand apart is being revealed as subjective fantasy. All of us, says Levinas, fall prey to the temptations of modernity. We are preoccupied with finding our place in the meaning and direction of history, or more precisely, "with not finding ourselves opposed to the meaning and direction of history" (EDM 136/278–9/200). But, he insists, to be a Jew, even today, is to resist the temptation to draw the meaning of people and events from a conception of the meaning of history. History threatens the other, and above all the Jews. Thus the Jew has been and must continue to be the pre-server of the idea critical to the continuing existence of human relation, the idea that one must stand outside of his-tory. It is at this point that Levinas describes structuralism or indifferentism as a further degeneration of the modern comprehension.

Most of the comments in the discussion focus on the issue of the meaning of history. There are two main attacks, the first led by Jean Wahl who is, if possible, more antihistoricist than Levinas-Rosenzweig, and the second by M. W. Rabi, who argues in favor of the idea of a meaning of history.

Wahl opens the debate with two interconnected arguments. He begins by referring to Levinas-Rosenzweig's analysis of the Jewish calendar and suggesting that it compromises his ahistorical stance. "That one must stand free from events," says Wahl, "no one is more persuaded than I. That which you condemn, I condemn just as energetically. But in spite of everything, what remains? What remains is what the Chris-tians call sacred history. I would like to say that you erase all of history . . . but, implicitly at least, you reintroduce it — I do not say surreptitiously, but implicitly. Thus in a sense I go much further than you." To this he adds the question of why, given that to stand outside of history ought to be a feature of all existence, Levinas wishes to call it distinctly Jewish? In his view, he says, "there is only truth," thus if it is true that one ought to "say no to history," all human beings should say it. But, Wahl concludes, "I will not therefore say that all human beings should be Jewish" (EDM 138).

Both of Wahl's points are well taken, but the first is more easy to treat than the second. The cyclical calendar is not intended as a new sacred grove, but as a breaking of the Hegelian sacred grove. Neither Levinas nor Rosenzweig understands history to be a process of eternal return any more than a process of gradually augmenting fulfillment. The cyclical calendar is not a plan that replaces a plan, but rather a device for promoting a kind of anamnesis. Somewhat later in the session Arnold Mandel argues, correctly I think, that Rosenzweig and Levinas have not spoken for sacred history (which he calls a "profoundly Catholic" concept), but for something that might be called holiness: "Holiness is precisely not a history in the evolutionary sense of the word. Holiness excludes and dominates history. It has its very real presence at each instant, like a kind of incarnation. So it is presence and much more than history. It is an incessant stream and an eternal presence" (EDM 143). Levinas defends himself similarly in his final remarks: "The rhythm of the Jewish year is the mode of existence that preserves the person against all the glamour of events and of human beings. The person living, really individual and living, living the eternal life according to the terminology of Rosenzweig, places himself in the religious community. Religious community, in distinction to the Hegelian or political totality . . . is for Rosenzweig a promotion of the person and not his invisibility in the system" (EDM 147–48). Certainly, then, Levinas rejects any understanding of sacred history, any understanding by which history, as an entirety, has a purpose or a meaning.[19] Nevertheless Wahl is right to point to the resurrection of sacred history as the danger of adopting a cyclical understanding. Levinas-Rosenzweig uses the symbol of the cycle in an effort to reclaim the broken or diachronous instant brought to me by the other, but it may be that the cycle does not actually offer "a promotion of the person" but rather precisely "his invisibility in the [new] system." It must be said that nowhere outside of his writings on Rosenzweig does Levinas call the Jewish understanding of history cyclical. Moreover, in "Messianic Texts" he suggests, as we will see, that the Hegelian conception of history can itself be seen as presenting an 'infernal cycle'. Thus Wahl's point is well taken, and I believe that Levinas later rethinks the question, perhaps on its basis, and rejects the Rosenzweigian idea that cyclical history breaks linear history.

But Wahl's second critique is more difficult to treat. Arnold Mandel makes an attempt to address it, arguing that it is quite legitimate to say that all human beings should be Jewish. "I believe," he says, "that every kind of conduct that has a pretension to value dignity must in some way proselytize. According to the Jews, in effect, all human beings should be Jewish, in the sense that the term [Jewish] shows the way a human being ought to comport himself. And if a human being comports himself thus, he is called Jewish" (EDM 144). But this is not at all the gist of the response later given by Levinas. On the contrary, Levinas reasserts Rosenzweig's scheme in which it is necessary for Jews to stand outside of history, and equally incumbent on Christians to enter history. To this he adds that "in order to judge history, you do not necessarily have to be Jewish, but it is Judaism — by virtue of its concrete existence — which has perhaps made it possible to be free of history, without necessarily being Jewish oneself. It is perhaps the subsistence of Judaism, in the empirical sense of the term, that still guarantees this freedom. This empirical presence is one of the coordinates of the Western consciousness" (EDM 148). Because the Jews do not

enter history, they make it possible for the Christians to remain free enough of history that they, like the Jews, can stand
in judgment over it.

But this does not entirely solve the problem, which is, in
fact, quite a sticky one. We must begin by acknowledging
the fact that, since we are on Rosenzweig's ground, we are
speaking only about Judaism and Christianity. Rosenzweig
does not approve of Islam and does not here treat the Eastern religions, and thus his theory of religion effectively
divides the religious world — or the world of truth — into two
camps, Judaism and Christianity (the latter of which also
has dealings with those who are more or less outside the
world of truth, the 'pagans'). The question Wahl raises, in
Rosenzweigian terms, is how the distinction between Jew
and Christian is to be mapped onto the distinction between
particular and universal. Of course, no one present at this
Colloquium is likely to propose a Hegelian mapping; no one
will argue that Judaism is a particularity that must be subsumed into the more universal and synthetic Christianity.
But the Rosenzweigian mapping, in which Christianity and
Judaism are two particularities that together offer a universal truth is also attacked. First, Wahl proposes a mapping in
which both Jews and Christians should come to the awareness of the universal necessity of standing *against* Hegel and
saying no to history. Second, Mandel (ostensibly arguing
against Wahl) points out that not only should everyone stand
against history but that this means that everyone should be
Jewish. And third, underneath all of this, is the fact that
Levinas-Rosenzweig has suggested (and this is perhaps
Levinas himself coming to the fore) not only that everyone
should say no to history, but that everyone *does* say no to
history insofar as love or relation persists always outside of
and prior to historical determinism. This debate may shed
some light on why Levinas, in all of the works on Judaism
written after these discussions, does indeed come close to

adopting the Wahl-Mandel position and, indeed, taking it a
step further. Judaism, in the majority of Levinas's works, is
the antithesis of systematization and especially historicism,
and all human beings insofar as they stand outside of avoidable totalities or systems can be said to be enacting Judaism,
or indeed, to be Jews.

But on the occasion of the delivery of "Between Two
Worlds," Levinas is presenting Rosenzweig's ideas and feels
it necessary to defend them. He is on difficult ground. As we
have seen, he speaks of Rosenzweig's 'religion' — referring
both to Judaism and to Christianity — as the conception that
ruptures the totality philosophy has erected of God, World,
and Man. But he has also said that only Judaism stands
entirely outside of history, and implied therefore that only
Judaism offers the ground for a rupture of the specifically
Hegelian totality. If Christianity is unlike Judaism in that it
participates, to a certain extent, in history, how is he to avoid
charging it with Hegelianism? Claude Vigée appears to hold
that such a charge has actually been brought. "With regard
to history," says Vigée, "Christianity, as Rosenzweig has said,
consists of marching towards a being, towards a Parousia
for human beings, a Parousia that has already taken place,
theoretically, through the incarnation of Christ. But we are
not saved. It is a march in the desert. Christianity, you said
and repeated, is proselytizing; it wants to encompass the
world, history, etc. This is the modern conception of history,
which follows directly from Christianity" (EDM 145). Vigée
is arguing for a direct connection between the Christian
conception of providence and the Hegelian conception of
historical necessity as guided by the cunning of reason.
Moreover, he is arguing that the connection is implicit in
Levinas-Rosenzweig's argument. He also holds that Levinas-
Rosenzweig has described Judaism as the one form of understanding that does not commit the error of postulating an
overarching historical or providential scheme. He explains:

"During your exposition you made a digression. You cited a magnificent passage that is ultimately the key to all this: *Vous êtes aujourd'hui dans ce lieu.* This is to say, *we* are today in this place, here. . . . The Jewish conception of time is that the time of manifestation is always now; . . . it is always now and for always now; . . . even as space is always manifested, time manifests being always now. . . . I believe that this is quite right; it is our principle insight. . . . Eternity is in time" (EDM 145). Then, in polar opposition to the thrust of Vigée's intervention, Starobinski argues that both Christianity and Judaism are Hegelian: "This axiality of time and irreversibility of time that has been called something entirely Christian . . . has always seemed to me to be where Christianity held onto Judaism; after all, the revelation of the Decalogue is an event with the same character of decisive apparition after which things are not as before. It seems to be simply that this progressivity, this character of tending towards an end, was what Christianity owed to Jewish messianism. I don't know if I am correct historically, but it seems to me that Hegel and the philosophy of history are less separated from Judaism than was said a while ago" (EDM 146). The problem is thus complicated and recomplicated in the course of the discussion.

Levinas's response does not provide a decisive solution. He agrees with Vigée to an extent — as he must in order to maintain, contra Wahl, that Judaism and Christianity have different roles to play vis-à-vis history — but expresses his agreement by saying little more than: "M. Claude Vigée was right to underline a difference between the Jewish institution of time and the Christian one" (EDM 147). Then, later in the discussion, he makes what may be an attempt to redeem Christianity from the charge of Hegelianism, saying that Christians have their own experiential access to eternity. "Religion is not only Judaism, it is also Christianity. Rosenzweig thinks that Judeo-Christianity is the axis of

the world. . . . [His] analyses (which I could not summarize)
of the manner in which the cycle — the anticipation of
eternity in time — is accomplished through the Jewish and
Christian experience sustain, at least in [his] view, this fundamental character of the eternal life of Judaism and the
eternal path of Christianity" (EDM 148). Thus, in this lecture, Levinas maintains a Rosenzweigian mapping of Judaism and Christianity onto universal and particular. Both
religions are particularities that must be maintained and
that cannot be synthesized.

The main difficulty here with respect to Judaism — laying
aside the matter of the relation of Christianity to Hegelianism — exemplifies the general problem of parts and wholes.
If Levinas agrees with Wahl and Mandel, he is making an
argument that all human beings or the whole of humanity
should take a stance against history, and by dictating to the
all he is erecting a totality. If, on the other hand, he continues to defend Rosenzweig, he is adopting a kind of universal
scheme in which two parts have different roles to play in
history, and thus still dictating to the all and erecting a totality. The impulse to defend Rosenzweig contra Wahl and
Mandel is intensified by the fact that if the whole of humanity
were to stand against history there would be no history to
stand against and Levinas's analysis would lose its meaning.
But this means that his account of Rosenzweig depends on
understanding Judaism as a part rather than a whole — and
yet a part is a part of a whole and therefore, according to his
philosophical comprehension, necessarily an element of a
totality. The move he makes in "Messianic Texts" and subsequent works, perhaps partly in response to the Wahl-Mandel
barrage, is to stop speaking of parts and wholes at all. In
"Messianic Texts," as we shall see, he begins to develop the
concept of the universal-each, as opposed to the universal-
all that is the whole of humanity or the sum of its parts.

It is not until roughly half way through the debate that a

voice is raised on behalf of progressive history. M. W. Rabi is surprised, he says, at the general affirmation that the essence of Judaism is to be outside of history. For a long time, he continues, we were 'objects' of history — or pawns in the historical game — now we are 'subjects' — or players. Without becoming subjects of history we would have had no emancipation from the ghettoes, and we would have no Zionism. The idea that Jews should live outside of history is not only an error, but a version of escapism; it is "the refusal to make choices when confronted with the problems that interest the modern world." Either our debates here "have absolutely no importance" or else we must see ourselves as "one of the currents of history, participate with other collectivities . . . in the gestation of the new world, and risk our lives and our doctrine in the face of the problems that concern it" (EDM 144–45). Rabi may well express the reaction of many people to Levinas's ahistoricist stance. If one says no to history, if one assumes that history is not progressing — or cannot progress — toward better societies or understandings, what is the motivation for acting in the world?

But Levinas is not at all denying action in the world, or the efficacy of such action. He does not stand against the attempt to create a better world, only against the conviction that the world *is* getting better. Attempts at betterment have their place, as long as they are enacted without being understood as elements in the process of history-at-large. He begins his response by speaking of a "misunderstanding." Existence outside of history "does not at all mean, as M. W. Rabi thought, the comfort of neutrality, of a wait-and-see policy, or non-engagement, the ivory tower." Rather, he repeats, it is to refuse to identify events and others by a function defined by history and to retain the capacity to judge them. Existence outside of history does not put an end to action. On the contrary, it is accounts of the meaning of history that, taken to the limit, "would prohibit us from thinking or speaking." Free thought and speech breaks the force of the overarching structure: "to think and to speak is the interruption of the course of history" (EDM 147).

By the end of the discussion it is clear that there are several difficulties that require further address. This may be partly because Levinas's idea that the Talmud desacralizes the Bible, presenting the ethical experience that underlies its images, is not raised until Levinas's response, which comes at the end of the discussion. Several of the participants in the colloquium are unwilling to accept the here-and-now — the eternity — of Levinas-Rosenzweig's Judaism, and want, on the contrary, to preserve more sacralized conceptions: ontological conceptions of religion as faith in a locatable divine, and historical conceptions of Judaism as a part of the progressive scheme of world history. Levinas must show further how it is that the Talmud desacralizes; he must vindicate his definition of Judaism as ahistorical and clarify the nature of its ahistoricism. Only then will he be able to claim that his argument against Hegel and Kojève is a Jewish argument. Bearing on the question is the problem raised by Wahl of whether and to what extent Judaism is a universal or a universally necessary particular, and whether this status is compatible with an anti-Hegelianism. Levinas must resolve or at least shed some light on this problem as well.

Wahl's issue, already much discussed, is raised twice more in the course of the debate. First, Dr. Fouks argues, contra Vigée and also contra Levinas, that the only reason Jews do not participate in world history is because they are rejected by the world-historical community for following God's laws, including the laws that speak of a sacred history or providence that "guides us to the end of the world and to the final community" (EDM 142); Fouks is entirely unwilling to accept a desacralized or desacralizing Judaism. Second, and finally, Mme. Amado Lévy-Valensi attempts a resolution, suggesting that there may be a Jewish "history of fulfillment" — a history apart from history, linked to eternity — which is still not a sacred history in the strictest providential sense. "The history that we challenge," she says, "is the history of fatality, of a material determinism of which the meaning is not tied to human action. But there is a history of fulfillment that is creation, a newness, a Bergsonian time if you will, and that is itself messianism" (EDM 146). The nature of the history of fulfillment or messianic history of which she speaks is not immediately clear. What is clear, however, is that in order to complete the discussion of the Jewish conception of history, Levinas must take up the question of the nature of Jewish messianism. If he can draw from the texts of the Talmud that deal with messianism (and, thus, one would think, with the meaning of history) an ahistorical comprehension, he will have shown most adequately that Judaism, conceived through the Talmud, is a desacralized religion. But to take the texts that seem more than any others to deal with a providential conception, and to show that they are asacral or ahistorical, is not an easy task.

Messianic Texts

In "Messianic Texts" Levinas exegetes a number of talmudic passages in an effort to complete the argument against Hegel and Kojève.[20] Desacralization appears here under two aspects. First, Levinas explains during a digression that he understands the words of the rabbis to have as much to do with our time as with their own; indeed, he makes a joke at Hegel's expense, claiming that the rabbis, having already thought the homogenization of the technological modern state, had, in effect, absolute knowledge. In other words, Levinas holds that the Talmud is intended to be read with reference to the reader's experience rather than as a historical document. This seems innocuous enough, but it becomes important, and perhaps more controversial, when it is understood as the justification for the second aspect of dehistoricization: reading the text's own images and meaning as ahistorical and aontological. This is more problematic. Having been introduced to the concept of desacralization by the examples given in Levinas's first intervention and offered further explanation of it in "Between Two Worlds," we are now ready to consider the question of its legitimacy more closely. Did the rabbis intend to speak ahistorically and aontologically? Who is desacralizing here? The question — at least as far as it concerns the dehistoricizing aspect of desacralization — can be taken up fruitfully through a comparison between two accounts of the ahistorical or antihistorical nature of the rabbinic hermeneutic, Levinas's and Jacob Neusner's.

In a recent article, Neusner has argued that the rabbis understood meaning not in terms of history but in terms of what he calls "paradigms," that is, sets of symbols ordered as narratives. Rabbinic paradigms, according to Neusner, were based originally on historical accounts in the Bible, but in becoming paradigms were denuded of historical status and so became timeless models that could be used to impose order and meaning on subsequent events. The Bible, he contends, is "a set of writings of a one-sidedly historical character," and the rabbis subverted that history when they reinterpreted the Bible "in an utterly ahistorical way." The rabbinic practice of ahistorical reinterpretation, he continues, came about as a result of the destruction of the second Temple in 70 CE. When the first Temple was destroyed (in the sixth century BCE), the event was seen by the Bible as a world historical, one time event, a radical break with the past. But the second time, precisely because it was the second time, destruction appeared as a repetition that could provide a certain continuity with the past. "Paradigm replaced history because what had taken place the first time as unique and unprecedented took place the second time in precisely the same pattern and therefore formed an episode in a series."[21] Moreover, the second destruction threw into question providential notions that had previously been taken for granted. In short, the event shattered any conception of history as leading linearly towards a telos thus suggesting the need for a new ahistorical or nonlinear comprehension, and at the same time provided such a comprehension by becoming the first paradigm, the first example of a repeated set of symbols. Like Levinas, then, Neusner feels that the Bible is dehistoricized in the postdestruction rabbinic writings, especially the Talmud. No doubt Levinas would object to certain parts of Neusner's analysis. For one thing, Levinas suggests that the Bible is not a fundamentally historical document — that it was always intended, as it were, to be read with rabbinic eyes. For another, he might point out that Neusner's account of rabbinic ahistoricism is itself a historicist account, and add the idea that the rabbis were blessed with a genius not determined into existence by the event of the destruction of the Temple. Nevertheless, we can find some support in Neusner's argument for Levinas's idea that the Talmud dehistoricizes the Bible.

But though Neusner and Levinas share an understanding of the rabbis as ahistorical, they mean somewhat different things by it. On the central point they are compatible. Neusner (perhaps overstating the case somewhat) says that "the paradigm obliterates distinctions between past, present and future, between here and now and then and there." By this he means that the paradigms lessen the importance of linear history, allowing the rabbis to allocate significance to events based not on whether they are world historical but on whether they seem to fit and reinforce the paradigm. This is analogous to Levinas's understanding of rabbinic ahistoricism, by which ahistoricism and the dehistoricization of biblical images is an attack on an understanding that regards linear history as the source of the meaning of events. But

Neusner also argues (perhaps with some self-contradiction) that the paradigms that 'obliterated linear history' were often used to predict the course of the future. A paradigm, he writes, is a "model — the past that is present — [that] accounts for how things now are, and also explains what is going to happen in time to come."[22] Here he departs from Levinas, for whom the rabbinic subversion of history implies that they do not — or cannot or must not — speculate about the end of history. "What does the end of history matter?" say Levinas's rabbis with their God. They judge each person and event in the here and now. The difference between Neusner and Levinas is manifest again in their opinions of cyclical thinking. Neusner holds that though cyclical thinking was the great temptation after the destruction of the Temple, Jews could never accept such a comprehension, remaining tied, at least to some extent, to the biblical conviction that history was going somewhere. But according to Levinas-Rosenzweig, Judaism does at least partly adopt a cyclical comprehension in the institution of its ritual year. This adoption supports Levinas's idea that, according to the Talmud, history is not going anywhere, at least nowhere that is within the bounds of legitimate speculation.

To the extent that Levinas and Neusner are in agreement, we can assume that their analysis is correct. The rabbis are focused on present experience at the expense of linear history, and they employ hermeneutical schemes to break the idea of linear history as it appears in the Bible; in other words, they dehistoricize the Bible and to this extent desacralize it. But the question on which Neusner and Levinas disagree remains open. Are the dehistoricized biblical symbols used to predict the future, as Neusner thinks? Or, as Levinas thinks, are the very symbols that appear to treat the end of time being used consciously to express the present? For this will be the basis of Levinas's interpretation of the passages from the end of *Tractate Sanhedrin*: that when the rabbis speak of the end times they are expressing experience in the diachronous here and now. For Levinas, in order to break the back of a theory in which linear history is paramount, it is necessary to destroy entirely the idea of a judgment made by history or a meaning of history — and thus to abandon the idea of an end of history — and this, he holds, is what the rabbis were about. From a historian's point of view, it may be necessary to side at least in part with Neusner. While the rabbis, good phenomenologists that they were, were undoubtedly thinking primarily about the experience of human beings in this world, at least some of them were also speculating with utmost seriousness on the end of the world as we know it and the advent of a new ontological and historical dispensation. Levinas, in distinction, moves his reading of the talmudic texts on messianism gradually but surely always towards its aontological, ahistorical culminating claim: that the messianic era or world is not a location in time or place; that it is here already for those who choose it; that messianism is ethical responsibility; that "the messiah is me; to be me is to be the messiah. . . . everyone is the messiah" (DF 89). The voices in the debate which present the historical and ontological case are heard, but eventually passed by along the way to the concluding claim: there is no historical, ontological messianic era; there is no meaning of history. We may, however, speculate that Levinas's reading is not an attempt to determine the spectrum of views held by the rabbis as historical figures. Indeed, this is where the first aspect of his desacralized hermeneutic becomes critical: Levinas's lecture itself has as its purpose philosophically to challenge our desire to take a historical viewpoint. We will keep this in mind, and return at the end of the chapter to the question of the legitimacy of his hermeneutic, at which point the matter may appear in a clearer light.

I will discuss here only a few passages from "Messianic Texts" from the perspective of its culminating claims: that 'I'

am the messiah and that there is no meaning of history.
These few passages should be enough to show that, as I argued above, Levinas's battle with Hegel is also a battle with
Kojèvian indifferentism, with the utterly open stance of the
egalitarian citizen of the universal and homogeneous state.
For though Levinas delights in the lack of conclusiveness of
the rabbinic give and take, he does not draw from it the idea
that one opinion is as good as another, but shows rather how
an ethically decisive truth emerges from the interplay. A first
glance at the lecture suggests that he begins with a neutral
exegesis, clarifying the poles and positions in the rabbinic
discourse and refusing to take sides, and then moves gradually toward eisegesis, taking sides (or even inventing sides)
as the argument against the Hegelians becomes more and
more explicit. A closer reading, however, reveals his guiding
hand there all the time, breaking open the text in a way that
is profoundly directional, a way that moves always toward
the culminating claims. Levinas's openness is thus not arbitrary but directional, and his rupture of the talmudic text is
a structured rupture. Moreover, the text's closing claims
themselves constitute another structured rupture: the rupture of history and being by ethics. At four points in the lecture he argues or implies that Hegel was right, within the
boundaries of Hegel's own ontological and historical logic. It
is these boundaries, therefore, that must be seen through or
ruptured in the name of ethics. The hermeneutical structured
rupture opens upon a philosophical structured rupture.

The first passage Levinas discusses records a debate between Johanan and Samuel.

> Rabbi Hiyya ben Abba said, in Rabbi Johanan's name: "All
> the prophets prophesied only about the messianic era. As for
> the world to come, no eye has seen apart from you, O Lord,
> what is prepared for the one that waits for you."
>
> There also exists on this point an opposing opinion, that of
> Samuel. Samuel says: "Between this world and the messianic

era there is no difference other than the end of the 'yoke of
the nations' — the end of political violence and oppression."
(DF 60)[23]

I will skip over Johanan's distinction between the messianic
era and the world to come — already a partial refusal to
speculate about an ultimate future or meaning of history —
and move directly to his debate with Samuel about the
nature of the messianic era. Levinas's interpretation of
the debate is straightforward. Johanan sees the messianic
era as the institution in the world of everything good the
prophets prophesied, thus the end of all injustice both 'social' (which Levinas uses here to mean interpersonal) and
political, while Samuel sees the messianic era only as the
end of political injustice. This interpretation lays the ground
for Levinas's comments.

Johanan, he begins, believes that it is possible to have "a
pure and gracious spiritual life" in which difficulty in the
form of need or moral dilemma is done away with. He envis-
ages a life in some way stripped of difference, of struggle and
of drama, a life in which the other will no longer be the different one but a 'companion', and there will be "no more
professions, only arts" (DF 62–63). In effect, Johanan is an
idealist. Moreover, Levinas implicitly links him to Kojève,
who likewise holds it possible for there to be a society with
no radical difference between beings, a society in which there
will be full equality and mutuality; no more conflict, only
free play. Then, in distinction to the Kojèvian Johanan,
Levinas offers up a relatively Levinasian Samuel. Samuel,
according to Levinas, would like to see a world rid of political injustice or inequality but knows that interpersonal
injustice, or inequality between subject and other, must continue to exist because the root of goodness is the gift to the
other. This is not, as Levinas points out, to say that we must
keep the poor poor so as to be able to give them charity. It is

rather to say that difference is the mark of human life, and that the different one, the other, is always worthy of whatever one can give. Unlike Johanan, then, Samuel "knows the permanent effort of renewal which the spiritual life demands" (DF 63). He is the realist to Johanan's idealist;[24] he stands for difference where Johanan stands for commonality.

But despite the fact that Samuel appears Levinasian, Levinas refuses to take his side in the argument, saying instead that the two positions are poles "between which thought oscillates eternally" (DF 64). Why? We can begin by speculating that Levinas wishes to preserve something from both sides of the debate. From Samuel's position he takes, first, the idea that human interaction cannot be made perfect, that it cannot be radically or ontologically transformed in history, and, second, the ground for this idea: that poverty and inequality are the foundations of ethical action, i.e. that ethics is not found in a Johananian commonality but in difference. From Johanan's position he takes the idea — echoing Rabi's defense of 'subjects of history' from the previous year's discussion — that we should nevertheless struggle for a better world, and even perhaps for a world where there is more equality and more commonality. The two poles must be maintained in tension: we should strive (with Johanan and contra Samuel) for commonality while recalling (with Samuel and contra Johanan) that such striving is conditioned by fundamental difference, or, in Levinas's more usual terms, we should make a totality of equality without forgetting that it is ruptured by inequality. But already we run into a problem, namely, that this whole understanding seems already to be expressed by Samuel. Samuel suggests that equality and commonality are the proper modes for politics, while inequality, poverty and asymmetry are the proper modes for interpersonal relation: in other words, he seems to allow for striving towards a third-level equality while preserving rupture on the level of the two. And this is precisely Levinas. We must therefore seek another, deeper answer to the question of why Levinas refuses to take either side in the debate.

I believe what holds him back is that the debate as it stands is not yet situated on the level on which he prefers to think. Johanan seems certainly to be speaking of a historical, ontological messianic era in which everything will be common. Samuel has laid the ground for a dehistoricization and deontologization of the idea of the messianic era by suggesting that the status quo, in which not everything is common, will and should in part remain, and thus that there is to be no complete ontological transformation in history. But Samuel still seems to argue that messianism resides in political commonality rather than in interpersonal difference; in other words, he links human commonality with the human relation to God. And while this is not the utter opposite of Levinas's way of thinking, it is a shift in emphasis, since Levinas, to a very great extent, understands the human relation to God, or messianism, as an aspect of interpersonal difference. The shift means that the messianic era as described by Samuel is in fact close to the self-understanding of the liberal regime, where 'the good' is defined by the fact that everyone is equal politically, and the fact that inequalities persist in the private realm is irrelevant. If I am correct about Levinas's uneasiness with the goals of liberalism — if I am correct to say that, according to Levinas, the political equality imposed by liberalism tends to distract one from interpersonal inequalities — then it becomes amply clear that Levinas cannot quite take Samuel's side, or at any rate not without reservations. In short, if Johanan is a Kojèvian idealist, then so, to some extent, is Samuel: for according to both rabbis the messianic era has to do with a teleological commonality, even if Samuel's teleological commonality is compromised or ruptured and thus more Levinasian.

Thus while Samuel has begun to show the way the Johananian understanding might be dehistoricized and deontologized, he has not gone far enough; he is still speaking of a partial perfection, a partial telos, a partial position of rest or wholeness or harmony. What is missing, even in Samuel's position, is Levinasian rupture, by which not just interpersonal relation but also politics is never allowed to come to rest or to assume it has achieved perfection. That Samuel sees commonality as the good and understands that good to be *partially* achievable by an ontological transformation in history, means that he does not provide an adequate corrective to Johanan, who sees commonality as the good and understands that good to be *entirely* achievable by an ontological transformation in history. A Levinasian messianism would, in effect, be more like Samuel's position than Samuel's itself: it would be uneasy about any imposition of equality, either between two people who would then become 'companions', or between the citizens of a political body; it would hold that such equalities are imposed on the differences in reality (to be sure, often with justice in mind) and thus in a fundamental sense at odds with those differences. It would be a position that, while preserving some of the Johananian revolutionary spirit, holds that there can be no radical wiping away of difference — that is, no ontological transformation in history of either interpersonal relations or politics — and thus that attempts at such ontological, historical transformation are violent, unjust, and grotesque. Levinas is waiting until the text offers a shift in context or level, a shift that will clarify and transform both Johanan's and Samuel's positions.

Now to the analysis of the passage at hand, Levinas adds an analysis of the two comments that follow directly in the Talmud on the one quoted above. Hiyya, speaking again in the name of Johanan, sets out to explain for whom the prophets prophesied, and answers the question with a ranking of human beings. The messianic era, he says, is for repentant sinners, the world to come for those who have never sinned; the messianic era is for those who feed scholars or marry their daughters to scholars, the world to come for the scholars themselves (DF 63). From these passages arise two new issues: whether or not the messianic era is for everyone or only for the righteous, and whether or not its coming depends on merit. Johanan clearly holds that the messianic era is not for everyone and that its coming depends on merit; in short, that certain people are going to press for the end, and that they are the ones who will get it. Samuel (and Levinas draws this not directly from the text but from a rather sweeping extension of the thrust of Samuel's earlier comment) would seem to stand for the position that the messianic era, being political, is for everyone and also for the position that human beings, frail and limited as he understands them to be, cannot bring it about. Again, Levinas seems to remain neutral, and again, his is not the neutrality of utter openness, but has to do with the fact that there is something true in both positions and something that is not quite true or not as yet quite true. He cannot side with Johanan, whose idealist position that there can be a new ontological dispensation for human beings in history is now shading into a position analogous to that of Marxist Hegelians: that it is possible for human beings, or some human beings, to bring about the historical shift and usher in the new dispensation for themselves. But, on the other hand, it now appears even more clearly that Samuel is also postulating a quasi-Kojèvian historicist sacred grove with his idea that the messianic era is for everybody and that it comes objectively in history, regardless of merit. In a later section of "Messianic Texts," Levinas effectively repudiates the position he here applies to Samuel, commenting: "Not everyone enjoys the messianic era. One must be worthy of it, and in this messianism differs from the End of History, in which objective events free everyone who has the good fortune or grace to be present at the final hour of History" (DF 80). So, once again, Levinas cannot quite take either side. Nevertheless, he may now see the truth in both positions even more clearly than before. For, if we stop now and put the whole debate together, we see that already the strands of Levinas's position are assembled.

There are three issues. (1) Is the messianic era an ontological transformation that takes place at the end of history
and reveals the meaning of history in complete equality and
mutuality — or is it a matter of political equality without
interpersonal equality? (2) Is the messianic era only for some
people — or is it for everybody? And (3) can the messianic
era be brought about from below, from inside the human being or the world — or is it imposed from on high or from
outside the human being and the world? The two rabbis have
offered opposing answers to the three questions; each has
apparently made his position clear. But Levinas is going his
own way, or rather, he is going the way the text is going to go
in a moment. As we have seen, he uses the first debate to
suggest a partial answer to the first question. There can be
no ontological transformation of the human being or human
relation in history and thus the messianic era must refer to
something else, something nonontological and nonhistorical.
He preserves Johanan's desire to change the world for the
better and tempers it with Samuel's understanding that the
world cannot be perfected and that inequities must remain;
in other words, he draws from the first debate the idea of
ethical action in a history that is not ultimately going anywhere and does not have an overarching meaning or telos.
Now, if we carry the Levinasian answer to the first question
into a discussion of the second and third questions, the answers given those questions by the two rabbis begin to look
different than they did at first glance. For if the rabbis are
talking about ontological, historical transformation, their
understandings are providential[25] and, as Levinas sees it,
proto-Hegelian: they disagree only insofar as Johanan holds
that the ontological, historical transformation to commonality
or rest or telos is brought about by the few for the few and
Samuel that the transformation is brought about by God for
everyone. But if they are not talking about ontological, historical transformation, but rather about ethical action, then:

(a) Johanan's ranking of individuals is the expression of an ethical truth — some human beings are good and some bad, or some are ethically better than others; (b) Samuel's refusal to rank human beings is also the expression of an ethical truth — somehow, all human beings are on the same footing ethically; (c) Johanan's assertion that the messianic era may be brought from within or by human beings is the expression of an ethical truth — the necessity of ethical effort; and (d) Samuel's assertion that the messianic era must be imposed from without or by God is also the expression of an ethical truth — that human beings do not strive ethically in solitude. In effect, a dehistoricization and deontologization of the discussion reveals that the concept of the messianic era and the arguments about the concept are ways of expressing human ethical experience and of bringing into play the contradictions inherent in that experience.

Now let us watch the text going this way. In the next passage I want to look at Levinas turns back to Sanhedrin 97b,[26] where Rav is representing Johanan's side of the argument, and Samuel appears again in the role of antagonist. Here, at last, Samuel's response is cryptic enough to bear the weight of Levinas's understanding of Jewish messianism. The passage reads,

> Rav said: All the dates of extension have expired, and the matter depends only on repentance and good deeds. And Samuel maintained: It is enough for the mourner to keep his period of mourning. (DF 69)[27]

Of course, the crucial interpretive question is: whom does Samuel mean by "the mourner"? Levinas offers three traditional interpretations, the third of which brings Samuel into concurrence with Rav so that they are standing together for the position that Levinas himself also takes up. The first interpretation says that God is the mourner; that is, God will bring about the messianic era. Here we find the exact opposite of Rav's position that the matter rests on the shoulders of human beings. Levinas says, however, that the insight at the root here is the recognition of the need for something external to make messianism possible. The second interpretation says that the mourner is Israel, who must suffer to bring about the messianic era. This is a little closer to Rav's position, since suffering is fundamentally human, an aspect of the human condition. But, for Levinas, what is important here is still the recognition of the necessity of external force, of movement from without, movement suffered. The third interpretation, that of Maharsha, says that the mourner is Israel who must suffer *and repent*. By this interpretation, Samuel is finally in concurrence with Rav, who also spoke of repentance. But by adding the necessity of suffering, he is seen to be standing for more than Rav, representing a position in which the external and the internal, the 'from without' and the 'from within' are brought together.

Here we find an anticipation of the theme that closes *Otherwise Than Being*, the theme that we discussed in chapter two: that the revelatory relation involves an ambivalence in which the order from beyond appears only in the response from the human being. The inside and the outside are linked. Our actions and natures are at once our own and formed from without. It is almost impossible to distinguish the active from the passive, the autonomous desire from the response to external stimulus, the 'from within' from the 'from without', the subjective from the objective, the repentance from the suffering. Ontological distinction has become blurred; its oppositions are merged and, as a category, it is rendered useless or marginalized. To the three interpretations, Levinas now adds a fourth of his own: the mourner is the messiah. He finds precedent for this idea from the image of the leper-messiah drawn from elsewhere in the Talmud. The leper-messiah, the story goes, tells Rabbi Joshua that he will come "today." Today is traditionally interpreted, following Psalm 95.7 as "today if you will hear my voice."

Today: this effects another blurring, a historical blurring of this world and the next into a single today in which history is rendered useless as a category, or marginalized. *If you will hear my voice*: this adds to the motif of suffering and repentance Levinas's other great motif for the 'from without' and the 'from within', namely hearing and speaking. The command appears as the response; in other words, hearing the divine word appears as speaking the ethical word, and suffering appears as repentance. We now have a full Levinasian understanding of messianism. The messiah is here, "today"; the messianic moment is the moment of the meeting of the 'from without' and the 'from within', the future and the now; and the paradigms for the meeting are suffering and repentance, and hearing and speaking.

Agreement has been reached through a gloss in the interpretive tradition (Maharsha's, with a little help from Levinas) that takes the words of Samuel and uses them to bring forth the nonsacral meaning of the entire debate. The debate has shifted its context or level, to the point where the reason for Levinas's prior hesitations becomes clear. Difference is vindicated over commonality, for difference is the root of potential error, of suffering, of repentance, of hearing and of speaking. But what is more important is that the difference in question is not a matter of an ontological or historical transformation, but of a diachronous meeting 'today', that is, a meeting in which any teleological understanding of time is inexorably broken. Johanan and Samuel no longer appear as Kojèvian idealists; they are revealed to be using the symbol of the messianic era to discuss what human beings should do, and what human beings do do.

Levinas sees the strength of Hegel's philosophical account of reality: philosophical polarities, like historical polarities, *do* merge into syntheses. But what must be remembered is that the truth does not lie in the polarities, historical or philosophical, but outside them. The rupture of which Levinas speaks is different from Hegelian rupture in two respects.

First, it is ultimate; it precludes any coming to rest or fulfillment; and thus it reveals all rests or fulfillments that exist ontologically and historically to be conditional. Second, it is ethical, and it reveals all rests or fulfillments that exist ontologically and historically to be at least unethical, and maybe also antiethical. What Levinas has done so far in "Messianic Texts" is to show us the rabbis showing us this. Through his eyes, we have watched them take up two dialectical oppositions — one historical and one ontological — allow them to merge into two syntheses, and then juxtapose them to something outside history and ontology, something that always ruptures and is thus unassailable and unsynthesizable. This world fades into the next, objective fades into subjective, and up against the new syntheses is the always available diachronous here and now of anarchic ethics, an element that cannot be made to play a role in the Hegelian drama. Johanan/Rav fades into Samuel, Samuel into Johanan/Rav, but what emerges is Johanan, Samuel and Rav all treating the contradictions and difficulties of ethics. This movement — thesis, antithesis, synthesis, and something beyond — is, as I have said, the leitmotif of "Between Two Worlds" as well as "Messianic Texts." In "Between Two Worlds," Levinas gave a first example of the movement when he suggested that Hegel was right, that philosophical contentions coming into conflict in history have indeed led to the universal synthesis characterized as the end of history — and yet that there was an element of human experience outside the synthesis, an element he called religion. So far in "Messianic Texts" we have been offered two further illustrations of this movement.

Two more illustrations emerge in the course of the lecture, and, once again, one is historical and one ontological. Both illustrations take up the question of the 'each' — and so both return to the problem touched on in the first half of this chapter, the problem of parts and wholes and the need to turn away from that problem. The second historical opposition is between the temporally relative and the absolute, that is, between acting for one's own time and acting for all times. It arises in the course of the discussion of the following passage:

> R. Giddal said in Rav's name: Israel, in the future, will enjoy the messianic era. Rav Joseph objected: Isn't that obvious? Who else, then, would enjoy it? Hilek and Bilek? (DF 80)[28]

The commentators are aware of the plain sense of Rav Joseph's words. The phrase 'Hilek and Bilek' generally comes into English as 'any Tom, Dick or Harry', and thus Joseph means that not just anyone will enjoy the messianic era, but only Israel. Nevertheless the commentators also interpret the passage in less nationalistic ways. One of them, Levinas relates, suggests that 'Hilek' and 'Bilek' are the names of the judges of Sodom. Now one would presume the judges of Sodom were righteous men, so why are they excluded from the messianic era? Because, says Levinas, "the judges, even if they are judges of Sodom, in their capacity as judges place their action under the sign of universality. The judges of Sodom are people who are still familiar with political life and the State; and according to the theoreticians of the end of History, people who act under the sign of universality, act just for their era. All politics, through the universality of its designs, is moral and every intention is directed towards the unfolding of history" (DF 81). Levinas is arguing the case as a theoretician of the end of history. Those absolutists who claim to be acting for all of history, such theoreticians say, are actually acting according to what the overarching plan demands for their particular era, and those relativists who claim to be acting for their own era and disregarding history at large cannot by this claim escape the overarching plan. So the two positions, relativism and absolutism, are equivalent, and Hegel is right again. But his triumph is complete only if the distinction, or its synthesis, is held onto as a principle.

To this principle Levinas now opposes a different kind of judgment, one made in immediacy: "Our text would therefore teach us that the simple fact of acting under the sign of universality does not justify entry into the messianic era. . . . Hilek and Bilek, judges of Sodom, are not judged in relation to their historical situation — they are at every moment ready for absolute judgment" (DF 81). Hilek and Bilek wish on the one hand to be judged relative to their historical era, in which case they must be vindicated for being better than the Sodomites, and on the other hand to be judged relative to history as a whole, in which case they must also be vindicated for having condemned Sodom. But actions are not, according to Levinas, judged either by a historically relative standard — which in any case is merely a matter of a division of the 'absolute' plan of history into a series of phases — nor are they judged by the absolute standard of the course of history — which in any case is merely a matter of adding up the results of all historically 'relative' periods. Rather, each action is judged in itself and each human being in herself. Judgment depends on one's relation to the other and the others, not on whether one is better or worse than the others, nor on how one furthers the course of history. The relative/absolute synthesis has been admitted and transcended in the idea of a judgment that comes 'at every moment' from beyond time, or from the meeting of two times, and thus in the idea of a time that is neither the 'my time' or the 'all time' of history, but the 'each time'.

This dynamic — 'one time' is equivalent to 'all time' and opposed to 'each time' — is also what underlies Levinas's claim that 'I' am the messiah. He works his way to the claim gradually in the next few pages of the lecture, taking up a number of the passages that follow in the tractate. In the first, various rabbinic schools put forward their best guesses as to the name of messiah. In each case, the name they offer resembles the name of their teacher, which suggests, says

Levinas, that "the pupil-teacher relationship, which seemingly remains rigorously intellectual, contains all of the riches of a meeting with the messiah" (DF 85). But the names proposed are also words, and the rabbis reference the words to biblical verses, verses that speak of peace, justice, and love. Other passages follow in which other names are proposed; each name carries an ethical significance, and the sequence culminates in a name which implies that the messiah suffers for the suffering of others. Finally, Levinas cites R. Nahum saying: "If he is among the living, it might be me."[29] And Levinas, after exclaiming on the extraordinariness of the statement, explains: "We have just seen that the messiah is the just man who suffers, who has taken on the suffering of others. Who finally takes on the suffering of others if not the being who says '*Moi*'? The fact of not evading the burden imposed by the suffering of others defines ipseity itself" (DF 89). This is the lecture's highest point. Messianism is now most clearly connected to Levinasian responsibility and separated from eschatology, both future and 'realized'. For any eschatology suggests a Meaning of History; any eschatology bespeaks something that is (or will be) finished and done. It is not 'one time', and not 'all times'. Nor is it 'any time', or some arbitrary time. It is always 'this time', only just this time, never before and never again. Or rather, because it is a diachronous 'this time', it is five minutes ago, yesterday; for I am late and must hurry up.

The second ontological opposition is the distinction between ethnic Jews and the other nations, between the particular and the universal understood as 'all peoples'. Robert Gibbs has worked through the problem of particular and universal in Levinas under the rubric of the status of 'Hebrew' and 'Greek' in Levinas's thought. As we saw in chapter one, these are terms that Levinas employs occasionally to distinguish coherent, conceptual speech and thought that tends toward totality ('Greek'), from polysemic dialogical speech and

thought that tends toward relation or ethics ('Hebrew').
'Greek' thought is universalizing; it seeks to absorb and syn-
thesize everything around it into a coherent whole. It reaches
out to the 'Hebrew' in an effort to absorb it — and finds that
at the same time, the 'Hebrew' is reaching out to it. Gibbs
has carefully documented Levinas's understanding that Jews
should translate their 'Hebrew' into 'Greek': "The Talmud
breaks with the particularism of the Bible and universalizes
through reason. Thus the only legitimate reading of the
'Hebrew' of biblical thought is one that seeks a universalized
reading. The best reading of 'Hebrew', therefore, is philosophical — is in 'Greek'!"[30] Judaism wants its concepts to be intelligible to the world at large; its role, as we saw in the first
part of this chapter, is not only to remain distinct from history with its tendency to universality, but also to teach others to remain free enough of history to be able to judge it.
This Jewish outreach occurs, in Rosenzweig's Star, through
Christianity, but Levinas's attempt to translate his 'Hebrew'
into 'Greek' shows that he holds that Jews, or at least some
Jews, can play the role of both the Rosenzweigian Jew and
the Rosenzweigian Christian. How are they then to avoid
becoming part of, or even creating, a universal synthesis?

In fact, the problem of reconciling Judaism and universal
humanity — the problem raised by Jean Wahl, who says in
response to "Between Two Worlds" that he believes there is
only one truth, or 'one world' — should not arise at all for
Levinas. Levinas does not, in general, treat totalizing concepts like universal humanity and universal truth, replacing them instead with ethical ideas that are never universal
but always individual. The Levinas who is bold enough to
call himself an atheist in *Totality and Infinity* is surely bold
enough to tell Jean Wahl that there is no universal truth!
And if he does not, it is in deference to Rosenzweig, for whom
there still remains the idea of a universal truth and in whose
name there must be maintained a delicate balance between

the universal truth and various particularisms. That Levinas encounters the problem of the relation between Judaism and universal humanity at all in the meetings of the Colloquia is perhaps partly due to the fact that he has begun his series of speeches to them with "Between Two Worlds" and is reluctant thereafter to abandon the Rosenzweigian formulations. But towards the end of "Messianic Texts," he does point to a way of allowing this last distinction to be synthesized and then moving beyond it.

Still moving through the passage from *Tractate Sanhedrin*, he arrives at a description of a conversation between Rabbi Abbahu and a Min (a heretic or Christian).[31] The Min comes to the Rabbi and asks when the messiah will come. He answers: 'when darkness covers those people who are with you'. The Min is shocked, and responds: 'You have condemned me!' And Abbahu continues: 'It is but a verse: For behold the darkness shall cover the earth, and gross darkness the people, but the Lord shall shine upon thee, and his glory shall be sent upon thee' (DF 93).[32] The verse cited is Isaiah 60.2, and it is offered in support of what appears to be a strongly particularist condemnation of the Min. But, says Levinas, if one looks at the verse that follows in Isaiah, one sees that Abbahu is not at all speaking from a particularist perspective — or at least that he wishes to allude, for those who can hear, to an entirely different comprehension. For the next verse reads: "And the nations shall come to your light, and kings to the brightness of your rising." Abbahu points with the evocation of the unstated verse to the idea that redemption is available to all the nations. So it is not the gentiles who will be covered in darkness, and Abbahu is not to be understood as a particularist. And yet Abbahu does suggest that the darkness must cover some people — that not all will be redeemed — and thus he is not to be understood as a universalist either, if universal is conceived as referring to all human beings.

Before Levinas offers his final interpretation of Abbahu's words, he describes once again the Hegelian understanding of particularities and universals. First, he suggests that the Hegelian understanding is true.

> What is in fact the march towards the universality of a political order? It consists in confronting multiple beliefs — a multiplicity of coherent discourses — and finding one coherent discourse that embraces them all, which is precisely the universal order. . . . This situation can also be described as the beginning of philosophy. But it is precisely the destiny of Western philosophy and its logic to realize that it is a political condition. . . . The conflicts between men, the opposition of some to others, the opposition of each one to himself, create the sparks of an enlightenment or a reason that dominates and penetrates antagonists. The ultimate truth is set ablaze by all these sparks as the end of History embraces all histories. (DF 94)

Then he suggests that the Hegelian understanding, while true, is grotesque.

> Suppose for a moment that political life appears not as a dialectical adjustment which men make towards one another, but as an infernal cycle of violence and derision; suppose for a moment that the moral ends which politics prides itself on achieving . . . appear steeped in the immorality that claims to sustain them; suppose, in other words, that you have lost the meaning of the political and the consciousness of its grandeur, that the non-sense or non-value of world politics is your first certainty, that you are a people outside peoples . . . capable of diaspora, capable of remaining outside, alone and abandoned: then you have a totally different vision of universality, one no longer subordinated to confrontation. (DF 94)

The course of Western history follows Hegelian lines, and in so doing follows immoral lines, even horrific lines. Hegelian history appears as appalling, and particularly appalling to Jews. However, it still appears as the truth. For this second paragraph, surely one of the most moving in Levinas's *oeuvre*, does not offer anything that stands outside the Hegelian comprehension. From a Hegelian perspective, one could say that Levinas was defining the Jews correctly as a negative force. If the great march of the Hegelian dialectic could incorporate this antithesis once and for all, it would finally reach fulfillment. In short, the position that only the existence of the Jews keep Hegel from being right is itself a Hegelian position, and a position that, at its extreme, gives a perverse justification to the Shoah. Had the Shoah been successful, there would be a good deal less chance that infinity be remembered, that anything would rise up to call the state a totality. For a Hegelian to prove his case, or at least to make sure it will not be disproved, he must only slaughter all the Jews — a sentiment shared by some notable Hegelians.

But, in Levinas's interpretations of Abbahu's words, which follow directly after this paragraph in the text, it is not, in fact, particularly the Jews who stand between Hegelianism and the world. For now we are given the positive counterpoint to Abbahu's conception that the darkness does not fall on the gentiles, that is, we are told where it does fall. The darkness falls, suggests Levinas, on Hegelian dialectics; it falls on the understanding that forces one to pit particular against particular and squeeze them into a universal; it falls "on all those teachings that call you to fallacious confrontations" (DF 94). These teachings will be covered in darkness and reduced to silence. In effect, Levinas figuratively condemns Hegel to hell. But he refers here not to a future event but to something that is always taking place. For when the dialectic is in darkness, the "real light" behind it shines out. And this is the "true universal" that refers neither to everyone nor to a particular group, but to each individual person in her responsibility. The true universal, says Levinas is universal insofar as it "consists in serving the universe. It is called messianism" (DF 95).

Thus, once again, two sides of a dialectic merge. Levinas

is not remotely ironic when he says in "Between Two Worlds" that "the particularity of a people is identical to its finitude," that "Hegelian logic presides over this . . . disappearance" and that this must be so because "the particularity of a thing has significance . . . only in relation to a whole" (EDM 135/278/ 199). Hegel was right; all ethnic or national particularities do march in history toward universal identities. And, once again, if the distinction is held onto as a principle, Hegel has won. But to the particular/universal synthesis is newly opposed a different kind of universal, an unsynthesizable universal. We cannot put our faith in all human beings or in our kind of human being, but must put it, instead, in each human being. With Abbahu's answer to the Min, Levinas provides an answer to Wahl. The rubric of parts and wholes is abandoned, since any argument that stays within its boundaries stays within Hegelian boundaries and emerges in a call for violence. Levinas shows Abbahu turning away from Hegel, toward the other, or more specifically, toward each other.[33]

What, then, about the distinction between 'Greek' and 'Hebrew'? Gibbs defines three senses of the word 'Greek': one in which it stands for "the rule of the universal" in the sense of "the power of a political State," another in which it means "the desire to know in an a-ethical way" and a third in which it refers to the language of rhetoric. In the first two senses, 'Greek' is generally understood to be dubious or compromised; in the third sense, as Gibbs shows in a comprehensive argument, it is necessary and perhaps good. But it is the first two senses that interest us here. This kind of 'Greek' thought, best represented by Hegel, is overcome in "Messianic Texts," not because it loses its battle with 'Hebrew' but because the distinction between 'Greek' and 'Hebrew' — between universal and particular — is transcended. Gibbs points out that at times Levinas asserts that the Jews have something to teach the 'Greek' world that the 'Greek' world cannot find out on its own, while at other times suggesting that each human being has access to whatever truth arises from human ethical experience.[34] Of course, the evidence of "Messianic Texts" tends in the latter direction. Whenever Levinas maintains that the Jews know something, in a fundamental sense, that no other nation has access to except through the Jews, he opens up all the paradoxes of the universal/particular problem, and in doing so walks onto ground ruled by Hegel. Must all 'Hebrew' be translated into 'Greek'? He must answer yes (for the Jews have a duty to teach what they know), and he must answer no (for if all 'Hebrew' is translated, the Jews disappear). May the Jew play the roles of both the Rosenzweigian Jew and the Rosenzweigian Christian? Again, and for the same reasons, he must answer yes and no. If it is true that all particularities march, in history, toward universal syntheses, then the claim that Jews form a distinct polarity is simply a concession to Hegel. Levinas is at his best when he transcends the issue, and deals exclusively with the human individual. Which is not to say there is no place in the world for Judaism. At this point in time and at all previous points in time, Jews do carry and have carried conceptions that are different from and truer than the prevailing historical conceptions. They must continue to do so.[35]

Derrida asks Levinas to choose: is he Greek or Jew?[36] But Levinas is neither. He is not a universalist; he cannot identify his thought exclusively with that of a particular group; and he cannot be accused of arriving at some sort of synthesis of the two. In the roundtable discussion that follows the presentation of the first half of "Messianic Texts," Levinas says:

> That all their teachings remain without conclusion, in the state of pure dynamism, is in effect the characteristic trait of talmudic thought. It is a dialectic certainly. The theses return on themselves. But it is at least a dialectic without a synthesis. . . . The synthesis . . . is an idea of the mixed. In Talmudicism is produced something completely curious: a

> reason that, in the final analysis, is revealed as personal. . . .
> In the talmudic method, the solution is always the solution of
> a person who chooses, each time, in his way. (La Conscience
> juive 2: 289)

The intention of "Messianic Texts" is to show that most of
the distinctions with which we commonly view the world are
dialectical oppositions that seek to merge together into syntheses, or 'ideas of the mixed'. It is useless to search around
within them seeking the precise mix that will enable us to
live good lives. We must search outside them, using a 'personal reason', that is to say, asking the other.

So Levinas breaks open the text in a way that refuses the
finality of a version of Hegelian synthesis. Or, to be more
precise, he refuses to remain in indecision, torn between two
versions of that synthesis, Greekjew and Jewgreek; he refuses
to live in this kind of openness. He ruptures the text, but his
rupture is a structured one, it is a rupture that cannot be
accused of indifference or indifferentism. He never refuses to
make a choice; he does not vindicate debate for debate's sake
or say, after the manner of that great liberals, that opposed
and contradictory positions should nevertheless be preserved
and given hearing. What Levinas understands by 'these and
these are the words of the living God' is that within the opposition between these and these, a rich, complex and decisive truth is to be found. And this truth is itself a structured
rupture — or a "structure which is . . . dis-structure itself"
(GCM 199 n. 15) — the breaking of history and being by an
other meaning. Out of the breaking of text comes truth; out
of the breaking of history comes ethics: as the hermeneutics,
so the philosophy.

And finally it can be said that the question of the legitimacy
of Levinas's reading — of who is doing the desacralizing —
involves one more false distinction, the distinction between

exegetical readings and eisegetical readings. In the round-table discussion that follows the presentation of the first half of "Messianic Texts," Levinas is asked whether human beings can speed up or slow down the course of history. Since he is arguing that there is no "course of history" in the sense of a pattern or plan that could be sped up or slowed down, he is quite distressed by the question. (It must be recalled, in support of the questioner, that Levinas's argument is unclear, given how often he overtly champions the Hegelian understanding before turning away from it.) "The manner in which you pose the question," Levinas responds, "shows that you take these texts — which I have tried above all to transpose — in their strictly theological sense. Thus it is extremely difficult for me to answer. . . . I am very embarrassed by the theological question you pose: can good action speed up history? I think that if you read these texts as texts of pure piety you will perhaps find your problem in them. . . . For me, I wanted to find in these texts a conception of the role of the individual in history" (La Conscience juive 2: 287). With these words he suggests that his method is eisegetical insofar as it depends on coming to the text with certain questions. Later in the discussion, however, he explains that his teacher, Chouchani, has taught him an exacting method of talmudic criticism, one that refuses to settle for platitudinous meanings, but instead assumes that the Sages thought "everything," or at any rate, *could* think "everything" (DF 68). With these words he suggests that his method is not strictly eisegetical, that the meanings he finds are in the text to be found. Both are true. For the distinction between exegetical and eisegetical is merely the 'from without' and the 'from within' applied to text, and like the 'from within' and 'from without', it may be allowed to merge, following the pattern we have traced, and can then be put up against the unsynthesizable hermeneutic, the ethical reading. All exegetical readings, as recent theorists assure us, are in actuality, eisegetical — and the opposite is also true: there is no eisegetical reading that does not refer to a text and is not therefore in some sense exegetical. Levinas's reading stands in opposition to the entire distinction.

For even if one takes what is apparently a strictly exegetical reading, and assumes that rabbis are speaking of a historical and ontological messianic era, the philosophical problems Levinas deals with would remain. He finishes his answer to the question of whether human beings can speed up the course of history with a meditative statement which may provide the best answer to the question of the legitimacy of his readings: "Even if God allowed the course of history to be bent by human beings, it would be necessary that God resolve, for his own account, the problems over which [these rabbis] are opposed. Even if the messiah arrives as in the popular imagination, it would be necessary to unravel these contradictions" (La Conscience juive, 2: 287). Levinas's questions are necessary questions, and his readings may likewise be necessary readings — not for all times or our time, not for history at all, but for us, or, since one can only speak for oneself, for me. We who live in the second half of the twentieth century can hardly deny that history does march under the banner of the progressive augmentation of the realm of the same, whether the same be the fascist state or the universal and homogeneous state. Therefore it is critical for us not to put our faith in a historical plan but instead to remember that all determinations of such a plan are ruptured by a structure of meaning that lies outside and before them, a structure of ethical service to the different one. Otherwise the other is lost and so is the anachronistic Jew, always the victim of world-historical attempts to impose homogeneity on reality. The relation between philosophy and scepticism described at the end of *Otherwise Than Being* is paradigmatic for the relation between history and the Jews. History always has the last word; it always wins against the Jews. But the Jews refuse to admit defeat and return to harass history. And just as the sceptic must deny philosophy's claim to be an unbroken thread, the Jew must deny history's claim to be an unbroken march. It is true that history has never quite succeeded in defeating the Jews, but it has come very close; and this is what makes it possible for Jews to judge history. Ultimately it is for this reason, the reason of the ethical necessity to perform the tasks one can perform, that Levinas's reading of the Talmud is a legitimate Jewish reading. It undercuts the modern agenda, an agenda that is supported by a sacral, literal reading.

But let me conclude by undercutting my argument slightly, as Levinas, I believe, undercuts his. What happened to Johanan's idealism? It was dealt with in the way indicated — his hopes for the next world were dehistoricized, revealed as impulses or actions in this world springing from the ethical moment or the flash of eternity into time. But how well does this particular case of dehistoricizing work? The problem with it is that those who withdraw from history, while they may be able to judge history, also tend to get beaten up by history. At the very end of the lecture, Levinas returns to the polarity between idealism and realism and re-erects it as the polarity between political messianism (equivalent, for him, to Zionism) and messianism proper. There is room for a little political messianism, as there was room for a king in Israel — as long as it is understood that political results are necessarily of limited duration, since the course of world history shifts up and down, in no particular pattern, between its narrow poles of truly horrific and somewhat better. The question for Jews, he notes, is how to remain outside of history while also entering it, how to maintain true messianism while participating in political messianic movements. However we may answer this question, it seems clear that just as there is room in Levinas's understanding for political and historical action, there is also room there for some of the polarities of the common understanding.[37]

FIVE

Night Space

> *Interregnum or end of the Institutions, or as if being itself*
> *had been suspended. Nothing was official anymore. Nothing*
> *was objective. Not the least manifesto on the Rights of Man.*
> *No "leftist intellectual protest"! Absence of any homeland,*
> *eviction from all French soil! Silence of every Church!*
> *Insecurity of all companionship. So these were "the straits"*
> *of the first chapter of Lamentations: "None to comfort her!",*
> *and the complaint of the Yom Kippur ritual: "No high priest*
> *to offer sacrifices, nor any altar on which to place*
> *our holocausts!"*
> — *Levinas*, Proper Names

Having traced certain biblical, kabbalistic and talmudic
themes in Levinas's work, we turn now to the way his themes
arise from or are shaped by reflection on the Holocaust. Such
reflection, I argue, has in large part defined the space in which
Levinas philosophizes; it is not the source of his ideas but
their arena. As the Holocaust ruptured the souls and bodies
of its victims, so reflection on it ruptures any conviction that
there is a plan of the whole, be it historical, ontological,

founded on a conception of the good, or founded on the idea of a present and accessible God. All the totalities of previous philosophy and theology are swept away in a shift so radical that it demands to be described with images of the death of God or of apocalypse. In the wake of this occurrence, a movement toward the other is possible. The movement is not new, but it is demanded now more than ever before. It is the movement Levinas describes in all of his work.

This chapter does not take up in detail the destruction of previous philosophy; instead we focus on the destruction of previous theology. We begin with four stories, briefly told, each of which, in its own way, describes that destruction and the subsequent movement toward the other.[1] From the stories we turn to Levinas's discursive account of the movement in "Useless Suffering," and the first half of the chapter closes with a discussion of that essay's critique of Emil Fackenheim. The second half moves to a more general discussion of the way Levinas's ethics is shaped by the Holocaust.

Nights

Four Stories

1) Elie Wiesel's *Night* was the one of the first literary works to describe the horrors of the Holocaust, and may remain the best description of the crisis of faith in the camps. Wiesel opens the memoir with an account of his childhood in a shtetl in Transylvania, focusing on his faith, which is centered in complete trust in God's presence in history, his providence over history and, as the culmination of this presence and providence, the historical coming of the messiah. Wiesel-the-author sees this faith as childish, but he does not attribute his earnest adoption of it to the fact that he was a child at the start of the war; rather he portrays the entire shtetl as mired in a religious infancy. Convinced that since God is good

historical events must ultimately be just, the Jews pray to be forgiven for whatever sin brought the Nazis upon them, or for a miracle to free them from the ghetto or the roundup or the camp. The most reflective of the men Wiesel meets in Auschwitz are twisting themselves desperately to find a way to maintain their belief in the good God's involvement in the events of the world, claiming for instance that the evil of the camp is a test, and therefore a sign of God's love. For these Jews, faith in the God present in history and presiding over history is the only faith; the alternative is atheism and despair.

Wiesel is from the first uneasy about this alternative and hungry for something deeper. While still living in the shtetl, he takes up the study of the Kabbalah — stumbling fortuitously upon a master of the subject — and this study lends a humanistic thrust to his faith, allowing him a glimpse of the idea that humankind must redeem God and of the kinds of responsibility that this might entail. But the teaching does not stick, and the Kabbalah he encounters later in Auschwitz is not of this nature; the Kabbalist there clings to a faith as providential as that of the shtetl rabbis, murmuring numerological formulas ceaselessly in an effort to determine when Europe will be liberated. On his first night in the camp, Wiesel falls back on the traditional alternative and turns away from the God of history into a kind of atheism, writing of the turn: "Never shall I forget those moments which murdered my God and my soul and turned my dreams to dust." This is the first appearance in *Night* of the image of the dead God, which reappears most effectively in the famous story of the execution of the "sad-eyed angel." A young boy, beloved of all, has participated in an aborted insurrection and is subsequently tortured to reveal the names of his comrades. He is silent, refusing to name names; and he remains silent as he is hung in the square, refusing even to shout out his defiance at the last moment. Wiesel, forced to watching the hanging along

with the entire camp, hears someone behind him ask —
"Where is God? Where is He?" — and voice within Wiesel
answers — "He is hanging here on this gallows."[2] The story
belies its simplicity; it seems to constitute an admission that
Nietzsche's madman was right, both in his central claim that
God has been murdered and in his claim that he is ahead of
his time. God is dead, executed at Auschwitz.

But what does the death of God mean? Wiesel tells us he
has lost his faith, but nevertheless he continues to pray, if
strangely. He argues with God, asking neither the ontological question — where or what he is — nor the historical question — when he will come — but instead reproaching him. In
short, Wiesel experiences, in extraordinary circumstances
and thus in an extreme or twisted way, the phenomenon
Levinas calls contestation. He becomes aware that all the
responsibility lies on human beings. He denies God, but in
denying him, he seems to affirm him if only as the object of
his denial. Wiesel's densest account of contestation occurs in
the description of a Rosh Hashanah service when ten thousand inmates of the camp come together to pray. He inter-
polates his thoughts into a few lines from the liturgy.

> *Blessed be the Name of the Eternal!*
> Why, but why should I bless him? . . . Because He had had
> thousands of children burned in His pits? Because He kept
> six crematories working night and day, on Sundays and feast
> days? Because in His great might He had created Auschwitz,
> Birkenau, Buna, and so many factories of death? How could I
> say to Him: "Blessed art Thou, Eternal Master of the Uni-
> verse, Who chose us from among the races to be tortured day
> and night, to see our fathers, our mothers, our brothers, end
> in the crematory?"
>
> *All the earth and the Universe are God's!*
> And I, mystic that I had been, I thought: "Yes, man is very
> strong, greater than God. When You were deceived by Adam
> and Eve, You drove them out of Paradise. When Noah's

generation displeased You, You brought down the flood. . . .
But these men here, whom You have betrayed . . . what do
they do? They pray before You! They praise your name!"

All creation bears witness to the Greatness of God!

Once, New Year's Day had dominated my life. I knew that
my sins grieved the Eternal; I implored his forgiveness. Once,
I had believed profoundly that upon one solitary deed of mine,
one solitary prayer, depended the salvation of the world.

This day I had ceased to pray. I was no longer capable of
lamentation. On the contrary, I felt very strong. I was the
accuser, God the accused. My eyes were open and I was alone —
terribly alone in a world without God and without man.
Without love or mercy. I had ceased to be anything but ashes,
yet I felt myself to be stronger than the Almighty, to whom
my life had been tied for so long.[3]

Though he says he has refused to pray, Wiesel offers, in
effect, a new three-part prayer. First he refuses to bless the
God of history, the God who supposedly caused these events
to come to pass. Second, he discovers a new strength, but
can use it only to manufacture disgust for those who continue to worship this God. Finally he turns, in his new
strength, toward God and becomes his accuser. The prayer
makes it clear that what Wiesel means by saying that God is
dead is that a particular God — the present and providential
God, awaited by the camp theologians and the camp Kabbalist — is dead, or rather, that he can now see that this God
never was. In becoming the judge of history, he has become
the judge of the God of history. He is not a part of a grand
scheme but outside, alone, autonomous, counting on no one
and nothing; he is without totalities. But, having lost his
faith in the present God, he may nevertheless affirm an
absent God, a God who is met in contestation.

In the third and last tier of his prayer, Wiesel shifts grammatically from a second person address to the third person.
We are reminded of Levinas's description of the ancient

Hebrew blessing, which begins in the second person ('Blessed art Thou') and shifts to the third person ('He who creates all things', or etc.). Between the two forms of address sits the Tetragrammaton, which in this position, according to Levinas, encompasses God's presence and his absence, or functions as the gate from awareness of his presence to awareness of his absence (BTV 122). The one who moves from second person to third person in his prayer acknowledges a God who does not show himself, but whose absence is the absolute holiness which resonates in human relation (EI 106). Wiesel closes his account of the Rosh Hashanah service as follows: "I ran off to look for my father. . . . He was standing near the wall, bowed down, his shoulders sagging as though beneath a heavy burden. I went up to him, took his hand and kissed it. A tear fell upon it. Whose was that tear? Mine? His?"[4] The young man who is stronger than God turns toward his father. To continue to love the one he loves, to stay with his father in danger — these things are at the limit of Wiesel's strength, and, as it is perhaps the main purpose of *Night* to show, they are sufficient. Wiesel has turned away from the faith of his boyhood toward the other, away from structures that explain by imposing meaning on events toward ethical relation. In this turn, he lays the ground for a different understanding of God and a different understanding of faith: an 'adult' God and an 'adult' faith.

But the adult faith is — and here I understate — not nice and not easy. During the course of Wiesel's narrative several sons desert their fathers, allowing the fathers to die alone; in one episode a son steals a crust of bread from his father, a crust that the father has procured at great pains only to feed to his son. Wiesel, by great courage, does not degenerate this far, but he cannot save his father's life and he cannot even prevent himself from having the thought, at times, that he would be better off if his father were dead. Indeed, at certain points in the story, the utmost Wiesel can do to retain his humanity is to feel shame at the thought of deserting his father. The emptiness and fruitlessness of this kind of turn to the other — its pathos — is all that emerges from the Holocaust for Wiesel. Such pathos is also what drives Levinas in his own reflection on the Holocaust. Levinas's adult faith is the antithesis of resignation; on the contrary it is active — but the action that constitutes it is a passive action. In a word, adult faith is a 'passion', understood as a suffering or an undergoing. It is experienced as the passive actions of anger and love. It is not a matter of hope or of edification.

2) In "Loving the Torah more than God" Levinas speaks of a story called "Yossel, son of Yossel Rakover from Tarnopol, speaks to God."[5] It is set in the final hours of the Warsaw Ghetto rebellion, and relates the thoughts of a man whose family has been killed and who will soon be dead himself. Levinas does not retell the story, but instead offers an interpretation. He begins by saying that the most common response to the Holocaust is to claim that there is no God, and that this is also the sanest response, at least for those who had believed in the kind of God who "dished out prizes, inflicted punishments or pardoned sins" (DF 143). But it is not Yossel's response. Yossel sees, in a single moment, that there is no help, no intervention, no providence, no ultimate justice, and no promise of an afterlife; standing alone, he realizes that he must bear all the responsibility. But he arrives in this moment not at a denial of God, but at the idea that "the path that leads to the one God must be walked in part without God" (DF 143). This is the moment, writes Levinas, when "the adult's God is revealed precisely through the void of the children's heaven. This is the moment when God retires from the world and hides His face" (DF 143).

In this moment, Yossel sees himself as free; he is under no obligation; he is the hero of his own story. And therefore, he can love God freely, and at the same time — as an aspect of the same movement — can reproach God, calling him to show his hidden face. And because Yossel has come to this point, he does not love only God. The story ends with Yossel saying: "I love him, but I love even more his Torah" (DF 144). Above all he loves the Torah, that is to say, the words that express the ethical law. *The words*: for speech is the way relation is expressed, the way that autonomy and intimacy, presence and absence, are maintained together. *The ethical law*: for true relation is ethics. Yossel, alone, has no opportunity to turn to the other, but, according to Levinas, he shows us that this is the meaning of Judaism and its book. Words, ethics, Torah — these are the meaning of God, the expression or mode of the one who remains hidden. To love the Torah more than God is to love this God.

Both Wiesel and Yossel begin with faith in a God present in history; both must confront an ungodly manifestation of that history; both face this manifestation with lament and anger; both abandon all conceptions of providence, discovering themselves alone and strong; both turn, in the strength of their anger, towards a hidden God, different in nature from the present God they have rejected; both accuse the hidden God or contest with Him; and, finally, both turn to something else, Wiesel to his father and Yossel to the Torah. In *Night*, it is clear that this final turning is all that may be expected from a human being; this is how one's humanity is to be claimed and retained in extreme circumstances. In "Yossel speaks to God" it is clear that not only is this turn sufficient, it is itself the path to the hidden God, who, in his own person, can only be approached by means of reproach.

Again, though, this adult faith or path to God is an atrocious one. Yossel's shift can be described glibly as a turn from dogmatism to humanism: Levinas explains Yossel's adult faith as arising from "the internal evidence of morality supplied by the Torah" (DF 144). But what gives the shift its meaning are the circumstances under which it takes place, and the fact that they are paradigmatic for the circumstances of Jewish faith. According to Yossel, God has always attempted to discourage the Jews' love by heaping miseries upon them, but the Jews in turn have always refused to stop loving God — and thus their very love exists as reproach. "To be a Jew," says Yossel, "means . . . to swim eternally against the filthy criminal tide of man," to be aware that this swimming accomplishes practically nothing, to be, therefore, "the most unhappy people on earth," but also, and finally, to be "happy [to be] unhappy" (DF 144). Levinas ends his interpretation with the following description of Yossel's adult faith: "This is a long way from a warm and almost tangible communion with the Divine and from the desperate pride of the atheist. It is a completely austere humanism linked to a difficult adoration! . . . A personal and unique God is not something revealed like an image in a dark room! The text I have just commented on shows how ethics and principles install a personal relationship worthy of the name. Loving the Torah more than God means precisely having access to a personal God against Whom one may rebel — that is to say, for Whom one may die" (DF 145). Yossel's awareness of the futility of counting on God is matched by an awareness of the futility of human action in the world — is the same awareness. His rebellion against God is not made in the name of a humanity without God, but is precisely a rebellion against the human condition. But this rebellion means also that God, and humanity, are worth dying for. It is the simultaneity of anger and love, reproach and adoration, which constitutes Yossel's turn.

3) In "Beyond Memory" (ITN 79–91), Levinas speaks of Vasily Grossman's *Life and Fate*, a novel about the victory of Stalingrad. Grossman was at one time a good Bolshevik, which is to say that he adopted a faith comparable in its naiveté to the one held by Wiesel as a child, believing, as

Levinas has it, with 'hope' as well as 'faith', that in October of 1917, "he had entered into the times of eschatological events" (ITN 88). By the time of the writing of *Life and Fate*, however, he has changed his mind, and that work portrays the circumstances of the battle of Stalingrad blended and thus compared with an account of other Nazi atrocities. Like *Night* and "Yossel Speaks to God," *Life and Fate* describes the triumph of horror: "an uninhabitable world in the abyss of its dehumanization. The breakdown of the very basis of European civilization. A . . . world of people who have been degraded, stricken in their dignity, delivered to humiliation, suffering, death" (ITN 88–89).

Perhaps surprisingly, Levinas does find a kind of eschaton in the wake of this shattered world. The war as Grossman describes it appears, to Levinas if not to Grossman, as the war of Gog and Magog, and the dehumanization of the world of the war heralds an apocalypse that brings an end to "the theologies of a past, shaken to the point of atheism" (ITN 90). The remnant that emerges from this apocalypse is not, however, a group of human beings fit to enjoy a millennium of freedom and peace, but a particular kind of human activity, namely, simple kindness stripped bare of the trappings it wears as part of 'the good'. The description of kindness is not offered as 'part of the story' but as something outside the linear course of historical events; it is given in words spoken not by Grossman's narrator but by a minor character, one who has been able to watch events pass by because he is 'feeble-minded' as well as 'inspired'. Levinas closes his essay with a long selection of the words of this feeble-minded sage, of which I will cite an abbreviated version.

> Last year, on September 15, I saw 20,000 Jews — women, children and old people — executed. On that day I understood that God would not have allowed such a thing. It seemed obvious to me that God did not exist. . . . When violence is carried out, calamity reigns and blood flows. I was there for

the great suffering of the peasants . . . and yet the goal of the collectives was good. . . .

What did [the Christian] doctrine of peace and love bring to humanity? The tortures of the Inquisition, the struggle against heresies in France, Italy and Germany, the war between Protestants and Catholics. . . .

I have been able to see in action the implacable force of the idea of social good born in our country. I saw it again in 1937; I saw that in the name of an idea of the good as humane as that of Christianity, people were exterminated. I saw entire villages starving; in Siberia I saw the children of deported peasants dying in the snow. . . .

There exists, side by side with this so terrible greater good, human kindness in everyday life. It is the kindness of an old lady who gives a piece of bread to the convict along the roadside. It is the kindness of a soldier who holds his canteen out to a wounded enemy. The kindness of youth taking pity on old age, the kindness of a peasant who hides an old Jew in his barn. It is the kindness of those prison guards who risk their own freedom to smuggle the letters of prisoners out to wives and mothers. That private goodness of an individual for another individual is a goodness without witness, . . . without ideology, . . . without thought. (ITN 90–91)

Again the childhood theologies give way to an adult understanding. Again, the new understanding begins from the idea that 'God does not exist', and is therefore able to answer what Levinas calls, in "Loving the Torah more than God," "the legitimate demands of atheism" (DF 143). And again it is constituted by the turn to the other. But here, in addition, we find a new motif. To rid religion of the notion of providence is a move radical enough to be referred to as an apocalypse. What is gone is not merely the conviction that God is involved in history or that all will come out right in the end, but all overarching ideas of what is good, theological, or secular. The idea of the good is a totality, a monism, an attempt to make plurals singular; thus Grossman's feeble-minded sage can express it using generalizations like "the goal of the collectives," or "Christianity." Kindness, which replaces the idea of the good after the apocalypse, is and must be in the plural; the sage's kindnesses are described one by one, not classified or defined but only told. In this way kindnesses emerge as the many ways of an ethics of diversity or plurality, the infinity to the good's totality. And like the Levinasian infinite in all its manifestations, they show three aspects. They are prior to the good, as a primary human impulse. They give rise to the good — as in the case of Christ's doctrines, which began in kindnesses and yet had to speak of a good and thus "weaken the power" of kindnesses (ITN 91). And they follow the good and break it, allowing Grossman's sage to say: "I do not believe in the good, I believe in kindness" (ITN 91). Kindnesses precede, condition, and rupture the good.

4) The image of the apocalypse and the kindness that is its remnant is found again in "Wholly Otherwise," where Levinas relates his own experience of the retreat of 1940:

> A retreating military unit arrives in an as yet unsuspecting locality, where the cafés are open, where the ladies visit the "ladies fashion store," where the hairdressers dress hair and bakers bake; where viscounts meet other viscounts and tell each other stories of viscounts, and where, an hour later, everything is deconstructed and devastated: houses closed up or left with their doors open, emptied of their occupants who are swept along in a current of cars and pedestrians, through roads restored to their "former glory" as roads when, in an immemorial past, they were traced by great migrations. In these in-between days, a symbolic episode: somewhere in between Paris and Alençon, a half-drunk barber used to invite soldiers who were passing on the road to come in and have a free shave in his shop; the "lads" (*"les petits gars"*) he used to call them in a patriotic language which soared above the waters or floated up from the chaos. With his two companions he

shaved them free of charge — and it was today. The essential procrastination — the future *différance* — was reabsorbed into the present. Time came to its end with the end of the interim period in France. (WO 4)

Here is an apocalypse. The "immemorial past" is here "today," as is the future or "essential procrastination." The beginning and end are now; the world and time are at an end. And this fourth and final story adds to the image of apocalypse an image of the messiah. The barber who stands outside his door also stands outside history, watching it pass by. His gesture, magnificent for its magnanimity despite or because of its simplicity, says, with Levinas or to Levinas, that the messiah is here, that there is no further coming, that one does what one can for the other. The barber's language "soared above the waters" of history just as the "one-for-the-other of responsibility . . . 'float[s] above the waters' of ontology in its irreducible diachrony" (OB 167).

The today of the barber is surely any day. The Levinasian apocalypse — the shift from providential theologies to ethical relation, forced by extreme circumstances — is not once and for all, but takes place in various places at various times; it may indeed take place in many places frequently, or perhaps even everywhere all of the time. Still, it is particularly linked, in Levinas's writings, to the horrific events of the twentieth century — to the experience of men like Wiesel in Auschwitz, of Yossel in Warsaw, of Grossman in Stalingrad, and of Levinas in France. And it is linked especially to the event which, for Levinas, is paradigmatic for all historical horrors, the Holocaust. In another essay — "Useless Suffering," where Levinas reflects more deeply on the Holocaust — it becomes clearer how that event has made this apocalypse more possible or more likely now than ever in the recent past.

Useless Suffering

Levinas begins "Useless Suffering" with a complex phenomenology of pain or suffering in which it appears as the enemy of all peace, indeed, as utter negation. In Levinas's analysis, suffering is not something one does, but something done to one. Moreover, it is not an experience, or a characteristic or an affectivity, for although it is done to one all the time it cannot be fitted easily into our understanding of what it means to be a human being or a particular human being. It is a sensation-destroying sensation; in other words, it is both a sensation that stops us from thinking — a negative of a positive — and the sensation of the stoppage — a positive of a negative. Suffering, pain, *mal*: these are "contradiction by way of sensation" (PL 157), but the contradiction is not a strict one, for both sides are negative. Suffering, then, is utter negation, "pure undergoing," a passive that has no corresponding active. It is the referent of all evil, and it offers a 'not' that is more negative than the apophatic 'not', for there is nothing beyond it; "the *not* of evil is negative right up to non-sense" (PL 157). Suffering destroys meaning and *is* the destruction of meaning. It is utterly without purpose, entirely useless.

But, Levinas continues, human beings cannot bear these truths. They attempt always to find purpose in suffering, to impose meaning on it. Some suffering can easily be given meaning as a means to an end — as in the case of hard work that produces an effect or a product, or the case where bodily pain is understood as a warning sign leading one to seek treatment. Then there are more abstract justifications, where suffering appears as necessary to the life of the mind properly lived, or as producing moderation in the otherwise wayward soul, or as a force necessary to the health and continuing dynamism of society or political life. Levinas understands there to be a certain kind of truth in all this, for all these rationalizations are taken up in the spirit of good will. But he does not believe that they go to the heart of the matter. As he has it, all these 'rationally' inflicted or 'rationally' tolerated pains somehow 'rejoin' the pains that are inflicted unjustly and the pains that are given in nature (PL 160). There is something in every pain deeper than considerations of justice and injustice, voluntary and involuntary, means and ends; at bottom, it is all of a piece, all malignant, negative and useless. So it is that human beings have been forced to come up with a greater justification, an absolute rationalization: a theory of providence in its aspect as theodicy. We make pain bearable by totalizing it within the idea that God has a "plan of the whole" (PL 160), a plan in which each pain or the totality of all pain has purpose.

Levinas does not analyze the theodicies of various traditions or periods in any detail; he merely sketches their basic characteristics. They tend to attribute evil to human fallibility or finitude; the fulfillment of the plan of the whole generally involves atonement or compensation or both; the whys and wherefores of the plan are, as a rule, understood to be invisible in nature and history — in effect, theodicies subordinate pain to a metaphysical ultimate "in one way or another" (PL 160). Levinas contends that the idea of theodicy has dominated Western thought since biblical times; it held and still holds empire over our thinking. It has survived the Enlightenment in the form of a theory of progress, in which the plan is no longer hidden to nature and history but revealed in them, and in this form has made its way into the canon of Western secular thought as the source of the moral norms — the ideals or utopias — of triumphalist progressivism. Whether explicit, as in the premodern world, or implicit, as in the modern world, it was and remains the foundational idea of our theology and philosophy.

At this point in "Useless Suffering," Levinas turns to a description of the movement we have been looking at. We saw in the four stories that the suffering at Auschwitz could be called an apocalypse or a deicide; in "Useless Suffering" Levinas reminds us of this asking, in the manner of Wiesel: "did not the word of Nietzsche on the death of God take on, in the extermination camps, the signification of a quasi-empirical fact?" and explaining further that Auschwitz reveals with "a glaring, obvious clarity" the inadequacy of any idea of a plan of the whole (PL 162). In short, Levinas claims that after Auschwitz it is possible for us to rid ourselves of the idea that has dominated and defined our thinking for centuries. Moreover, it is in "Useless Suffering" that he makes his clearest statement about what remains after this apocalypse. He begins by explaining that the double negative that is suffering-as-a-phenomenon can also be described as a complete passivity: the sensation of suffering is suffered and the destruction of sensation in suffering is also suffered. Thus the one suffering has no foundation for activity and there is nothing there except a reaching out. In other words, because suffering is suffered, because it is not something the subject does or an aspect of the subject, assumed into the subject, there appears in suffering a space for the other. The "evil of suffering [is] extreme passivity, impotence, abandonment and solitude [but] also the unassumable and thus the possibility of a half opening, and, more precisely, the possibility that wherever a moan, a cry, a groan or a sigh happen there is the original call for aid, for curative help, for help from the other ego whose alterity, whose exteriority promises salvation" (PL 158). While the other's suffering is useless, it calls out to me, and my compassion, my pity, my charity toward the other in suffering is not useless. Suffering for suffering carries meaning; intrinsically meaningless, suffering takes on meaning in the interhuman sphere. The central content of the essay, then, is a call to suffer over the other's suffering. Levinas calls this call "the supreme ethical principle — the only one which it is not possible to contest" (PL 159).

The supreme ethical principle takes over the role played in previous theology by one of a number of layers of meaning beyond ethics and reinscribes those layers into the ethical; it is relation beyond relation as opposed to providence beyond relation. It is also true messianism as opposed to false. For the error of providence is also the error of historical and ontological messianism. These ideas are violent in two ways or on two levels: first, insofar as they ignore the other except as a function of a plan of the whole, promoting complacency with suffering, allowing us passively to close our eyes to the other's pain and do nothing when we should be doing everything; and second, in cases where they allow us actively to subjugate the other to the needs of the plan, where they lend support "to a dialectic of progress that requires war, violence, and economic depression," a dialectic in which suffering is not merely legitimized but required by "a teleological drama."[6] The way to avoid both kinds of violence — complacency with suffering and the dangerous 'alliance of God with the self'[7] which calls for suffering to be inflicted — is to understand God to be hidden or absent, to be a reality which, in itself, can only be contested, but which appears also in the incontestable form of a trace in the face of the other. Once the present God is abandoned, in its wake arises the acknowledgment of evil and suffering for what they are, and consequently, pity for the suffering other; in its wake, as well, arises messianic expectation understood as a spiritual orientation and the recognition that this orientation is equivalent to an ethical order. Our four stories attest to these truths when they suggest that the hidden God is God, and that he is expressed with a messianic gesture that turns from the ashes of historical and ontological expectation to compassion, or more specifically, to the father, to the Torah, to kindnesses, or to the world as it passes before one's door. This is the messianism of the rabbis described in "Messianic Texts," a messianism that counts on nothing, that says that the messiah is here, today; that I am the messiah. It is the messianism that comes when one 'soars above' or stands outside of the course of world history, or that consists of standing outside of world history.

But in all likelihood one does not choose to stand outside of history. One stands there because — like Wiesel, Yossel, Grossman's sage, or the barber — one has been thrust there: either pushed out or simply left behind. Perhaps only in this position, once one has been forced to acknowledge that there is no meaning *of* history, can one discover a meaning *in* history. For there is indeed meaning *in* history for Levinas, in two senses. First in a simple sense: because all human events take place on a literal level in time, history is a forum where meaning appears; in other words, the ethical relation — as the diachrony of time — takes place in history. Second in a more complex sense: because different societies and epochs have different characteristics, a particular society or epoch may be more or less open to ethics or diachrony; in other words, the history of political, social, and economic changes can be understood as the story of the rise and fall of structures that encourage or discourage human encounters with the divine trace. In the first sense, meaning can be had in any age or any society. In the second sense, our age and our society are, according to Levinas, poised on the edge of an unprecedented realization of meaning. Having lived, as a society, through the apocalypse described in the literary accounts above, we have together been stripped of the imperial grip of theodicy and made fit as never before to realize the supreme ethical principle, to suffer for the other's suffering.

This is what Levinas means when he refers to Auschwitz, and the destruction of theodicy it initiates, as an event in sacred history (PL 161). He does not mean that Auschwitz reveals a plan of the whole, or that our new fittedness to realize the supreme principle is a sign of any continuing progress; he speaks rather of a sacred history "without rhetoric or theology," without the illusion that history has led us inevitably to our elevated state or that we will necessarily retain it and improve it — indeed, this sacred history is even without the certainty that we will take up the new ethical possibilities in the first place.[8] The destruction of the Good at Auschwitz is an event in sacred history insofar as it creates a space for ethics — and, as I maintain, a space for Levinas's philosophy of ethical rupture. The idea is crystallized into a few lines in an interview: "I want to say that this business of Auschwitz did not interrupt the history of holiness. God did not reply, but he has taught that love of the other person, without reciprocity, is a perfection in itself" (RM 21). The event in sacred history, the apocalypse of the Holocaust, does not 'interrupt the history of holiness'; it does not usher in anything radically new. Judaism has always, according to Levinas, been a 'religion of adults'. And yet, through the Holocaust, God has taught again, and perhaps taught better, that suffering for the suffering of the other is the supreme ethical principle. Levinas speaks in "Useless Suffering" of "a still uncertain and blinking modernity" which "at the end of a century of nameless sufferings" is now capable of the "elevated thought" in which suffering can take on meaning in the interhuman perspective (PL 159). This elevated thought is not exclusive to the late twentieth century, but it is nevertheless our call and thus the mark of our age.

Towards the end of "Useless Suffering" Levinas turns to the topic of how Jews, in particular, should live in the wake of the Holocaust, and, as a framework, to the treatment of this question in Emil Fackenheim's *God's Presence in History*. But the discussion that follows is somewhat confusing for anyone who knows Fackenheim's book well. Levinas cites an extended passage in which Fackenheim argues for the uniqueness of the Holocaust, saying that it differs from other genocides not only because it is evil for the sake of evil rather than for the sake of acquisition, but also because the Jews died not on account of their faith but on account of the faith of their great-grandparents.[9] But he does not cite

Fackenheim's subsequent argument: that because they did not choose to die for their faith, because often they did not even die for a faith they had chosen, and because even those who had chosen Judaism were stripped, before their deaths, of their faith along with their humanity — that because of all this, those who died cannot be understood as martyrs. Instead, he proceeds, in his own voice, to call the victims martyrs and to contend moreover that "the final act of [the Nazi] destruction is accomplished today in the posthumous denial of the very fact of martyrdom by the would-be 'revisers of history'" (PL 163).

A brief examination of the relevant themes in Fackenheim's book will help us to understand the nature of the critique here. The burden of *God's Presence in History* is to describe the crisis in providential faith. Fackenheim argues, like Levinas after him, that none of the theodicies of biblical and midrashic Judaism is equal to the Holocaust. It cannot be accounted for as punishment for sin because children and other innocents were murdered. It cannot be accounted for with the midrashic rubric of martyrdom because of the reasons stated above. It cannot be explained as a lesson to the gentiles since its existence in history renders a second Holocaust not less likely but more. It cannot be accounted for with the biblical rubric of a test since in the biblical accounts of such tests — in the stories of Abraham, Jeremiah and Job — a restoration follows unlike anything that happened in the camps. And finally, it cannot be accounted for with the idea of the absence of God for a theory of absence relies on the hope that God will reappear when he is needed, and yet at Auschwitz he did not appear.[10] This series of repudiations leads Fackenheim to an impasse. On the one hand, the fact that none of these theodicies is adequate suggests the conclusion that there is no good God, and leads therefore to the abandonment of Judaism. On the other hand, to abandon Judaism is to give Hitler a "posthumous victory,"[11] and for this reason, if for no other, the conclusions that there is no God or that Jews should stop being Jews are the most unacceptable of possible conclusions.

When Fackenheim retreats from the edge of his impasse, it is to return to the God of Judaism, and thus, necessarily as he sees it, to the God of history and providence. He does not conceive of Judaism as a religion of difference or brokenness; he does not make use of any conception like that of the Levinasian face or the God who appears only in the relation with the other. On the contrary, he seeks God always in the overarching structure or the plan of the whole. The origins and foundations of Judaism, he contends, are found in 'root experiences', which he explains, quoting Martin Buber, as moments in which the "laws of nature" and the "laws of history" become "transparent, and permit a glimpse of the sphere in which a whole power, not restricted by any other, is at work."[12] And though he speaks in this description of root experiences of the "laws of nature" as well as the "laws of history," when he speaks in his own voice rather than Buber's, it is the laws of history, not the laws of nature, which reveal the "whole power" of God, or God's plan of the whole. Moreover, according to Fackenheim, all religions and philosophies are based on a plan of the whole; other conceptions depart from that of Judaism only insofar as they discover or situate the plan elsewhere than in history. Much of *God's Presence in History* consists of a list of the rubrics that thinkers have used to replace the God of history and an account of what is wrong with each one; what is interesting here is not, however, the argument between these rubrics and Fackenheim's, but the fact that all of them are versions of the plan of the whole. Fackenheim explains that one may turn away from the God of history "to eternity above history, to nature below it, . . . to an individualistic inwardness divorced from it," to the positivism of Laplace, to the messianism of the Marxists, or to the humanism of Nietzsche.[13] But the turn to the other does not arise. At the end of the book, having repudiated the alternatives just mentioned and also Jewish theodicies listed above, he presents part of a new plan of the whole, a renewed Jewish providential framework in which the Holocaust itself becomes a revelation, comparable to the Exodus and Sinai.

At certain points, Fackenheim comes close to expressing a Levinasian understanding. In one passage, he suggests that God-talk that is adequate to the human condition cannot take place within philosophy but only within midrash. Philosophical reflection would destroy the root experience by focusing on its contradictions: the involved God in contradiction with evil; the involved God in contradiction with human freedom; and the involved God in contradiction with the transcendent God. In distinction, midrash, which is "fragmentary," and which expresses rather than explains, can hold these things together in tension without attempting to reconcile them logically; as Levinas would say, it can preserve an enigma without having it become a dilemma. But, according to Fackenheim, traditional Jewish midrash also insists that these tensions will one day be resolved, and in this sense it is not only fragmentary but at the same time whole. Thus while Fackenheim appears here to acknowledge the idea of rupture or enigma, he cannot rid himself of the conviction that all rupture must one day give way to the wholeness guaranteed by the existence of the plan, and all enigma to the ultimate answers the plan will offer. Again he comes close to Levinas when he says that in the Bible, God is not an explanatory concept. Rather than presenting God as what explains or does not explain, he argues, the Bible presents God as revealed and concealed.[14] But, the upshot of this discussion is only that Fackenheim's God does not function as an etiology, a projection, or a stopgap. For although he is not an explanation, he nevertheless has an explanation, which he will eventually make manifest to human beings in a messianic era. Fackenheim's critical ire is directed not at

those who say there is a plan of the whole, but at those —
like Laplace, Marx and Nietzsche — who think they can grasp
the plan prematurely.

Let us return now to "Useless Suffering." Levinas's charge
against Fackenheim is on the one hand radical and, on the
other hand, unexplicit to the point of obscurity. That it is
radical is obvious: Fackenheim denies the victims the name
of martyrs; Levinas says that those who deny the victims
the name of martyrs finish Hitler's work posthumously.
Moreover, Levinas makes his claim not only in a discussion
of Fackenheim, but in a discussion of the very argument
Fackenheim uses to support his denial of martyrdom, and
thus he makes it quite clear that he is not merely mistaking
Fackenheim's meaning but consciously criticizing it. However, the radical nature of the critique is mitigated by the
fact that it is not stated explicitly. Since Levinas makes use,
for the purpose of the critique, of something very close to a
phrase Fackenheim himself is famous for coining — 'posthumous victories' — it must sound to a reader only partly
familiar with *God's Presence in History* as if Levinas's accusation is being made in Fackenheim's name against others.
The radical nature of the critique shows that something
in Fackenheim's book, or perhaps a number of things, have
offended Levinas gravely. Its implicit or covert nature suggests that Levinas respects Fackenheim's experience, and
perhaps some of his ideas.

What is behind the critique? I see three ways in which
Levinas may be offended or distressed by Fackenheim's book.
First, I believe that Levinas may be put off by Fackenheim's
extended discussion of the question of martyrdom, in which
he rejects its usefulness as a midrashic theodicy piece by
piece.[15] He begins by noting that unlike in previous cases of
martyrdom, the Nazis did not offer their victims the choice
of conversion, and suggests that there can be no martyrdom
without choice. He then presents the argument that there

may still be found among the victims "a faithfulness resembling" martyrdom, but casts doubt here as well, since the Nazis made every effort to destroy souls before bodies and thus to force their victims into faithless deaths. Finally, he notes that the Nazis did not always succeed in destroying faith — some victims died in the gas chambers with the shema on their lips — and in this context he begins tentatively to use the word martyr again. His general point is merely that a theodicy of martyrdom is not sufficient to reconcile the deaths of the victims with the existence of the good God, a point with which Levinas would certainly agree. But the point is developed through what might appear to Levinas an excessive interest in the grizzly details of how the killing was carried out and in what state of mind or soul the victims died. To make distinctions between those who died piously and those who did not, and to accord the name martyr to one group and not the other — this may seem to Levinas an unworthy way to think. The existence of ethical behaviour in the camps, documented for instance by Wiesel in *Night*, is evidence of God's trace, and in any case the awareness of the infinite in the individual human heart is not something that can be disclosed, defined, or designated. God is not present in a particular set of historical circumstances and absent in others; he is always absent, and always present in the trace of his absence. But if it is saying too much to say that Levinas finds Fackenheim's discussion unworthy, it is certainly legitimate to say that it must seem to him to be missing the point, that is, misunderstanding the meaning of the word martyr. For Levinas, the word is connected to the supreme ethical principle; to accord the term is not to designate a certain state of mind or status, but to suffer for the other's suffering.

The second issue at stake in the critique is Fackenheim's impasse: that he finds theodicy unacceptable and also the rejection of theodicy unacceptable, that he both repudiates

theodicy and reassumes it. I believe that Levinas sees the
two sides of the impasse together in Fackenheim's denial of
martyrdom. Immediately after Levinas speaks of that denial as the "the final act of . . . destruction," he adds: "this
[denial] would be pain in its undiluted malignancy, suffering for nothing" (PL 163). This is to say that the denial of
martyrdom shows, in part, that Fackenheim, like Levinas,
rejects theodicy in the awareness of the uselessness of
suffering. But, for Levinas, it is from this position that the
shift to adult faith is accomplished; it is from this position
that one moves to the other, to the supreme ethical principle,
to suffering for the other's suffering. And Fackenheim's
denial of martyrdom means not only that he has reached
this position, but also that he is unable to recognize this
movement, or unwilling to make it. In short, the denial signifies both that he knows something true — that there can be
no theodicy — and that he does not know something true —
that beyond theodicy is the supreme principle. Levinas's
critique is covert out of respect for Fackenheim's arrival at
the impasse. It is radical because Fackenheim falls away
from the impasse, choosing the wrong side of the dialectic.

Were Fackenheim to remain torn between the two sides of
his impasse — theodicy and the critique of theodicy — he
would perhaps be on the verge of the discovery of the supreme principle. The critique of theodicy would harass
theodicy continually; like scepticism harassing philosophy it
would tear down any version of completeness or providence
Fackenheim presented to it; in the end he would surely be
forced to abandon the impasse, choosing the sceptical, harassing apocalyptic side, and, in its light or in its darkness,
would be left with nothing grand but only the turn to the
other. And the impasse *could* be preserved as a tension for a
time and expressed in the style of Fackenheim's fragmentary midrash, if he were to argue that the Holocaust was
both a sign that God was not present in history and also a

sign that he was, both a destruction of structures and also a structure, and that the God above the Holocaust was both silent and also revealed. But Fackenheim does not keep revelation and silence together in tension and nor does he opt in favor of silence; instead he discards silence and verbalizes the assignation conveyed by the 'Commanding Voice of Auschwitz', which orders the Jew to remain a Jew. It is at this moment — the moment when it becomes clear that "according to [Fackenheim], Auschwitz would paradoxically entail a revelation of the very God who was nevertheless silent at Auschwitz" (PL 163) — that he falls away from the potentially fertile position of the impasse toward the wrong side. Fackenheim is simply too profoundly attached to the plan of the whole.

The third and most important element in Fackenheim that has perhaps offended Levinas, is the nature of the assignation conveyed by the 'Commanding Voice of Auschwitz'.[16] Fackenheim argues that Auschwitz, or rather God-through-Auschwitz, reveals what he calls the 614th Commandment, namely, that the Jew must not abandon Judaism and thus give Hitler a 'posthumous victory', or in short, that the Jew must remain a Jew. If the Holocaust also brings a command to the Gentiles, it is only that they must allow the Jews to remain Jews. Levinas cites this idea, but then adds a reflection of his own, one that critically undercuts Fackenheim's idea. "This final reflection of the Toronto philosopher, formulated in terms which render it relative to the destiny of the Jewish people, can be given a universal signification. From Sarajevo to Cambodia, humanity has witnessed a host of cruelties in the course of a century when Europe, in its 'human sciences', seemed to reach the end of its subject, the humanity which, during all these horrors, breathed — already or still — the fumes of the crematory ovens of the 'final solution' where theodicy appeared impossible" (PL 164). All of humanity, not just the Jewish part, has experienced horrors that are perhaps unprecedented. Therefore, as Levinas goes on to say, all human beings should be "pledged" to the supreme ethical principle and to a faith without theodicy. This is a far cry from Fackenheim's point both in the sense (on which we have focused above) that Fackenheim does not, ultimately, think that anyone should be pledged to a faith without theodicy, and in the sense (on which we will focus now) that the lesson Fackenheim draws from the Holocaust is strongly particularist and cannot be universalized.

We have seen that Levinas tends to use the word 'Judaism' to represent characteristics common to humanity that appear paradigmatically in Jews. This is especially the case with respect to what might be called the negative aspect of Judaism: antisemitism, for Levinas, is quintessential hatred, the hatred not of gentile for Jew but of one — any one — for the other: it "is not simply the hatred felt by a majority towards a minority, nor just a xenophobia or some form of racism, even if it is the ultimate reason for these phenomena which are derived from it. For antisemitism is the repugnance felt toward the unknown of the other's psyche, the mystery of his interiority, or, beyond any conglomeration into a whole or organization into an organism, the pure proximity of the other man — in other words, social living itself" (BTV 190). Judaism stands, in Levinas's thought, for a certain way of being in which other peoples can also engage; it is common to Jews perhaps because they are, by nature or by circumstance, quintessentially involved in what he here calls "social living itself"; Jews are social beings. The way of being is best expressed, I think, by Yossel, when he says that to be Jewish is to be happy to be unhappy. It is to understand and accept that history or reality is mainly a matter of misery and injustice and to be happy with this history or reality; and it is to do this without becoming resigned, but instead continuing to swim against the tide of misery and injustice. This comprehension — by which one's love of God is equivalent to one's reproach of God, and is also equivalent to one's love of one's fellows, and also to one's suffering for their suffering — this is Levinas's Judaism. It is profoundly nonexclusive; it expresses the experience of all who suffer, all who undergo passion. And to hate the Jew is, for Levinas, to hate this way of being, to fight it in an attempt to grasp a happiness more certain than the Jewish happiness to be unhappy.

The third element of Levinas's critique of Fackenheim is thus connected to the second element. Fackenheim's struggle with the question of universal and particular which ends with the assertion that the Holocaust brings a message exclusively for Jews reveals, once again, his attachment to the God of history or the plan of the whole, and his own desire for a happiness more certain than that of Levinas's Judaism. Fackenheim is thinking in ontological or overarching terms: he is thinking of humanity as a whole divided into groups rather than as a collection of alterities; he is thinking of the 'all' and the 'Jew' rather than the 'each', and he is thinking in this way in order to facilitate the postulation of a plan in which, to speak bluntly, people like Fackenheim are looked after. For what is behind the fact that Fackenheim both reasserts providence and insists on the continued exclusive survival of the Jews? What stops him from moving into adult faith? In part, it is probably simply the understandable desire to live in the awareness of a God who will put things right; certainly this is what is suggested by Levinas's analysis of theodicy as having as its sole purpose making life's suffering bearable. But there is also an anger here — an anger that is not, like Wiesel's and Yossel's directed at God, and not, more surprisingly, directed at the Nazis — an anger that is directed at the rest of the world, at non-Jews. It emerges most clearly, perhaps, in his unwillingness to offer, ethically, more than he receives; he finds "totally unacceptable" the idea that "because of Auschwitz the justification of Jewish existence depends on Jews behaving like superhuman saints toward all other peoples ever after";[17] here, the overstatement betrays his anger. And he falls back into theodicy and into an insistence on exclusivity in order to provide an ontological philosophical framework for what is essentially an ideological statement: Jews for the Jews.

With this in mind, we can return to the first element of the critique. Fackenheim returns at the end of his account of martyrdom to the idea that some of the Nazis victims, those who died with the shema on their lips, might be called martyrs. But he begins the account by saying that the victims, in general, cannot be called martyrs. Clearly, he does not think that most of the Nazi victims died with the shema on their lips. How, then, does he see the Nazi victims? As liberal, enlightened Jews like himself. Without doing Fackenheim too much injustice, I think it is possible to suggest that his book is not actually an attempt to deal philosophically with the Holocaust at all, but an attempt to deal ideologically with the contemporary question of Judaism and liberal assimilation. The morally bankrupt use of the Holocaust by flag-waving Jewish ideologues is described in some detail by Jacob Neusner in his book *Stranger at Home*. Levinas's critique of Fackenheim's discussion of martyrdom in which it becomes clear that Fackenheim's concern is the loss of Jewish identity rather than the loss of life, his critique of Fackenheim's historicism in which it becomes clear that Fackenheim is erecting a grand historical scheme in which Auschwitz becomes a buttress for historical ontology rather than its end, and his critique of Fackenheim's exclusivism in which it becomes clear that for Fackenheim that historical ontology has as its sole function to ensure continued Jewish existence — all of these critiques may suggest that, as Levinas sees it, Fackenheim is engaged in an endeavor that could be classified as the same kind of flag waving criticized by Neusner.

Levinas's most radical critique of Fackenheim may appear

in a passage in which he does not seem to be addressing him at all. He comments that there are only two philosophical positions open in light of the experience of the Holocaust: "to abandon the world to useless suffering ... or ... in a faith more difficult than ever, in a faith without theodicy, [to] continue Sacred History, a history which now demands even more of the resources of the self in each one, and appeals to its suffering inspired by the suffering of the other person, to its compassion which is a nonuseless suffering (or love), which is no longer suffering for nothing and which straight-away has a meaning" (PL 164). If one clings to theodicy, one "abandon[s] the world to useless suffering." Fackenheim clings to theodicy and thus, we are forced to assume, Fackenheim abandons the world to useless suffering.[18]

If my contention that the Holocaust defines the space in which Levinas philosophizes is correct, then the lack of movement toward the supreme principle in Fackenheim is of great personal concern to Levinas. The point of "Useless Suffering" is that modern society as a whole is now ready to understand the supreme principle because of the events in which we have been involved. But Fackenheim, who was incarcerated in a labor camp for a short period before the war and thus is more closely involved with these events than most of us, is quite evidently not ready. Moreover, his attitude is indicative of the general trend. Jewish theological treatments of the Holocaust have tended either to defend providence or to give up on or repudiate the entire Jewish tradition.[19] This range of treatments — described perfectly by the categories of Fackenheim's argument — represents a threat to Levinas. For in light of this range, what is the status of Levinas's claim that human beings are more than ever ready to understand the supreme ethical principle? And — and this is the critical question — if we are not ready to understand the supreme principle, have we ears to hear any of Levinas's prophecy at all? The critique of Fackenheim is not only an argument for

Levinas's understanding of the Holocaust, it is a plea for a hearing of his entire philosophy.[20]

The space of his ethics

Levinas's ideas do not arise directly from his experience of the Holocaust. His philosophy, as he often explains, is first and foremost the stuff of life lived, confirmed in encounter and desire — and some of these erotic encounters are relations with old books, books of philosophy, and, as I have tried to show, the sources of Judaism. Nevertheless, the track he lays down in "Useless Suffering" — from reflection on the Holocaust with its rupture of certainties, to the supreme ethical principle — functions, in part, as an intellectual autobiography. For though his ideas occur in his reading, it is the Holocaust that makes him read — and if it does not tell him what and how to read, at least it gives him some guidance in what and how not to read.

At one point in "Useless Suffering" Levinas suggests that the notion of providential theology "is in a certain sense implicit in the Old Testament, where the drama of the Diaspora reflects the sins of Israel," a teaching he compares to the Christian doctrine of original sin (PL 161).[21] However, in another essay, "Jewish Thought Today," he claims that Jews who abandon providential theology in the wake of the Holocaust do not, in fact, abandon their own texts, but the texts of Christian Europe.

> The fact that the monstrosity of Hitlerism could be produced in an evangelized Europe shook within the Jewish mind the plausibility which Christian metaphysics could have for a Jew used to a long acquaintance with Christianity. This plausibility involved *the primacy of supernatural salvation with regard to justice on earth.* Has not this primacy made at least possible a great deal of confusion on earth, and this extreme

> limit of human dereliction? The famous incomprehension to-
> wards supernatural salvation shown by supposedly worldly
> Jews . . . appeared abruptly not as an example of pigheaded-
> ness but as a moment of supreme lucidity, and the Jews
> began to believe that their stiff necks were the most meta-
> physical part of their anatomy. (DF 161)

Jews turn away from Christian texts with their explicit providence — and presumably also from the texts of secular
modernity that express an implicit version of that providence — back to their own books. But do they not find there a
comparable theory of providence? To answer the charge it is
only necessary to see that, in "Useless Suffering," just before
saying that providential theology is 'in a certain sense
implicit' in the Bible, Levinas says that theodicy is as old as "*a
certain reading* of the Bible" (PL 161, my emphasis). He thus
slips in the suggestion that the entire Old Testament might
be read without any conception of theodicy or providence
appearing there. Such a reading, if one were to attempt it,
would certainly have to be performed using the Talmud as a
screen or interpretive code; it would be a sustained example
of the kind of desacralized reading we discussed in the last
chapter. This is the kind of reading he means when he speaks,
in "Jewish Thought Today," of studies that "aim to return to
the rabbinic texts, which offer a true illumination of the
Bible, the law and the prophets" (DF 161).[22] For Levinas, the
Holocaust not only sends the Jew back to the text but takes
him there armed with a rabbinic hermeneutic and a new
motivation to apply it.

This is something Levinas knows from experience. For
what Jews find when they return to their old books, according to Levinas in "Jewish Thought Today," is ethics — by
which he means *my ethics* that *I* found when *I* turned back
after the Holocaust to these texts. It is an ethics particularly
fit to deal with the crisis of our time: an ethics given by a
God who provides no source for static certainty in the worldly

sphere, nor any conclusions about the ultimately good ends to which political evil is turned; an ethics of diversity that stands against the rigid claims and commonalities of ideologies; an ethics discovered by means of an ethical hermeneutics — itself discovered — in which ideas acquire and maintain authority by movement and not by rest. This way of thinking is *there* in the old books, and is at the same time is arrived at *because of*, or *for*, the Holocaust. The double source is possible because Levinas's readings of the Jewish sources are neither exegeses nor eisegeses but relations, because his interpretations are speakings that follow listenings, which is to say, responses. They exist in the space between Levinas and the text, a space that is defined neither by Levinas, nor by the text. The space exists because Levinas is reading, and Levinas is reading because of the Holocaust; the space is therefore predicated on the Holocaust, and its borders are, at least in part, defined by the Holocaust.

Insofar as his philosophical space is defined by the Holocaust, he reaches out not only to the past, but also to the future. His thought, he says, in a much-quoted line, is "dominated by the presentiment and memory of the Nazi horror" (DF 291). Presentiment *and* memory. Already in itself the statement plays with time — perhaps conflating two times into one, perhaps splitting one time into two — but one must see the statement as it is originally placed to understand its impact and its import. The essay "Signature" — which is presented as a short intellectual autobiography — begins with a staccato catalog, one paragraph in length, of the events of Levinas's philosophical life. The verbs in this first paragraph are almost all in particle form, that is to say, the paragraph contains no complete sentence until its closing sentence — "This disparate inventory is a biography" — a sentence that has as its function only to close. The sentence, "It is dominated by the presentiment and the memory of the Nazi horror," forms on its own the second paragraph, and is thus only the second complete sentence in the essay. Its succinctness and clarity, in stark contrast to the drone that precedes it, makes it striking. And so does its solitude. Its context is a noncontext; it is not explained; it is not referred to in the list that precedes it and has barely an echo in the extended account that follows. Why does it not appear in its place in the catalog or the later account? Because the Holocaust has no time of its own in Levinas's thought, no once-present; it is out of time; it does not 'appear'. However, its absence — its pastness and futureness — occurs throughout the essay, as it does throughout the life and the work. The image or dynamic here is the opposite of the messianic barber. For Levinas watching the barber, yesterday and tomorrow fade into today; for Levinas in "Signature," the today of the Holocaust fades into yesterday and tomorrow. And yet the two images mean the same thing: that yesterday and tomorrow are orientations in the soul today; that the past and the future are products of a broken now. In "Signature," Levinas takes the now of the barber's apocalypse and uses it to orient himself to what was and what will be, to listen and speak to the dead and to those he has not yet met, that is, to us; the space of the relation that is defined by the Holocaust is the space of a relation with this past and this future.

Levinas's Judaism — and Levinas's philosophy — are thus not merely speech about nonuseless suffering, or about the for-the-other; they *are* a nonuseless suffering and a for-the-other; they are acts of compassion. They honor the martyred dead, and they offer words to those yet to come, words of warning and also of welcome. The Holocaust sends Levinas to the texts of tradition — to the past — but the tradition is one in which rethinking and reshaping — the renewal demanded by the future — is at all times a possibility. And the possibility of rethinking and reshaping, even unrealized — indeed, the antithesis of the realized — may be sufficient. In its plurality and plasticity, his Judaism and his philosophy may be adequate to the task of addressing a people who has suffered at the hands of a totalitarian movement.

Let us now look at the way some of the peculiarities of the ethics arising in Levinas's relation to old texts are driven and bordered by the Holocaust. The defining characteristic of Levinas's ethics is asymmetry. This has two aspects: *the differential of identity*, that is, the realization that the other is unlike me rather than like me, and, following from it, *the differential of responsibility*, that is, the realization that the other is higher than me so that my duties to him increase infinitely. I want to take up the relation of these aspects to the experience of the Holocaust at some length.

Let us begin by approaching the question of the differential of identity from the other side, asking: what kind of ethics might arise in the wake of the Holocaust, an ethics of commonality or an ethics of difference? We can begin by acknowledging the basic truth Plato expresses when he has the Stranger explain in the *Sophist* that everything has within it, as well as being, motion and rest, *same and different* (255c–e), and once again when he has Socrates suggest to Callicles in the *Gorgias* that if the two of them had nothing in common they could not speak to one another and if they had everything in common there would be no point in speaking to one another (481c–482c): that is, that human beings are in part the same and in part unique. I believe that Levinas understands this, and that his emphasis of difference over commonality takes into account the fact that we are not utterly strange to one another in *all* respects, though we are *all* utterly strange to one another in *some* respects. He bases his ethics primarily on difference simply because an ethics of difference is more demanding. But the matter comes into better focus if the question of difference or commonality is rephrased, in light of the fact that we are all same and different, in a more sophisticated form; namely, should I believe that what concerns me concerns the other, or that what concerns the other concerns me? The first idea — that what concerns me concerns the other — expresses the basic truth of likeness or commonality but carries little authority and may be overlooked in a case where violence is deemed necessary; it may occur, for example, in the fellow feeling that arises at times between soldiers fighting for opposing armies, or in the empathy of the executioner for the executed. The second idea — that what concerns the other concerns me — expresses the basic truth of unlikeness or difference and carries complete authority; it is the shock of alterity, an invitation to discovery, and a command that may not be overlooked. Certainly, both were missing at Auschwitz. The Nazis were often almost without a sense that the Jews were like them, part of the common brotherhood of humanity; they attempted to dehumanize their victims until no feeling of brotherhood could grow up between them and their executioners. But the very fact that this was attempted, perhaps in part successfully, is reason to turn in the wake of the Holocaust to the command that cannot be refused, to the conviction that what concerns the other concerns me, that I am the other's keeper; in short, to the for-the-other of responsibility. Brotherhood or fellow feeling is not a sufficient definition of what was missing, or of what is now necessary.

To conceive of difference as the basis of our ethics — and indeed as the basis of our humanity — is necessary after the Holocaust for another reason as well. Levinas's main charge against Buber is that he overemphasizes commonality. This may or may not be true of Buber's thought generally, but it does seem to emerge in his attitude toward Adolph Eichmann.[23] Because Buber emphasizes what is common to the point where it becomes the mark of one's humanity and because he has nothing in common with Eichmann, he comes close to refusing him the status of human being. It seems to me that what is wrong with this is not so much that it is ungenerous to Eichmann, but that, taken to its logical limit, it means that Eichmann cannot be tried in a human court. In order to put the Nazi on trial and condemn him, we must recognize that he is not a different species or an inexorably evil alien, but one of us. Because of the necessity of war trials, then, the Holocaust calls us to find a way of conceiving human beings that includes the Nazis. Not that it must understand them; indeed it must not even attempt it, both because the Nazis thought they could understood the plan of the whole and the human role in it, and also because, with Buber, we find it impossible to understand the Nazis. On the contrary, it must surely have as one of its premises that none of us can ever explain or understand another; it must be founded on difference. Only it must not exclude the Nazis from the ranks of human beings, and therefore, if it is not to account for their behaviour, it must in some way be accountable for it.

So much for the differential of identity. We move on to the differential of responsibility, the idea that the other is higher than me and that my responsibilities to him increase infinitely. The limit case of this phenomenon is expressed in the several passages in which Levinas says that I must be responsible for my persecutor and my persecutions, that "the nonindifference of responsibility . . . is responsibility for the very outrage that the other, who qua other excludes me, inflicts on me, for the persecution with which, before any intention, he persecutes me" (OB 166). How are we to explain this?

Let us first try out the explanation offered by Bernhard Waldenfels.[24] Waldenfels argues that Levinas is speaking in the passages that treat responsibility for the persecutor in same way as Socrates speaks in book 2 of the *Republic*. Socrates, we recall, begins book 2 willing to defend ethics[25] as something that is both good in itself and also good in its consequences, but this does not satisfy his young interlocutors, who insist not only that he defend ethics as something good in itself regardless of consequences, but that he reverse the consequences, attributing to the ethical man all the material circumstances that might be thought to accrue to immorality; in short, they demand that he prove that ethics is good in a case where the ethical man is friendless, abjectly poor, tortured, and finally put to death. We should add to Waldenfels's argument the fact that Socrates does not take up the challenge explicitly in the *Republic*, although the vision of the good in book 6 and the vision of the heavenly spheres in book 10 certainly offer between them an implicit answer. He takes it up explicitly, however, in the *Gorgias*, where he presents a most convincing argument that the tyrant is unhappy, more unhappy even than the tyrant's victim. Thus Levinas may be called Socratic when he suggests that we should pity the persecutor: that "the face of the neighbor in its persecuting hatred can by this very malice obsess as something pitiful" (OB 111). More to the point, though, and returning to Waldenfels, Levinas's and Socrates' arguments are correlative insofar as, in both, what is defended is defended in every case; thus, in the view of Socrates, ethics that excludes the extreme case would be worthless and, "in the view of Levinas, responsibility that excludes the extreme case would be worthless."[26] Levinas must include the extreme case if he is to have any case at all. A passage that illustrates the point can be culled from a section of *Ethics and Infinity*.

> EL: I have previously said elsewhere . . . that I am responsible for the persecutions that I undergo.
> Nemo: You go that far!
> EL: Since I am responsible even for the Other's responsibility. . . . [J]ustice only has meaning if it retains the spirit of disinterestedness which animates the idea of responsibility for the other man. (EI 99)

The excerpt makes it fairly clear that Waldenfels argument is sound. Levinas reaches the difficult position of bearing the responsibility for his own persecution because of the need to apply his ethics in all cases.

But by itself Waldenfels's argument is inadequate. It depends on the idea that when Levinas speaks of persecution he uses that term in the common sense, referring to a case where the other torments me in some fashion or other. But — pace Waldenfels — persecution, as Levinas uses the term, is never explicitly connected to a particular set of circumstances; and thus it cannot refer only to a Socratic limit case. Or perhaps it can. Perhaps it would be most accurate to say that Levinas admits and extends Waldenfels's point, suggesting with the frequency with which he tosses out the term persecution that *every* ethical encounter is a limit case. For persecution, as Levinas uses the word, refers simply to the command from the other.[27] We recall that in the passage cited above it was not 'the other qua Nazi' who persecuted me, but the "other qua other." In another passage Levinas writes that passivity, which is the characteristic of ethical subjectivity "deserves the epithet of complete or absolute only if the persecuted one is liable to answer for his persecutor. The face of the neighbor in its persecuting hatred can by this very malice obsess as something pitiful. . . . In the trauma of persecution [passivity] is to pass from the outrage undergone to the responsibility for the persecutor, and in this sense from suffering to expiation for the other" (OB 111).[28] "The persecuted one" is "the self," the one who "is accused beyond his fault before freedom"; and "persecution is the precise moment in which the subject is reached or touched without the mediation of the logos" (OB 121). The face persecutes me.

To begin to explore this usage, let us recall our discussion in chapter one of Levinas's ontic levels, and redescribe them, following Edith Wyschogrod, as levels of violence. We may divide 'Levinasian violences' into the violences of the human being alone, the violences of relation, and the violences of society or politics: this is to say, the violences of the one, the two and the three. (1) First there is the *il y a*, being itself, existence that is prior to and underlies separate existents, the absolute neutral 'it is' of 'it is raining' or 'it is night' in which the 'it' has no referent except the "rumbling silence" the human being feels when she thinks that "even if there were nothing, the fact that 'there is' is undeniable" (EI 48).[29] This impersonalization is the primary violence, but it is evaded through another act of violence, the "wrenching free from undifferentiated being" which is the development of the subjective consciousness of the separated self.[30] In addition, the human being alone lives in the element — a kind of beneficent lack of differentiation — from which she wrenches herself by means of the violence of work. These are violences of one, the violences of being and nature. (2) The separated self, separated from violence by violence, is now able to meet another existent in relation. She desires to kill him; this is the primary violence of this level. But she is called into question by the command coming from his height and destitution, 'thou shalt not kill'; this is seldom described as a violence, but *is* called a 'trauma' and of course a 'persecution' — words that are, in effect, euphemisms for the memory of violence and for violence itself, and seem to take their place in the discourse precisely so that Levinas does not have to call this event a violence. In any case, these events are categorically different from the violences of the one alone: the persecution of the face is not the violence of being or nature but diachrony rupturing the subject's being, and the subject's impulse to kill the other is not mere subjectivity or mastery but an attack on diachrony. The dynamic of violence at this ontic level can also be described as a dynamic of power: murder is a power over power, but the other has recourse to further power, a power that "paralyses the power of power" (TI 198). (3) With the entry of the third, we find the new violences of justice, calculation, knowledge, writing, philosophy, and also those of avoidable totalities or bad regimes, of force as opposed to authority. Here, in addition, there are the violences that politics do to ethics, and those that ethics do to politics. For example, the violence of the logos or said that emerges at the second ontic level and is mitigated in the saying is recomplicated at this level when the address is made not to the other but to the many; the solution offered by Levinas is the preservation of the saying by means of what might well be understood as another violence, that of abusive speech or scepticism.

Violences upon violences. Some are unmitigatedly evil, like the *il y a*, or murder, while others are more or less good, like the violences of justice; then, in addition, there is persecution, which seems to be an unmitigated good. The blurring here gives rise to a question: how can we tell which violences open on diachrony and which seek to destroy it? The problem must strike any reader of Levinas. It may come to our attention first when we look at his reflections on suffering or the Holocaust and compare them to what he says about infinity. Both suffering and the idea of the infinite are described in Levinas's works as the 'passivity of passivity' or 'passivity more passive than any passivity' (PL 157, GCM 64); moreover, the Holocaust, as suffering par excellence, ruptures certainties and renders those who experienced it or reflect on it open to the supreme principle and thus seems to function traumatically in the same way as the idea of the infinite or the command from the other. How are we then to distinguish, on Levinasian grounds, the malignant rupture from the divine one?[31] Another way the problem may strike us is in the similarity between the formulations '*il y a*' and illeity: Levinas does not seem to provide criteria for distinguishing between these two movements or experiences. And, finally, in the designation of the command from the other as a persecution, Levinas seems to make no provision for an ethical distinction

between the command from the Nazi (which, qua persecution is not violent, but will obviously be combined with
violence) and the command from the orphan (which is nonviolent but remains a persecution).

Let us start with the easy question — the relation of the
Holocaust to ethical rupture — before turning to the relation of the *il y a* to illeity and the Nazi to the orphan. I have
suggested that the Holocaust functions in Levinas's thought
to rupture certainties, to destroy the consolations and justifications of totalizing systems, and also that it effects this
rupture from a nontime beyond time. It would indeed appear therefore to function in essentially the same way as the
diachronous command from God. But a closer look at what
Levinas says about the Holocaust shows that this is not so.
The movement in our four stories is not simply from security
to rupture; rather, it is a three-part movement from the
security of third-level structures, to atheism, and thence to
rupture. In all of Levinas's descriptions of events connected
to the Holocaust he stresses that the subject suddenly finds
himself alone, thrust out of history or the story, not counting
on God; in short, the subject becomes an atheist, which is to
say that he takes up a position that has a specific meaning
in Levinas's understanding, namely, an inhabiting of the first
ontic level. What the Holocaust does is to throw people from
the third level to the first; in this sense it is a rupture of
certainties but not yet an ethical rupture. From the first level
it is possible to realize that one is in relation; but the Holocaust does not itself put one into relation. To say this is essentially to say again that Levinas's ethics does not arise
from the Holocaust, but arises from his reading in the wake
of the Holocaust. And to say it is also to begin to address a
slightly different problem: the problem of whether Levinas
draws a lesson from the Holocaust and in this way does what
providential schemes do, namely, turns the bad to a good.
We will take this up briefly later; it can already be said,

though, that the Holocaust does not teach us the supreme ethical principle. It shakes up our reliance on systems, but it does not shake up our reliance on ourselves.

The question of the relation of the *il y a* to illeity is best examined by looking at an argument made by Jeffrey Kosky, and we can also use his argument to segue into the question of the Nazi and the orphan. Kosky begins his article on the subject by noting what we described in the first half of this chapter, that "according to Levinas, after the death of God, philosophy is open to the significance of God only insofar as it describes the ethical situation of the responsible self."[32] He does not link the death of God to the Holocaust, but to the demise of metaphysics, that is, the demise of ontology and the modern conception of the autonomous subject; nevertheless, he traces Levinas's movement in the same order as I have traced it above, namely backwards, as it takes place, from the collapse of philosophy into the ethics that is prior — in support of which ordering he cites Levinas: "after the death of a certain God inhabiting the world behind the scenes, [responsibility] discovers the trace" (OB 185). But, Kosky asks, how can this trace be identified as God's trace? "How . . . can that which survives the death of God be identified with or determined as God?"[33] The problem, more specifically, is that the trace signifies God's absence, and is thus difficult to distinguish from the absence that constitutes the *il y a*. In fact, there are a number of points of possible confusion. The trace is the trace of illeity — the pronoun-for-a-pronoun with which Levinas designates the divinity. Illeity and *il y a* are constructions of *il*; which is to say that both seem to describe an anonymity, a neutrality, that takes place in the midst of — or above or below, before or after — relation. But it is the essence of anonymity to oppose the uniqueness of the other qua other, and thus an anonymity in the midst of relation would seem to undercut the subject's attention to that uniqueness. Moreover, both illeity and the *il y a* are, to speak loosely,

violent; both are inflicted on the subject and rupture her being. The *il y a*, writes Levinas at one point, is "an obscure
invasion [before which] it is impossible to take shelter in
oneself, to withdraw into one's shell. One is exposed" (EE
59). Illeity, he suggests elsewhere, bespeaks "the impossibility of escaping God [that] lies in the depths of myself as a
self, as an absolute passivity. . . . [It is] the impossibility of
slipping away, absolute susceptibility" (OB 128).[34] The potential confusion between the two strikes Kosky as a critical
problem in Levinas's thinking: "For Levinas, then, everything
hinges on distinguishing two types of anonymity. Without
distinguishing these two forms of anonymity. . . . [t]he self
may be a witness, but it . . . cannot say or identify . . . that to
which it is a witness. Is it God or the *il y a?* . . . Why is the
trace a trace of God and no other?"[35]

I want now to propose two solutions to Kosky's problem,
one of which arises in the context of ethics and the other in
the context of politics. I will take up the first at some length,
since it is, I believe, the key to Levinas's ethics as an entirety. Very broadly: one cannot be called, in the moment of
ethical decision, to distinguish between illeity and the *il y a*,
because one does not in that moment distinguish between a
good persecution and a violent persecution, or between the
command of the orphan and the command of the Nazi. Kosky
notes that Levinas himself describes God as "transcendent . . .
to the point of his possible confusion with the agitation of
the *il y a*" (GCM 69) and thus that he may intend to invoke
a certain confusion, but he does not see that this confusion
is equivalent to the refusal to judge the other, and is thus
Levinas's central ethical criterion. For in one's daily life —
say, on the street — one does not run across illeity or the *il y
a*; one runs across the other. The other may caress one, or
punch one in the face; quite likely the other will ask one for
money. But one does not stop to ask oneself whether the command issuing from his mouth — or only from his eyes — has

as its ultimate source illeity or the *il y a*. Rather, one offers oneself, body and soul; one is the other's hostage; one is the other's martyr; one is the other's expiation; one suffers for him and bears his suffering. To ask to know the source of his command is simply something we do not do, at least not then, not immediately, not in the ethical moment.

And though we do ask such questions afterwards, for the sake of the third — thereby raising all the problems of what, exactly, justice demands, problems that Levinas almost always refuses to discuss in detail — it remains the case not only that we act with kindness solely on the basis of our initial response, but also that our initial response was truer than anything that follows. One could only properly classify the command of the other as good or bad if the command were a facet of the other; one could only define the source of the trace if the trace were *there*. But the command and the trace are not facets of the other; they are not there. The command, which is the mark of the trace, takes place in the subject's response to the other; the other expresses the trace only insofar as he elicits that response; the movement that is analyzed in Levinas's ethics takes place in the subject's soul, and it is she who is ethically in question, not the one who commands her. In short, any attempt to distinguish illeity and the *il y a* must take into account that they appear only in her response. And while one can say, broadly, that if she responds by offering herself she responds to the trace of illeity, and if she slits the other's throat her actions are correlative with the workings of the *il y a*, practically this serves only to bring us back to the critical point: that one distinguishes between illeity and the *il y a* only in oneself, and between good and bad others only for the sake of the third — and in both cases one does so after the fact.

Kosky's desire, as I see it, is for criteria that will allow him to make distinctions between types of others or rank them on a scale of worthiness; moreover, he seems to hold that such criteria are necessary to an understanding grounded in the differences between people. He implies that the only way to distinguish God, understood as alterity, from the *il y a*, understood as the lack of alterity, is to reerect ontology; in other words, that only an ontological structure, a structure that classifies, will keep us from blending into the all-in-all of the *il y a*. But this idea depends on his critique of the anonymity of Levinas's God, a critique that seems at first glance to be well taken but that does not ultimately hold up. The critique arises because, in Levinas's descriptions of the face or of the trace of illeity, uniqueness often seems to give way to the idea of the face qua face, or the trace qua trace, an idea that seems to allow for a diversion of the attention away from the needs and commands of the particular other. To put the matter as clearly as possible: it sometimes seems as if the subject is responding to the same thing in every other, 'the trace' or 'otherness', and not to the particular person at all. But this, I believe, bespeaks a flaw in philosophical language rather than a flaw in Levinas's ethics. Levinas is not Shakespeare; he cannot describe the effect of the face without generalizing, even though the effect of any particular face is never general.[36] The need to generalize in language extends into the further need to speak of a God who is One and Whole but somewhere else than here, and thus absent and anonymous.

In reality, however, Levinas's God is not encountered as One or as Whole because infinity appears precisely as plurality and as difference; and God is not encountered as anonymous, because he is only encountered in the face and the trace, which are personality. Indeed, the concept of absence employed by Levinas in his description of God in human relation functions not to add an element of anonymity or sameness, but precisely to mitigate the anonymity and sameness that would be imposed on the other were God present in the relation. When the absence of Levinas's God appears, and because it appears only as absence, it is not at all anonymous or same-making; and therefore, while God may be confused with the *il y a* in a reading of Levinas's philosophy, the confusion cannot occur in experience. The *il y a* has no trace. Thus it is not necessary to parachute ontology back into the picture to protect alterity. And, of course, for Levinas, such a move is not merely unnecessary. For Levinas, ontological structures, far from supporting difference, compromise it, either by allowing us to believe that we are all equal under God and thus undercutting the asymmetry — the *you* are higher than *me* — in which God's absence resonates, or else by allowing us to commit the error of ranking human beings as unequal on an objective rather than subjective scale, defining some as more godly than others.

At the core, what I am saying here is something that has been said many times by Levinas and Levinasians, that the asymmetrical nature of his ethics means that the ethics cannot be presented as a set of rules that could be applied universally. But the discussion above serves also to make clear something that is said less often, namely, that because Levinas's ethics is not a set of rules, it does not provide any grounds by which human relations can be made smoother or easier. Levinas was frequently asked in interviews what happens if the self or the other, instead of responding to the encounter ethically, responds with physical violence or murder.[37] Behind the question lies one of two ideas, either (a) that Levinas's ethics suggests that we *always or often* respond to one another with responsibility, and that the truth of the ethics is therefore compromised by the mundane fact of murder, or (b) that Levinas's ethics suggest that we *should* respond to the other with responsibility, and that the ethics ought therefore to offer a set of objective rules. In other words, the question presents one of the central scholarly dilemmas about the ethics: that they seem to be insufficient as description and insufficient as prescription. Levinas almost always answers the question by dismissing the first consideration immediately. To Phillipe Nemo, in 1981, he says something close to 'I thought you'd ask me a harder one', changing the subject as soon as it is decently possible to do so,[38] and to the group of students who interview him in 1986, he says simply that he is fully aware that murder is a common occurrence or even that "the law of evil is the law of being" (PL 175). With these dismissals, he suggests that insofar as his ethics are descriptive they are not intended to describe every case from start to finish; as we have seen, the descriptive element of the ethics refers to a prior shouldering of responsibility and does not at all preclude the fact of murder; on the contrary, it invites it.

After these dismissals, Levinas sometimes invokes Auschwitz. By this he means not only to play trump, reminding the questioner that he understands first hand the most inhuman of violences, but, more than this, to shift to an address of the second idea that underlies the question and to explain why it is that he cannot provide an objective set of rules. For Auschwitz does not only destroy theodicy and totalities of the good — that is, any ideology that assumes that all will come out right in the end — it also undermines any theory of justice or practical ethics that suggests that humanity in general can be forced or coaxed or taught or even encouraged to do what is right in the here and now. To the students he says that Auschwitz repudiates the 'Happy End' in every sense, that it leads us to an ethics or "a piety without reward" (PL 176); and to Ralph Mortley he explains that "living through Auschwitz" teaches us that "we must still take account of the other man, even if taking account of him is not recompensed" (RM 21). Even *if* taking account of him is not recompensed — to this we may add, drawing on the description of the encounter with the other as a persecution: even *though* taking account of him is not recompensed. What Levinas points to here is surely the single most radical aspect

of his ethics: because Auschwitz almost succeeded, our ethics after Auschwitz must be one that fails; because Auschwitz
'worked' so efficiently, our ethics must be one that does not
'work'. Levinas's ethics does not show us a way to avoid an
Auschwitz, for a society inured against Auschwitz is another
Auschwitz. For the same reason, it does not show us any
way to moderate our Auschwitz-causing impulses, pitting
them against one another in an effort to create a 'harmony',
or twisting out of Auschwitz a political theory of force against
force; this kind of dialectical fiddling is still a play with certainties, a play performed in the name of an ideal or a solution. The second intention behind the question put to Levinas
by the students, Nemo, and Mortley — where in your ethics
are the criteria by which I can judge the one who persecutes
me? — bespeaks the desire for certainty on either a worldly
or a cosmic level. Such certainty can no longer be had; indeed, it never could.

'Unworkability' as the critical aspect of Levinas's ethics is
thus the first answer to Kosky's question about illeity and
the *il y a*, and also a first answer to the correlative question
about the orphan and the Nazi, or why Levinas calls any
encounter with the other a persecution; it is also a defense of
the differential of responsibility as the ethics most adequate
to the circumstances of the Holocaust. For unworkability —
while it has precedent in all the Jewish sources that repudiate the idea of the plan of the whole, and in all the sources
that speak giving without expecting to receive or suffering
for the suffering of the other[39] — takes its place as the critical characteristic of the ethics because of, or for, Auschwitz.
And the second answer to our question, the political answer,
also arises in the wake or for the sake of the Holocaust. It is
simply that although I do not distinguish, for my own part,
between Nazi and orphan, I do make such distinctions on
behalf of the other's other, that is, the orphan's other or, more
pertinently, the Nazi's other. On their behalf, I must step

outside the bounds of ethics and make a claim for justice. Earlier we discussed the fact that it is necessary to regard the Nazi as human in order to put him on trial; now we may add that the fact that one must put him on trial despite being responsible for his responsibility is the whole distinction between ethics and politics. To illustrate this we look again at the passage from the interview with Phillipe Nemo, cited above, this time including the lines previously omitted.

> EL: I have previously said elsewhere — I do not like mentioning it for it should be completed by other considerations — that I am responsible for the persecutions that I undergo. But only me! My 'close relations' or 'my people' are already the others and, for them, I demand justice.
> Nemo: You go that far!
> EL: Since I am responsible even for the Other's responsibility. These are extreme formulas which must not be detached from their context. In the concrete, many other considerations intervene and require justice even for me. Practically, the laws set certain consequences out of the way. But justice only has meaning if it retains the spirit of dis-interestedness which animates the idea of responsibility for the other man. (EI 99)

Anyone who has given a paper on Levinas in public has been confronted by a member of the audience offended by Levinas's claim that I am responsible for the persecution that is done to me. They ask: what would Levinas have me do if someone were to break into my house and rape my wife? The answer is simple. Kill him. This is a case in which the other other demands justice; this is a case of what Levinas calls politics. The example illustrates the ethics/politics distinction fairly well; it also illustrates the fact that the distinction plays such a large role in Levinas's thought because of the need to make an unworkable ethics work. But actually we do not need hypothetical rapists to make our point. In the wake of the Holocaust, Levinas must present an ethics

of service, an ethics that pays no attention to what is successful or what is smooth, but he must also present an ethics
that makes room for punishment. The two requirements do
not sit easily with one another. In experience, it is difficult to
tell when one should serve, and when punish. But the dilemma of the Ezekiel's judgment-dispensing prophet is, if
not unsolvable, at least beyond the bounds of this book. We
need only note that Levinas speaks more often of ethics than
of politics, and more often of inequality than of the need for
an equalitarian society; the distinction between the two is
demanded in the wake of Auschwitz, but so is the primacy of
ethics. Indeed, the fact that Levinas uses the word persecution for any encounter with the other rather than for a phenomenon occurring on the third ontic level — that he thus
compels us to think first of everything, even politics, in ethical terms, rather than, as we have been inclined in recent
decades to do, to think first of everything, even ethics, in
political terms — depoliticizes our thinking, drawing us away
from the dilemma of the justice-dispensing prophet and towards self-sacrifice. In any case, it is certain that Levinas's
reflection on the complex relation between rupturing ethics
and structuring politics — ethical love and the delicate judgments of *halachah* — becomes more urgent in light of the
need to execute judgment on the Nazi for whose responsibility one is responsible.

That ethics is prior to and regulates justice — that the
for-the-other rules the for-the-other's-other — is manifest
in another set of reflections called up in Levinas for the sake
of the Holocaust, a set of reflections that lie under everything I have so far written. In the same way that it is not
legitimate to attempt to account for the Holocaust, it is
also, according to Levinas, not legitimate to draw a lesson
from it. The Holocaust, as the event that ruptures all theories, is also, as it were, the teaching that ruptures all teachings, for any teaching one draws from it acts only to justify
or give meaning to suffering, while the Holocaust repudiates

such impositions. "Accusing oneself in suffering . . . [or] the for-the-other," Levinas writes, "is the most profound adventure of subjectivity, its ultimate intimacy. But this intimacy can only be discreet. It could not be given as an example, or be narrated as edifying discourse. It could not be made a prediction without being perverted" (PL 163). And yet what Levinas says elsewhere in "Useless Suffering" about the supreme principle does look like an edifying discourse, or even a prediction. The difficulty cannot be overcome, but it can for the most part be avoided: since Levinas cannot talk about the Holocaust for fear of sacralizing its commanding voice after the manner of Fackenheim, he seldom speaks of it. He does, however, occasionally retell its stories, which he can describe as "true as only fiction can be" (DF 142), because in them, character and author speak for themselves. And he reads in its wake, drawing from the sources of Judaism every available image of alterity, discourse, difficulty, and error — every image that will allow him to show the fixed structures of modern totalities as broken and incoherent at the core. "Useless Suffering" is unique in Levinas's corpus in its explicit, discursive account of the turn after Auschwitz to the supreme principle, and it may have been written with the sole purpose of disassociating himself from Fackenheim's conception of Judaism, or criticizing it.[40] But what Levinas wants to say about Auschwitz — that in its wake, in the absence of all lessons, one reaches out toward the other — emerges in all his work, in his reaching out to the future for the past, and to the past for the future.

Levinas's idea that Judaism stands for ethical rupture is fast becoming familiar to us, in a way. But it is prone to misinterpretation. For instance, one can combine the fact that Levinas abandons the idea of God's 'plan of the whole' with the idea that his ethics has no fixed rules, and arrive at the belief that he repudiates the idea of God as a lawgiver. But this is not so, for the *halachah* remains, according to Levinas, the signature of the absence of the divine. When Levinas reinterprets the most sacred of God's laws — the proscription of murder — as the existential occurrence of the awareness of alterity, Judaism is opened up; but it does not thereby become a mere openness.

What we learn from Levinas is that Judaism is made of rupture and disjunction. We learn that the Jewish people was born from the breaking of commonalities: once with the expulsion from the security of the garden of Eden, twice when Abraham left stable Ur to parts wild and unknown, and a third time when we were drawn out of that great ancient imperial order, mother Egypt. We learn that Judaism is nondogmatic and nonauthoritarian. We learn that we stand before the world as representatives of difference and uncertainty. But Levinas's desacralizations show more than this. For they stand against the openness of relativism as much as they stand against the closure of authoritarianism; and against progressivist liberalism almost as much as against totalitarianism. Indeed, they function to rupture not only authority, but the entire opposition between authority and spontaneity that is the foundation of most ethical and political thought; they repudiate the paradigm of ethics and justice as the balance between license and law or custom. For the rupture that is Judaism is a law itself, but one that cannot be written down or enforced, the law of personal responsibility, the law of service. This Judaism-that-is-rupture can therefore be called the good, or the godly, if these are phrases that please. But it cannot be called happiness, at least not in any simple sense.

Levinas liked to tell two talmudic stories to illustrate the openness of Judaism; they have since been retold often enough to become familiar. In the first story, God spirits Moses into a class being taught by Rabbi Akiva, some 1,500 years after Moses' time. Sitting at the back of the class, Moses is stunned what he hears; he doesn't understand a word. But then he hears Rabbi Akiva defending the authority of a teaching with the words, "this is the law given to Moses on Mount Sinai," and he is comforted.[41] In the second story, four rabbis are arguing over whether or not an oven is kosher. Three rabbis take one side, but the fourth, Rabbi Eliezer dissents. He says: "if I'm right let this river prove it," and the river flows backwards, but the others say: "you can't prove anything with a river." He says: "if I'm right, let this carob tree prove it," and the carob tree is uprooted and flies 300 cubits through the air, but the others say: "you can't prove anything with a carob tree." And so it goes, until he says: "if I'm right, let it be proved from heaven," and a voice, a *bat kol*, speaks from on high, saying "why are you arguing with Rabbi Eliezer? You know the law always agrees with him." But the others say "it is not in heaven," meaning that the Torah has been given to human beings to interpret and that they need not listen now to a heavenly voice. And God laughs, and says: "My children have defeated me."[42]

Of course these stories suggest that Judaism is non-authoritarian; that not just its *aggadah* but also its *halachah* is within limits variable according to particular circumstances; that the tradition's glory is that it is made up of many voices; that the Torah can be turned and turned; that these and these are the words of the living God. But the ends of the stories — or, at any rate, their continuations, since nothing in the Jewish tradition ever really ends — reveal something else. As the second story goes on, Rabbi Eliezer, he with whom the law always agrees, is not only chastised but excommunicated; when Akiva goes to tell him this, Eliezer weeps, and as he weeps a third of living crops perish. And the first story has an even more grizzly finish. Moses says to God: "You have shown me his knowledge, show me also his reward," and God shows him Akiva's flesh being weighed out in the marketplace.

It is not that Akiva or the rabbis who dispute with Eliezer were somehow too sure of themselves, too systematic in their judgments, and therefore had to be punished. They were doing what Levinas thinks we must do, rethinking the old laws and the old stories in the absence of any certain interpretation; they were, in fact, calling authority into question, and they understood that they must allow themselves to be called into question as well. The point is that this is a job for which there is no reward; ethics is not recompensed. Indeed, quite the contrary. The ethical subject is perhaps always friendless, abjectly poor, tortured, and finally put to death. Every ethical encounter is a limit case. To be ethical is to be unhappy. But it is also to be happy to be unhappy. The love of the neighbor, the suffering for his suffering, is the reproach of God and also the love of God.

NOTES

Notes to Introduction

1. The confusion about his birthdate evident in his various obituaries results from the fact that Lithuania was at the time of his birth using the Julian calendar. His birthdate was therefore recorded as 30 December 1905.

2. From an interview with François Poirié, quoted in R. Cohen, *Elevations*, 116. I have drawn mainly on Cohen's biographical chapter for this short biographical sketch: 115–32.

3. Levinas never, or almost never, used Chouchani's name. Elie Wiesel, another student, says in his description of Chouchani that he did not even know the man's name. See Wiesel, *Legends of Our Time*, 87–109.

4. For a definitive analysis of contemporary continental philosophy as founded on the interaction of same and other, see Descombes, *Modern French Philosophy*.

5. This account of the life may be fleshed out by consulting Levinas's "Signature" in *Difficult. Freedom* (291–95); Lescourret, *Emmanuel Levinas*; and the chapter from R. Cohen, *Elevations* mentioned in note 2.

6. It is because of these trackings *back* that Levinas can be called a phenomenologist. Despite his arguments with Husserlian intentional phenomenology, he retains from the phenomenological method its basic aim: to move back from structures of representation or form to what is behind them and gives rise to them (see TI 21). He rejects Husserl only insofar as Husserl does not complete the phenomenological work, instead resting in the knowledge that the subject becomes master of

what he senses. Thus, as Susan Handelman puts it, "Husserl's idealist pure consciousness . . . represents the object to itself as a pure present, proceeding from the same and foreclosing alterity and temporality" (*Fragments*, 189). Whether or not Levinas's judgment of Husserl is legitimate is a subject I will not take up.

Other terms might also be applied, 'empiricism' for instance. Rosenzweig calls his philosophy an "absolute empiricism"; later, Levinas mentions this in one of his essays on Rosenzweig; later still, Derrida playfully charges Levinas with empiricism. See Rosenzweig, "The New Thinking," 207; DF 188; Derrida, "Violence and Metaphysics," 151–52. But empiricism — and this is the substance of Derrida's charge — still carries the cast of ontology.

Alternatively, because of Levinas's focus on experience, one might call him an existentialist, but, like everyone to whom the term has been applied except Sartre, Levinas rejects it, mainly in an effort to disassociate himself from Kierkegaard (see TI 40), but also because he is critical of most previous philosophies of experience (see DEHH 177; TI 109, 196; CPP 59).

See also R. Cohen, *Elevations*, 274–86, where he argues, on the basis of Levinas's rejection of Husserl, that his philosophy should technically be termed "an ethical overloading of phenomenology"; and Robert Gibbs, *Why Ethics?*, in which he argues that Levinas is to some degree a semiotician. I think it likely that Levinas would reject any term for his philosophy that ended with the suffix -ology or -ism, implying certainty or a static position. But, keeping this in mind, I continue to use term phenomenology, for the reasons stated at the beginning of this note.

7. Levinas always uses the male pronoun to refer to the human being in general in its function as the subject and *almost* always uses the male pronoun to describe the other. The points at which he refers to the other as female are specific descriptions of what he understands to be feminine aspects of the other, e.g. that aspect which is the homemaker, the lover, or the mother. This usage gives his work a cast of masculinity that offends some commentators; it is now, therefore, quite common to use the female pronoun ubiquitously in descriptions of Levinas's thought. I have not done this, but instead have adopted a strategy similar to Levinas's own, referring to the subject with the female pronoun (since I am female), and the other with the male pronoun (to emphasize an aspect of his difference from me or from the subject). Like Levinas, I do not wish these usages to be taken too literally. He writes:

> Perhaps . . . all these allusions to the ontological differences between the masculine and the feminine would appear less archaic if, instead of dividing humanity into two species (or into two sexes), they would signify that the participation in the

masculine and the feminine were the attribute of every human being. Could this be the meaning of the enigmatic verse of Genesis 1.27, "male and female created He them"? (EI 68–69)

For an extended account of some recent feminist articles on Levinas see R. Cohen, *Elevations*, 195 n. 1. Cohen documents the charges brought against Levinas by feminists, following Simone de Beauvoir's attack on him in 1949 and Derrida's assertion, in 1967, that "it seems to us impossible, essentially impossible, that [*Totality and Infinity*] could have been written by a woman" — and, later, the various feminist defenses of Levinas. See de Beauvoir, *The Second Sex*, xix; Derrida, "Violence and Metaphysics," 320–21 n. 92. Four interesting texts (besides Derrida's) on Levinas and feminism that Cohen does not discuss or does not do justice to are: Finn, "Space Between Ethics and Politics"; Oppenheim, *Speaking / Writing*; Chalier, *Figures du féminin*; and Irigaray, "Questions."

8. R. Cohen, *Elevations*, 121–23.

9. Levinas speaks often of the otherwise in Plato and Descartes; they are mentioned in a list that also includes Augustine and Pseudo-Dionysius in RK 25, but see also CPP 62 for Plato and CPP 159–61 for Descartes. That he finds the otherwise in the Hebrew Bible and the rabbinic writings is uncontroversial, and his mentions of it in the New Testament are also fairly frequent, see for instance RK 27. Robert Bernasconi adds Kant, Bergson and Heidegger to the list in "Scepticism," 152. Among these additions, Heidegger is the most dubious, for ultimately his philosophy is, according to Levinas, deeply ontological. Kant is less dubious; on the correlations between Levinas and Kant see Lyotard, "Levinas's Logic"; and see also OB 129. Bergson is mentioned frequently by Levinas as having laid the ground for an ontological position in his conception of time; see RK 13, TO 132. Adriaan Peperzak adds to the list, in his own name, Plotinus and Bonaventure, thus redeeming the central thrust of Christian mysticism along with Western philosophy; see A. Peperzak, "Presentation," 53; for Levinas on Plotinus see TrO 347. Finally, Wes Avram offers a long list that includes, besides those mentioned above, Kierkegaard (see CPP 66–67) and Marx (see RK 33); moreover Avram's short explanation of the various philosophical concepts that display the trace is useful; see W. Avram, "Priority." I leave Franz Rosenzweig out of this discussion, since he has his own ambivalent relation to the history of philosophy; it should be said, though, that his influence on Levinas is enormous. On it, see Robert Gibbs, *Correlations*, throughout; R. Cohen, *Elevations*, throughout; and Handelman, *Fragments*, throughout.

10. Bernasconi, "Scepticism," 152.

11. Let me lay out the three phenomena more slowly and describe their relation to the word 'other'. Until recently, the word 'other' in the

language of the social sciences generally denoted a pejorative designation used by one group of people to exclude or marginalize another; to call someone 'other' was understood to be committing an injustice. Levinas, of course, stands against such injustices; he repudiates all justifications of oppression on the basis of totalizing groupings. However, he does not repudiate them in the usual way, which is to claim that at bottom we are all the *same* or to privilege inclusion. Instead, he reclaims the word 'other' as a designation of something real (rather than something imposed by a culture) and, moreover, as something positive (rather than pejorative); the other, for him, is not just truly other but also *better than the same, better than I*. Thus he attacks the very possibility of the oppressive injustice, and at the same time, refuses to fall into the potential injustice of the second position mentioned in the body of the text, namely, the assumption of global sameness in the name of universalizing, totalizing shibboleths — which, for him, is tantamount to global same-making. But here, once again, he is not refusing the second (potential) injustice in the usual way; he is not at all moving in the direction of a politically correct vindication of cultural isolationism or particularism. Levinas's other is other in himself, not because he speaks a different language or eats a different food, or even because he follows a different religion — and to assume that his otherness stemmed from these things would only be to judge him on the basis of another, smaller totality, and thus, once again, potentially to do him an injustice. To clarify the point, Levinas *repudiates* the injustice of the imposed designation of otherness as a justification of oppression (you are other and therefore inferior), and *undercuts or calls into question* the other two alternatives, that of global democracy (there is no other) and that of identity politics or multiculturalism (we are other; my group is your other; your group is my group's other). That he repudiates the first injustice is un-controversial; that he undercuts the other two potential injustices is highly controversial. I speak at length in the course of the book about his undercutting of global democracy, especially in my discussion of his uneasiness about modern liberalism in chapter four. I speak more briefly of his undercutting of identity politics in the discussion of ethics, politics and 'community' in section three of chapter one; see especially note 36 to chapter one.

Notes to Chapter One

1. Levinas uses the word in four French forms: *autre* and *autrui*, capitalized and lowercase. At times, the forms seem to have some distinct nuances: thus *l'Autre* seems to mean the concept of the other, or otherness; *l'autre* means another; *l'Autrui* means another one, and

refers to another person or God; and *l'autrui* seems always to refer to another person. However, as I read Levinas, the forms are not used systematically, and he is more interested in how they cross one another or coincide than in maintaining the distinctions. I have, therefore, always used the simple lowercase form in my own descriptions, using the upper case only when transcribing someone else's work. Alphonso Lingis, with Levinas's permission, translates *autrui* and *Autrui* "Other," and autre and Autre "other," thus already obscuring any distinctions that might exist (see TI 24–25 note). I do not believe that a great deal is lost by Lingis's move, and some sense of connection or continuity may be gained.

2. Levinas at one point defines the face as follows: "the way in which the other presents himself before me, exceeding *the idea of the other in me*, we here name face" (TI 50). Handelman has an extended discussion of why Levinas chooses to use the image of the face, including descriptions of the work of other scholars on the issue; *Fragments*, chapters seven and eight, especially 208–23, 227–28 and 359 n. 5.

3. Levinas cites here the line from Pascal that he uses again as one of the five epigraphs of *Otherwise Than Being*: ". . .'That is my place in the sun'. That is how the usurpation of the whole world began." Pascal, *Pensées*, 112.

4. Levinas makes the distinction between responsibility *to* and responsibility *for* in various passages, speaking for instance of "the face of a neighbour, ambiguously him *before whom* (or *to whom*, without any paternalism) and *for whom* I answer" (OB 12).

5. Gibbs points out that "in French grammar, there is no informal plural of the second person: two *tu*'s must be addressed as *vous*." Gibbs, *Correlations*, 231. This comment offers insight into the formal nature of the Levinasian plural — with a *tu* there can be intimacy and ethical rupture, but with a *vous* there must be formality and the imposition of the same. A grammatological account of Levinas would, in fact, have to regard *vous* — and therefore two *tu*'s — as tantamount to *ils*.

6. In the interview with graduate students conducted in 1986, Levinas says: "In *Totality and Infinity* I used the word 'justice' for ethics, for the relationship between two people. I spoke of 'justice' although now 'justice' is for me something which is a calculation, which is knowledge, and which supposes politics; it is inseparable from the political. It is something which I distinguish from ethics, which is primary. However, in *Totality and Infinity* the word 'ethical' and the word 'just' are the same word, the same question, the same language" (PL 171). The way all these terms switch sides will be taken up later in this chapter; in addition philosophy will be further discussed in chapter two, religion in chapter four, and the good in chapter five.

7. Peperzak, "Preface" to BPW, x.

8. A great many passages from Levinas inscribing this ambiguity might here be cited. I content myself with two besides those that will be cited later in the body of the text: (1) "The signification of my responsibility for what escapes my freedom is the defeat or defecting of the unity of transcendental apperception, the originary actuality of every act, source of the spontaneity of the subject or of the subject as responsibility" (OB 141). Responsibility precedes every act, but it also defeats conceptions that assemble things into a unity of apperception, thus, presumably, following certain acts of conception. (2) "Critique [of dogmatism] precedes dogmatism" (TI 43).

9. The structure 'as it is' is probably best laid out in "God and Philosophy" (GCM 55–78), though the account of it offered here is drawn from *Totality and Infinity*. The structure as it occurs to us, or at any rate to Levinas, is what he generally presents in his philosophical writings; it is, indeed, the main thrust of *Totality and Infinity*.

10. I draw heavily in this sketch on Edith Wyschogrod's seminal article "Derrida, Levinas and Violence."

11. In his recent work, Peperzak gets at this dynamic more clearly than in the preface to BPW. In *Beyond*, he notes that Levinas criticizes some ontologies, accusing them of "not doing justice but violence to the Other's absoluteness and of ignoring transcendence" and also that Levinas connects ontology to the said and to totality in general. Then he writes:

> Does this mean that ontology, and even the Said of discursivity as such, is necessarily violent? I do not think that this is Levinas's thesis. Violence is rather the effect of the absolutization of ontology. Within its own limited horizon, ontology is innocent; in the dimension of philosophy, it is the expression of a necessary condition for a politics of general peace and justice. (225)

Peperzak's distinction between 'innocent' and 'violent' is precisely my distinction between endemic and avoidable. I would, however, defend my usage against his, since Levinas is occasionally willing to use the word 'violence' of all totalities.

12. Bernasconi, "Rereading," 24.

13. Donna Jowett, in "Origins, Occupation," is referring here particularly to the totalizing forms that pass these days under the name of 'communities'. She writes:

> This sameness is actually never successfully totalizing; these communities and regimes are never vigilant enough to completely succeed in guarding against 'impurity'. The Same exists only by displacing the difference within it to 'others' marked as inferior through the burden of difference they are forced to carry so that

the Same can continue to hallucinate its sameness, purity and
privilege to itself. (24)

While Jowett's condemnation of community as justifying prejudice is
intended to apply only to certain totalities, hallucination is a good
description of totality in general.

14. 'After you' occurs at OB 117 as well as EI 89. 'Here I am' occurs
frequently throughout *Otherwise Than Being*. My use of the phrase
'interrupt me' draws generally on Maurice Blanchot.

15. Bernasconi, "Rereading," 23.

16. For this account, I have drawn heavily on R. Cohen's chapter
entitled "On Temporality and Time," *Elevations*, 133–61.

17. R. Cohen, *Elevations*, 149.

18. I should further qualify the assertion that Levinas "partly
addresses" the problem of the identity of differences with this analysis.
It is not a problem to be solved easily; indeed, it is perhaps the issue
most commonly raised in critiques of Levinas's thought. I will take it
up briefly in the second half of chapter five.

19. R. Cohen, *Elevations*, 157. That time effects a curvature is
Husserl; the link between curvature and ethics is not, at least according
to Levinas.

20. The face is a metaphor. It may, thus, be taken too literally, which
is perhaps why Levinas insists that it would be best not even to notice
the color of the other's eyes (EI 85). But the fact is that the face mostly
drops out of *Otherwise Than Being*, replaced by the term 'proximity'.
The common argument is that *Otherwise Than Being* differs from
Totality and Infinity by being less ontological, following the critique of
Levinas made by Derrida in "Violence and Metaphysics." I am convinced
that this is not so. Some aspects of Derrida's charge of ontological
thinking are merely playful, some are critiques of Derrida himself as
much as of Levinas or laments about the necessary inadequacies into
which philosophy is forced, some are serious and trenchant. In the
sense relevant here, however, Levinas was never an ontologist. The
figures, times, and locations in *Totality and Infinity*, though described
in "ontological language" (DF 295) — as what is not? — are all meta-
phors (see GCM 82). They are made less metaphorical in *Otherwise
Than Being* simply because they were understood too literally — a
shift that comes, unfortunately, at the expense of some concreteness. I
will discuss the problematic loss of the knack of reading in any manner
except the literal in chapter two.

21. With the hyphens in the words 'inter-est' and 'disinter-est',
Levinas plays with etymology. Inter-est is intended to suggest 'being
between' or 'being among', that is to say living in society or with the

third, while disinter-est refers to the relation with the other, which is prior to the entry of the third and thus before 'being among'. This means that disinterestedness appears in Levinas's writings with quite a different meaning than is common; it does not refer to impartiality or objectivity, which are aspects of the relation with the third.

22. On justice see note 6 above. I will use the term justice in this book only in the sense that Levinas gives it after *Totality and Infinity*. Morality is a much more slippery term, and though I will use it, in this section, as synonymous with justice, it should be noted that Levinas very often uses it (perhaps indeed, everywhere except the Kearney interview) as a synonym for ethics.

23. Illeity is God, whose role in all of this is discussed in the fourth section of this chapter and then in greater detail in chapter two. The term allows Levinas to speak of a betrayal of responsibility without speaking of a betrayal of the particular other who stands before me.

24. Gibbs, *Correlations*, 229–54, 232, 233. He cites the extended discussion of the "we" at CPP, 43–44.

25. Gibbs, *Correlations*, 240.

26. *Ibid.*, 238, 240, 241, 242.

27. Caputo, *Nutshell*, 42.

28. Hobbes thinks that the distinction most important to an understanding of the world and politics is the one between 'man alone' and 'man in society'. So do many other thinkers. I have recently come to think that the single best way of quickly describing what is new and good about Levinas's philosophy is by saying that he takes this distinction and relativizes it with the face. He is probably the only philosopher ever to use — at least to such an extent and effect — the relation between two to point out the similarities between the one (man alone) and the three (man in society). Moreover, he would likely argue that unless one sees the one and the three together, and downgrades their importance with the two, one is forced to adopt some form of the nature/convention distinction. I should say also that Levinas allows us to see that the addition into the 'man alone/man in society' rubric of ideas like 'man and nature' or 'man and God' is a red herring. The critical distinction remains the one between all these things — which are, to be sure, real aspects of human experience — and the face.

29. Jowett, "Origins, Occupation," 21.

30. Benammar, "Absences of Community," 35. Benammar discusses Nancy, Bataille, Blanchot and Lingis.

31. Derrida, "Violence and Metaphysics," 80, 79.

32. This qualification has to be made because, although Levinas is scornful of idealism, he is rather fond of utopianism, which he defines distinctively as the movement toward a u-topos, a nonplace, a

transcendence that is not realizable in institutions but that is present as the 'site' of relation.

33. From an interview with Poirié, cited in Gibbs, *Correlations*, 252. See also TI 216, where Levinas writes that "idealism completely carried out reduces all ethics to politics."

34. Levinas is becoming increasingly popular among groups seeking a renewal of our government or society. See for instance Finn's "Space Between Ethics and Politics." Finn criticizes the position that reduces politics to ethics as 'idealist' and the position that reduces ethics to politics as 'materialist'. (Some semantic conflict between her claim and the statement by Levinas quoted in the last note may be remarked. Levinas would, I think, link idealism and materialism; both the reduction of everything to what might be called 'ethics' and the reduction of everything to what might be called 'politics' could be termed either idealism or materialism from his perspective.) Finn laments the fact that most feminist discourse, while it may not take up a strictly materialist position, remains on the level of the political without reference to the ethical, offering only 'technical' suggestions and thus working with the norms in operation instead of challenging them. Real political change, she holds, can only be brought about by referring from the political level (which feminism, qua collectivity, must exist on) back to an ethical level, back to a 'space' of 'desire', the "space of the specifically ethical encounter with others (otherness) as other and not more of the same: as otherwise-than-being simply a re-presentation of a pre-conceived, pre-scribed, pre-determined and thus pre-dictive category and class — a re-presentation which relieves us of the ethical responsibility of attending to the particularity of the other" (108). All political praxis speaks from this space, she argues, and if we want good politics we must understand this to be true. We must not 'obfuscate' or 'abandon' our reference back to the ethical space, while at the same time knowing that its demands must be rendered practical, subordinated to the political.

35. Levinas's distinction between ethics and justice is rewritten as Derrida's distinction between justice and law, of which Caputo writes, in *Nutshell*, 136–39: "Justice and the law are not supposed to be opposites but to interweave: laws ought to be just, otherwise they are monsters; and justice requires the force of law, otherwise it is a wimp." Having said this, Caputo proceeds to define three 'aporias' in Derrida's thought on the matter: (1) Judgment must reside in the space between the general rule and the particular case. The law must therefore be constantly reinvented by justice. Otherwise the judge is not a human being but a calculating machine. (2) Decision must be preceded and conditioned by a moment of indecision — or indeed, undecidability —

if it is to be anything other than mere calculation, and thus "deciding is a possibility sustained by its impossibility." (3) It is nevertheless urgently necessary to make judgments and to make them *now*, rather than waiting for 'all the facts to come in'. These aporias, which Caputo also describes as axiomatic for Derrida's 'inventionalism', describe the nature of Levinas's distinction quite well.

36. A short summary of scholarship is called for before leaving the subject of Levinas and community. Most people who write on Levinas's politics focus on its relation to the politics of identity. These people can be divided, broadly, into three types. First, there are those who read Levinas as a champion of identity politics, ethnicity politics, interest group politics, pluralism, multiculturalism, or even gender politics. Michael Oppenheim, for instance, argues in *Speaking/Writing* that Levinas's other can be understood to mean 'women' or 'non-Jews' both of which groups are marginalized by mainstream Judaism, and that his pro-other stance thus provides a recipe for a Jewish pluralism that would respect the two groups without making them same. Nancy Scheper-Hughes, for another instance, argues in "Primacy of the Ethical" that Levinas's critique of the objectivity and cultural relativism of the social sciences is a call for moral engagement, which is to say an "activism" that can be realized not only by teaching literacy and building infrastructure, but also by working to support the local (Brazilian) candidate of the Socialist Worker's Party. Both Oppenheim and Scheper-Hughes misunderstand Levinas's other as referring to marginalized groups of people. The second type of writer, like Oppenheim and Scheper-Hughes, is in favour of identity politics, but, unlike them, is aware that Levinas doesn't lend himself to its support. Thus Enrique Dussel writes in *Underside of Modernity* that "Levinas was a determinant in the late sixties in my development of a Philosophy of Liberation . . .: Levinas awakened us from the 'closed' ontological dream. But we had to go beyond him rapidly because of his inability to develop a politics of liberation" (39 n. 20). Thus, too, Andrew Shanks explains in *Civil Society/Civil Religion* that "a truly presuppositionless thinking must involve some consideration of the practical as well . . . Levinas's own morally therapeutic thought may be seen as a brilliant but nevertheless one-sided beginning. Given the complementary need for prophylaxis . . . its completion [i.e. the completion of Levinas's thought] will surely also bring us back into the Hegelian territory in the end (198–99). Dussel argues for a pluralistic Marxist regime, Shanks for a pluralistic communitarian regime in which interest groups receive government funding — but the point is that both understand that arguments for pluralisms leave Levinas behind. Dussel states why most

clearly: "Levinas showed us how to formulate the question of the irruption of the Other, but we could still not develop a politics . . . which placed in question the ruling Totality (which dominates and excludes the Other) and *would develop a new Totality*. This critical-practical questioning of a new Totality was exactly the question of 'Liberation' With this Levinas could not help us" (81–82, my emphasis). Dussel and Shanks do not misunderstand Levinas but know that, to use him politically, one must depart from him at least to the extent of interpreting the other as a group; they also know that this reinterpretation is precisely the creation of totality. The third type of writer can be represented by Simon Critchley and Geraldine Finn. Critchley argues in *Ethics of Deconstruction* that although Levinas does not support a particular politics — advocating instead a 'democracy' that is 'always not yet here' — he does understand that politics is both necessary and good as long as it remains open to the ethical critique that arises from the *single* other (see 219–47). Finn makes an analogous argument in "Space Between Ethics and Politics": that although Levinas does not support a feminism, he allows us to understand feminisms as necessary and good as long as they too remain open to the critique of the single other. Critchley and Finn, as I see it, take Levinas as far into the realm of interest politics or identity politics as he can be taken, without departing from him, or, as Dussel puts it, "radicalizing" him (17 n. 24). I will close this note with some words of Levinas:

> The sarabande of innumerable and equivalent cultures, each justifying itself in its own context, creates a world which is, to be sure, de-occidentalized, but also disoriented. To catch sight, in meaning, of a situation that precedes culture, to envision language out of the revelation of the Other . . . in the gaze of a human being looking at another human precisely as . . . human, disengaged from all culture, in the nakedness of his face, is to return to Platonism in a new way. It is also to find oneself able to judge civilization on the basis of the ethical. . . . Platonism [is] an affirmation of the human independently of culture and history."
> (BPW 58–59)

Here Levinas gently criticizes Edward Said in Plato's name. Groups do injustices to groups and groups do injustices to individuals — but groups cannot be ruptured by groups but only by encounters between individuals. Levinas's thought is not incompatible with a practical pluralism or multiculturalism; his aim, however, is not to advocate these alternatives but to open them up to be questioned by the incoming of the other.

37. Peperzak, *Beyond*, 224.

38. That this is the point he is at pains to deny in the quotation from TI 78–79 cited just above is indicative of the difficulty of understanding Levinas on God.

39. This is "Beyond Memory" in *Difficult Freedom*, discussed in chapter five.

40. In *Totality and Infinity*, he writes: "The place of the good above every essence is the most profound teaching, the definitive teaching, not of theology but of philosophy" (103).

41. The next chapter will take up the matter of the tension in Levinas himself between ontology and prophecy in the context of his acknowledgment of the necessity of ontological language and his attempt to subvert it through 'abuse'. At that point we will also take up again the existence of two philosophies in the discussions that close chapter five of *Otherwise Than Being*. It must be said, however, that Levinas almost always speaks of philosophy in the pejorative sense; he almost always uses the term philosophy to refer to the reason that seeks proof, that is to say, to ontology.

42. Llewelyn, *Genealogy*, 211.

43. *Greek is what Hebrew looks like after the entry of the third.* What we have here is a metaphor such that what is real is the two and the three, for which 'Hebrew' and 'Greek' are symbols. Derrida, in an interesting move, literalizes the metaphor, suggesting that if the seat of the rupturing encounter is Israel then the third must be the goyim — thus the two/three distinction becomes a figuration for Israeli border politics. Derrida's move is legitimate for two reasons: it is anticipated in certain of Levinas's alarmingly fervent essays on Zionism, and, more simply and importantly, it constitutes a call to Israel to act well. But it is troublesome that the move can only be made by shifting into and then back out of the realm of symbol. Or maybe it is more than troublesome. Narrowing Levinas's general meaning in this way results in a great many problems, not least a reversion to the elitism of the common understanding of 'chosenness', an elitism I believe Levinas to have overcome. See Derrida, *Adieu*, throughout.

44. In my paper, "Familiar Objections," I did, in fact, argue that, despite what one might think, Levinas is more Jewish (or more Jewgreekish) in the philosophical works, and more Greek (or Greek-Jewish) in the talmudic works.

45. The distinction between the all and the each has the virtue of being immediately intelligible, as well as going some way to clear up the problem of universality. What it leaves out is the level of the one, since each = two, and all = three. This is why, technically, same and other is a better distinction (same = one and three, other = two).

46. Levinas frequently refers to Judaism as an 'anachronism' (for instance at OB 148 or DF 80), meaning not only to refer to the Hegelian

notion that Judaism should, by rights, have disappeared by now into the universal all, but also to its status as happening in another time than world-historical time. See my chapter four on Rosenzweig on these matters.

47. There is also a rabbinic idea underlying Levinas's basic structure: the idea of the Good Impulse and the Evil Impulse. Take this passage from Genesis Rabbah, the ancient compilation of rabbinic comments on Genesis.

> Nahman said in the name of R. Samuel: 'Behold it was very good' refers to the Good Impulse; and 'behold it was very good' refers to the Evil Impulse. Can the Evil Impulse then be very good? That would be extraordinary! But for the Evil Impulse, however, no man would build a house, take a wife, or beget children. (Gen. Rabbah, IX.7)

It is the Good Impulse that moves one to responsibility, and the Evil Impulse that moves one to create structures, even structures that are necessary to life properly lived — which is to say that the Evil Impulse moves totalities, endemic ones as well as avoidable ones. The Good and Evil Impulses may thus provide a microcosmic source for the dynamic of infinity and totality, supplementary to the source that is the course of Jewish history. Note also that the passage comes close to suggesting that the Evil Impulse is called forth by the Good Impulse — while it remains true, of course, that they vie with one another. When R. Samuel — who emerges in Levinas's "Messianic Texts" as something of a proto-Levinasian — says that the Evil Impulse is 'very good', he does not suggest that all evil is ultimately good; he does not, as Levinas sometimes puts it "subordinate suffering to a metaphysical ultimate." He merely suggests that one needs the Evil Impulse (read totality) to get things done, things that are done for the sake of the responsibility to one's fellows and God that is at the core of the Good Impulse (read infinity).

48. Susan Handelman stresses the "as if." History, she points out, is not God; and Levinas is not Hegel. See *Fragments*, 291–92.

49. See, for instance, Levinas's forward to BTV. But if Levinas has rethought the matter through Derrida, there is some obligation on Derrida to be more generous on the matter than he appears in certain sections of *Adieu*.

50. His single favourite quotation is drawn not from any Jewish source but from Dostoyevsky. It is Father Zosima's line that we are all responsible for one another but that "I" am more responsible than anyone else. The line is cited in one form or another in at least half of Levinas's published works and almost all of the interviews. See for instance GCM 72, EI, 98, 101, RK 31, OB 146.

Notes to Chapter Two

1. Jacques Derrida's essay "Sauf le nom" is overtly a meditation on the Christian mystic Angelus Silesius. But in addition, it can be read as a running commentary on chapter five of *Otherwise Than Being*, to which it clearly owes a great deal. One of Derrida's opening questions concerns the nature of the 'desire of God': "does it come from God in us, from God for us, from us for God? . . . Who speaks to whom?" (37).

2. I put it this way to highlight the poetry of the idea. It reminds me of the mantra at the end of the Heart Sutra, which a teacher of mine, Robert Sharf of the University of Michigan, used to translate something like: "gone, gone, gone beyond, gone way beyond, enlightenment, yippee!" But what I mean is: the infinizing (rupturing, revealing) or the becoming infinite (accomplishment, actualization) of the infinite (the Infinite, the beyond being), in the infinity (endless number) of the infinitude (uniqueness, beyondness) of others.

3. Gibbs, "Name of God," 1.

4. Descartes's idea of the infinite is also anarchic; it stirs things up in the same way as Levinas's trace in the saying does. When Levinas writes of the word God as assembling the unassemblable, he seems to write as a Hebraic Descartes — rather than thinking more than he can think, the Levinasian subject is saying more than he can say. But while throughout his earlier writing, Levinas seems to hold the two notions — thinking the unthinkable, and saying the unsayable — to be equivalent, here he offers a short critique of Descartes's formulation. Descartes suggests, he writes, that the subject is "thematizing thought"; he does not take into account saying, or signification, which requires corporeality. The "I think" indicates a "unity of apperception or a representation," which does not admit of responsibility, of "the gravity of the body extirpated from its *conatus essendi* in the possibility of giving" (OB 142). Thus, while Descartes's idea of the infinite continues, for Levinas, to express the moment of passivity or "inspiration itself" (OB 146), it is important to realize that Descartes is not able to understand that this "passivity breaks out in a saying" (OB 147).

5. Levinas does not speak at length here about the link between poetry and prophecy, though he makes its existence quite clear. The link is obviously in part biblical — the prophetic books of the Bible tend also to be works of poetry — but it is also classical, emerging from Hesiod; see Bowra, *The Prophetic Element*. In and after Hesiod, the poetry/prophecy duo became one side in the battle between poets and philosophers, which later informs and in part fuels the battle between Jerusalem and Athens. As we have seen, Levinas undercuts this debate, but at times also makes use of it, putting prophecy up against ontological

philosophy. In *Otherwise Than Being* chapter five, as will emerge presently, Levinas wishes both to undercut and also to utilize the debate; this is one of the things that makes the chapter so confusing. It may be well to keep in mind that the link he employs here to save his own work from the charge of being ontology is Greek in origin as well as Hebrew.

6. There is, in fact, a larger aggregate of blurred terms here. In "Presentation," Peperzak names as occurring together, "saying, responsibility, goodness, proximity, subjectivity and spirituality" (63); and Fabio Ciaramelli writes in "Levinas's Ethical Discourse" that "language itself is always ethical, prophetic, sceptical, religious, and inspired" (98).

7. In BTV, Levinas writes: "one may wonder whether man, an animal endowed with speech, is not, above all, an animal capable of inspiration, a prophetic animal" (110).

8. Peperzak, in "Presentation," voices the question that must be foremost in the minds of many who read Levinas on scepticism. Does scepticism — the position that all theses are false — really argue from a different ground than that of philosophy, a diachrony opposed to philosophy's synchrony? Does it really hold the saying distinct from the said? Peperzak thinks not. He argues that philosophy can indeed refute scepticism logically, or incorporate it (he illustrates the incorporation that I have called the second, grander refutation with reference to Kant and Hegel) precisely because scepticism does *not* argue from a different ground than that of philosophy. Therefore, Peperzak would prefer that Levinas continued to present his case using the terminology of saying and said without recourse to the weak term scepticism. "Levinas's great discovery is that he found a way beyond the solidarity of logic and its sceptical denial, in the difference between the said and the saying" (58).

Robert Bernasconi, in full understanding of the problems Peperzak discerns, nevertheless defends Levinas's use of the term *scepticism*. He points out that Levinas is not supporting the antiphilosophical school of that name as much as he is using the term as a model or metaphor. Scepticism is useful to Levinas because its contestation of truth stands in proximity to Levinas's subordination of truth to ethics — a proximity that is recognizable in the fact that the refutation of scepticism (that its theses contradict the ground for holding theses) stands in proximity to the familiar objections. Levinas himself is not contesting truth in the manner of a sceptic. See Bernasconi, "Scepticism," 152. Bernasconi opens his article with an epigraph from Holderlin that helps to explain what Levinas may be thinking of in his choice of scepticism as a model: "Believe me, the sceptic finds contradiction and imperfection in all that is thought, because he knows the harmony of the perfect beauty, which is never thought. The dry bread that human reason well-meaningfully offers him, he disdains only because he is secretly feasting at the table of the gods." But, of course, to be useful, Holderlin's lines must be denuded of their gnostic implications, desacralized, or made metaphysical. Other good discussions of Levinas on scepticism can be found in Jan de Greef, "Scepticism and Reason" and Maurice Blanchot "Our Clandestine Companion."

9. Derrida, in "Sauf le nom," is only slightly more willing to use the term 'negative theology' to describe the ambivalent phenomenon of witnessing: "[in] the way of theology called or so-called negative, [the] voice multiplies itself, dividing within itself: it says one thing and its contrary, God that is without being or God that (is) beyond being" (35). Derrida is aware of the Levinasian critique of the very idea of a 'negative' theology, explaining later in his meditation that negative theology must involve 'translation', and thus must ultimately be positive (47, see 41). But although this stops him from using the term negative except "provisionally" (61), it does not stop him from interpreting what has traditionally been called negative theology in terms that are clearly borrowed from Levinas. According to Derrida, Silesius writes of

> the singularity of the unknown God [which] overflows the essence and the divinity, thwarting in this matter the opposition of the negative and the positive, of being and nothingness, of thing and non-thing — thus transcending all the theological attributes. . . . This excess or this surplus (with regard to language) . . . [leaves] some remains on the body of a tongue. . . . Some trace remains in right in this corpus, becomes this corpus as *survivance* of apophasis (more than life and more than death), survivance of an internal onto-logico-semantic auto-destruction. . . . In effect, this theology [i.e. negative theology] launches or carries negativity as the principle of auto-destruction at the heart of each thesis; in any event, this theology suspends every thesis, all belief, all doxa . . . in which its *epokhe* has some affinity with the *skepsis* of scepticism. (52, 55, 67)

In short, Derrida sees an affinity between Silesius (and other apophatic mystics) and Levinas.

10. Derrida speaks of a "New Testament eventness" ("Sauf le nom," 71), meaning a tendency to locate or objectify. But he also undercuts this himself, quoting Silesius: "It is not you in the place, the place is in you! Cast it out, and here is already eternity" (57).

11. Though Levinas does not adopt either an ontological or a psychological perspective — and thus neither an ontological nor a psychological hermeneutic — he is often read in one of these two ways. Language tends in one or the other direction; this is its deficiency.

In *Totality and Infinity*, Levinas's language tends toward ontology or third level images — he speaks of being and of things, and he personifies his others into iconic figures. In *Otherwise Than Being*, he attempts — largely as a result of others' misunderstanding and subsequent critique — to correct this tendency. As a result, *Otherwise Than Being* tends unfortunately to be somewhat psychological in its language, allowing a new misunderstanding. Levinas's problem with respect to psychological language can be described more specifically. He wishes to retain the phenomenological insight that one cannot know the other, that one knows only what happens to oneself, or, more specifically, that one only knows what happens *within* oneself. However, he does not wish this insight to degenerate into a solipsism or an egology, as he understands most phenomenology to do. Therefore, while he speaks of the encounter with the other as a 'psychism', or a split in the subject, in which the subject "is divided from himself" or "cannot return to himself," he insists: (a) that this analysis of levels in the psyche has nothing to do with the distinction between consciousness and self-consciousness and everything to do with the distinction between same and other, and (b) more simply, that the movement is not psychological (see OB 147). Critique of *Totality and Infinity*'s ontologism has forced him to shift the locus of the movement to within the subject, and thus *Otherwise Than Being* has a new problem: it allows us, at times, to forget that the movement within is a movement from or to without.

12. I leave the question open in the understanding that no simple answer is admissible, especially not the one usually offered, namely, the Greeks. Caputo, for instance, writes that a sort of scholasticism "has overrun the biblical traditions ever since Philo Judaeus decided that Yahweh needed to square accounts with Greek ontology, the result being that Greek ontology settled the hash of Yahweh and Elohim" (*Prayers and Tears*, 113). While I agree that Philo is part of the problem, I find the blanket use of the term "Greek" here, and in many similar passages, at the very least unrigourous; such an attempt to establish philosophical evidence for a theological argument is useful only if one wishes to preach to the converted.

13. Handelman, in *Fragments*, 265–68, also treats the first two references, and discusses Levinas's debt, in his use of these passages, to Rosenzweig.

14. Biblical quotations not cited directly from Levinas's text are taken from the JPS, though some I have modified.

15. Any nuances implied in these grammatical characteristics are lost in the English, 'here I am'. However, like Levinas's translators, I retain 'here I am' for the sake of its resonance with English Bibles, eschewing more grammatically accurate forms such as 'behold me'.

16. Derrida, "Violence and Metaphysics," 150–53.

17. Levinas's debt to Rosenzweig is always great, but perhaps especially so in the midrash in this chapter. The Levinasian Adam's 'as-for-me' is drawn from the 'He-She-It' of the Rosenzweigian Adam. See Rosenzweig, *Star*, 175. In addition, Levinas's surrounding midrash may be compared to Rosenzweig's midrashic accounts of revelation (173–78, 199–204 and 151–55).

18. With reference to Moses, we may add two biblical references that do not appear in this chapter of *Otherwise Than Being* but are common in Levinas's work. In Exodus 33, a problem of interpretation arises. We are told that "The Lord would speak to Moses face to face, as one man speaks to another" (v. 11) and also that "He said, 'you cannot see My face, for man may not see Me and live. . . . See, there is a place near Me. Station yourself on the rock and, as My presence passes by, I will . . . shield you with My hand until I have passed by. Then I will take My hand away and you will see My back; but My face must not be seen'" (vv. 20–23). How may the two passages may be reconciled? Read the first passage with emphasis on its second half, and its 'as' (*ke-*) as 'while' rather than 'like'. Moses sees God, as it were, face to face, as or *while* he sees *the other* face to face. God, in himself, can only be seen in the trace, which is, as it were, his back or his passage. The image of the face to face does not occur quite as often in *Otherwise Than Being*, where Levinas tends instead to speak of the 'one-for-the-other', an expression that more obviously suggests responsibility and is less spatial or ontological. Clearly, though, the trace in the face, common in other works, arises in some measure from reflection on Exodus 33. See BTV 144, 213.

19. See also Lamentations 3.30.

20. Actually this conjunction of images is not quite Levinasian. Levinas connects seeing to ontology but hearing to the approach of the other. Indeed, to be able to 'hear the seeing', or to use "the eye that listens" (OB 30) is already to see through seeing, to move beyond space into time, beyond location into diachrony. However, since hearing seems to function for Isaiah in the same way seeing functions, as a sense that absorbs data, Isaiah and Levinas appear to be in philosophical agreement and to differ only in their use of images.

21. Levinas cites this passage relatively often; see GCM 75, OB 148, ITN 174.

22. Llewelyn, *Genealogy*, 185.

23. See for instance Chalier, "Hebraic Tradition," 4; Handelman, *Fragments*, 180.

24. Gibbs, "Responsibility and Pragmatics," 15–16.

25. But lest we get too carried away glorifying the third level, we should note that Levinas warns us away from a direct association of

illeity, as a kind of thirdness, and the 'third man'. Prophecy ruptures all the thematization demanded by the third man.

It is in prophecy that the Infinite escapes the objectification of thematization and of dialogue, and signifies as illeity, in the third person. This 'thirdness' is different from that of the third man; it is the third man that interrupts the face to face of a welcome of the other man, interrupts the proximity or approach of the neighbour, it is the third man with which justice begins. (OB 150)

There are at least three different 'thirds' in Levinas: (a) the third man or third party, with which we are most familiar, (b) the thirdness of God, which is mentioned only very seldom, and (c) the 'third term' which is the rubric under which a totality is constructed. All of these are thirds because they come after the primary experience of relation between the subject and the other (one and two), but none of them is synonymous with another. The third *man* demands the imposition of the same under a third *term* ("a neutral term which is not itself a being" TI 42), and it all happens under and in the name of God. The problem of thirdness is immensely sticky. My analyses here remain provisional.

26. Levinas cites the passage again in "Demanding Judaism," BTV, 9.

27. Chalier, "Hebraic Tradition," 8.

28. Derrida, *Gift of Death*, 53–115.

29. Kierkegaard, *Fear and Trembling*. For a discussion of Kierkegaard and Derrida on this point and others, see Caputo, *Prayers and Tears*, 188–222.

30. This is the interpretation Levinas gives the passage in his talmudic reading "The Temptation of Temptation" in NTR, 30–50, 42.

31. Derrida, "Violence and Metaphysics," 312 n. 7.

32. Handelman, *Fragments*, 180. She cites Annette Aronowicz as the source of this idea, offered in personal conversation.

Notes to Chapter Three

1. Technically, the terms Jewish mysticism and Kabbalah should not be used synonymously. Jewish mysticism includes certain ancient mystical works, Kabbalah, Ashkenazi Hasidism, modern Hasidism, and perhaps other movements or trends. I use both terms here in the understanding that I am examining only a small part of Jewish mysticism, and indeed, only a small part of the kabbalistic tradition.

2. Scholem, *Kabbalah*, 3.

3. Quoted in Idel, *Kabbalah*, 59.

4. Hagigah 14b. For a short history of the story's interpretation, see Jacobs, *Jewish Mystical Testimonies*, 21–25.

5. It is quite possible, given that his subject at TI 77 is the mystical tradition, that Levinas is actually thinking about the story of the *pardes* while writing the passage. But, if he is, he leaves Aher out. Why? Aher, the heretic, is, I suspect, problematic to Levinas. One account of his heresy describes him having a vision of Metatron, Prince of the Face, and exclaiming: "Perhaps there are two powers in heaven!" — which is, in effect, to say that perhaps the face is another god. This must strike close to the bone for Levinas. From one perspective it is the error he spends all his time trying to correct. And, yet, from another, it is his whole philosophy. If we note in addition to these speculations that "Aher" means "the other" we may be led to ask whether the figure of Aher does not teach Levinas something or indeed everything about alterity — the way the other is wont to do. But, then, what Aher teaches may be something Levinas does not wish to ascribe to a heretic. On Aher's vision, see Segal, *Two Powers*, 10 and throughout.

6. Idel, *Kabbalah*, 60.

7. To pull a relational meaning out of the line is, however, to read against the grain. When Levinas uses the line as the epigraph to "Substitution," the central chapter of *Otherwise Than Being*, he seems to read it relationally. But Celan appears, at least on the surface, to be writing about the invisible meshes. The poem, called "Praise of Distance," is short enough to cite in its entirety:

> In the springs of your eyes live the nets of the fishers of Wildsea . . .
> Blacker in black, I am more naked. Only faithless I am true.
> I am you if I am I . . .
> A net trapped in a net: embracing we sever.
> In the springs of your eyes a hanged man strangles the rope.

Translated (though I have modified the translation at one point) and quoted in Felstiner, *Paul Celan*, 52–53.

8. In an essay on Rosenzweig, Levinas says, speaking partly in Rosenzweig's name and partly in his own, that "in the general economy of being a union can take place between irreducible and absolutely heterogeneous elements, a union of what could not be united, because of life and time" (DF 189).

9. See Bernasconi, "Scepticism," 152.

10. Peperzak, "Presentation," 53. Bernasconi treats the philosophic straw man in Levinas; Peperzak treats the theological or mystical straw man. It is left to Robert Eaglestone to treat the aesthetic straw man. He writes, in *Ethical Criticism*, that there is "a profound tension in [Levinas's] work between his claims against the aesthetic access to transcendence and his use of the aesthetic" (125).

11. Tracy, "Response," 197. Tracy proceeds to cite the work of Eliade, Scholem, Idel, Ricoeur and Marion as exemplary for the phenomeno-

logical study of mysticism All of these thinkers, he suggests, conceive of mysticism as non-totalizing and ethical.

12. I am aware that using Eliade's work in this context raises a host of questions about the nature and status of his understanding of mysticism and his political leanings. It has recently come to light that Eliade supported the Romanian Iron Guard during the 1930s; in addition George Steiner and others have argued that Eliade's journals from that period reflect xenophobia and antisemitism, and, moreover, that he never abandoned the fascistic understanding that provided the underpinning for these attitudes. If all of this is placed alongside Eliade's commitment to the project of comparative mysticism, which may (or may not) rest on the idea of universal hermeneutical and spiritual participation in various manifestations of The One — then Eliade emerges as a notable spokesman for the invisible meshes, and an exemplar par excellence of the deformed fruits they bear, or, in short, as a figure rather like Levinas's Heidegger. If this is so, then my comparison of Levinas and Eliade — which certainly shows Levinas using symbols that can be called shamanistic — should suggest, at least, that there are two ways of using those symbols, an Eliadean participatory way and a Levinasian relational way. But then it becomes possible to ask whether Eliade himself was not using the symbols relationally, and indeed to reassess the idea that his mysticism is fundamentally fascistic. See Steiner, "Ecstasies, not arguments"; and see especially the discussion of some of the evidence, Steiner, and several other scholars in John R. Mason, *Reading and Responding*, 60–75.

13. I narrow our focus here from Levinas's proximity with the Western mystical tradition (as suggested by Peperzak) to Jewish mysticism in particular. The beginning of a case for proximity between Levinas and Christian mysticism is made by Derrida in "Sauf le nom."

14. Mopsik, "Cabbale," 428.

15. Wolosky, "Derrida, Jabès, Levinas," 284, 300.

16. R. Cohen, *Elevations*, 241–73. Handelman, *Fragments*, throughout.

17. R. Cohen, *Elevations*, 251–52, 252, 252 n. 11.

18. See Idel, *Mystical Experience; Ecstatic Kabbalah*; and *Language, Torah and Hermeneutics*. See also the seminal *Kabbalah*.

19. Abulafia was influenced in his development of this practice by the ancient Sefer Yetzirah, with its strange speculations about the power of the Hebrew letters, and in addition by the writings of Eleazar of Worms. For a short history of the practice of letter recombination, see Idel, *Kabbalah*, 97–103.

20. Quoted in Jacobs, *Jewish Mystical Testimonies*, 57–62, 60–61.

21. Idel, *Language, Torah and Hermeneutics*, ix, x.

22. Both passages are cited in Wolosky, "Derrida, Jabès, Levinas," 292, 293.

23. Idel, *Kabbalah*, 235.

24. Idel, *Language, Torah and Hermeneutics*, xvi.

25. Scholem, *Major Trends*, 131–32.

26. Quoted in Idel, *Mystical Experience*, 136; see also 174 n. 305.

27. *Ibid.*, 136–37.

28. See Bokser, *Jewish Mystical Tradition*, 99. Bokser cites at length the passage in which Abulafia describes the movement from light to speech. We may note that the distinction derives from Maimonides, who speaks of 11 levels of prophecy. The first two levels are not yet true prophecy, and can be left aside. Levels three to eleven fall into two groups:

(A) 3. seeing in a dream, 4. hearing in a dream, 5. being addressed in a dream, 6. being addressed by an angel in a dream, and 7. being addressed by God in a dream.

(B) 8. seeing a vision, 9. hearing in a vision, 10. being addressed in a vision, and 11. being addressed by an angel in a vision.

The obvious twelfth level does not arise, explains Maimonides, for the human imagination could not bear it. In any case, the once-repeated pattern is a movement from sight to speech (*Guide* II 45–46).

29. Idel, *Mystical Experience*, 83; see 139.

30. *Ibid.*, 139. Abulafia cites Isaiah 50.6 which we saw Levinas cite in the previous chapter. And this is not the only time that Abulafia cites a biblical passage of which Levinas is fond. Abulafia describes his call to prophecy as beginning in *hineni*: "A spirit came and made me stand on my legs, and called me twice by my name, 'Abraham, Abraham', and I answered 'here I am'." Abulafia refers here to Genesis 22.1 and 11 — the first appearances of hineni in the Scriptures. He goes on to explain that after the call and response, he is taught by a voice the way of justice, knowledge, and understanding. See Idel, *Mystical Experience*, 140.

31. Idel, *Mystical Experience*, 84.

32. *Ibid.*, 84. Idel gathers the testimony of many mystics in whose thought "the idea of the human speech as an expression of the reception of prophecy" occurs, among them Hayim Vital. See *Mystical Experience*, 85.

33. Idel, *Mystical Experience*, 86–87.

34. *Ibid.*, 88–89; see also 152 n. 82. The symbol of the *kavod* as a mediator is common in Kabbalah. J. Dan, in *Jewish Mysticism*, 49, describes the centrality of the image for the Ashkenazi Hasidim.

35. Idel, *Mystical Experience*, 90.

36. Quoted in Idel, *Mystical Experience*, 126.

37. Scholem, *Major Trends*, 138, 141.

38. Idel, *Kabbalah*, 302 n. 21.

39. Quoted in Idel, *Mystical Experience*, 135.

40. There is no doubt that *halachah* (or *mitsvot*) are not synonymous with ethics in most of the several ways in which ethics is usually understood. For instance: (a) It may be that ethics is understood as 'more' than the *halachah*, or the 'spirit' of the *halachah*, or the reasons for the *halachah* — but here the two are already blended. (b) It may be that ethics is understood as indeterminate, and indeed, can come to refer to any logical or quasi-logical justification of one's actions, while *halachah* is fixed and unwavering. Levinas disputes both sides of this argument. (c) It may be that ethics is understood as something like a natural law that arises from human beings and is linked to their rationality, while the *halachah* is comprised of rules given by God and quite difficult to account for by reason. Again, Levinas disputes both sides, replacing the distinction with the witnessing structure. Levinas does not conflate ethics and *halachah*, as I explained in section three of chapter one, but neither does he maintain the distinction on any of the usual bases. Both ethics and halachah come to the subject from the other.

41. Idel, *Kabbalah*, xvi.

42. I cited this list at the beginning of this chapter; see Mopsik, "Cabbale," 428.

43. In *Kabbalah*, Scholem writes: 'The common order of the *sefirot* and the names most generally used for them are: (1) *Keter Elyon* ("supreme crown") or simply *Keter*; (2) *Hochmah* ("wisdom"); (3) *Binah* ("intelligence"); (4) *Gedullah* ("greatness") or *Hesed* ("love"); (5) *Gevurah* ("power") or *Din* ("judgment," or "rigour"); (6) *Tiferet* ("beauty") or *Rachamim* ("compassion"); (7) *Nezah* ("lasting endurance"); (8) *Hod* ("majesty"); (9) *Zaddik* ("righteous one"); (10) *Malchut* ("kingdom") or *Atarah* ("diadem")' (106).

44. Scholem, *Kabbalah*, 90. Kosover is late (c.1770) but Scholem notes that this understanding of the *En Sof* dates from the thirteenth century or before.

45. R. Cohen, *Elevations*, 254.

46. Scholem, *Kabbalah*, 402.

47. *Ibid.*, 402.

48. Luria wrote little; he explained this, but it is unclear whether his explanation implies that his thoughts could not be committed to paper because they are unsystematic and should remain so, or because his system was too complicated, or simply because he wished his ideas to remain esoteric (see Scholem, *Major Trends*, 254). We have four main versions of his cosmogony written by his disciples or their disciples:

that of Moses Jonah of Safed in *Kanfei Yonah*, that of Joseph ibn Tabul, that of Hayim Vital in *Etz Hayim*, and the less reliable account of Israel Sarug in *Limundei Azilut*. The best English descriptions of the Lurianic cosmogony can be found in Scholem's works: *Major Trends*, 260–78, *Kabbalah*, 128–44, and *Kabbalah and its Symbolism*, 109–17. These three accounts contain different details and complement one another. In the first, Scholem describes the relation of the cosmogony to earlier kabbalistic ideas. In the second, he is primarily interested to explain it as a myth of exile, a cosmic account of the expulsion of the Jews from Spain. In the third, he compares elements of it to philosophical concepts such as the *anima mundi,* and certain Platonic and neoplatonic themes.

49. Scholem, *Major Trends*, 262.

50. *Ibid.*, 273–74.

51. Scholem, *Kabbalah*, 141.

52. In the narrative line of *Totality and Infinity*, the subject comes across (1) in section 1, the teacher, (2) in section 2, the homemaker or 'woman', (3) in section 3, the fellow citizen or 'brother', (4) in section 4 the lover, and (5) the son.

53. Mopsik, "Cabbale," 432.

54. Handelman makes a different connection between a Levinasian motif and *tsimtsum*, one that I find breathtaking, but cannot yet place in my own analysis. She links *tsimtsum* to Levinasian passivity.

> Passivity in [Levinas's] work means that the access to the 'other than being' requires a kind of "holding back . . . breathlessness of the spirit" because being as essence is the principle of self and same as egoism — a self-expansion and filling up of everything (OB 5). Although Levinas is by no means a mystic, nor does he draw his inspiration from Jewish mystical sources, there is an interesting analogy here to the kabbalistic idea of God's . . . self-contraction. . . . [F]or Levinas, the emptying out or contraction of the subject is what opens it to the positivity of the ethical relation . . . the subject is . . . opened, hollowed out, traumatized, wounded, deposed, and subject to the other. (*Fragments,* 259)

Handelman goes on to link her analysis of tsimtsum as breathlessness (and in fact, the root word of *tsimtsum* does mean a contraction or drawing in of breath) to Levinas's use of the metaphor of the 'lung' to describe the subject (260). As I have used the Levinasian categories so far in this book, God has been the only lung — he breathed over the spirit of the waters at the end of chapter two. But it is possible that a kind of human breathlessness or passivity might correlate with a divine breathing over the waters, just as a divine contraction of breath might correlate to humanity as lung, as subjectivity, as separated essence, or in short, as life. In this case the human drawing in of the breath of life, her 'in-spiration' would be a reference to the in-drawn breath of the withdrawn God, or, by the ambiguity of the witness structure (which Levinas precisely describes as inspiration), a breathing for-God or to-God or even in-the-place-of-God. Handelman goes on to write of 'inspiration' as a breathing-like movement of "'oscillation'... between withholding and assertion, withdrawal and expulsion, philosophy and nonphilosophy, soul and body, language and what is beyond representation and speech" (261).

55. See Sacks, "Practical Implications."

56. Dan, *Jewish Mysticism*, 100.

57. This scheme is ably expounded by Harold Bloom in *Kabbalah and Criticism*, 36–37. Also see Bloom's comparison between Cordovero's *behinot*, Proclus's emanations, and the epistemology of C.S. Peirce (53–58), which is impressionistic but thought provoking.

58. See Idel, *Kabbalah*, 136–46; also Jacobs, *Jewish Mystical Testimonies*, 81.

59. Idel, *Kabbalah*, 254.

60. *Ibid.*, 146–53.

61. Handelman, *Fragments*, 96.

62. Dan, *Jewish Mysticism*, 90–91.

63. Handelman, *Fragments*, 97. An argument similar to Handelman's is made by Richard Cohen who notes that the Jewish prohibition against idolatry ensures that the symbols of supernal entities will not be understood literally. The symbols, he says, are not reified angels or divinities but 'openings'. The difference between Abulafia or Levinas, in these terms, is whether the portal to God is within, or in the human other. See *Elevations*, 256.

64. Gibbs, *Correlations*, 210–11, 214–15.

65. Bloom, *Kabbalah and Criticism*, 53.

66. Scholem, *Kabbalah*, 427.

67. Bokser, *Jewish Mystical Tradition*, 26.

68. Quoted in Idel, *Kabbalah*, 57.

69. Scholem, *Major Trends*, 275. I have altered his usage, rendering the Tetragrammaton as YHVH instead of JHWH.

70. Handelman, *Fragments*, 300. The central story is taken from Solomon, *Lire Lévinas*.

71. Handelman's general discussion of Levinas and Scholem is, however, excellent — and much more detailed than mine. See especially *Fragments*, 313 and thereabouts.

72. Handelman, *Fragments*, 299.

73. Representations of this conception are numerous. For Scholem's version, see *Major Trends*, 7–8. Also interesting is Idel's comparison between Scholem's version and that of Eric Voegelin. Idel, "Voegelin's Israel and Revelation."

74. A similar understanding emerges in Walter Benjamin's essays

on Kafka. Benjamin makes a distinction between myth and fairy tale, whereby the mythic structures that discourage free thought can be subverted by the fairy tale trickster. He then implies a comparison between myth and *halachah*, and contiguously, between the fairy tale trickster and *aggadah — aggadah* perhaps standing in for the Kabbalah or a proto-Kabbalah. This interpretation emerges from dialogue with Gershom Scholem and is certainly compatible with Scholem's understanding of the relation between myth and *halachah*, and between myth and Kabbalah. See Walter Benjamin, "Franz Kafka" and "Some Reflections on Kafka," 117, 144.

75. Nadler, *Faith of the Mitnagdim*.
76. See Gibbs, "Blowing on the Embers."
77. Quoted in Nadler, *Faith of the Mitnagdim*, 25.
78. Handelman, *Fragments*, 302.
79. The public argument between Levinas and Scholem, if there can be said to have been one, is entirely constituted by Scholem's passing remark quoted above, and by Levinas's passing remark in a footnote to "Messianic Texts," a reading we will take up at length in the next chapter. After praising Scholem for his "remarkable intuition" in distinguishing between apocalyptic anomian messianism and the rationalist messianism of the rabbis, he writes: "Not everything has been said, however, as Scholem sometimes seems to think, when one has affirmed the rationalist character of this messianism. As if rationalization meant only the negation of the miraculous and as if, in the realm of the spirit, we could abandon debatable values without setting other values in motion. It is this positive meaning of the messianism of the rabbis that I want to show in my commentary" (DF 296–97 n. 1). One can see why Levinas is uneasy with Scholem here. Scholem divides the tradition into rationalists (who are nomian, and want little to do with the miraculous) and apocalypticists (who have a virtual monopoly on the miraculous, and are anomian). Levinas would like to see all Jewish anomianism (with the possible exception of Hasidism) as attacks on the law for the sake of the law; he would like to see all of this as rational, all of it as miraculous, and, as we will see, all of it, in a certain carefully defined sense, as apocalyptic.
80. Quoted in Jacobs, *Jewish Mystical Testimonies*, 66.

Notes to Chapter Four

1. The three lectures discussed at length in this chapter come from the proceedings of the colloquium of French Jewish intellectuals. They and transcripts of the discussions that followed them were first published in volumes 1 and 2 of *La Conscience juive* (Les Presses

Universitaires de France, 1962–63). Later, the lectures were republished without the ensuing discussions in *Difficile liberté*, (Editions Albin Michel), the third and last edition of which is dated 1976 and appears in a *Livre de poche* reprint. For *Difficile liberté*, Levinas conflated his second and third talks under the title "Textes messianiques," though the first talk appears intact under the title "Entre deux mondes." *Difficile liberté* also appears in English translation as *Difficult Freedom*.

All references to Levinas's first lecture in this chapter are in the following form: (a) the abbreviation of the French title of the lecture (EDM), (b) the page reference for the first volume of *La Conscience juive*, (c) the page reference for the Livre de poche edition of *Difficile Liberté* , and (d) the page number for the English translation in *Difficult Freedom*. The roundtable discussions that followed the delivery of the lectures appear only in *La Conscience juive*, and citations of them are followed by only one page reference. References to the second and third lectures cite only the English version in DF; references to the roundtable read *"La Conscience juive* 2: [page]." The single citation of an intervention by Levinas in the discussions of someone else's paper is footnoted in full (in the note that follows this one). All translations appearing in this chapter are my own. The epigraph comes from the midrash Levinas cites toward the end of the first lecture (EDM, 137/280/201).

2. The intervention occurs toward the end of the discussions of the of the colloquium's first paper, "Sens de l'histoire juive," given by Edmond Fleg: *La Conscience juive* 1: 5–21, Levinas's intervention, 15–16.

3. Sanhedrin, 101b. Levinas's commentary adds much embellishment to the story.

4. Avodah Zarah, 3a–b. Levinas tells the story as it stands in the Talmud, omitting only some rabbinical asides.

5. Although I argued in the last chapter for the existence of a Levinasian mysticism, I shall use the term in this chapter as Levinas uses it. Thus 'mysticism' must be understood henceforth as the perverse craving for ontological union with the divine, or, more broadly, for any conception of a totality encompassing God and human beings. The fact that Western mystics do not, in general, have any such conception is from now on bracketed.

6. Thus the most famous of Levinas's discussions of desacralization is found in the talmudic reading "Desacralization and Disenchantment" (1971) which presents the move from 'sacred' (mystical, magical, same) to 'holy' (ethical, Jewish) as it is expressed in Sanhedrin 67a–68b. The essay appears in NTR, 136–60.

7. Gibbs, *Correlations*, 158, my emphasis.

8. Moreover, Levinas's presentation of his ideas in *Otherwise Than Being* can be understood as a desacralizing of *Totality and Infinity*: thus Levinas desacralizes the Jewish texts; the Jewish texts desacralize one another; Levinas desacralizes himself.

9. Peperzak, *To the Other*, 11–12. To this we may add the concrete fact that Levinas attended many of Kojève's lectures on Hegel at the Sorbonne. But whether Peperzak and I are right, it remains true that no commentator, including Peperzak, has looked in any detail at the relation between Levinas and Kojève's Hegel, while the subject of Levinas and Hegel himself has been written of extensively. I attempt here to remedy this gap. For Kojève's Hegel see Kojève, *Introduction to Hegel*. Incidentally, Kojève and Levinas led similar lives up to a point. Both were born in Eastern Europe in the first decade of this century, both left home before the age of twenty to travel, both spent time in the 1920s in Germany studying with Heidegger and Husserl, both moved to Paris around 1930, and both fought for France in the war.

10. The fact that these comments are 'interpolated' is an innovation. I have reorganized the discussion by issue, although it took place literally 'roundtable', i.e. moving from person to person rather than issue to issue and ending with a single long response by Levinas to all his supporters and detractors.

11. Levinas quotes a letter to Rosenstock-Huessey, where Rosenzweig writes, "Hegel spoke the truth when he (implicitly) said what he (explicitly) knew: that he was the end of philosophy." The letter in its entirety can be found in Rosenstock-Huessey, *Judaism Despite Christianity*, letter 2, p. 83. See also the two letters to Hans Ehrenberg in December 1913, cited in the introduction to Rosenstock-Huessey's book, in one of which Rosenzweig describes Hegel as the "last philosopher" and "the first of the new Church fathers."

12. "This resembles a poem by Mayakovsky, in which everyday things and even emblems of signs begin to live on their own account among men, concepts go out into the street, arguments become events, and dialectical conflicts become wars" (EDM 124–5/259/185).

13. Cooper, *End of History*, 25.

14. Levinas writes somewhat more cautiously, in the 1990 preface to an article from the thirties:

> We must ask ourselves if liberalism is all we need to achieve an authentic dignity for the human subject. . . . Such a society loses living contact with its true ideal of freedom and accepts degenerate forms of the ideal. It does not see that the true ideal requires effort and instead enjoys those aspects of the ideal that make life easier. It is to a society in such a condition that the

Germanic ideal of man seems to promise sincerity and authen-
ticity. (RPH 63).

15. Like those who cry, against Kojève: "History hasn't ended! We're
still *doing things*."

16. Derrida, "Violence and Metaphysics," 152.

17. It is incidental, but somewhat interesting in light of what we
shall shortly say about Levinas's treatment of the Rosenzweigian
analysis of the relation between Judaism and Christianity, to note that
Levinas is himself one of these 'Western Jews'. Any reader of his
philosophical works must be aware of how often he cites the gospel
and alludes to Christian images. Indeed, at times he seems to envision
himself a modern Jewish Jesus, universalizing the Christian images
or ideas as Jesus is said to have universalized the Jewish images or
ideas. In any case, the frequency of his references to things like 'the
resurrection of the son' (TI, throughout) — always a reference to the
subject's relation with the other who appears as his *own* son — deserves
scholarly attention.

18. That the Talmud desacralizes the Bible is only part of Levinas's
justification for desacralizing, at least in this instance. He has proved,
with the example of Jonah and the examples offered the previous year,
that the Talmud does desacralize the Bible. But this work is continued,
profoundly, in Rosenzweig's *Star*. Arguably, it is the *Star*, even more
than the Talmud, which has taught Levinas that the whole of the Bible
has love as its content.

19. However, in certain texts he does reclaim the term 'sacred
history' and redefine it as the history of ethical encounters, a move we
will look at briefly in the next chapter.

20. The passages are from Sanhedrin 99a and 97b–98a.

21. Neusner, "Paradigmatic Thinking," 371, 375.

22. *Ibid.*, 354, 362.

23. The Soncino edition of the Babylonian Talmud renders this
passage as follows: "R. Hiyya b. Abba said in R. Johanan's name: All
the prophets prophesied [all the good things] only in respect of the
Messianic era; but as for the world to come, 'the eye hath not seen, O
Lord, beside thee, what he hath prepared for him that waiteth for him'.
Now he disagrees with Samuel who said: This world differs from [that
of] the days of the Messiah only in respect to the servitude to [foreign]
powers."

24. I wish to avoid any crude associations of naiveté or belligerence
associated with the term 'realist.' I intend, on the contrary, to evoke an
echo of the term 'empiricist', which Levinas used of Rosenzweig
in "Between Two Worlds" (EDM 126/263/188). But I do not use the
term empiricist here because that term implies the awareness of a

metaphysical element in reality which is missing in Samuel's understanding. Samuel, as Levinas renders him, does not fully grasp that part of the structure of reality that is the effect of the desire for the beyond.

25. Levinas's rejection of providential conceptions will form much of the subject of the next chapter. I can now, however, quote again a passage I quoted in chapter one, but here at greater length:

> Here again I must express my reservations about the term eschatology. The term eschaton implies that there might exist a finality, an end to the historical relation of difference between man and the absolutely other, a reduction of the gap that safeguards the alterity of the transcendent, to a totality of sameness. To realize the eschaton would therefore mean that we could seize or appropriate God as a telos and degrade infinite relation with the other to a finite fusion. This is what Hegelian dialectics amounts to . . . (RK 30).

See also on this point Maurice Blanchot, "Our Clandestine Companion," 41–50. Blanchot's and Levinas's clandestine companion is a post-end-of-philosophy philosophy, a philosophy that appears in different guises such as literature, or 'standing outside', or love.

26. This point marks the beginning of what was originally the second talmudic lecture of the two which Levinas later conflated into "Messianic Texts." The first deals with Sanhedrin 99a, the second with 97b–98a.

27. Here Levinas renders the talmudic passage accurately.

28. The Soncino edition has: "R. Giddal said in Rab's name: The Jews are destined to eat their fill in the days of the messiah. R. Joseph demurred: Is this not obvious; who else should then eat — Hilek and Bilek?"

29. The Soncino edition has: "R. Nahum said: if he is of those living, it might be one like himself."

30. Gibbs, *Correlations*, 155–75, 171.

31. Handelman offers a close reading of almost the entire talmudic lecture in chap. 10 of *Fragments* (306–36). I refer to it here because her discussion of the last few references, from Abbahu and the Min on to the end (333–36), is particularly insightful.

32. Levinas renders the talmudic passage accurately.

33. I have here defended Levinas from Jean Wahl as well as I can. Ultimately, the defense is not entirely successful. Levinas does, in fact, offer something like a universal truth; this is why he can say that "all people *[tout le monde]* are the messiah" (DF 89). He *means* all here — not each. *All* of us feel the assignation that comes from *each* other; this is indeed the point of his account of the ethical encounter. But an account of what everyone experiences is not necessarily an ontology; we keep

in mind while making admissions to his critics that Levinas's account does not designate place; it does not rank; it does not order.

34. Gibbs, *Correlations*, 158, 155–75, esp. 164–67.

35. Is it actually possible to transcend the rubric of universal and particular? Not completely, or not for long. Jews, as a 'minority', will always return to the rubric. And so they should — but while they do so they should remember that all discussions of the issue are always already ruptured. The matter can be put generally. Levinasian postmodernism does not stand for ethnic autonomy as against universality but tries instead to reveal individuality and gift as the ground of the entire debate, and thereby to undermine the debate's primacy. But because the universal/particular debate cannot be done away with, only undermined, all its dangers remain alive. Elliot Wolfson, responding to discussions by S. Kepnes, P. Ochs, and R. Gibbs about Jewish postmodernism, writes:

> In spite of all [their] well-intentioned qualifications, one cannot help but come away from reading [the record of their discussions] with the feeling that there is a real potential in the postmodern Jewish project for a lapse into ethnocentrism that could promote rather than heal the suffering of others. . . . The challenge for postmodern Jewish philosophy is to facilitate the growth of a culture based on the textual specificity of the past without losing sight of the place that Judaism must occupy in the human community at large. We must get beyond the dichotomy of the universal and the particular, but not by reducing the one to the other. On the contrary, the particularity of the Jewish tradition is meaningful only to the extent that it improves on the moral condition of humanity.

Wolfson, "A Response," 102, 104.

36. Derrida, "Violence and Metaphysics," 153.

37. For a less radical interpretation of messianism, one need only turn to Levinas's articles on Zionism. See, for instance, "The State of Caesar and the State of David' in BTV, where he reinterprets a number of the talmudic sayings he treats in "Messianic Texts" in a way more friendly to the schwärmerei of conventional messianic expectation: here, not only is Johanan an idealist, but idealism is a reasonable position. But the Zionist essays and the (perhaps naive) hope they express should not be taken, as they sometimes are, to mean that Levinas eventually forgets or lays aside his sophisticated, antiontological messianism. On the contrary, the ideas laid out in "Messianic Texts" continue to inform his understanding, and, in addition, become central to the thought of Blanchot and Derrida.

Notes to Chapter Five

1. Levinas does not tell the first of these stories, which I nevertheless include because it expresses the movement in its entirety so well. The other three, which add particular aspects and symbols to the account of the movement, are drawn from his essays. A description of the movement in Levinas's thought is offered by Wes Avram, "On the Priority of 'Ethics'," 273–78.

2. Wiesel, *Night*, 32, 61–62.

3. *Ibid.*, 64–65.

4. *Ibid.*, 65.

5. DF 142–45. Levinas says that the story was originally published anonymously (DF 142). In fact, this is not so. The author, Zvi Kolitz, published the story in 1946 in an Argentinean Yiddish paper; it was then republished without the author's name in Israel. Zvi Kolitz called it fiction; when it was anonymously reprinted it was represented as fact. See Kolitz, *Yossel Rakover*, which includes the story, an account of the controversy, and several interpretations including a new translation of "Loving the Torah More than God." But a glance at the story reveals that Levinas's commentary misrepresents it — deliberately, I think, and for the better. There are at least three noteworthy scholarly discussions of Levinas's commentary on the story: Handelman's discussion (275–78 of *Fragments*), Oppenheim's discussion (41–52 of *Speaking / Writing*) and the commentary by Sugarman and Stephenson.

6. Gibbs, "Unjustifiable Suffering," 7.

7. See Oppenheim, *Speaking / Writing*, 47.

8. Levinas clarifies the difference between the common conception of sacred history and his own in "Poetry and the Impossible," one of his essays on Paul Claudel. Claudel holds, at least for a time, a strong belief in providence which leads him to research prefigurement imagery in the Old Testament and to attempt to define the continuing role of the Jews in sacred history. To this Levinas contrasts his own conception, saying that there is a kind of sacred history in "the life and death of the Jews under the Nazi occupation, the life and death of the Jews who built the State of Israel," but it is a sacred history "without rhetoric or theology." It is not the secret significance of these events but their literal meaning where sacredness lies. It is in the daily reality of lives lived, and in Jewish life in general (DF 129).

9. PL 162. Levinas omits the gritty centre of Fackenheim's argument, that Hitler killed anyone with one Jewish grandparent, and that therefore the supposed sin belonged to the victim's great-grandparents and consisted of raising Jewish children (*God's Presence*, 70). The argument comes through, however, without this detail.

10. Fackenheim, *God's Presence*, 69–70. This is a longer version of the two-theodicy scheme he describes in the middle of the book, in which the first theodicy, where evil is punishment for sin, gives way after the Bar Kochba rebellion to the second, where God feels remorse and laments the evil he has allowed, and goes into exile with us. See 25–31.

11. *Ibid.*, 84.

12. *Ibid.*, 12–13. Fackenheim quotes here from Buber's *Moses* (see *God's Presence*, 32 n. 14). Levinas implicitly but obviously addresses this idea in his essay "Demanding Judaism," where he writes: "Judaism, rather, is a rupture of the natural and the historical that are constantly reconstituted" (BTV 4). It might be possible to sum up the whole difference between Levinas and Buber using the various nuances inscribed in this juxtaposition: for Buber, the natural and the historical are transparent for God; for Levinas, Judaism is a rupture of the natural and the historical.

13. Fackenheim, *God's Presence*, 6, 35–43, 52–59, 49–52.

14. *Ibid.*, 20–21, 39.

15. *Ibid.*, 74–75.

16. I am in debt in this discussion of the third element in the critique to Robert Gibbs, who sketched it for me in conversation.

17. Fackenheim, *God's Presence*, 103 n. 51.

18. Other thinkers have formulated similar critiques of Fackenheim. Michael Wyschogrod, for instance, argues in "Faith and the Holocaust" that Fackenheim places the Holocaust — or rather, a drive to thwart Hitler posthumously by ensuring the survival of Judaism — at the centre of his religion, where it does not belong. He shows, further, that Fackenheim dismisses Richard Rubenstein only because Rubenstein's argument would divide Jews so that they could no longer stand against assimilation, rather than on any theological or philosophical basis. Fackenheim attempts, he writes "to turn the state of affairs into an ideology. . . . One is almost driven to the conclusion that in the absence of the Holocaust, given Fackenheim's profound understanding of the irreversibility of the secular stance, no justification for the further survival of Judaism could have been found. With the Holocaust, amazing as this may appear, Judaism has gotten a new lease on life" (289–90). In the same article, Wyschogrod deconstructs the notion of 'uniqueness' on which Fackenheim pins so much of his argument; the claim of 'uniqueness' — if it is not to be relativized by the simple fact that all events are unique — can only mean 'worse than anything else', despite Fackenheim's insistence that it does not mean this (291–92).

In "On Fackenheim's *To Mend the World*," Arthur Cohen, in distinction to Wyschogrod, takes issue with Fackenheim in a way that makes Fackenheim sound a little like a late-in-life Levinasian — though we should note that he is speaking not about *God's Presence* but about a later work. He points to Fackenheim's early ambitions toward developing his own philosophical system and notes that he pins similar sentiments on others, for instance Franz Rosenzweig whose hope that *The Star of Redemption* is 'unfanatical' is translated, by Fackenheim, into the distinctly un-Rosenzweigian hope that it is an 'unfanatical *system'* (227). Cohen proceeds to argue that when Fackenheim abandons the desire to systematize, in the wake of the Holocaust, he moves either into nonphilosophical homiletics or into nonphilosophical anecdote. On the "other side" of philosophy, "Fackenheim's book [*To Mend the World*] utterly collapses" (231). There, "where theology might have begun again, he surrendered intellection for the sake of moralizing examples of superlative human witness that are offered naked, without examination of their cognitive significance, their metaphysical situation, their ethical contribution either to the demolition of old views of God or to the construction of a new view of God formed in the aftermath of the Holocaust" (232).

19. Richard Rubenstein in *After Auschwitz* and Arthur Cohen in "Thinking the Tremendum" speak, like Levinas, of the death of God, and mean by it the death of previous theologies or theology at large. But unlike Levinas, they see no resources in the tradition describing a way of life 'otherwise than theology', and their arguments therefore emerge as props for modern secularism. Jacob Neusner in *Stranger at Home* argues, like Levinas, that nothing can be learned from the Holocaust, for God had no hand in it. But unlike Levinas, he does not allow this understanding to challenge the notion of theodicy or providence at large. Eliezer Berkovits in *Faith and the Holocaust*, Irving Greenberg in *Image of God*, and, as we have seen, Fackenheim, in complete distinction to Levinas, each find ways to fit the Holocaust into a providential framework.

20. Not, of course, that what Levinas sees as the deficiencies in Fackenheim's understanding come as any surprise to him. It is common to reaffirm providence after reflecting on the destruction of theodicy at Auschwitz; Levinas is surely familiar with the tendency in both Judaism, as described in the previous note, and Christianity, as represented, for instance, by François Mauriac who reaffirms providence in his foreword to Wiesel's *Night*. In addition, Levinas is familiar with the more dangerous deformations of modernity. Fackenheim is much closer to the supreme principle than the thinkers we saw Levinas take on in chapter four, Kojève and Lévi-Strauss, and a great deal less threatening to Levinas than they. It is only that because he comes so close to a repudiation of providence, his falling away is more to be

lamented, or more worthy of address. Or perhaps the only substantial difference is that Fackenheim's Hegelianism is better disguised than Kojève's and Lévi-Strauss's. In any case, the critical point is that the expressions in "Useless Suffering" that appear hopeful should be read carefully, in the understanding that they constitute lament and call rather than prediction.

21. This apparent criticism of biblical theology (and I argue presently that it is only apparent) is prefaced by two minor criticisms. First, in discussing one of the elementary ways pain can be made 'useful' and suffering overlooked — by linking pain to wisdom — he cites Ecclesiastes: "he that increaseth knowledge increaseth sorrow" (1.18, PL 159–60). Then, in discussing a more abstract rationalization of pain — the notion that a healthy society requires some suffering in the form of discipline — he asks: "is not fear of punishment the beginning of wisdom?" (PL 160) — a rhetorical question that functions as a critique of at least one interpretation of the biblical verse "the fear of the Lord is the beginning of wisdom" (Proverbs 1.7).

22. However, in a footnote in "Useless Suffering," Levinas says that he is thinking of Job, and appears to suggest that to perform a nonprovidential reading would be to read the Bible back through this late book (PL 167 n. 8). During the 1980s, Levinas was inclined to say that he drew on the Bible more than the Talmud, as in "Useless Suffering" (1982) and the interview with the graduate students published in PL (1986). This may represent a shift in thinking away from the talmudic emphasis of "Jewish Thought Today" (1961) and the earlier talmudic readings we discussed in the last chapter (1950s and 1960s). Or it may merely represent the way he addresses certain audiences.

23. See Arendt, *Eichmann in Jerusalem*, 251–52.

24. Waldenfels, "Response and Responsibility."

25. Socrates calls it 'justice'. I have used 'ethics' in this paragraph instead because, in Levinas's later thought, justice becomes a technical term distinct from ethics, meaning the symmetrical imposition of what once was asymmetrical ethics on a political body. In distinction, justice in the *Republic* is a fairly wide term covering moral behaviour in general; it is legitimate to translate it as ethics here.

26. Waldenfels, "Response and Responsibility," 48.

27. Robert Bernasconi objects to Levinas's use of the term 'persecution' for what we have called a second-level violence when it is almost always experienced as a social or political phenomenon: one group persecutes another. See " 'Only the Persecuted . . .'," 82. Bernasconi's article as a whole, however, deals mainly with the question of whether persecution, understood as an aspect of the encounter with

the other-qua-other is a formal notion that defies what is particular. I take up this question at length, though with reference to an article by Jeffrey Kosky, rather than to Bernasconi.

28. The idea appears Christian, which is perhaps why Levinas brings in both a biblical reference and a rabbinic reference to illuminate it: "to tend the cheek to the smiter and to be filled with shame" (Lamentations 3.30, OB 111); and, from the previous chapter in *Otherwise Than Being*, "responsibility '. . . to the point of being delivered over to stoning and insults'" (Rashi's Commentary on Numbers 12.12, OB 192 n.24).

29. Incidentally, some pages after Levinas illustrates the *il y a* with the phrase, "it is raining" (EI 48), he mentions the rain again, in the context of one of his most compellingly quotidian descriptions of how one enters into relation with the other: "It is difficult to be silent in someone's presence; this difficulty has its ultimate foundation in this signification proper to the saying, whatever is the said. It is necessary to speak of something, of the rain and fine weather, no matter what, but to speak, to respond to him and already to answer for him" (EI 88). Thus in the phrase "it is raining" there is horror. But the horror is overcome if one turns to the other and *says* it is raining; the horror is overcome by the quotation marks I have put around the phrase.

30. E. Wyschogrod, "Derrida, Levinas and Violence," 183.

31. Susan Shapiro writes, in terms borrowed from Lyotard, that "Levinas does not skip over the Shoah, [but] he does not — in my opinion — focus sufficiently on its immemorial character or on its difference from and relation to the transcendental Immemorial." See Shapiro "Response," 86.

32. Kosky, "After Death," 237.

33. *Ibid.*, 253.

34. For both passages and others that reveal the same correlations, see Kosky, "After Death," 255.

35. *Ibid.*, 256–57.

36. The problem of the anonymity of the other is raised by many commentators, usually as a critique of Levinas. Very occasionally, however, one hears it raised in praise of him. In such cases, the interchangeability of the other is seen as a positive thing, and even perhaps "a point of resonance with the Christian claim that the neighbor is always Christ." Let me say in response that I believe that for Levinas the neighbor is never Christ, despite the homiletical comparison he makes between Matthew 25 and Judaism in ITN 161–62. If there is a problematic anonymity in Levinas it is anonymity in the subject: all subjects respond, initially, with an awareness of responsibility; indeed, all subjects are the messiah; all subjects are, if

you like, Christ. Without defending the claim at any length, I will add that I see here and elsewhere a profound difference between Levinas's understanding and the main thrust of doctrinal Christianity. Of course the famous comment of John's Jesus "No one comes to the father but by me" (John 14.6) can be interpreted relationally to mean that everyone who comes to the father comes, whether he knows it or not, through Christ. But from a Levinasian perspective this is still too exclusive. In Levinas, the other is my route to the father not by virtue of some special quality, but by virtue of being whoever he is.

Levinas's flip here (the other is not the messiah, I am) has a great many implications. The golden rule will serve as just one example. The Christian formulation (do unto others as you would have them do unto you) presumes something about the other; like the presumption that the other is Christ, it imports a genericness into alterity. The Jewish formulation (do not do unto others as you would not have them do unto you) is merely a safeguard against bad behavior; it presumes nothing about the other. Moreover, in Hillel's famous statement of the principle, he follows it with the words: "The rest is commentary. Go and learn." Certainly Hillel means "go and learn" the Torah. But perhaps he also means "go and learn" from the other. Do not presume that he is like you, and likes what you do. Ask him what he needs and wants; then give it to him.

But let me return from theology to the technical question of the other's anonymity, and trace it through section 1 of TI. At 35, Levinas opens up the possibility of formality because of his attempts to avoid reversibility: in order for the other's relation to me to be different from mine to him, he must be otherness itself. At 38, Levinas denies form in favour of the other's content. At 50, he embarks on a "deformalization" of the idea of the other. At 51, the distinction between form and content is bracketed. At 66, a new term, "expression," is put up against the bracketed form/content distinction. Finally, at 74, the term "nakedness" is coined to refer to the individual's breaking out of his form. It remains throughout that "the other qua other is the Other" (71). But it is fairly clear that Levinas is always trying to load this formulation with a uniqueness he cannot describe.

37. See EI 89; PL 175; RM 21.

38. His words are rendered less colloquially by Richard Cohen: "I feared a much graver objection" (EI 89). Before saying this he does, however, take up briefly the question of his ethics as description, asserting that they are prior to hatred and ground it, a matter we have discussed in chapter one.

39. In the notes to "Useless Suffering," Levinas refers to the Song

of Songs 5.8 "I am sick with love," and also to Tractate Brachot of the Babylonian Talmud, 5b (PL 166 n. 5, n. 4). Obviously a great many more passages could be conscripted here.

40. Another piece that gives an account of the Holocaust and 'draws truths' from it is the essay "Nameless" (1966) which appears at PN 119–23, and from which the epigraph to this chapter is taken. Here Levinas suggests three things that can and must be taught in the wake of the Holocaust: (a) that our material needs are very few, (b) that we should continue to hope in evil times for restoration, and (c) that, rather than pinning everything on this hope, we should always be strong in isolation. This essay may possibly be understood as a trial run for "Useless Suffering," but is perhaps better understood as a nonphilosophical presentation of 'home truths' addressed to people who will not read many of Levinas's writings.

41. Menachot, 29b.

42. Baba Metzia, 59a–b.

BIBLIOGRAPHY

Note: For a bibliography of works by Levinas, see the Key to Abbreviations at the beginning of this book.

Arendt, Hannah. *Eichmann in Jerusalem: A Report on the Banality of Evil.* Harmondsworth: Penguin, 1963.

Aronowicz, Annette. "Translator's Introduction." In *Nine Tamudic Readings*, Emmanuel Levinas, ix–xxxix. Bloomington: Indiana University Press, 1990.

Avram, Wes. "On the Priority of 'Ethics' in the Work of Levinas." *Journal of Religious Ethics* 24, no. 2 (1996): 261–84.

Benammar, Karim. "Absences of Community." In *Who Is This 'We'?*, edited by E. M. Godway and G. Finn, 31–43. Montreal: Black Rose Books, 1994.

Benjamin, Walter. "Franz Kafka." Trans. H. Zohn. In *Illuminations*, edited by H. Arendt, 111–40. New York: Shocken Boooks, 1968.

———. "Some Reflections on Kafka." Trans. H. Zohn. In *Illuminations*, edited by H. Arendt, 141–46. New York: Shocken Books, 1968.

Bergo, Bettina. *Levinas Between Ethics and Politics: For the Beauty That Adorns the Earth.* Phaenomenologica 152. Dordrecht: Kluwer, 1999.

Berkovits, Eliezer. *Faith and the Holocaust.* New York: KTAV, 1973.

Bernasconi, Robert. "Deconstruction and the Possibility of Ethics."

In *Deconstruction and Philosophy*, edited by J. Sallis, 122–39. Chicago: University of Chicago Press, 1987.

———. "Hegel and Levinas: The Possibility of Reconciliation and Forgiveness" *Archivo di Filosophia*. 54 (1986): 325–46.

———. "'Only the Persecuted . . .': Language of the Oppressor, Language of the Oppressed." In *Ethics as First Philosophy*, edited by A. Peperzak, 77–86. New York: Routledge, 1995.

———. "Re-Reading *Totality and Infinity*." In *The Question of the Other*, edited by A. Dallery and C. Scott, 23–34. Albany: SUNY Press, 1989.

———. "Scepticism in the Face of Philosophy." *Re-Reading Levinas*, edited by R. Bernasconi and S. Critchley, 149–61. Bloomington: Indiana University Press, 1991.

Bernasconi, Robert, and Simon Critchley, eds. *Re-Reading Levinas*. Bloomington: Indiana University Press, 1991.

Blanchot, Maurice. "Our Clandestine Companion." In *Face to Face with Levinas*, edited by R. A. Cohen, 41–50. Albany: SUNY Press, 1986.

Bloom, Harold. *Kabbalah and Criticism*. New York: Seabury Press, 1975.

Bokser, Ben Zion. *The Jewish Mystical Tradition*. New York: Pilgrim Press, 1981.

Bowra, Maurice. *The Prophetic Element*. Oxford: Oxford University Press, 1959.

Butler, Judith. *Subjects of Desire: Hegelian Reflections in Twentieth Century France*. New York: Columbia University Press, 1987.

Caputo, John. *Deconstruction in a Nutshell*. New York: Fordham University Press, 1997.

———. *The Prayers and Tears of Jacques Derrida: Religion without Religion*. Bloomington: Indiana University Press, 1997.

Chalier, Catherine. "Emmanuel Levinas: Responsibility and Election." In *Ethics*, Royal Institute of Philosophy Supplement 35, edited by A. Phillips Griffith, 63–76. Cambridge: Cambridge University Press, 1993.

———. *Figures du féminin: Lecture d'Emmanuel Lévinas*. Paris: La Nuit Surveillée, 1982.

————. "The Philosophy of Levinas and the Hebraic Tradition." In *Ethics as First Philosophy*, edited by A. Peperzak, 3–12. New York: Routledge, 1995.

Ciaramelli, Fabio. "Levinas's Ethical Discourse between Individuation and Universality." In *Re-Reading Levinas*, edited by R. Bernasconi and S. Critchley, 83–105. Bloomington: Indiana University Press, 1991.

Cohen, Arthur. "On Emil Fackenheim's *To Mend the World*: A Review Essay," *Modern Judaism* 3 (1983): 225–36.

————. "Thinking the Tremendum," In *An Arthur Cohen Reader*, edited by D. Stern and P. Mendes-Flohr, 234–50. Detroit: Wayne State University Press, 1998.

Cohen, Richard A. *Elevations: The Height of the Good in Rosenzweig and Levinas*. Chicago: University of Chicago Press, 1994.

————. ed. *Face to Face with Levinas*. Albany: SUNY Press, 1986.

La conscience juive. Volumes I and II, Les Presses Universitaires de France 1962–63.

Cooper, Barry. *The End of History: An Essay on Modern Hegelianism*. Toronto: University of Toronto Press, 1984.

Critchley, Simon. *The Ethics of Deconstruction*. Oxford: Blackwell, 1992.

Dallery, A. and C. Scott, eds. *The Question of the Other*. Albany: SUNY Press, 1989.

Dan, J. *Jewish Mysticism and Jewish Ethics*. Seattle: University of Washington Press, 1986.

de Beauvoir, Simmone. *The Second Sex*. Trans. H. M. Parshley. New York: Vintage, 1974.

de Greef, Jan. "Scepticism and Reason," Trans. D. White. In *Face to Face with Levinas*, edited by R. Cohen, 159–79. Albany: SUNY Press, 1986.

Derrida, Jacques. *Adieu To Emmanuel Levinas*. Trans. P. Brault and M. Naas. Stanford: Stanford University Press, 1999.

————. "At this very moment in this work here I am." Trans. R. Berezdevin. In *Re-Reading Levinas*, edited by R. Bernasconi and S. Critchley, 11–48. Bloomington: Indiana University Press, 1991.

———. *The Gift of Death*. Trans. D. Wills. Chicago: University of Chicago Press, 1995.

———. "Of an Apocalyptic Tone Newly Adopted in Philosophy." In *Derrida and Negative Theology*. Translated and edited by J. P. Leavey, 25–71. Albany: SUNY Press, 1992.

———. "Sauf le nom." Trans. J. P. Leavey. In *On the Name*, edited by Thomas Dutoit, 35–85, 144–46. Stanford: Stanford University Press, 1995.

———. "Violence and Metaphysics: An Essay on the Thought of Emmanuel Levinas." Trans. A. Bass. In *Writing and Difference*, 79–153. Chicago: University of Chicago Press, 1978.

Derrida et al. "The Villanova Roundtable." In *Deconstruction in a Nutshell*, edited by J. Caputo, 3–28. New York: Fordham University Press, 1997.

Descombes, Vincent. *Modern French Philosophy*. Trans. J. M. Scott Fox and J. M. Harding. Cambridge: Cambridge University Press, 1980.

Durfee, Harold A. "War, Politics and Radical Pluralism." *Philosophy and Phenomenological Research*, 35 (1975): 549–558.

Dussel, Enrique. *The Underside of Modernity: Apel, Ricoeur, Rorty, Taylor and the Philosophy of Liberation*. Translated and edited by Eduardo Mendieta. New Jersey: Humanities Press, 1996.

Eaglestone, Robert. *Ethical Criticism: Reading After Levinas*. Edinburgh: Edinburgh University Press, 1997.

Eliade, Mircea. *Shamanism: Archaic Tasks of Ecstasy*. Trans. Willard R. Trask. New York: Bollingen, 1964.

Eisenstadt, Oona. "The Familiar Objections and the Old Accusations," paper delivered at the annual meeting of the Association for Jewish Studies, Chicago, December 1999.

Fackenheim, Emil. *God's Presence in History*. New York: Harper & Row, 1972.

Felstiner, John. *Paul Celan: Poet, Survivor, Jew*. New Haven: Yale University Press, 1995.

Finn, Geraldine. "The Space Between Ethics and Politics." In *Who Is This 'We'?*, edited by E. M. Godway and G. Finn, 101–16. Montreal: Black Rose Books, 1994.

Gerber, Rudolph J. "Totality and Infinity: Hebraism and Hellenism — The Experimental Ontology of Emmanuel Levinas." *Review of Existential Psychology and Psychiatry* 7, no. 3 (1967): 177–88.

Gibbs, Robert. "Blowing on the Embers: Two Jewish Works of Emmanuel Levinas: A Review Essay." *Modern Judaism.* 14 (1994): 99–112.

———. *Correlations in Rosenzweig and Levinas.* Princeton: Princeton University Press, 1992.

———. "The Name of God in Levinas's Philosophy." Paper delivered at McMaster University, November, 1996.

———. "The Other Comes to Teach Me: A Review of Recent Levinas Publications." *Man and World* 24 (1991): 219–33.

———. "Responsibility and Pragmatics." Paper delivered at Pluralité/Alterité, McMaster University, March 1998.

———. "Unjustifiable Suffering." Paper delivered at the annual meeting of the American Academy of Religion, November, 1997.

———. *Why Ethics?: Signs of Responsibilities.* Princeton: Princeton University Press, 2000.

Godway, E. M. and G. Finn, eds. *Who Is This 'We'?* Montreal: Black Rose Books, 1994.

Greenberg, Irving. *Living in the Image of God.* Northvale, N.J.: Jason Aronson. 1998.

Grossman, Vasily. *Life and Fate.* Trans. R. Chandler. London: Fontana, 1986.

Handelman, Susan. *Fragments of Redemption: Jewish Thought and Literary Theory in Benjamin, Scholem, and Levinas.* Bloomington: Indiana University Press, 1991.

———. *The Slayers of Moses: The Emergence of Rabbinic Interpretation in Modern Literary Theory.* Albany: SUNY Press, 1982.

Idel, Moshe. *Kabbalah: New Perspectives.* New Haven: Yale University Press, 1988.

———. *Language, Torah, and Hermeneutics.* Trans. Menahem Kallas. Albany: SUNY Press, 1989.

———. *The Mystical Experience of Abraham Abulafia.* Trans. Jonathon Chipman. Albany: SUNY Press, 1988.

————. *Studies in Ecstatic Kabbalah*. Albany: SUNY Press, 1988.

————. "Voegelin's Israel and Revelation: Some Observations." In *Politics, Order, and History: Essays on the Work of Eric Voegelin*, edited by Glenn Hughes, Stephen A. Mc Knight, and Geoffrey L. Price, 299–326. Sheffield: Sheffield Academic Press, 2001.

Irigaray, Luce. "Questions to Emmanuel Levinas: On the Divinity of Love." Trans. M. Whitford. In *Re-Reading Levinas*, edited by R. Bernasconi and S. Critchley, 109–18. Bloomington: Indiana University Press, 1991.

Jacobs, Louis. *Jewish Mystical Testimonies*. New York: Schocken Books, 1977.

Jowett, Donna. "Origins, Occupation, and the Proximity of the Neighbour." In *Who Is This 'We'?*, edited by E. M. Godway and G. Finn, 11–30. Montreal: Black Rose Books, 1994.

Kepnes, S., P. Ochs, and R. Gibbs, eds. *Reasoning After Revelation: Dialogues in Postmodern Jewish Philosophy*. Boulder: Westview Press, 1998.

Kierkegaard, Soren. *Fear and Trembling* (Princeton: Princeton University Press, 1983).

Kojève, Alexandre. *Introduction to the Reading of Hegel: Lectures on the Phenomenology of Spirit*. Trans. James H. Nichols Jr. New York: Basic Books, 1969.

Kolitz, Zvi. *Yossel Rakover Speaks to God: Holocaust Challenges to Religious Faith*. Hoboken: KTAV, 1995.

Kosky, Jeffrey L. "After the Death of God: Emmanuel Levinas and the Ethical Possibility of God." *Journal of Religious Ethics* 24, no. 2 (1996): 235–59.

Lescourret, Marie-Anne. *Emmanuel Levinas*. Paris: Flammarion, 1997.

Llewelyn, John. *Emmanuel Levinas: The Genealogy of Ethics*. London: Routledge, 1995.

Lingis, Alphonso. *Deathbound Subjectivity*. Bloomington: Indiana University Press, 1989.

————. "Face to Face: A Phenomenological Analysis." *International Philosophical Quarterly* 19 no. 2 (1979): 151–63.

Lorenc, Iwona. "Philosophical Premises of Levinas's Conception of Judaism." *Dialectics and Humanism* 16, no. 1 (1989): 157–70.

Lyotard, Jean-François. "Levinas's Logic." In *The Lyotard Reader*, edited by Andrew Benjamin, 275–313. Oxford: Basil Blackwell, 1989.

Manning, Robert J. S. *Interpreting Otherwise Than Heidegger: Emmanuel Levinas's Ethics as First Philosophy*. Pittsburgh: Duquesne University Press, 1993.

Mason, John R. *Reading and Responding to Mircea Eliade's History of Religious Ideas: The Lure of the Late Eliade*, Lewiston: Edwin Mellen, 1993.

Meskin, Jacob E. "In the Flesh: Embodiment and Jewish Existence in the Thought of Emmanuel Levinas." *Sound* 76 (1993): 173–90.

Mopsik, Charles. "La Pensée d'Emmanuel Lévinas et la Cabale." In *Cahier de l'herne*, edited by C. Chalier and M. Abensour, 428–41. Paris: Editions de l'Herne, 1991. 428–41.

Nadler, Allan. *The Faith of the Mitnagdim: Rabbinic Responses to Hasidic Rapture*. Baltimore: Johns Hopkins University Press, 1977.

Neusner, Jacob. "Paradigmatic versus Historical Thinking: The Case of Rabbinic Judaism." *History and Theory* 36, no. 3 (1997): 353–77.

———. *Stranger at Home: The Holocaust, Zionism, and American Judaism*. Chicago: University of Chicago Press, 1985.

Oppenheim, Michael D. *Speaking/Writing of God: Philosophical Reflections on the Life with Others*. Albany: SUNY Press, 1997.

Peperzak, Adriaan. *Beyond: The Philosophy of Emmanuel Levinas*. Evanston: Northwestern University Press, 1997.

———. "Preface." In *Basic Philosophical Writings*, Emmanuel Levinas, edited by A. Peperzak, S. Critchley, and R. Bernasconi, vii–xv. Bloomington: Indianan University Press, 1996.

———. "Presentation." In *Re-Reading Levinas*, edited by R. Bernasconi and S. Critchley, 51–66. Bloomington: Indiana University Press, 1991.

———. *To the Other: An Introduction to the Philosophy of Emmanuel Levinas*. West Lafayette: Purdue University Press, 1993.

———. ed. *Ethics as First Philosophy: The Significance of Emmanuel Levinas for Philosophy, Literature, and Religion*. New York: Routledge, 1995.

Rosenstock-Huessey, Eugen. *Judaism Despite Christianity: The Letters on Christianity and Judaism between Eugen Rosenstock-Huessey and Franz Rosenzweig.* Trans. D. Emmet. University of Alabama Press, 1969.

Rosenzweig, Franz. *The Star of Redemption.* Trans. W. H. Hallo. Notre Dame: University of Notre Dame Press, 1970–71.

———. "The New Thinking." In *Franz Rosenzweig: His Life and Thought*, 2nd Edition, edited by N. Glatzer, 179–213. New York: Schocken, 1961.

Roth, Michael. *Knowing and History: Appropriations of Hegel in Twentieth-Century France.* Ithaca: Cornell University Press, 1988.

Rubenstein, Richard. *After Auschwitz: Radical Theology and Contemporary Judaism.* Indianapolis: Bobbs-Merrill, 1966.

Sacks, Jonathan. "Practical Implications of Infinity." In *To Touch the Divine: A Jewish Mysticism Primer*, 59–90. Brooklyn: Merkos L'Inyonei Chinuch, 1989.

Scheper-Hughes, Nancy. "The Primacy of the Ethical: Propositions for a Militant Anthropology." *Current Anthropology* 36, no. 3 (June 1995): 409–20, 438–9.

Scholem, Gershom. *Kabbalah.* New York: New American Library, 1974.

———. *Major Trends in Jewish Mysticism.* New York: Schocken Books, 1941.

———. *On the Kabbalah and its Symbolism.* New York: Schocken Books, 1991.

Segal, Alan F. *Two Powers in Heaven: Early Rabbinic Reports about Christianity and Gnosticism.* Leiden: E. J. Brill, 1977.

Shanks, Andrew. *Civil Society, Civil Religion.* Oxford: Blackwell 1995.

Shapiro, Susan E. "Towards a Postmodern Judaism: A Response." In *Reasoning After Revelation*, edited by S. Kepnes, P. Ochs, and R. Gibbs, 77–92. Boulder: Westview Press, 1998.

Smith, Steven G. "Reason as One for Another: Moral and Theoretical Argument in the Philosophy of Levinas." *Journal of the British Society for Phenomenology* 12 (1981): 231–44.

Solomon, Malka. *Lire Lévinas.* Paris: Editions du Cerf, 1984.

Steiner, George. "Ecstasies, Not Arguments," *Times Literary Supplement* (September 28–October 4, 1990): 1015–016.

Sugarman, Richard and Helen Stephenson. "Emmanuel Levinas's 'To Love the Torah More Than God' " *Judaism*, 28 (1979): 217–22.

Tallon, Andrew. "Emmanuel Levinas and the Problem of Ethical Metaphysics." *Philosophy Today* 20 (1976): 53–56.

Tracy, David. "Response to Adriaan Peperzak." In *Ethics as First Philosophy*, edited by A. Peperzak, 193–98. New York: Routledge, 1995.

Waldenfels, Bernhard. "Response and Responsibility In Levinas." In *Ethics as First Philosophy*, edited by A. Peperzak, 39–52. New York: Routledge, 1995.

Wiesel, Elie. *Legends of Our Time.* New York: Holt Rinehart and Winston, 1968.

———. *Night.* New York: Bantam, 1986.

Wolfson, Elliot R. "A Response to Dialogues in Postmodern Jewish Philosophy." In *Reasoning After Revelation*, edited by S. Kepnes, P. Ochs, and R. Gibbs, 93–104. Boulder: Westview Press, 1998.

Wolosky, Shira. "Derrida, Jabès, Levinas: Sign-Theory as Ethical Discourse." *Prooftexts* 2 (1982): 283–302.

Wood, D. and R. Bernasconi, eds. *Derrida and Difference.* Coventry: Parousia Press, 1985.

———. eds. *Time and Metaphysics.* Coventry: Parousia Press, 1982.

Wyschogrod, Edith. "Derrida, Levinas, and Violence." In *Continental Philosophy II*, edited by H. Silverman et al., 183–200. New York: Routledge, 1989.

———. "Emmanuel Levinas and the Problem of Religious Language." *The Thomist* 36, no. 1 (1972): 1–38.

———. *Emmanuel Levinas: The Problem of Ethical Metaphysics.* The Hague: Martinus Nijhoff, 1974.

———. "Exemplary Individuals: Towards a Phenomenological Ethics." *Philosophy and Theology* 1 (1986): 9–31.

———. "God and 'Being's Move' in the Philosophy of Emmanuel Levinas." *The Journal of Religion* 62, no. 2 (1982): 145–55.

————. "The Moral Self: Emmanuel Levinas and Hermann Cohen." *Daat* 4 (1980): 35–58.

Wyschogrod, Michael. "Faith and the Holocaust." In *In the Aftermath of the Holocaust* V. 2, edited by J. Neusner, 252–60. New York: Garland, 1993.

INDEX